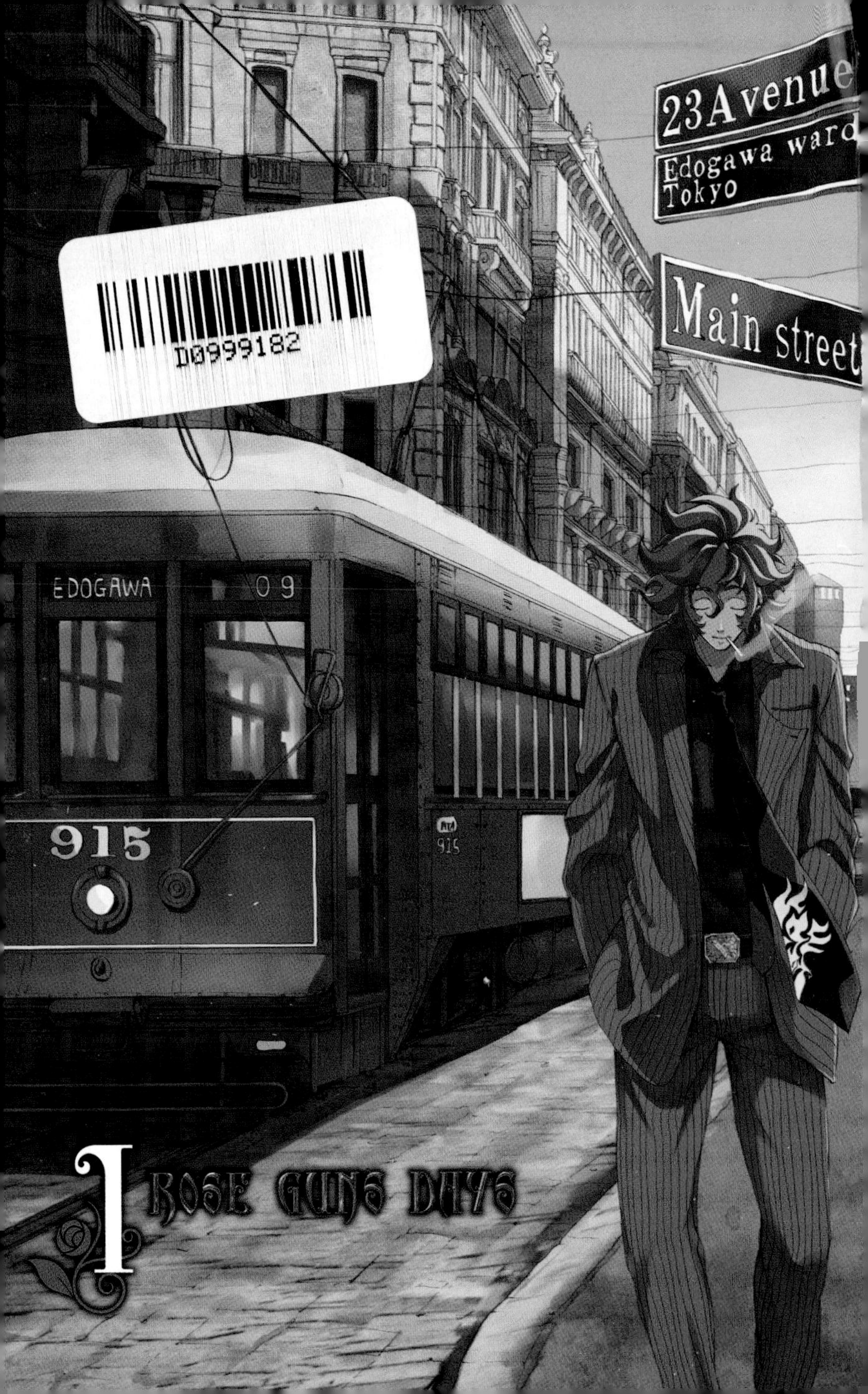
23 Avenue
Edogawa ward
Tokyo
Main street
EDOGAWA 09
915
915
1
ROSE GUNS DAYS

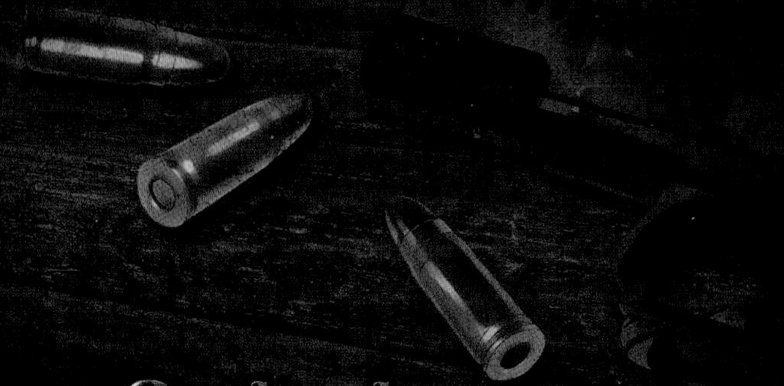

Contents

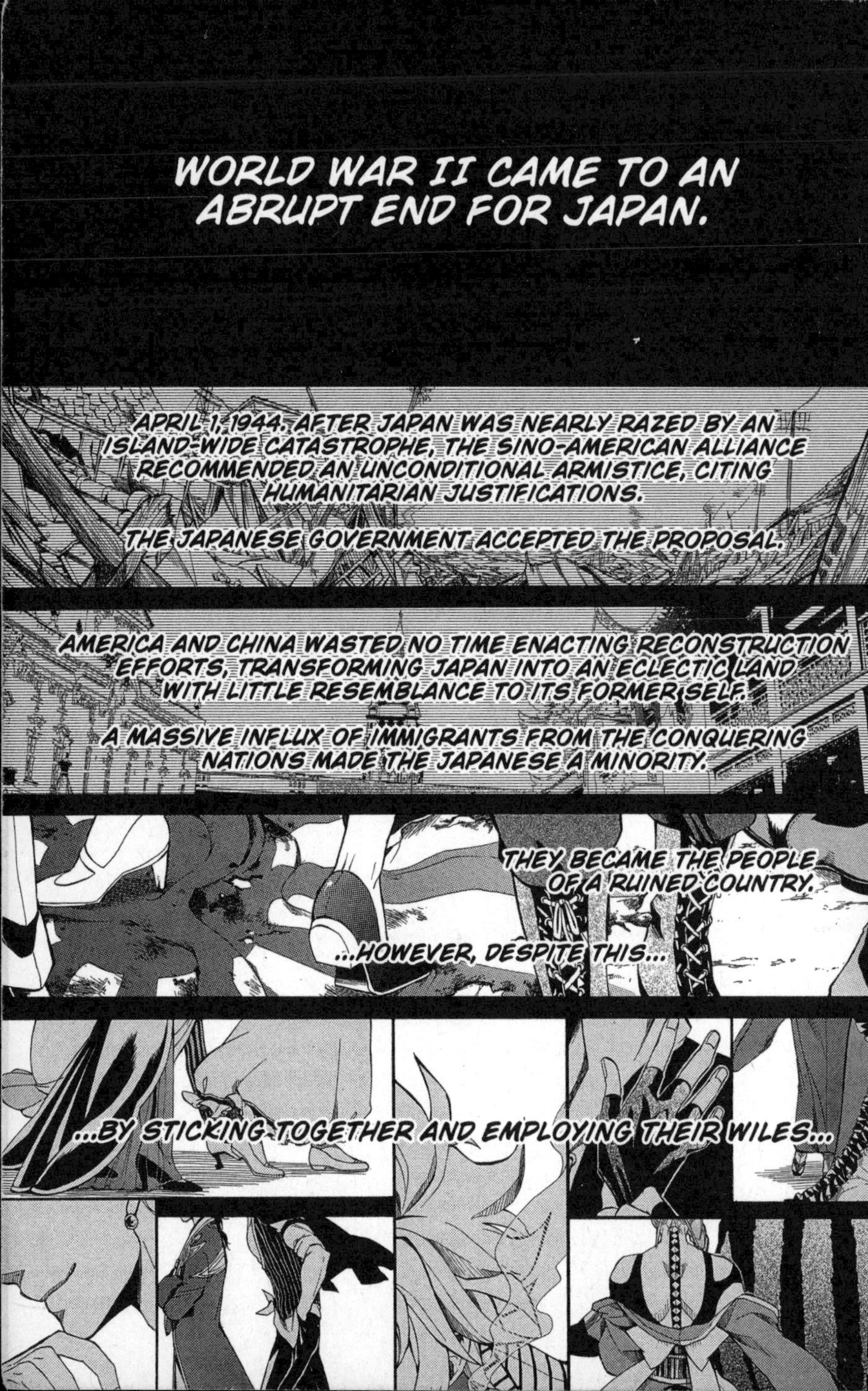
WORLD WAR II CAME TO AN ABRUPT END FOR JAPAN.
APRIL 1, 1944. AFTER JAPAN WAS NEARLY RAZED BY AN ISLAND-WIDE CATASTROPHE, THE SINO-AMERICAN ALLIANCE RECOMMENDED AN UNCONDITIONAL ARMISTICE, CITING HUMANITARIAN JUSTIFICATIONS.
THE JAPANESE GOVERNMENT ACCEPTED THE PROPOSAL.
AMERICA AND CHINA WASTED NO TIME ENACTING RECONSTRUCTION EFFORTS, TRANSFORMING JAPAN INTO AN ECLECTIC LAND WITH LITTLE RESEMBLANCE TO ITS FORMER SELF.
A MASSIVE INFLUX OF IMMIGRANTS FROM THE CONQUERING NATIONS MADE THE JAPANESE A MINORITY.
THEY BECAME THE PEOPLE OF A RUINED COUNTRY.
...HOWEVER, DESPITE THIS...
...BY STICKING TOGETHER AND EMPLOYING THEIR WILES...

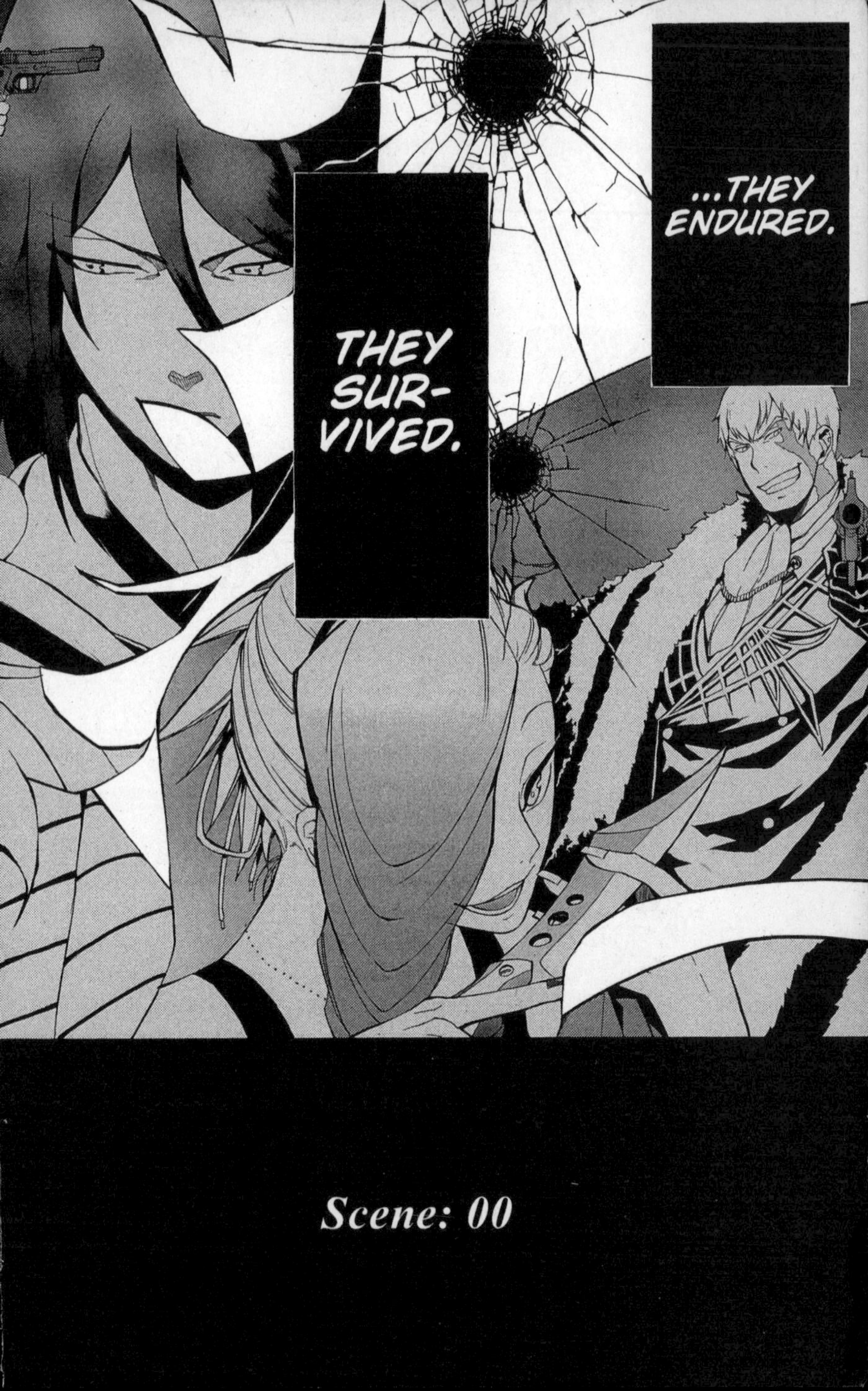
...THEY ENDURED.
THEY SUR-VIVED.

Scene: 00

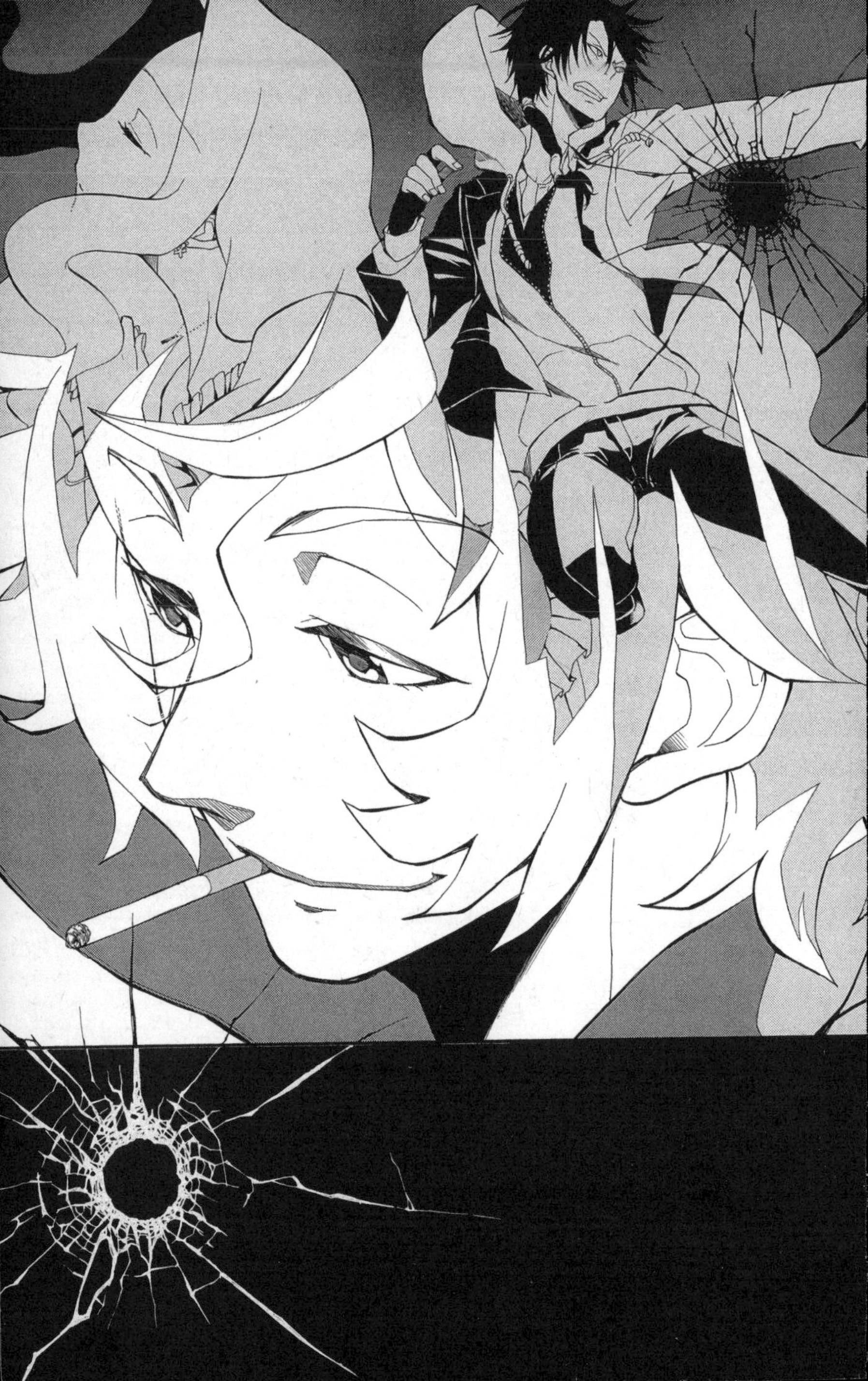

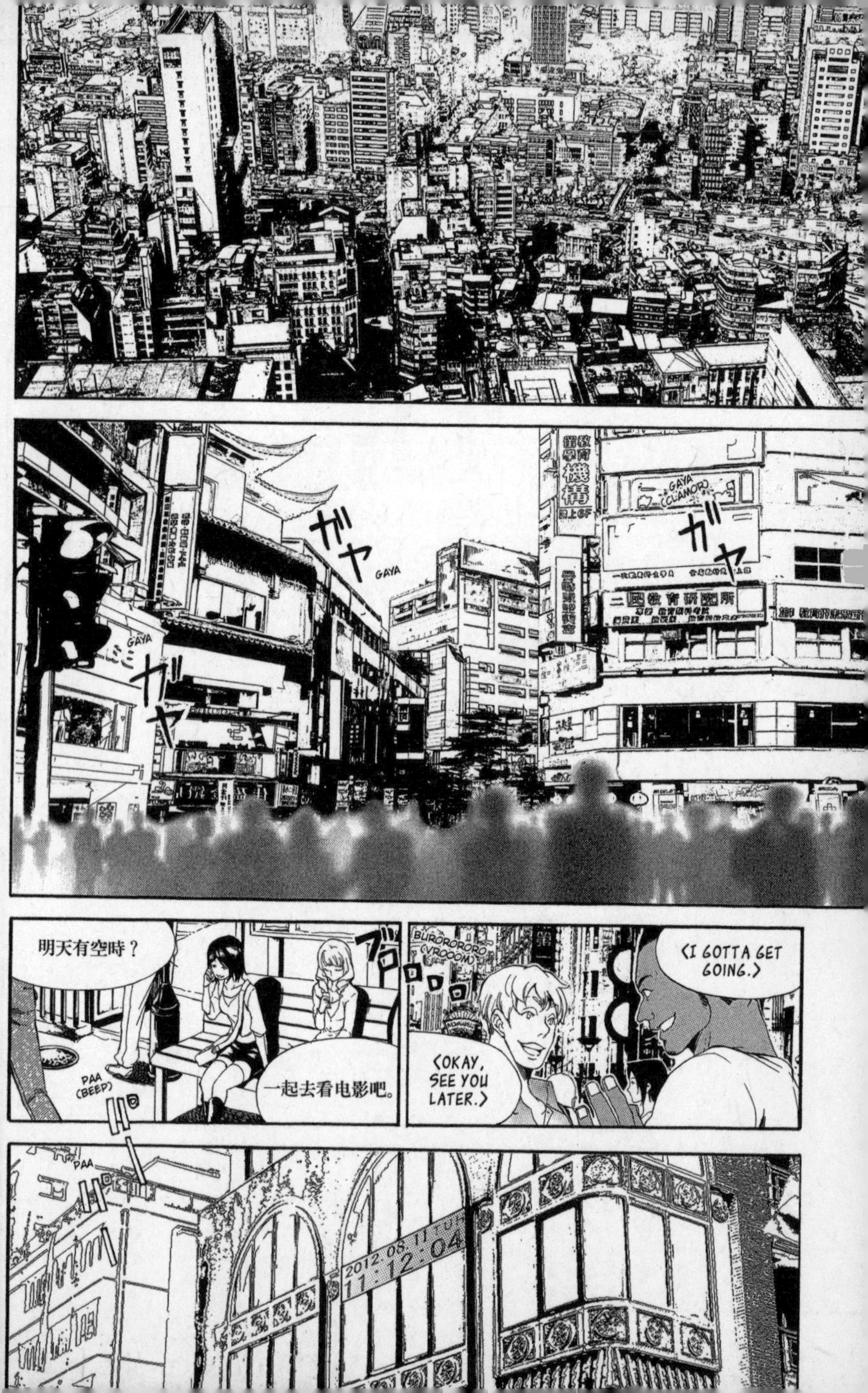ガヤ
GAYA (CLAMOR)
ガヤ
GAYA
ガヤ
GAYA
ブロロロロ
BURORORORO (VROOOM)
〈I GOTTA GET GOING.〉
〈OKAY, SEE YOU LATER.〉
明天有空時？
一起去看电影吧。
パー
PAA (BEEP)
パパー
PAA
2012.08.11
11:12:04

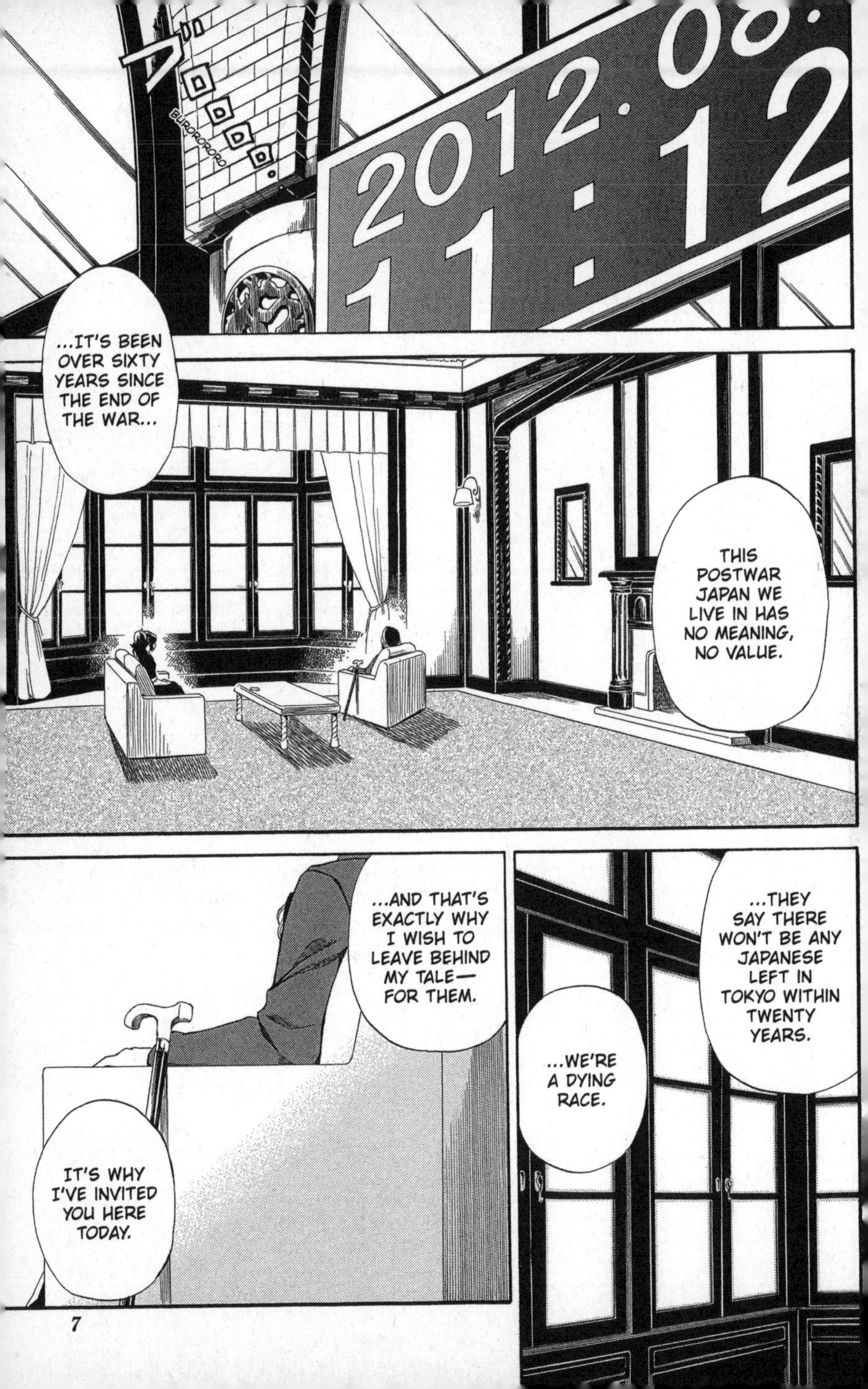
2012. 08.
11:12
BURORORORO
...IT'S BEEN OVER SIXTY YEARS SINCE THE END OF THE WAR...
THIS POSTWAR JAPAN WE LIVE IN HAS NO MEANING, NO VALUE.
...THEY SAY THERE WON'T BE ANY JAPANESE LEFT IN TOKYO WITHIN TWENTY YEARS.
...WE'RE A DYING RACE.
...AND THAT'S EXACTLY WHY I WISH TO LEAVE BEHIND MY TALE—FOR THEM.
IT'S WHY I'VE INVITED YOU HERE TODAY.

YOU'RE THE ONLY JAPANESE REPORTER AT THE TOKYO BRANCH OF THE HONG KONG DAILY, JYURI HAYASHIBARA-SAN.

YES.

AND YOU'RE THE HONORARY PRESIDENT OF "HARU-KAZE," THE ASSOCIATION FOR NATIVE JAPANESE...

...MADAM JEANNE.

YOU SURVIVED THE CHAOS OF THE POSTWAR PERIOD. EXACTLY WHAT SORT OF STORY DO YOU WANT TO BEQUEATH...

...TO US JAPANESE OF THE TWENTY-FIRST CENTURY?

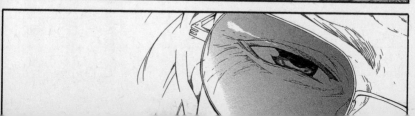

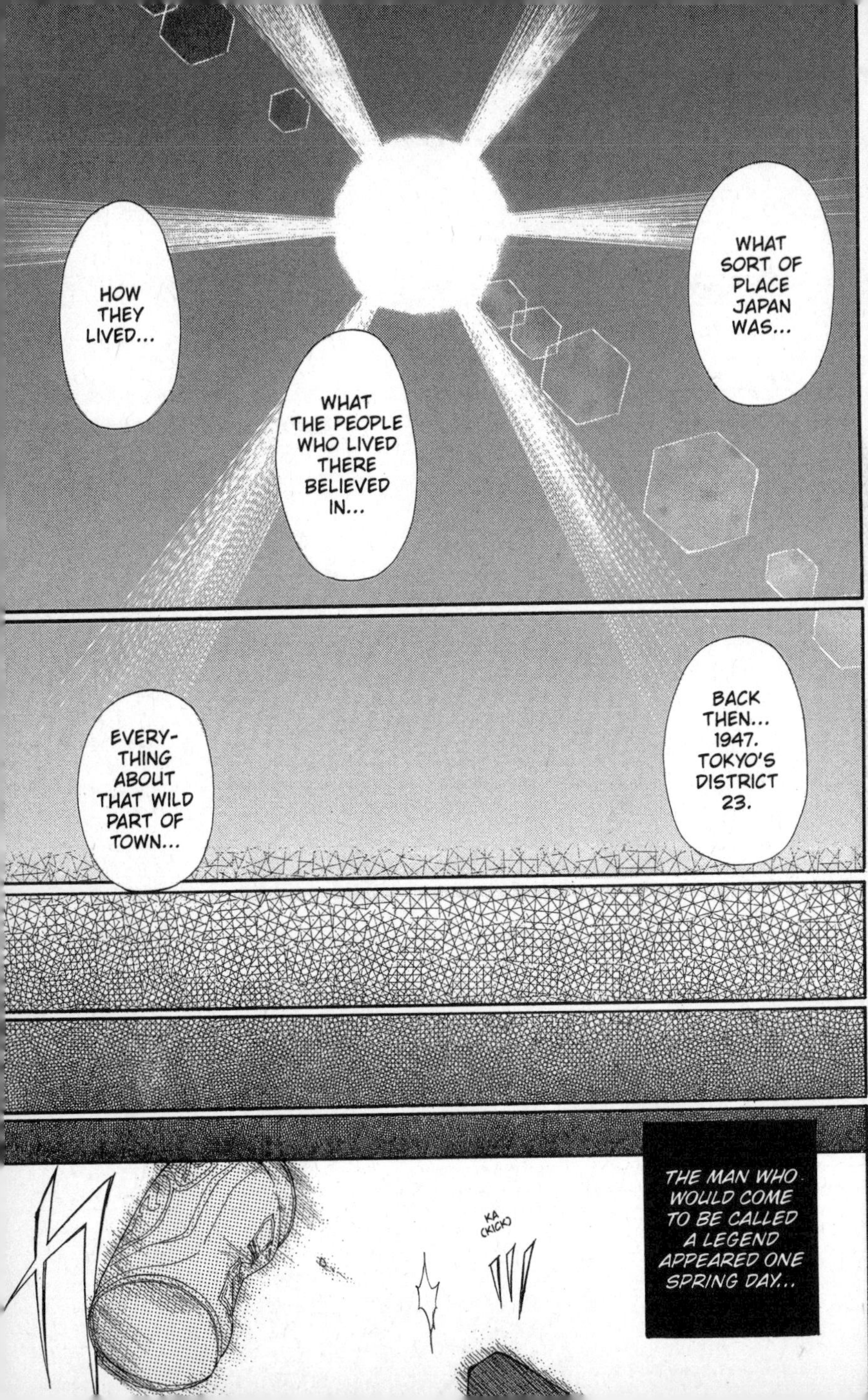
WHAT SORT OF PLACE JAPAN WAS...
WHAT THE PEOPLE WHO LIVED THERE BELIEVED IN...
HOW THEY LIVED...
BACK THEN... 1947. TOKYO'S DISTRICT 23.
EVERY-THING ABOUT THAT WILD PART OF TOWN...
THE MAN WHO WOULD COME TO BE CALLED A LEGEND APPEARED ONE SPRING DAY...
KA (KICK)

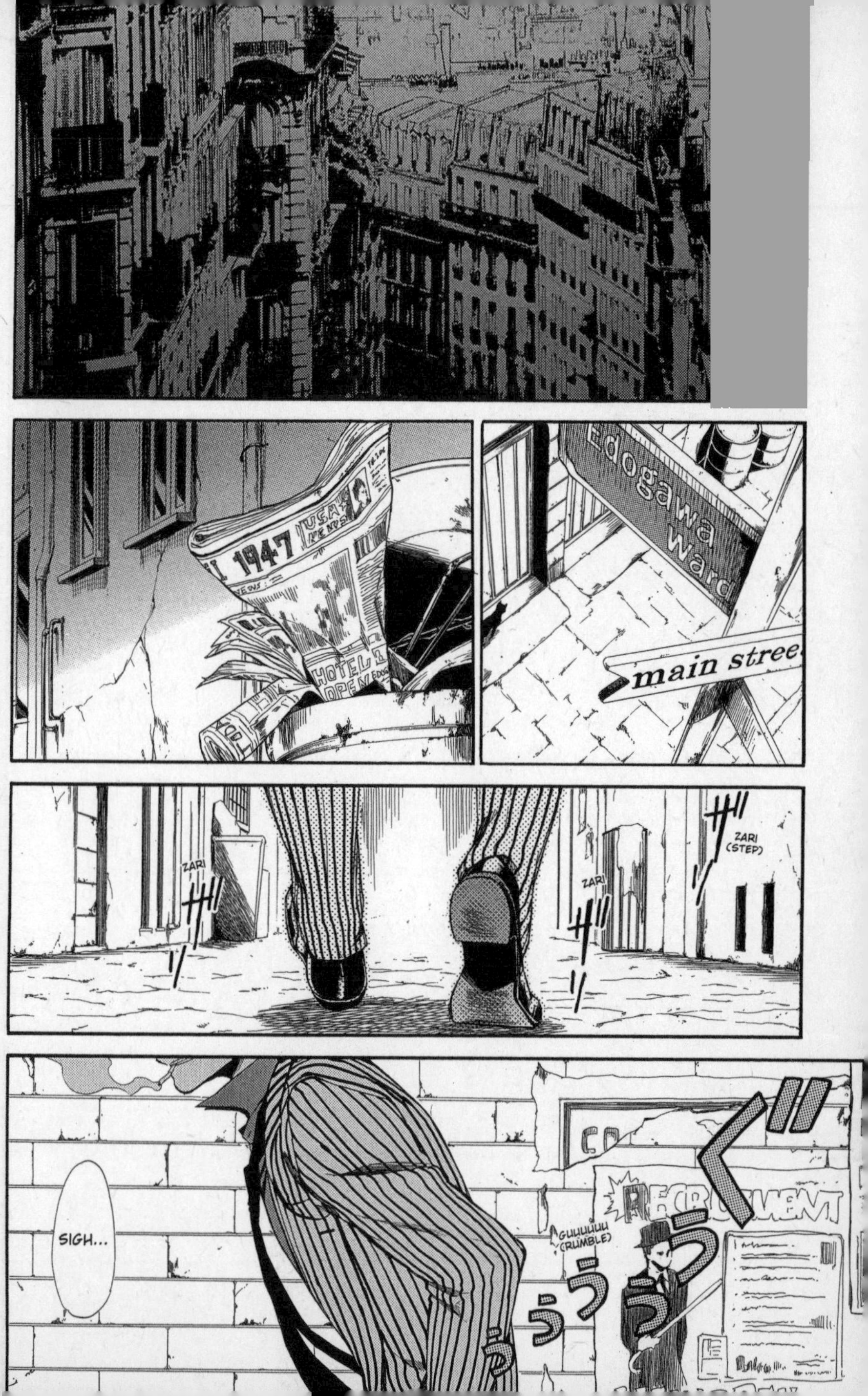

Edogawa Ward
main stree
1947
USA NEWS
HOTEL OPEN
ZARI (STEP)
ZARI
ZARI
GUUUUUU (RUMBLE)
SIGH...

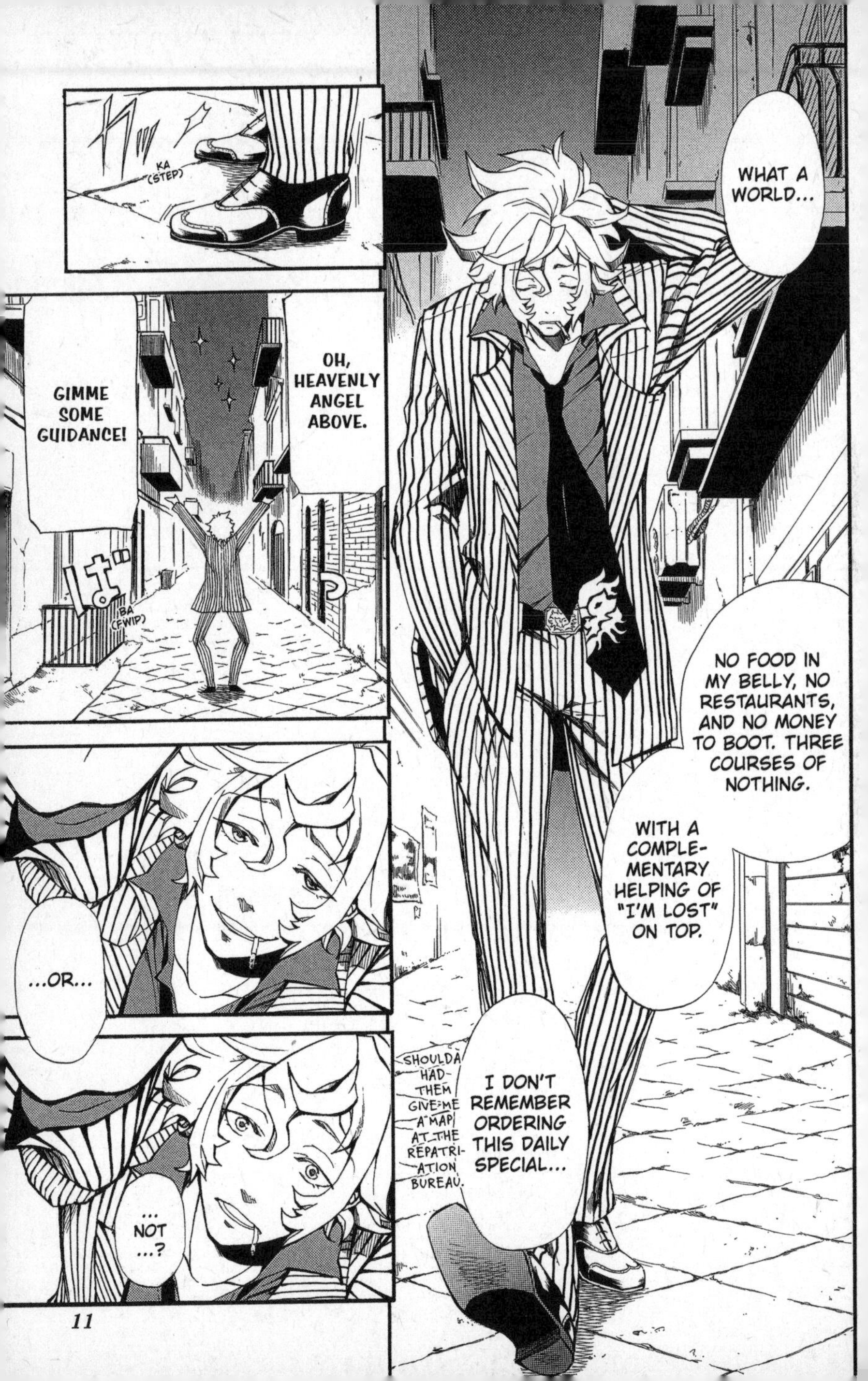
WHAT A WORLD...
NO FOOD IN MY BELLY, NO RESTAURANTS, AND NO MONEY TO BOOT. THREE COURSES OF NOTHING.
WITH A COMPLE-MENTARY HELPING OF "I'M LOST" ON TOP.
I DON'T REMEMBER ORDERING THIS DAILY SPECIAL...
SHOULDA HAD THEM GIVE ME A MAP AT THE REPATRI-ATION BUREAU.
KA (STEP)
OH, HEAVENLY ANGEL ABOVE.
GIMME SOME GUIDANCE!
BA (FWIP)
...OR...
... NOT ...?

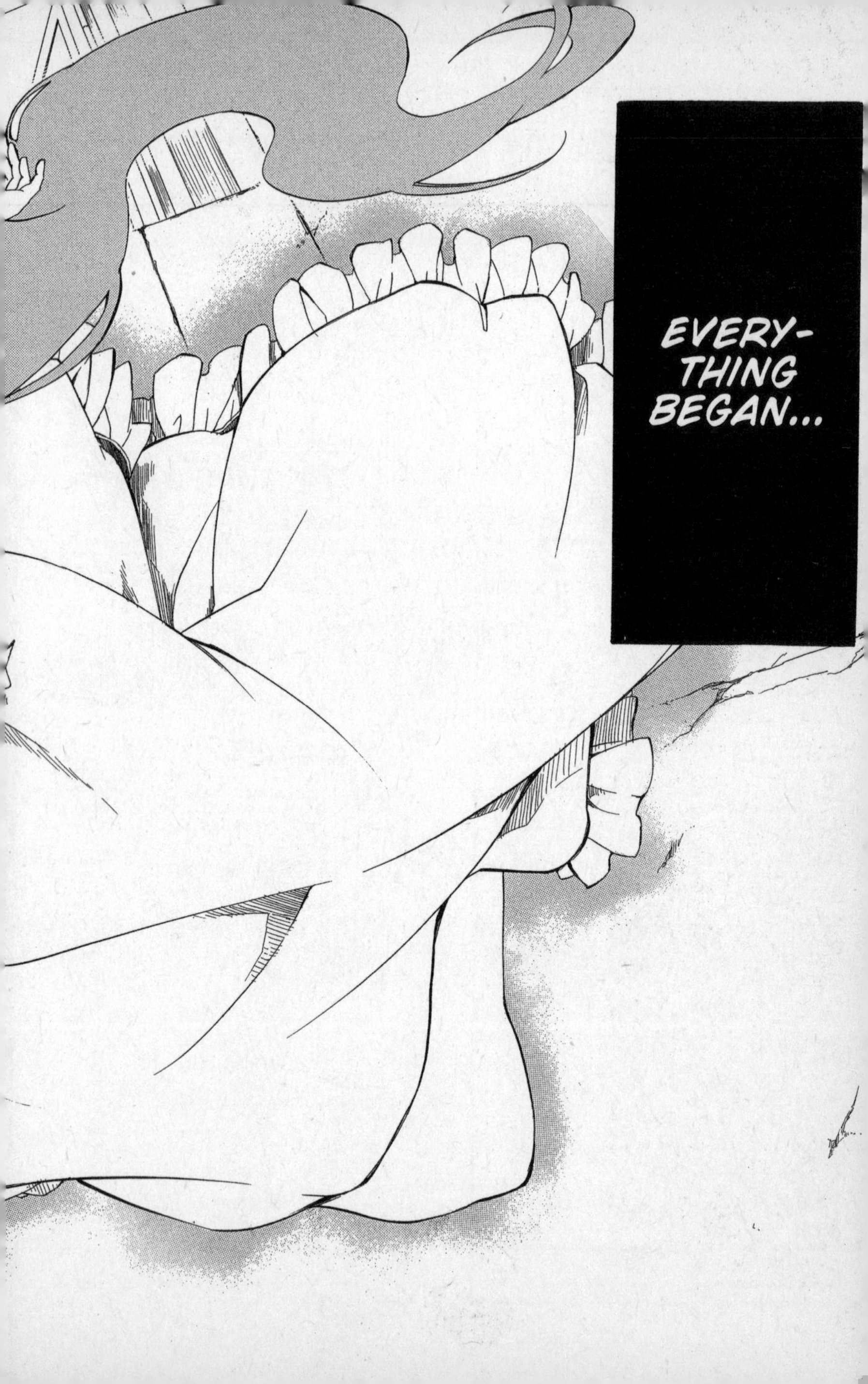
EVERY-THING BEGAN...

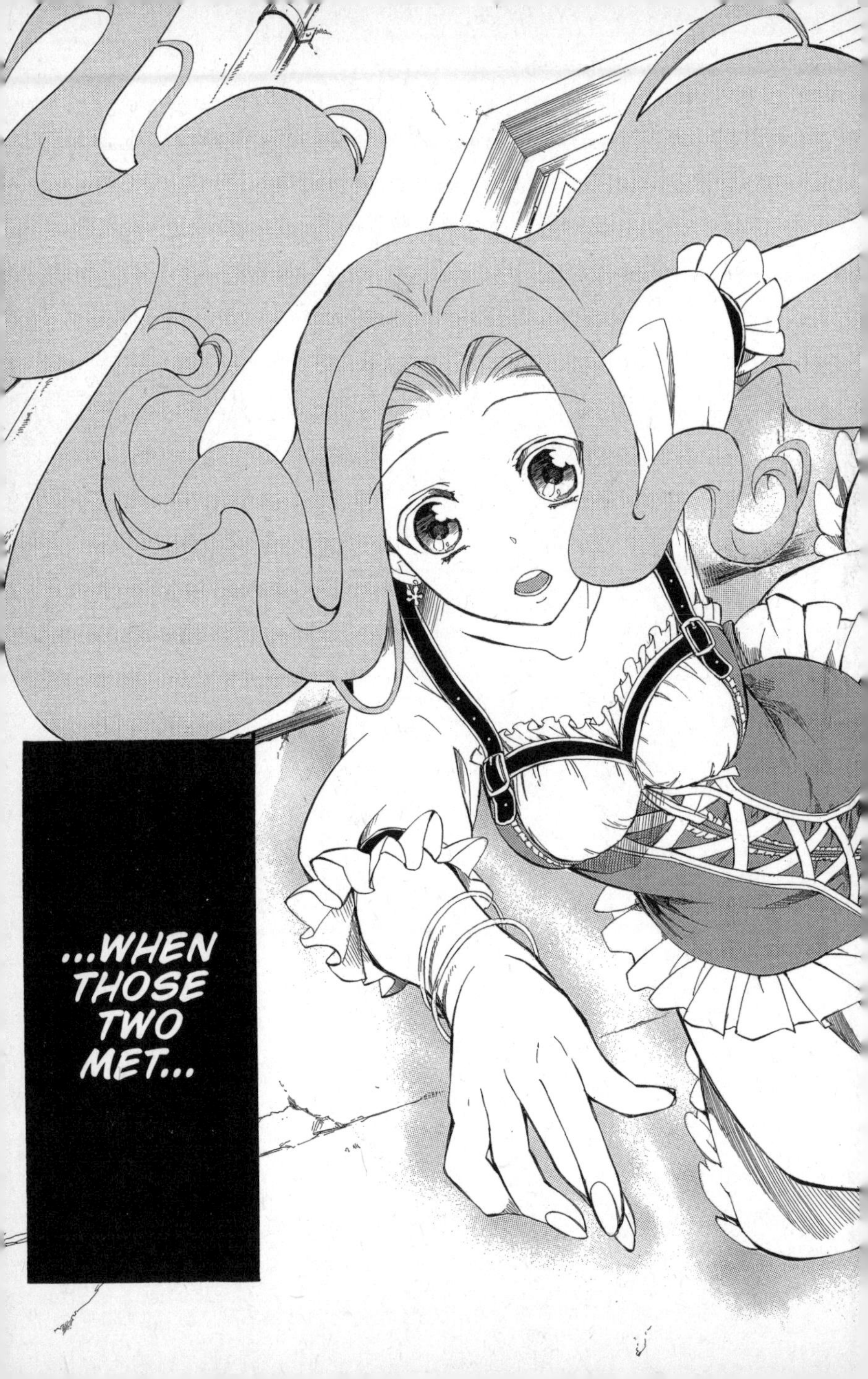
...WHEN THOSE TWO MET...

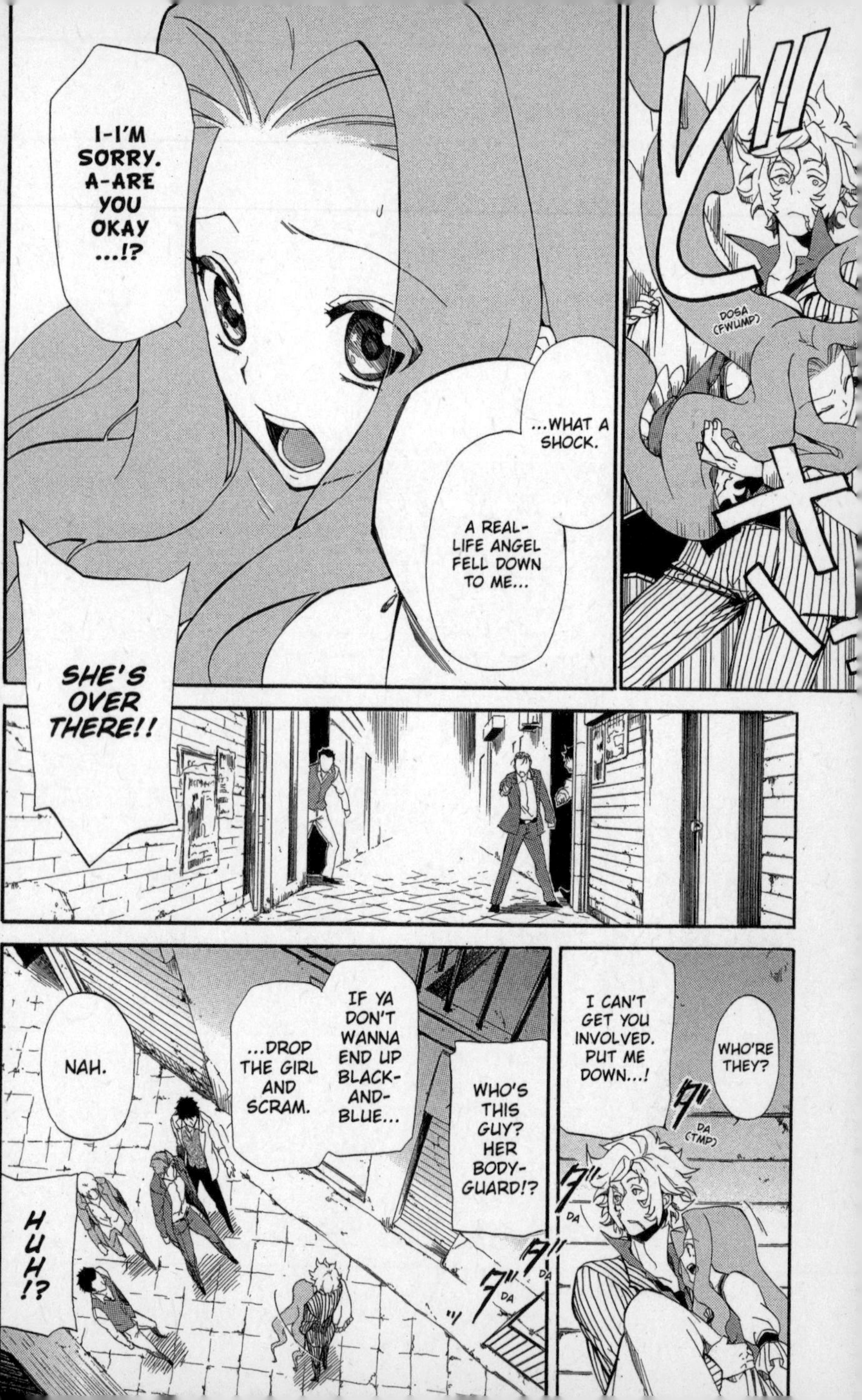
DOSA (FWUMP)
I-I'M SORRY. A-ARE YOU OKAY ...!?
...WHAT A SHOCK.
A REAL-LIFE ANGEL FELL DOWN TO ME...
SHE'S OVER THERE!!
WHO'RE THEY?
I CAN'T GET YOU INVOLVED. PUT ME DOWN...!
DA (TMP)
DA
DA
DA
WHO'S THIS GUY? HER BODYGUARD!?
IF YA DON'T WANNA END UP BLACK-AND-BLUE...
...DROP THE GIRL AND SCRAM.
NAH.
HUH!?

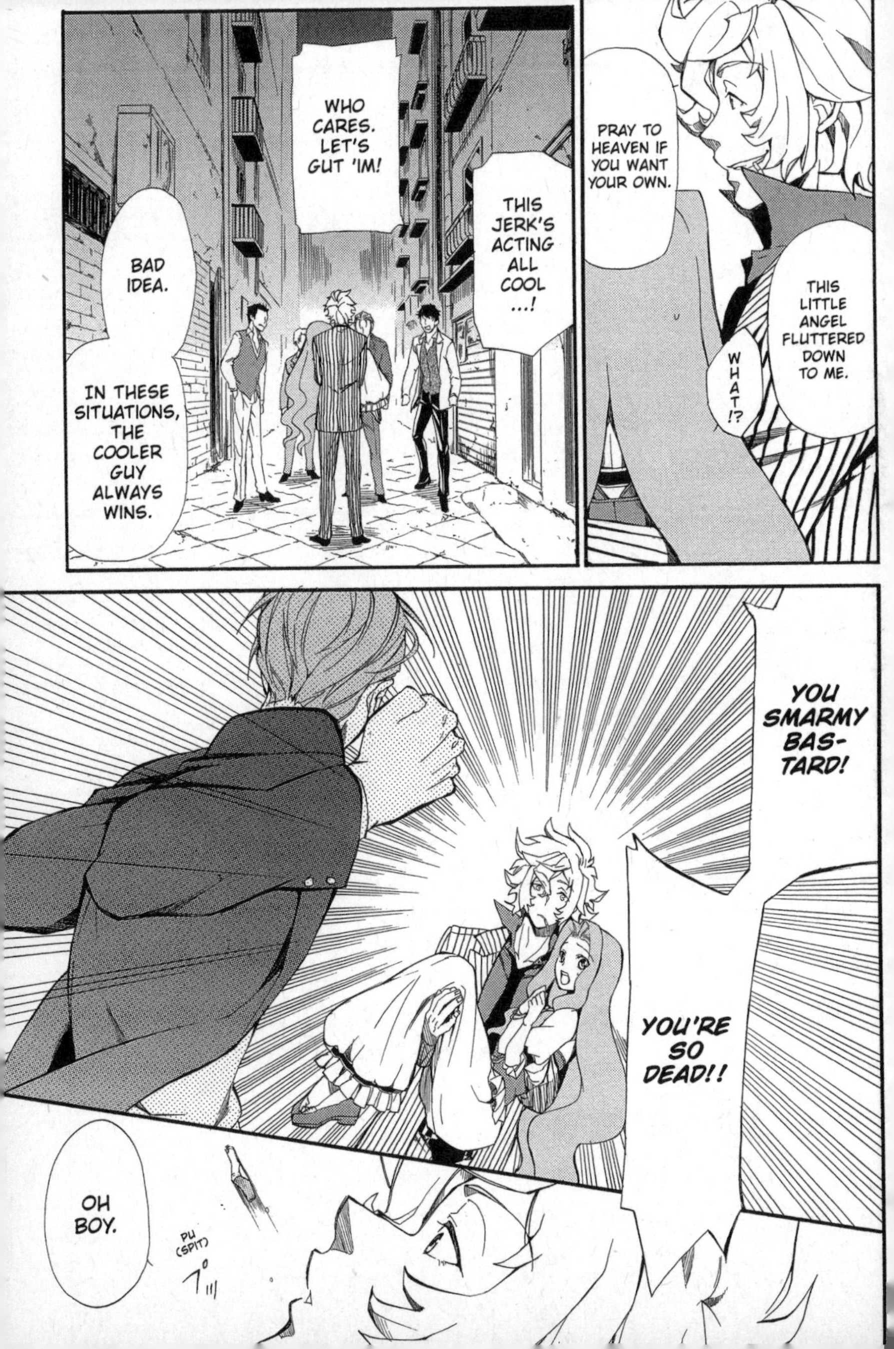
PRAY TO HEAVEN IF YOU WANT YOUR OWN.
THIS LITTLE ANGEL FLUTTERED DOWN TO ME.
WHAT!?
THIS JERK'S ACTING ALL COOL ...!
WHO CARES. LET'S GUT 'IM!
BAD IDEA.
IN THESE SITUATIONS, THE COOLER GUY ALWAYS WINS.
YOU SMARMY BAS-TARD!
YOU'RE SO DEAD!!
OH BOY.
PU (SPIT)

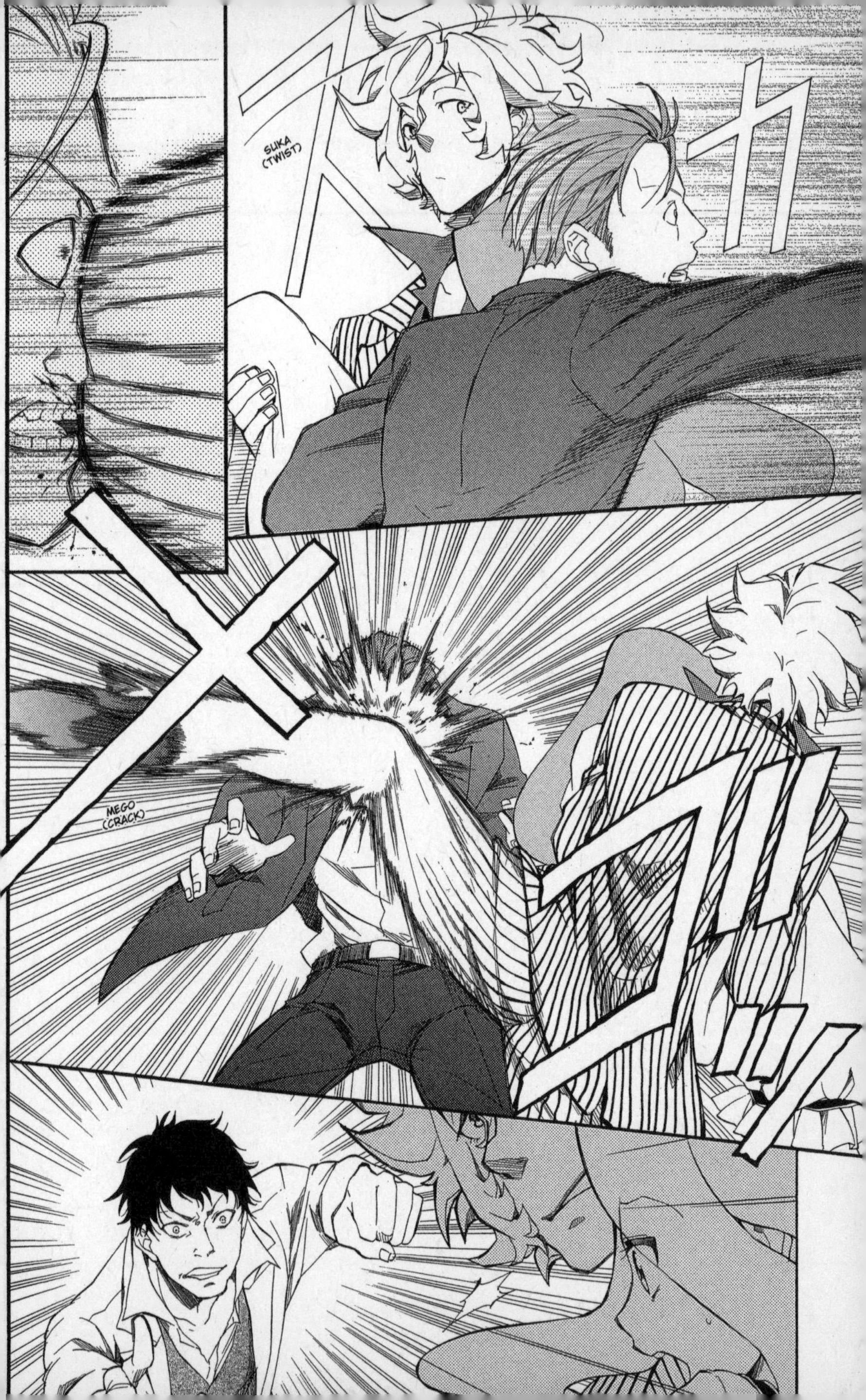
SUKA
(TWIST)
MEGO
(CRACK)

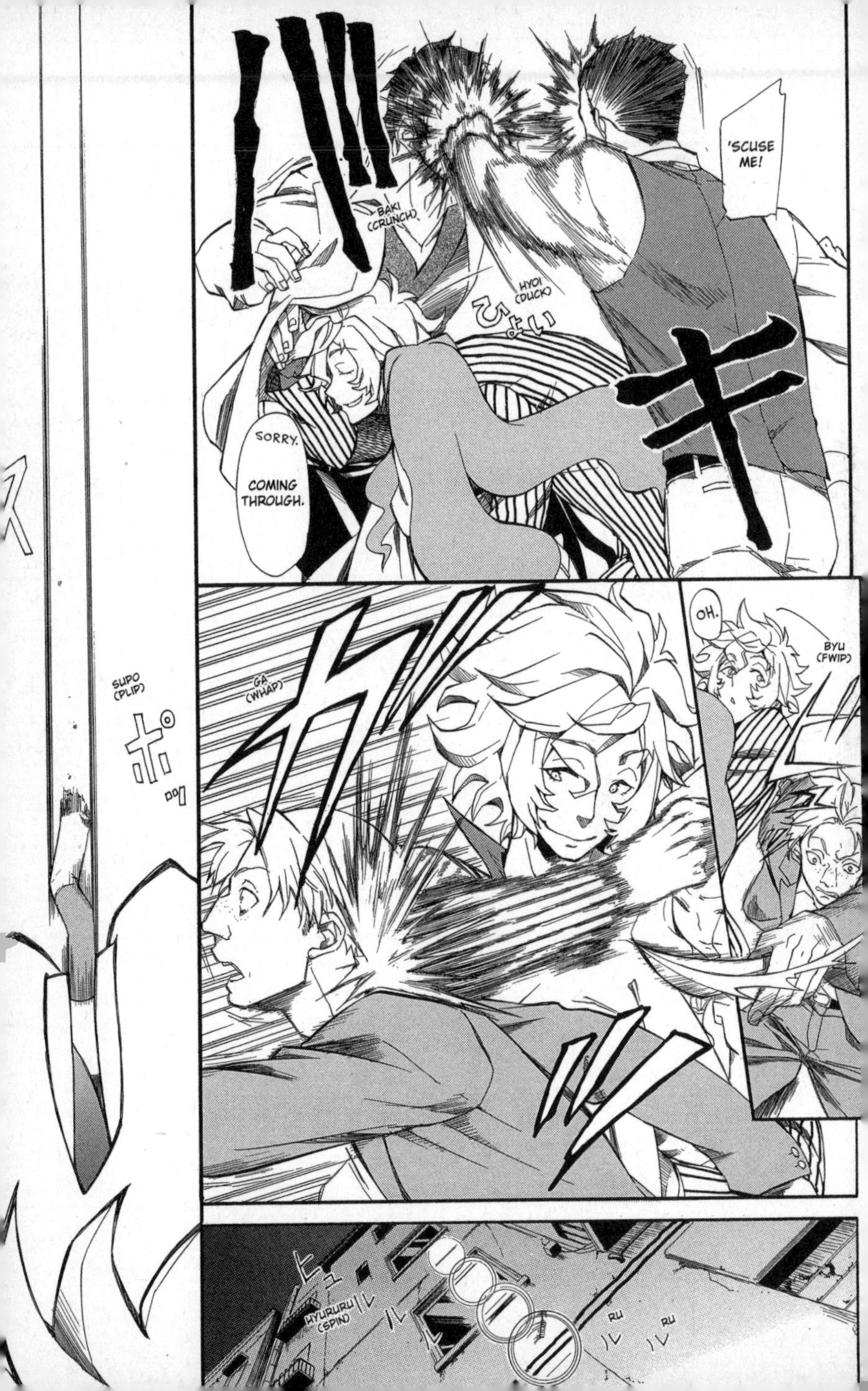
'SCUSE ME!
BAKI (CRUNCH)
HYOI (DUCK)
SORRY.
COMING THROUGH.
OH.
BYU (FWIP)
GA (WHAP)
HYURURU (SPIN)
RU
RU
SUPO (PLIP)

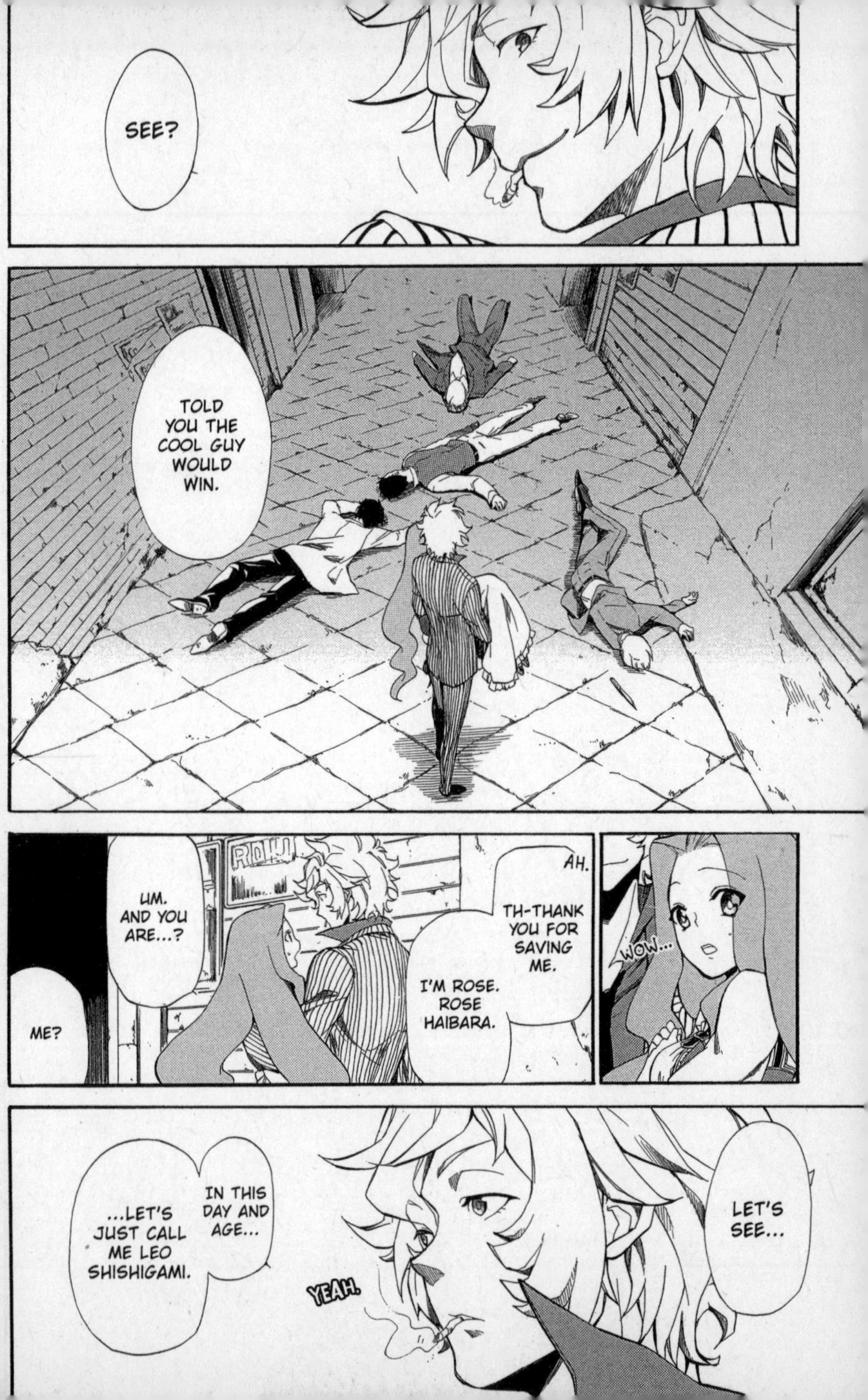
SEE?
TOLD YOU THE COOL GUY WOULD WIN.
WOW...
AH.
TH-THANK YOU FOR SAVING ME.
I'M ROSE. ROSE HAIBARA.
UM. AND YOU ARE...?
ME?
LET'S SEE...
YEAH.
IN THIS DAY AND AGE...
...LET'S JUST CALL ME LEO SHISHIGAMI.

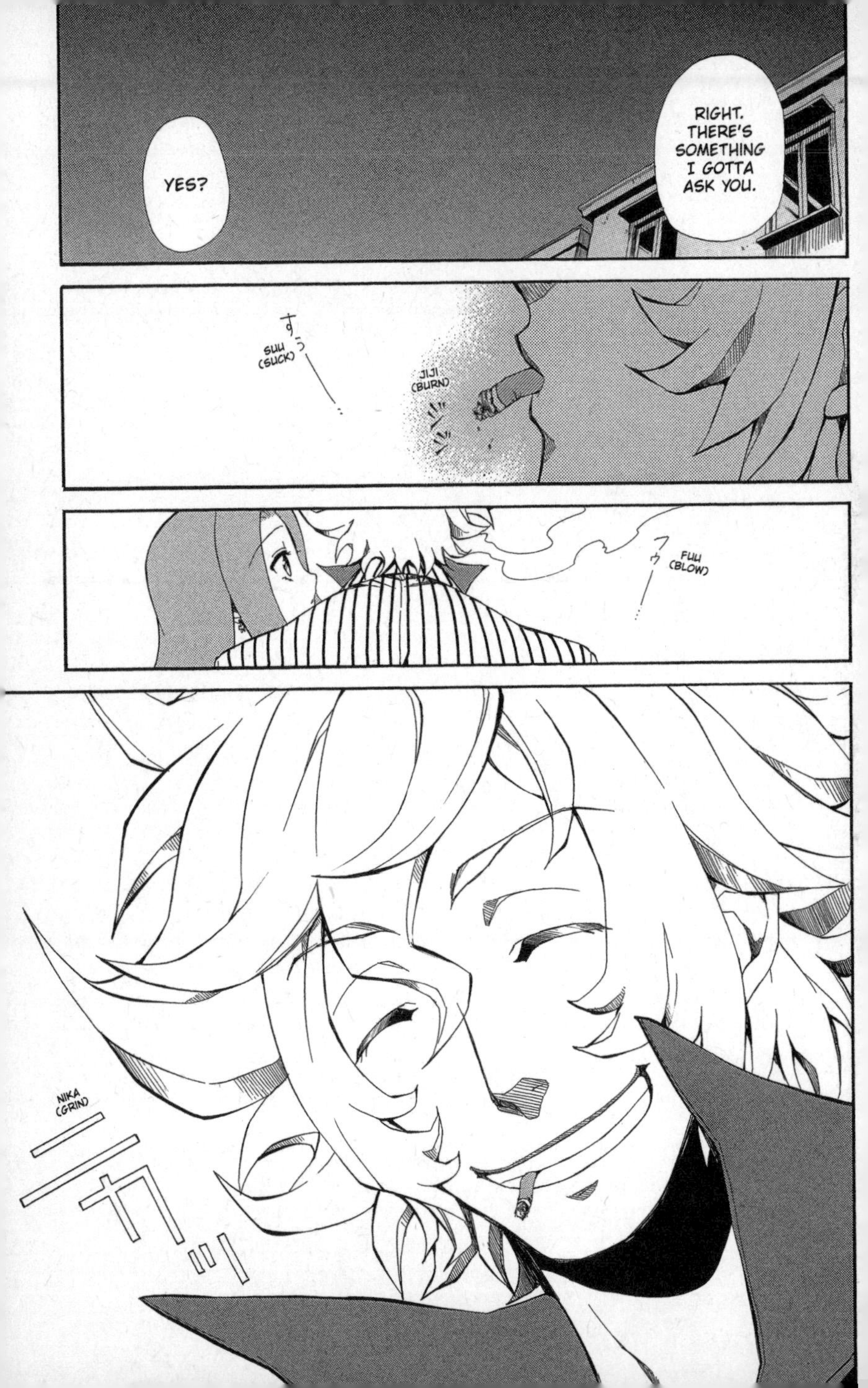
RIGHT. THERE'S SOMETHING I GOTTA ASK YOU.
YES?
JIJI (BURN)
すぅ
SUU (SUCK)
フゥ
FUU (BLOW)
NIKA (GRIN)
ニカッ

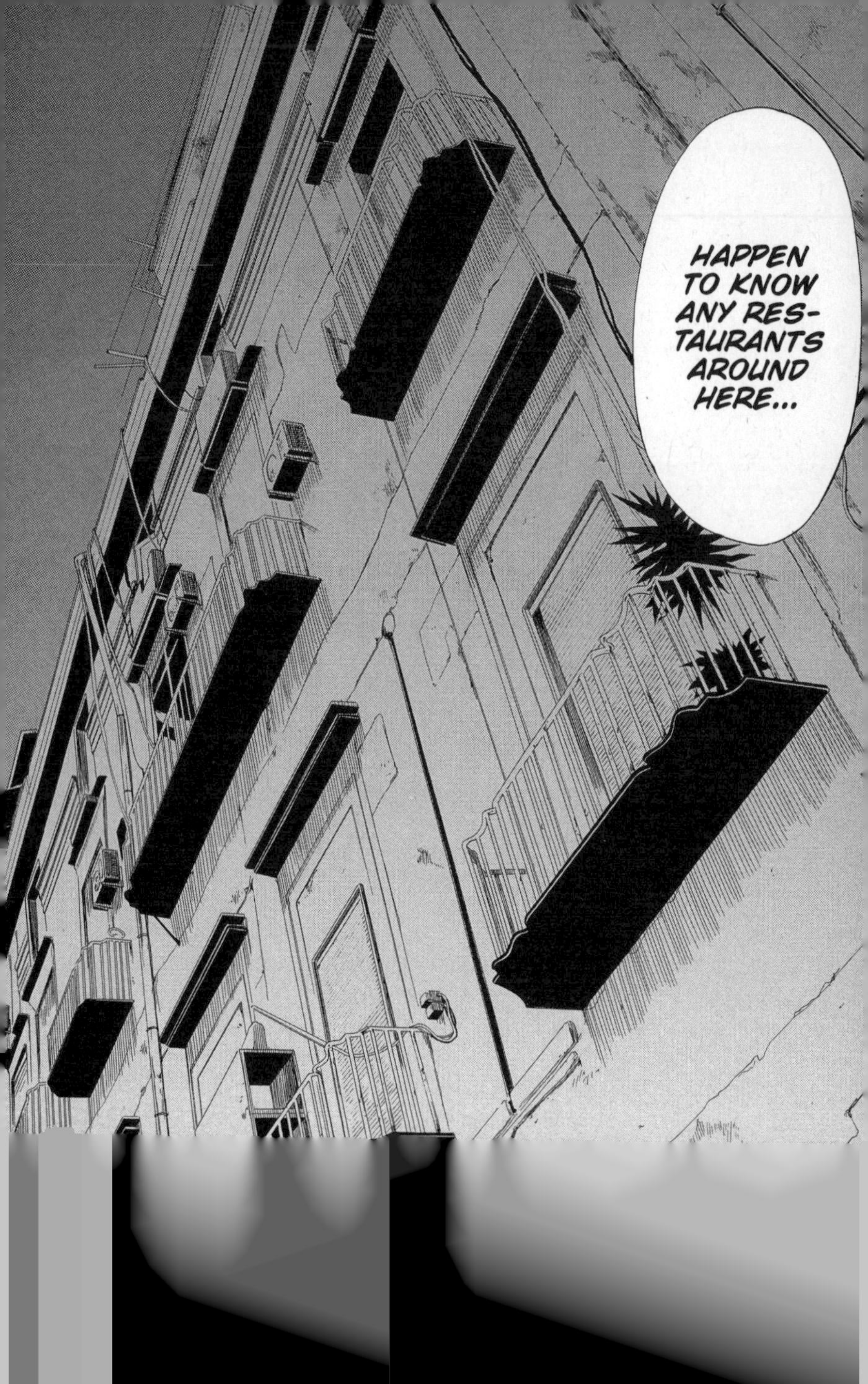
HAPPEN TO KNOW ANY RES-TAURANTS AROUND HERE...

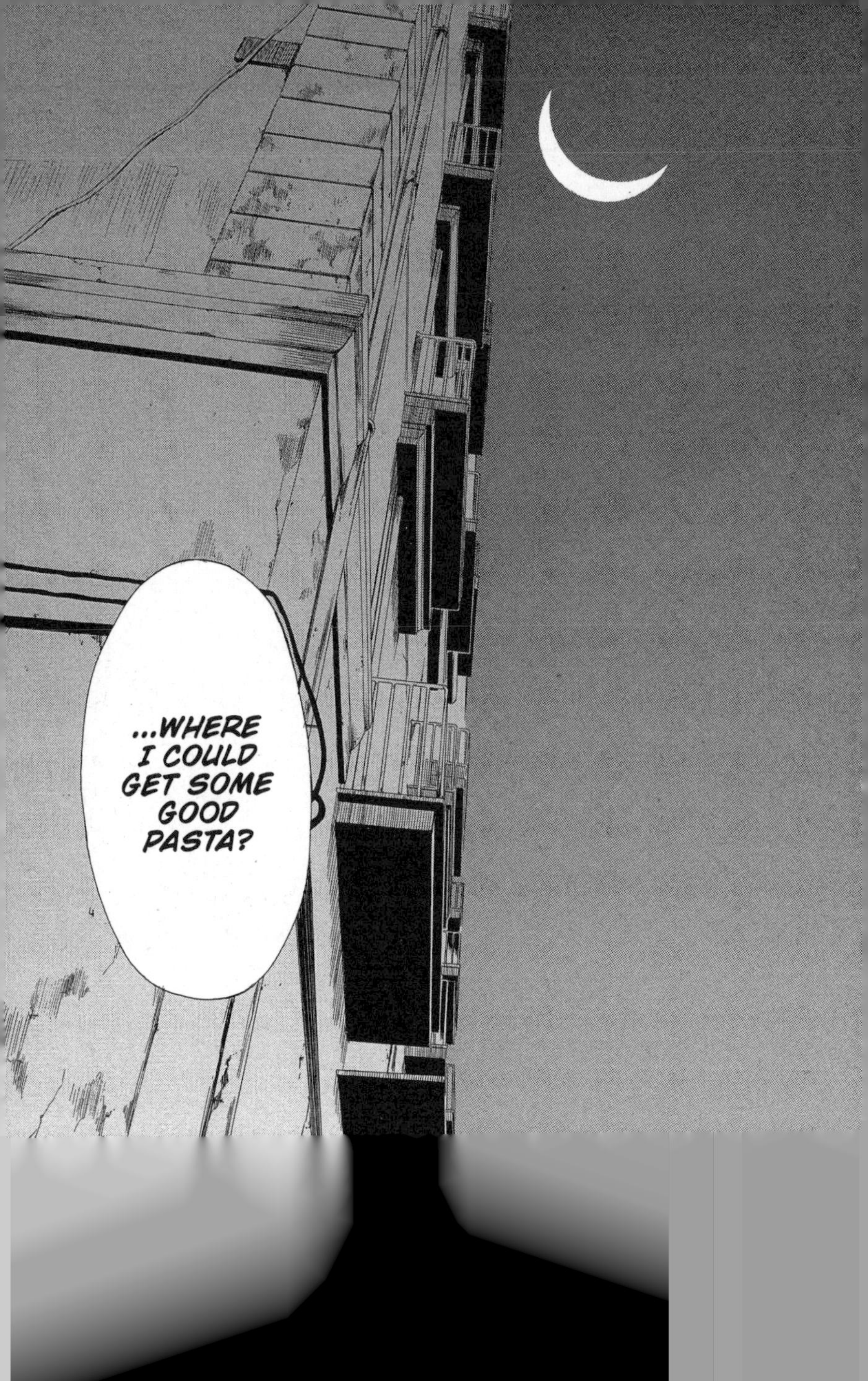
...WHERE I COULD GET SOME GOOD PASTA?

ROSE GUNS DAYS

Season 1

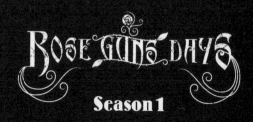

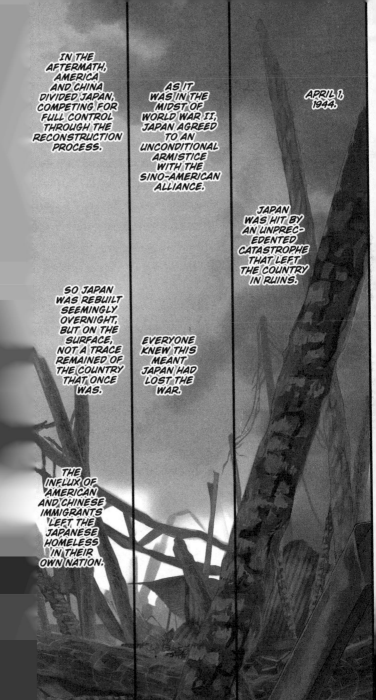

APRIL 1, 1944.

JAPAN WAS HIT BY AN UNPRECEDENTED CATASTROPHE THAT LEFT THE COUNTRY IN RUINS.

AS IT WAS IN THE MIDST OF WORLD WAR II, JAPAN AGREED TO AN UNCONDITIONAL ARMISTICE WITH THE SINO-AMERICAN ALLIANCE.

EVERYONE KNEW THIS MEANT JAPAN HAD LOST THE WAR.

IN THE AFTERMATH, AMERICA AND CHINA DIVIDED JAPAN, COMPETING FOR FULL CONTROL THROUGH THE RECONSTRUCTION PROCESS.

SO JAPAN WAS REBUILT SEEMINGLY OVERNIGHT, BUT ON THE SURFACE, NOT A TRACE REMAINED OF THE COUNTRY THAT ONCE WAS.

THE INFLUX OF AMERICAN AND CHINESE IMMIGRANTS LEFT THE JAPANESE HOMELESS IN THEIR OWN NATION.

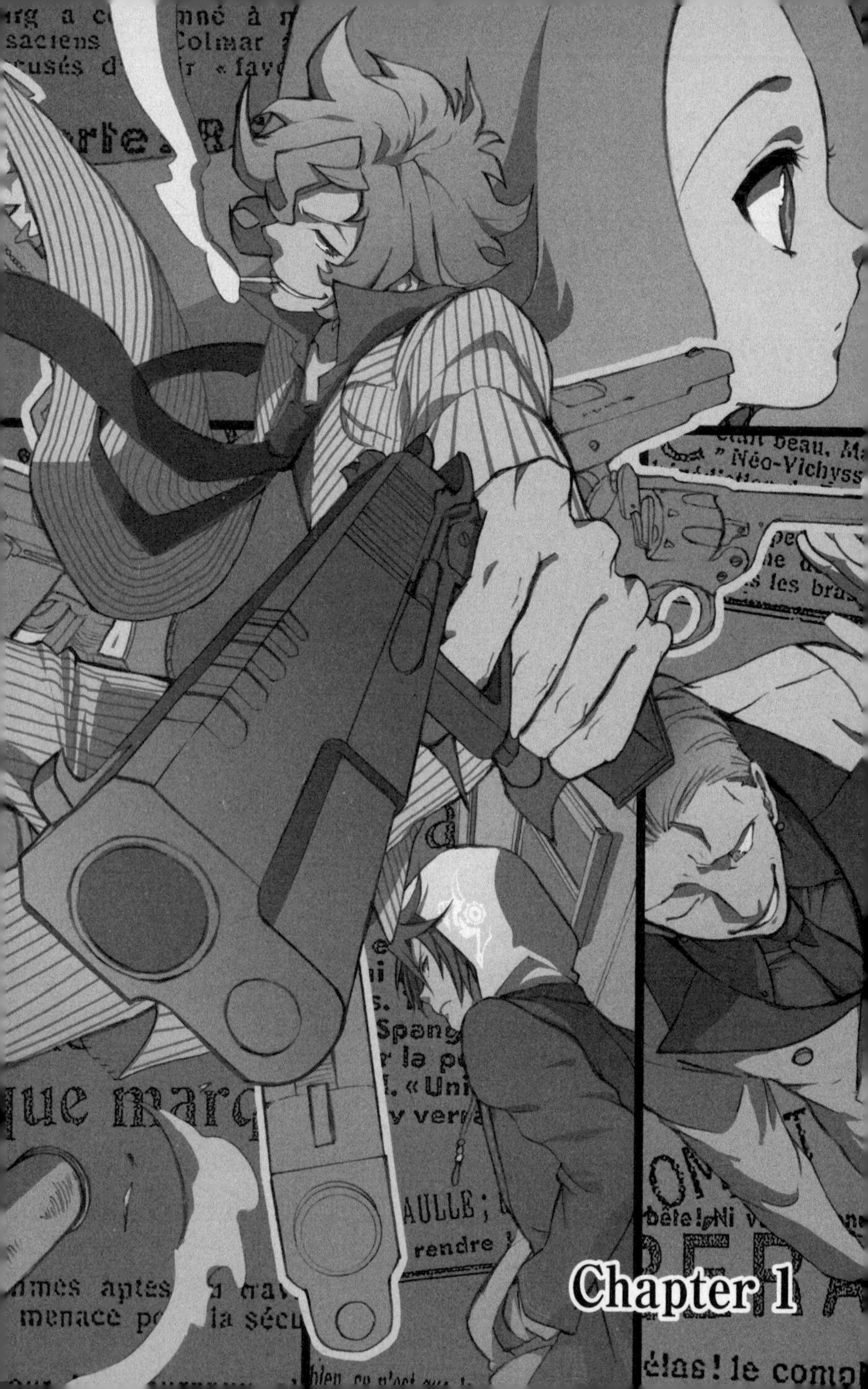

Chapter 1

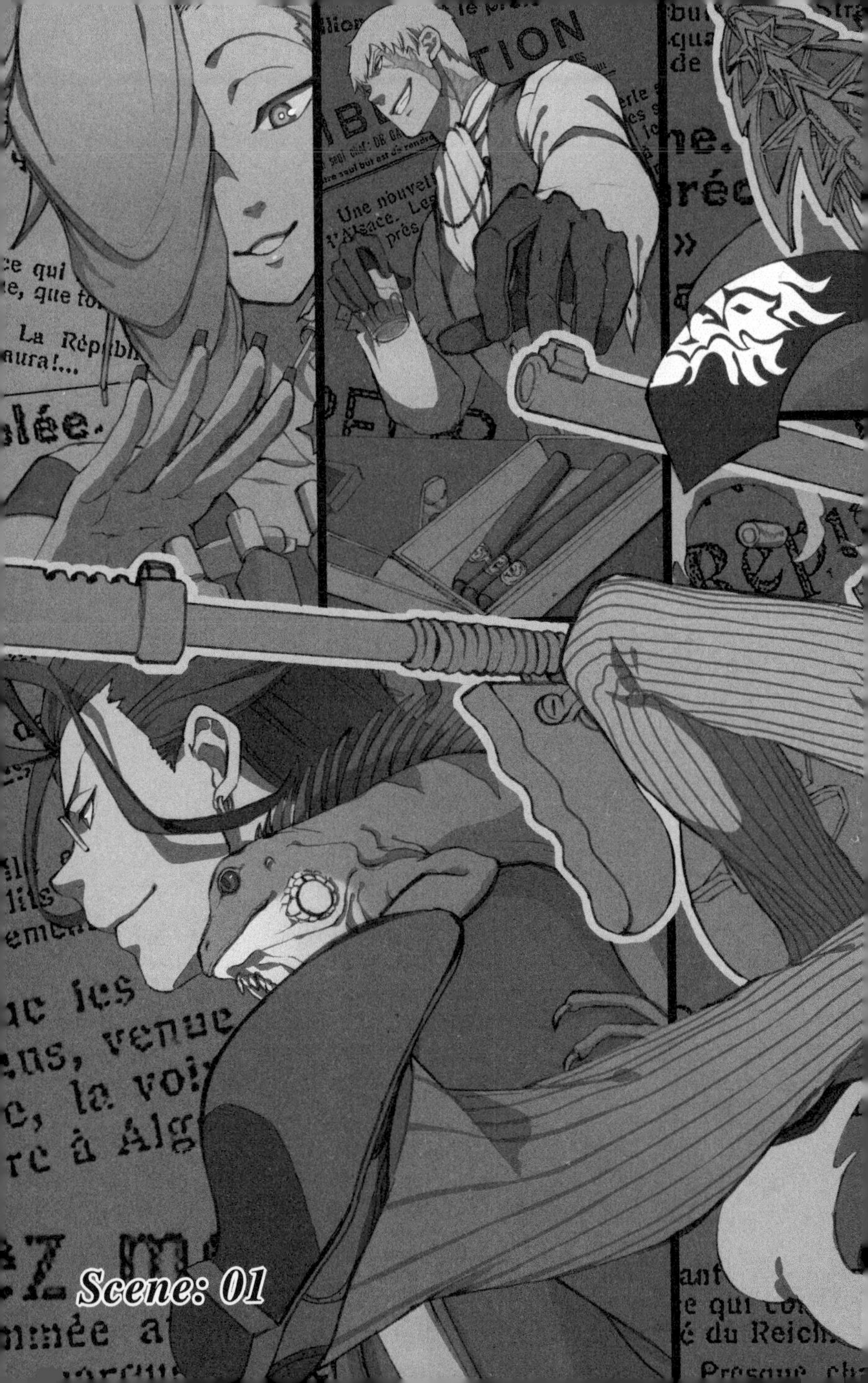
Scene: 01

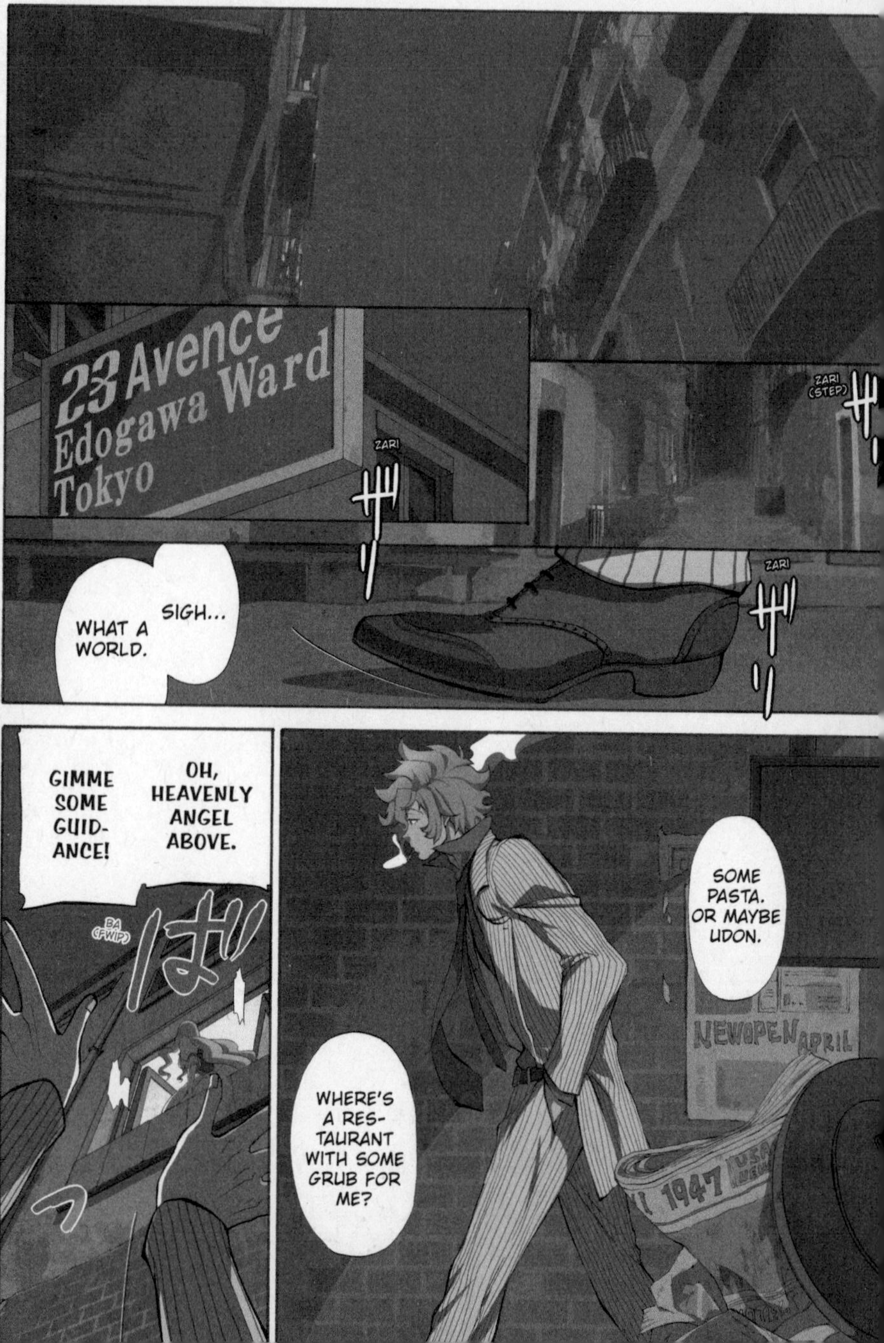
ZARI (STEP)
23 Avence
Edogawa Ward
Tokyo
ZARI
ZARI
SIGH...
WHAT A WORLD.
SOME PASTA. OR MAYBE UDON.
WHERE'S A RES-TAURANT WITH SOME GRUB FOR ME?
NEWOPEN APRIL
1947
OH, HEAVENLY ANGEL ABOVE.
GIMME SOME GUID-ANCE!
BA (FWIP)

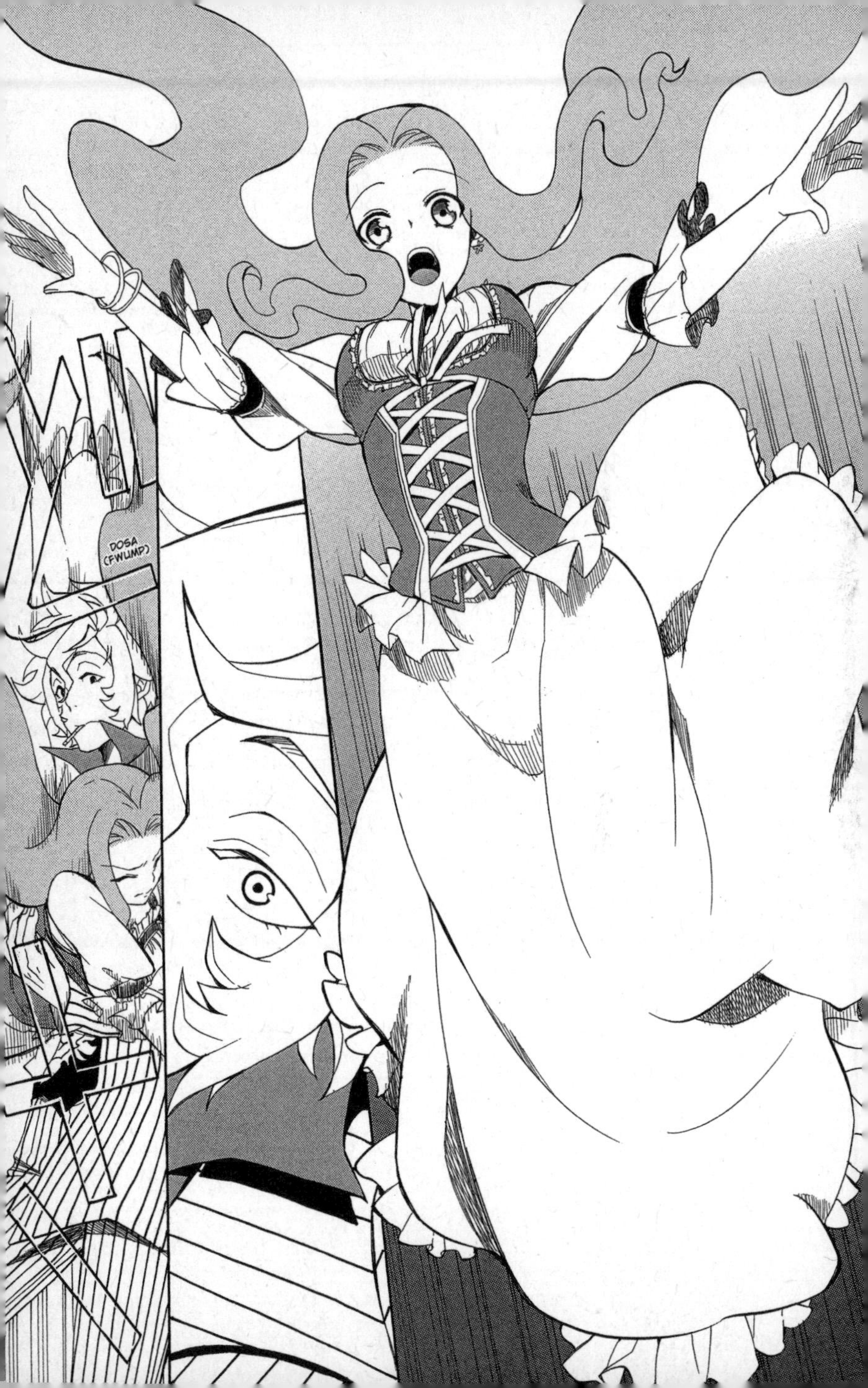
DOSA
(FWUMP)

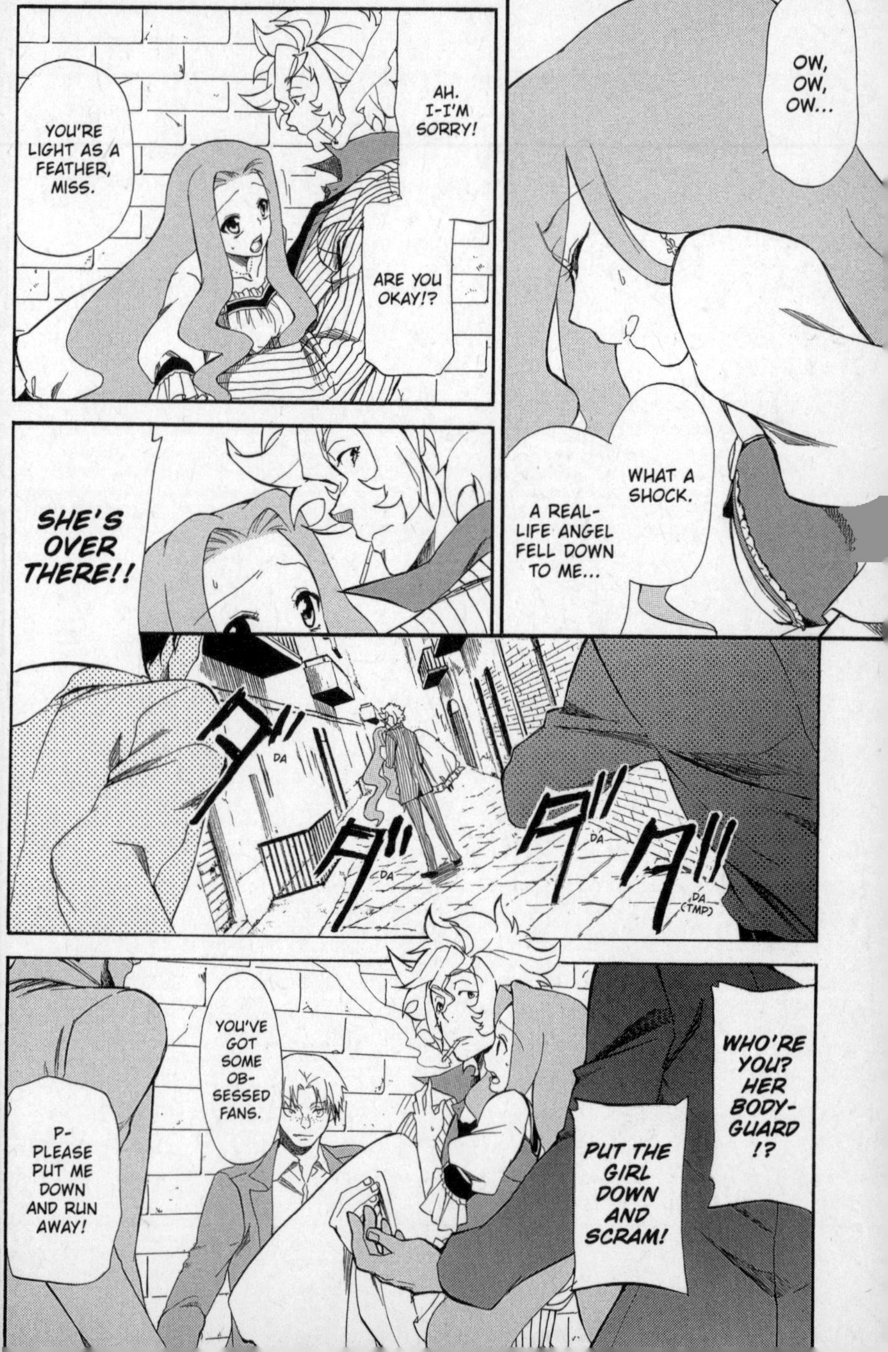
OW, OW, OW...
WHAT A SHOCK.
A REAL-LIFE ANGEL FELL DOWN TO ME...
AH. I-I'M SORRY!
ARE YOU OKAY!?
YOU'RE LIGHT AS A FEATHER, MISS.
SHE'S OVER THERE!!
DA
DA
DA
DA (TMP)
WHO'RE YOU? HER BODY-GUARD!?
PUT THE GIRL DOWN AND SCRAM!
YOU'VE GOT SOME OB-SESSED FANS.
P-PLEASE PUT ME DOWN AND RUN AWAY!

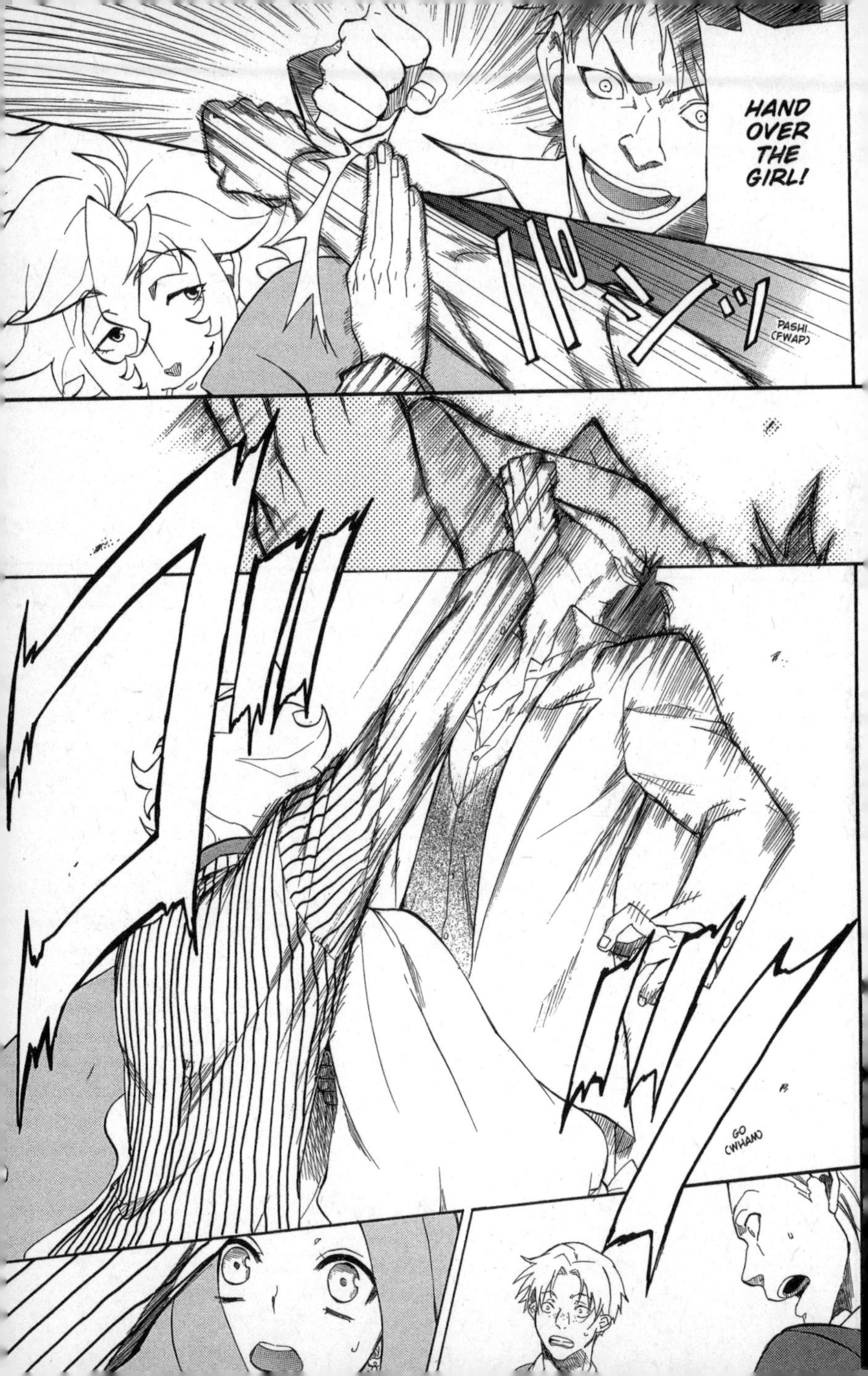
HAND OVER THE GIRL!
PASHI (FWAP)
GO (WHAM)

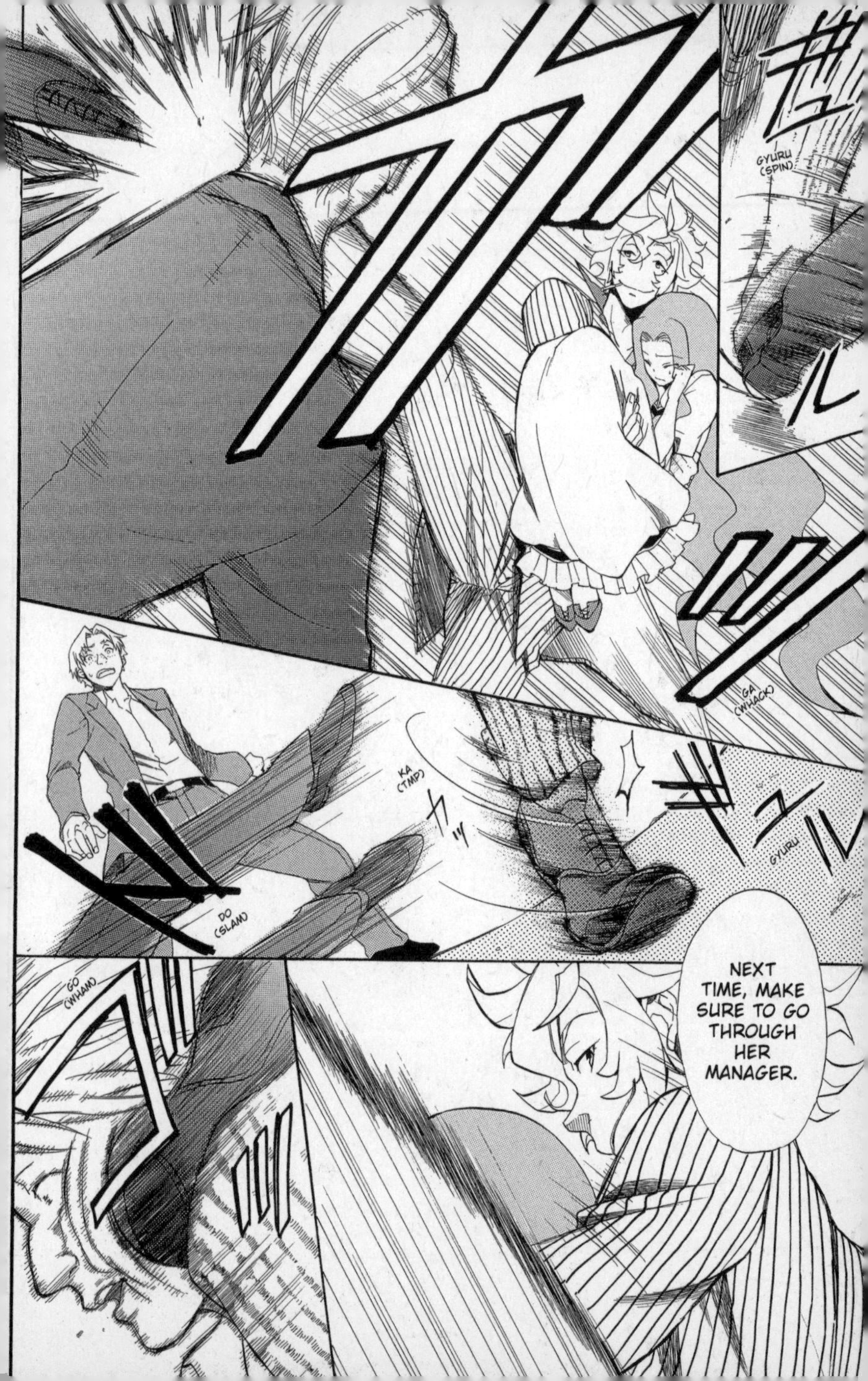
GYURU (SPIN)
GA (WHACK)
GYURU
KA (TMP)
DO (SLAM)
NEXT TIME, MAKE SURE TO GO THROUGH HER MANAGER.
GO (WHAM)

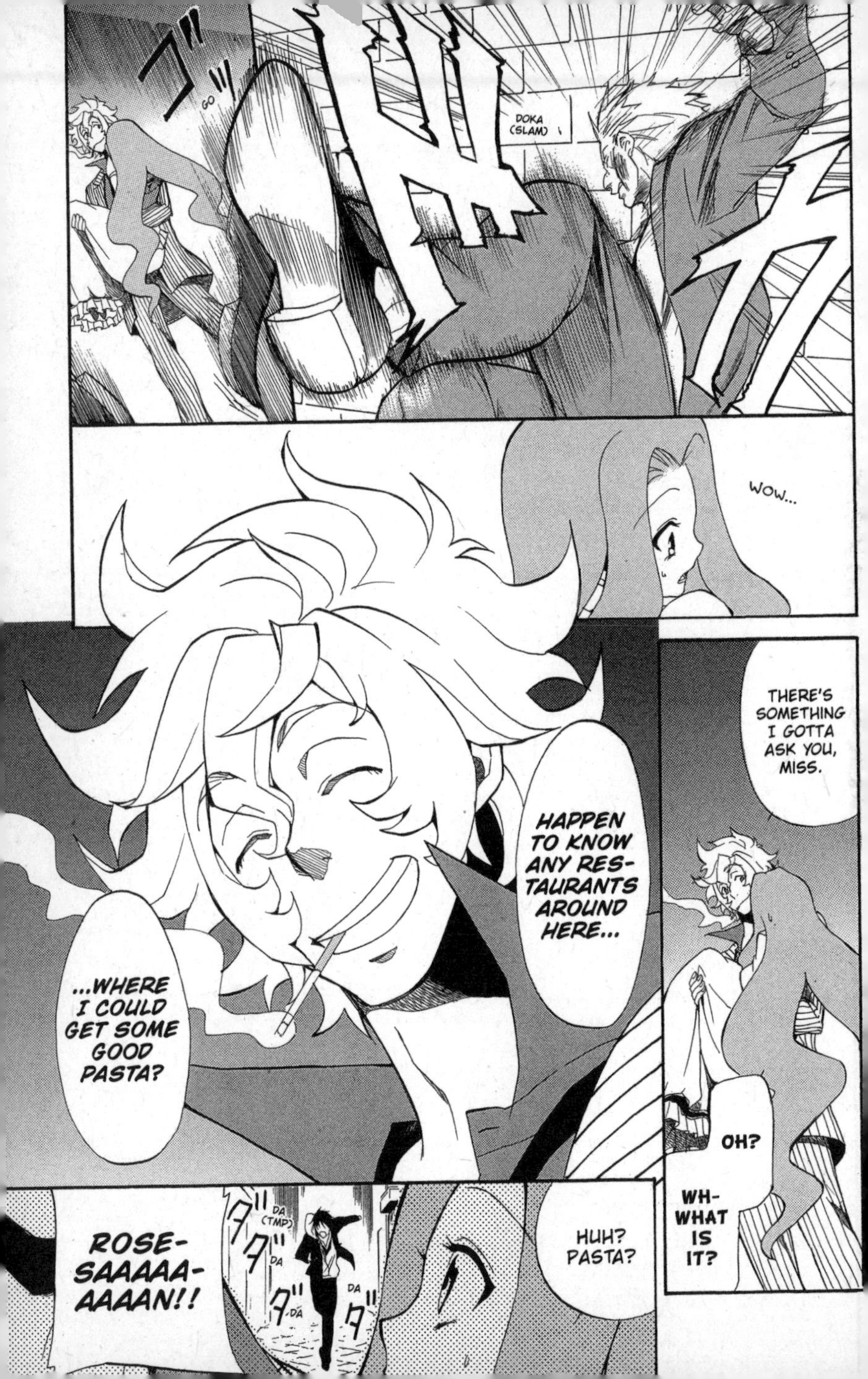
DOKA (SLAM)
GO
WOW...
THERE'S SOMETHING I GOTTA ASK YOU, MISS.
OH?
WH-WHAT IS IT?
HAPPEN TO KNOW ANY RES-TAURANTS AROUND HERE...
...WHERE I COULD GET SOME GOOD PASTA?
HUH? PASTA?
DA (TMP)
DA
DA
DA
ROSE-SAAAAA-AAAAN!!

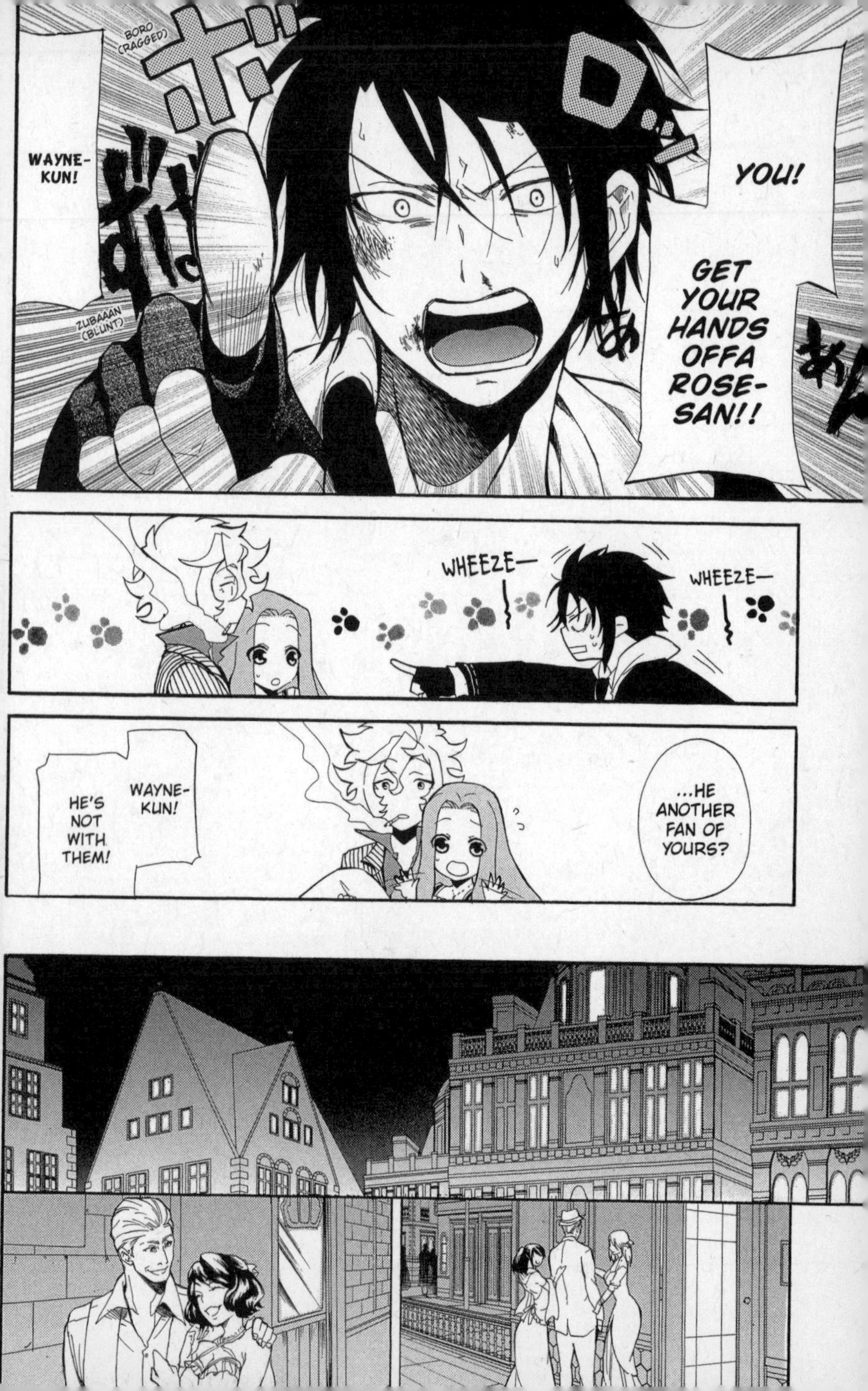
YOU! GET YOUR HANDS OFFA ROSE-SAN!!
BORO (RAGGED)
WAYNE-KUN!
ZUBAAAN (BLUNT)
WHEEZE—
WHEEZE—
...HE ANOTHER FAN OF YOURS?
WAYNE-KUN! HE'S NOT WITH THEM!

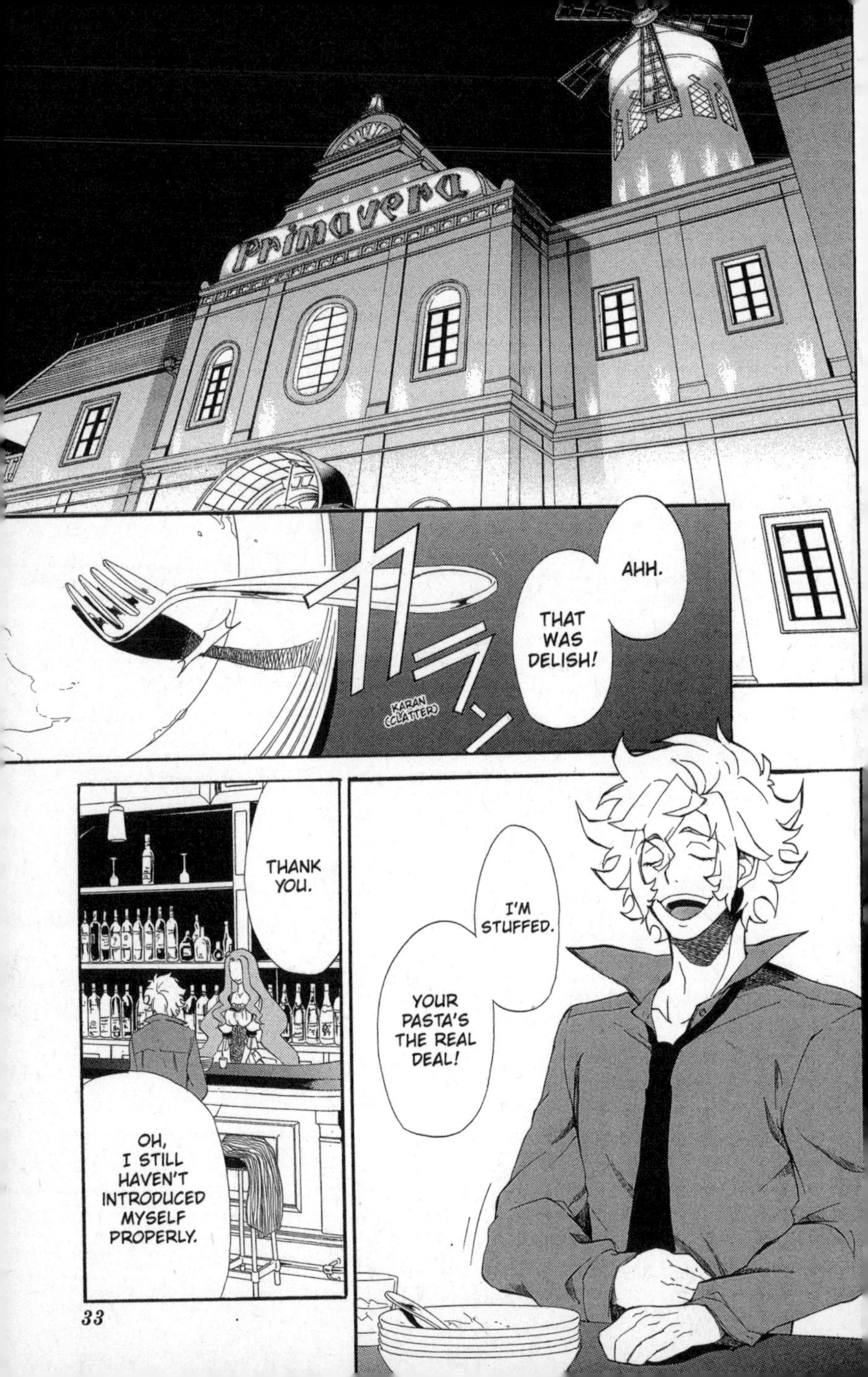
Primavera
AHH.
THAT WAS DELISH!
KARAN (CLATTER)
I'M STUFFED.
YOUR PASTA'S THE REAL DEAL!
THANK YOU.
OH, I STILL HAVEN'T INTRODUCED MYSELF PROPERLY.

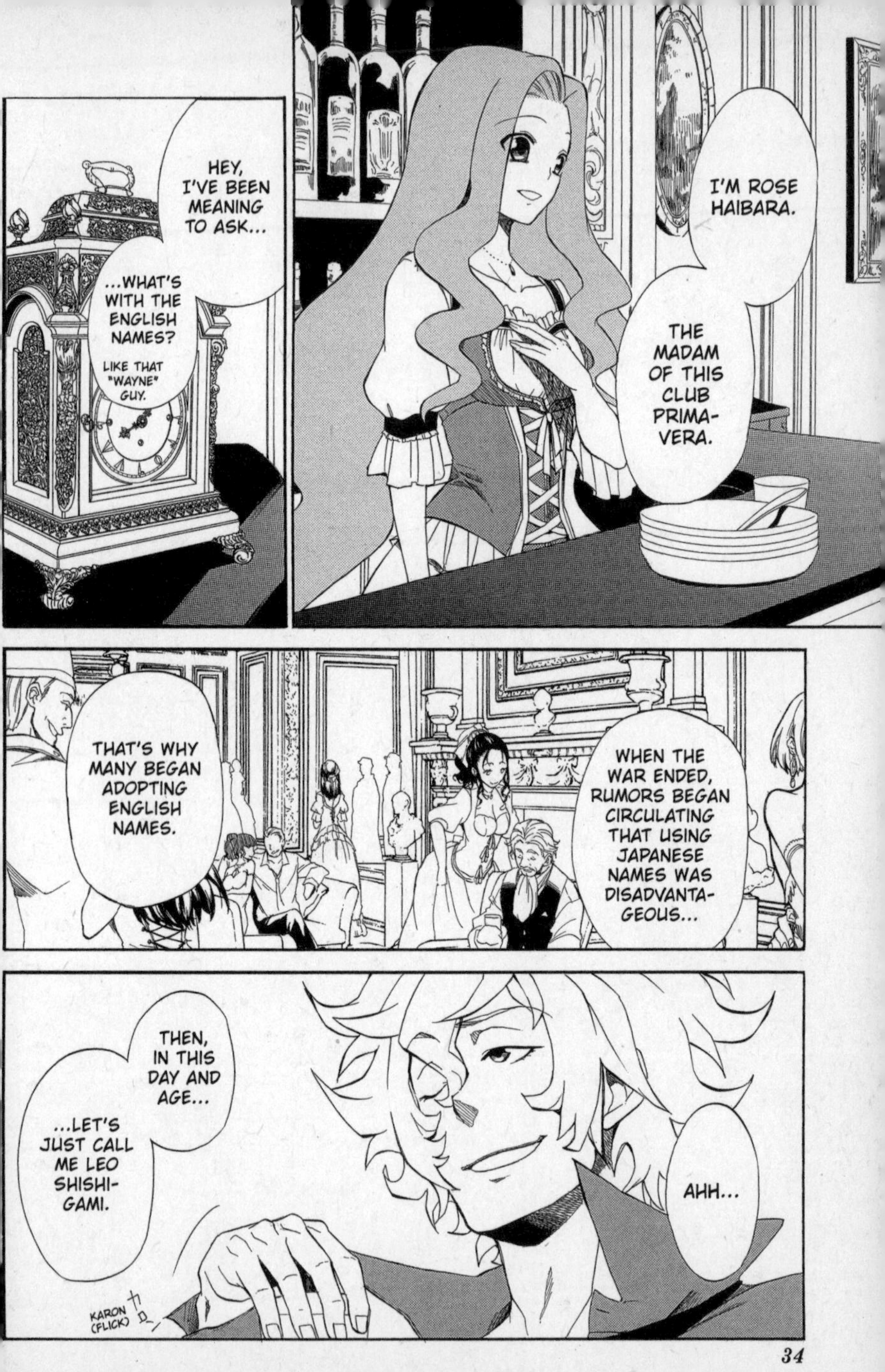
I'M ROSE HAIBARA.
THE MADAM OF THIS CLUB PRIMA-VERA.
HEY, I'VE BEEN MEANING TO ASK...
...WHAT'S WITH THE ENGLISH NAMES?
LIKE THAT "WAYNE" GUY.
WHEN THE WAR ENDED, RUMORS BEGAN CIRCULATING THAT USING JAPANESE NAMES WAS DISADVANTA-GEOUS...
THAT'S WHY MANY BEGAN ADOPTING ENGLISH NAMES.
AHH...
THEN, IN THIS DAY AND AGE...
...LET'S JUST CALL ME LEO SHISHI-GAMI.
KARON (FLICK)

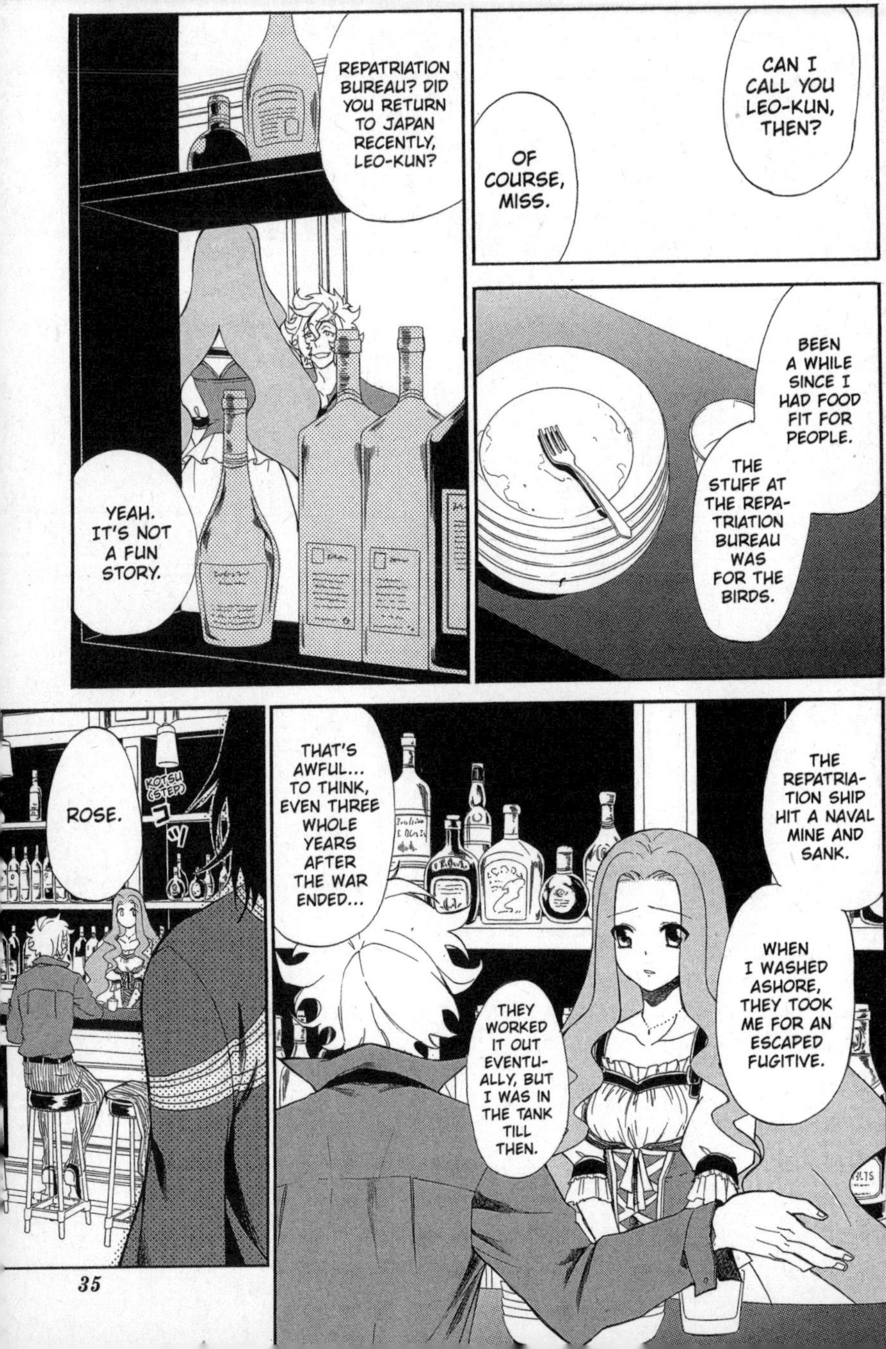
CAN I CALL YOU LEO-KUN, THEN?
OF COURSE, MISS.
BEEN A WHILE SINCE I HAD FOOD FIT FOR PEOPLE.
THE STUFF AT THE REPA-TRIATION BUREAU WAS FOR THE BIRDS.
REPATRIATION BUREAU? DID YOU RETURN TO JAPAN RECENTLY, LEO-KUN?
YEAH. IT'S NOT A FUN STORY.
THE REPATRIA-TION SHIP HIT A NAVAL MINE AND SANK.
WHEN I WASHED ASHORE, THEY TOOK ME FOR AN ESCAPED FUGITIVE.
THEY WORKED IT OUT EVENTU-ALLY, BUT I WAS IN THE TANK TILL THEN.
THAT'S AWFUL... TO THINK, EVEN THREE WHOLE YEARS AFTER THE WAR ENDED...
KOTSU (STEP)
ROSE.

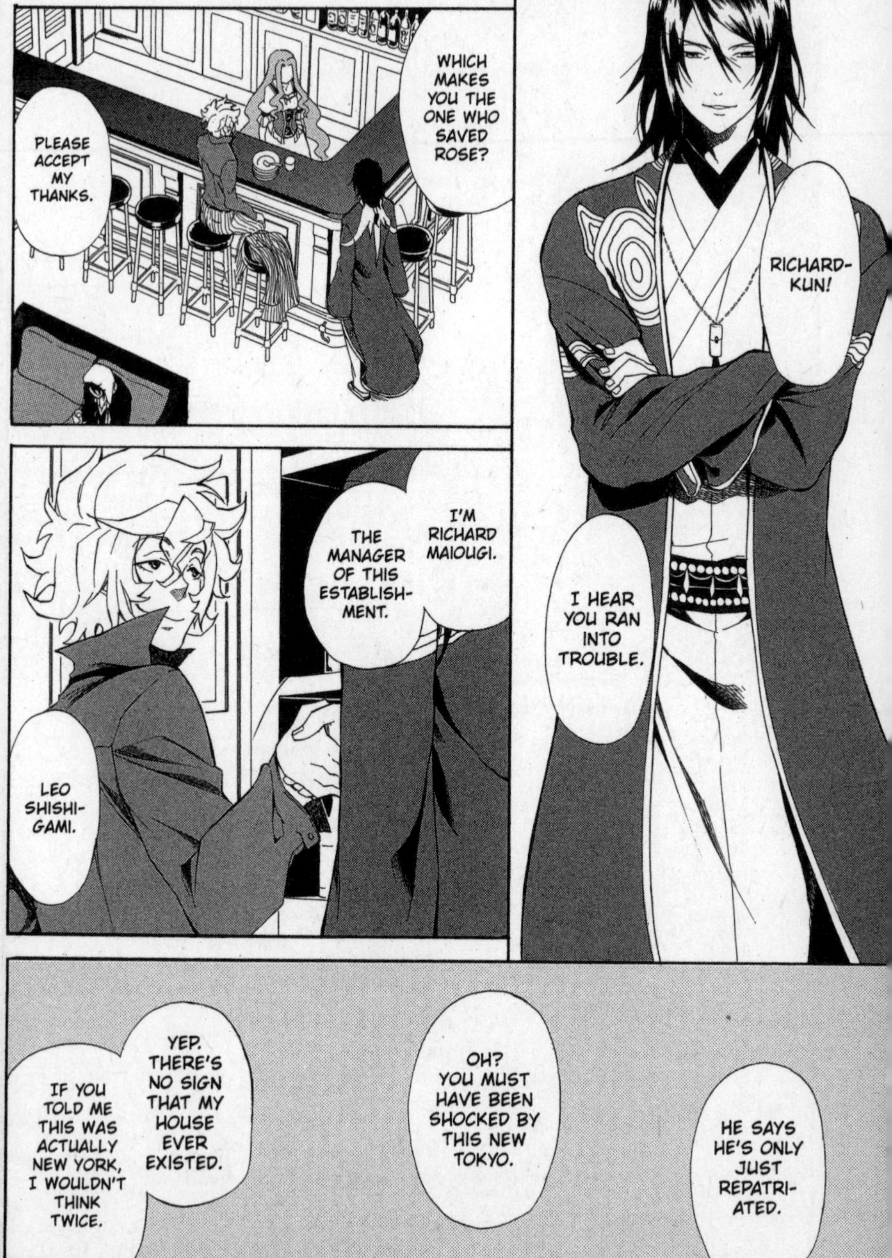
RICHARD-KUN!
I HEAR YOU RAN INTO TROUBLE.
WHICH MAKES YOU THE ONE WHO SAVED ROSE?
PLEASE ACCEPT MY THANKS.
I'M RICHARD MAIOUGI.
THE MANAGER OF THIS ESTABLISHMENT.
LEO SHISHIGAMI.
HE SAYS HE'S ONLY JUST REPATRIATED.
OH? YOU MUST HAVE BEEN SHOCKED BY THIS NEW TOKYO.
YEP. THERE'S NO SIGN THAT MY HOUSE EVER EXISTED.
IF YOU TOLD ME THIS WAS ACTUALLY NEW YORK, I WOULDN'T THINK TWICE.

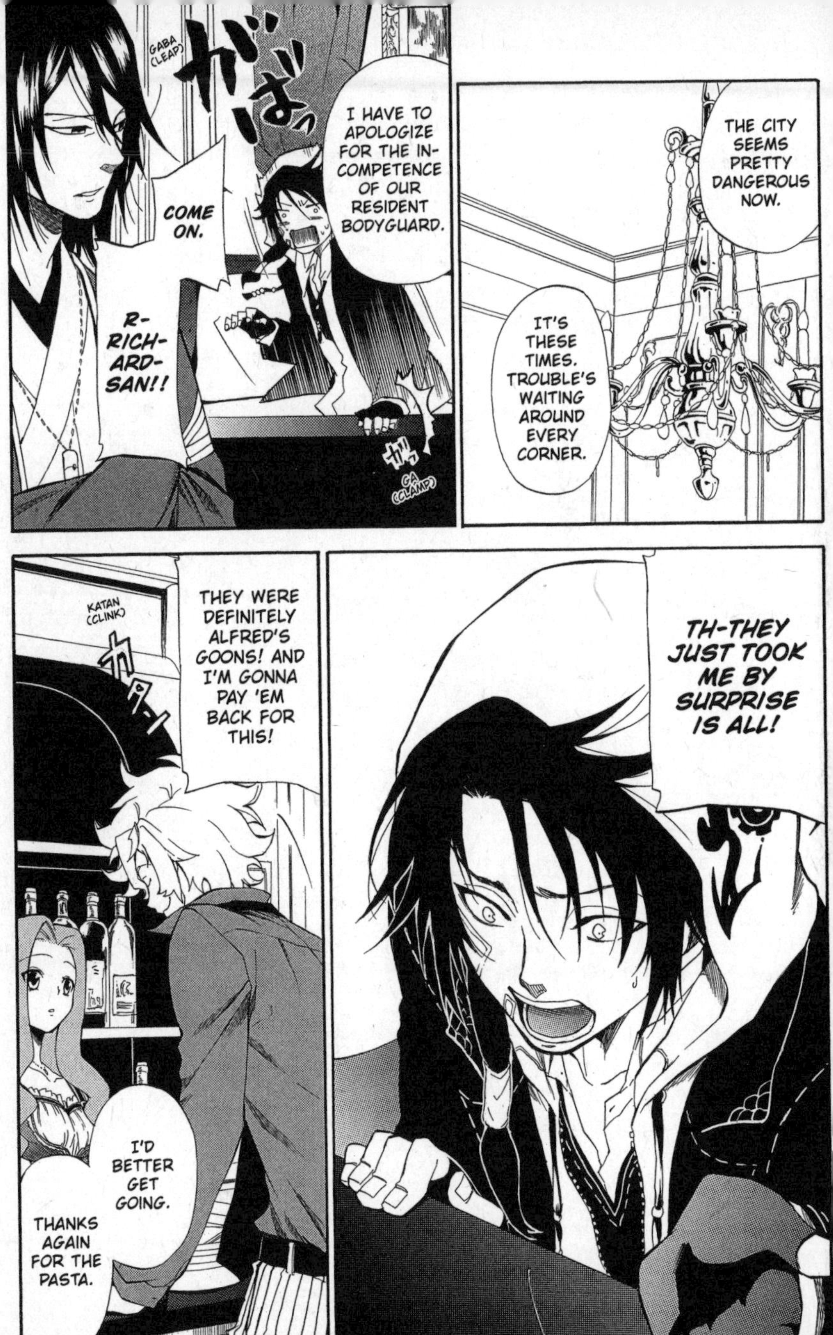
THE CITY SEEMS PRETTY DANGEROUS NOW.
IT'S THESE TIMES. TROUBLE'S WAITING AROUND EVERY CORNER.
GABA (LEAP)
I HAVE TO APOLOGIZE FOR THE IN-COMPETENCE OF OUR RESIDENT BODYGUARD.
COME ON.
R-RICH-ARD-SAN!!
GA (CLAMP)
TH-THEY JUST TOOK ME BY SURPRISE IS ALL!
KATAN (CLINK)
THEY WERE DEFINITELY ALFRED'S GOONS! AND I'M GONNA PAY 'EM BACK FOR THIS!
I'D BETTER GET GOING.
THANKS AGAIN FOR THE PASTA.

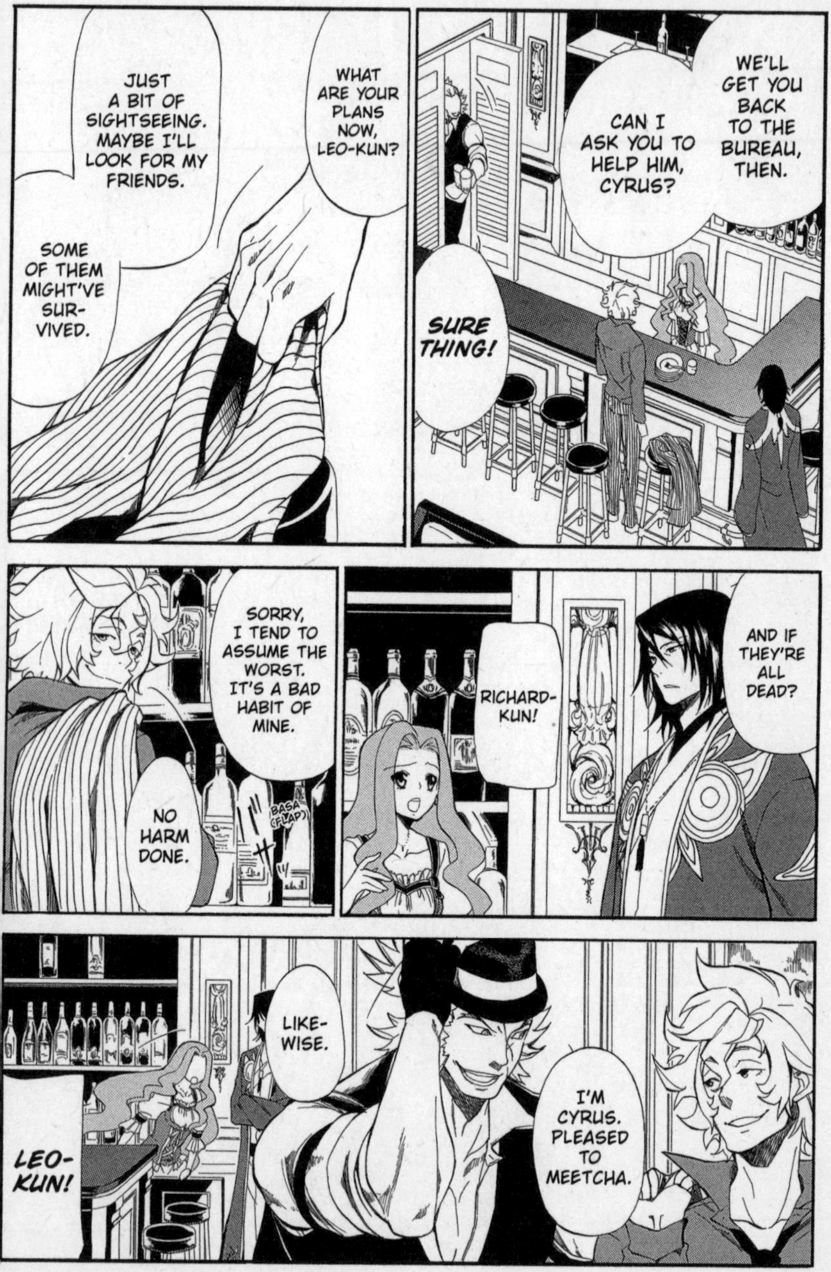
WE'LL GET YOU BACK TO THE BUREAU, THEN.
CAN I ASK YOU TO HELP HIM, CYRUS?
SURE THING!
WHAT ARE YOUR PLANS NOW, LEO-KUN?
JUST A BIT OF SIGHTSEEING. MAYBE I'LL LOOK FOR MY FRIENDS.
SOME OF THEM MIGHT'VE SURVIVED.
AND IF THEY'RE ALL DEAD?
RICHARD-KUN!
SORRY, I TEND TO ASSUME THE WORST. IT'S A BAD HABIT OF MINE.
BASA (FLAP)
NO HARM DONE.
I'M CYRUS. PLEASED TO MEETCHA.
LIKE-WISE.
LEO-KUN!

THANK YOU, REALLY, FOR SAVING ME.

I DON'T KNOW IF YOU'LL FIND YOUR FRIENDS, BUT...

...WE'RE FRIENDS NOW, LEO-KUN.

IF YOU EVER NEED SOMEONE TO TURN TO, YOU CAN ALWAYS COME HERE.

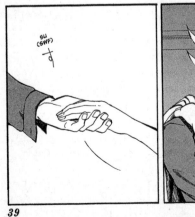

SU (SWF)

THANKS. YOU'VE GOT A BIG HEART, MISS.

39

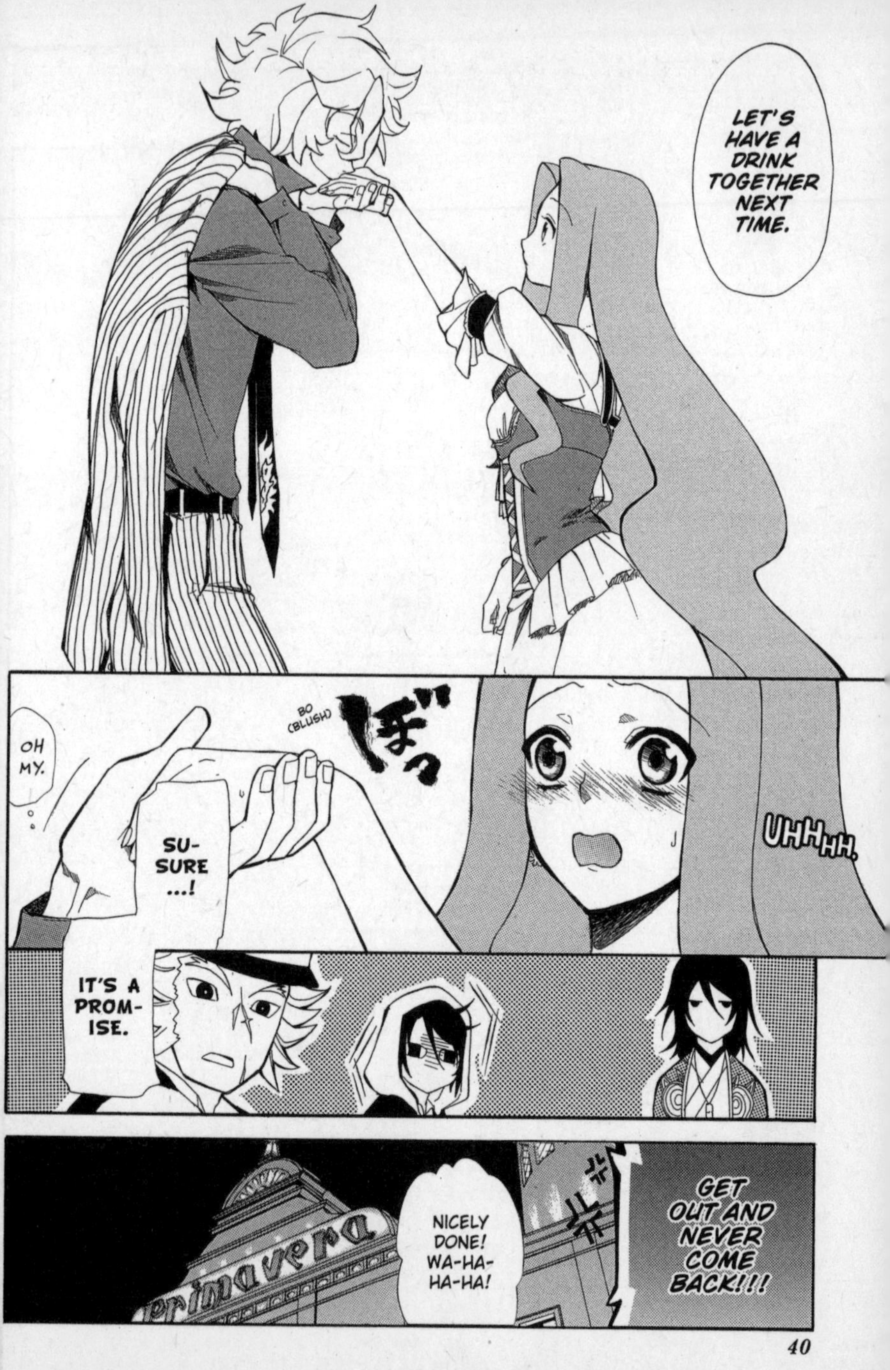
LET'S HAVE A DRINK TOGETHER NEXT TIME.
BO (BLUSH)
ぼっ
UHHHH.
SU-SURE...!
OH MY.
IT'S A PROMISE.
GET OUT AND NEVER COME BACK!!!
NICELY DONE! WA-HA-HA-HA!
primavera

BURORORORO
(VROOOM)

7"

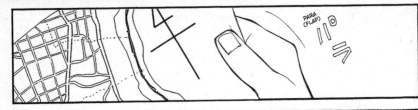

PARA
(FLAP)

WITHOUT THOSE, I'LL BE CALLING A BACK ALLEY HOME.

FIRST, I GOTTA FIND SOMEWHERE TO LIVE AND SOMEWHERE TO WORK...

LET'S SEE...

THEN...

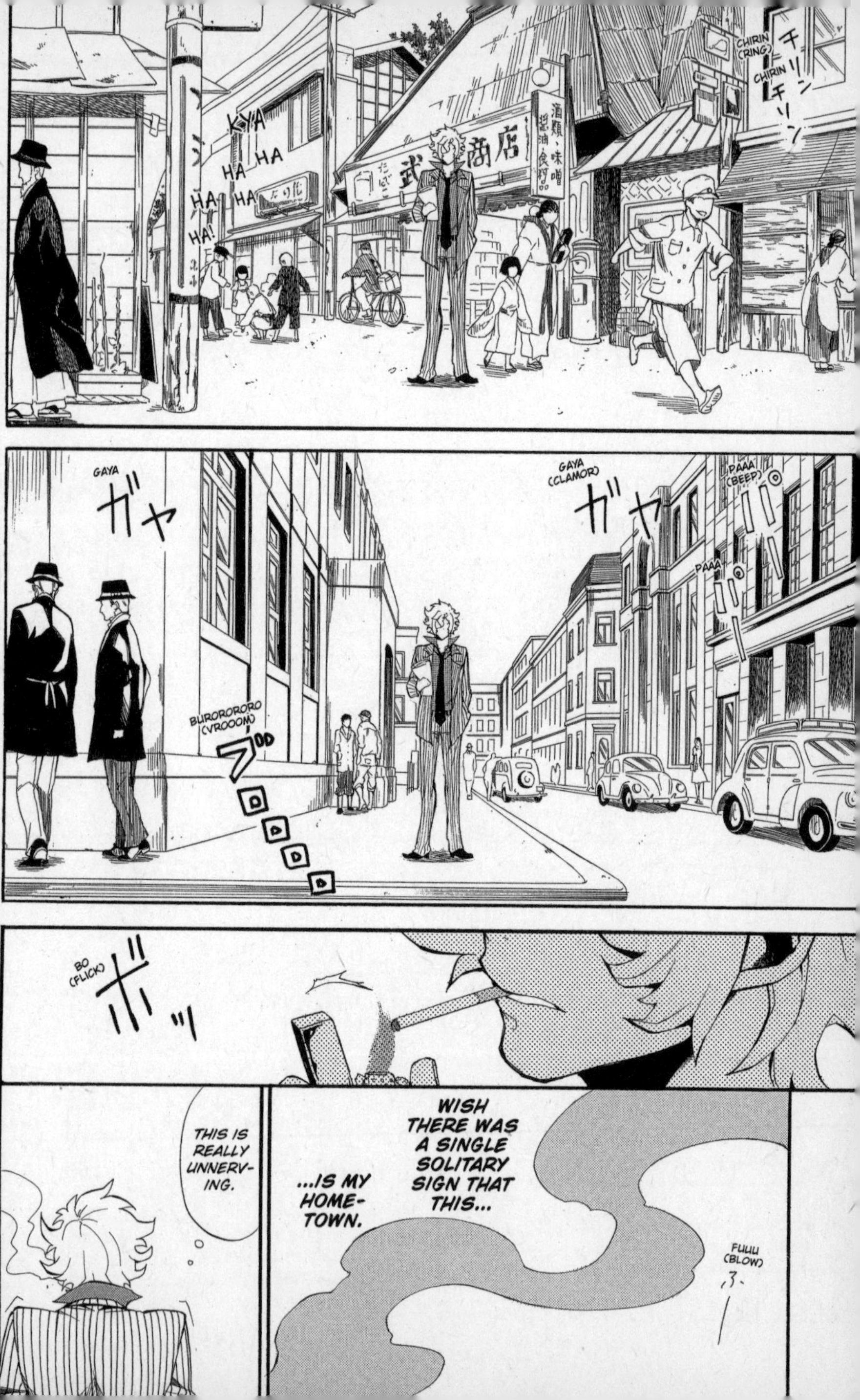
CHIRIN (RING) CHIRIN
チリンチリン
酒類、味噌 醤油食料品
武商店
KYA HA HA HA HA HA!
PAAA (BEEP) PAAA
GAYA (CLAMOR)
ガヤ
GAYA
ガヤ
BURORORORO (VROOOM)
BO (FLICK)
ボッ
FUUU (BLOW)
WISH THERE WAS A SINGLE SOLITARY SIGN THAT THIS...
...IS MY HOME-TOWN.
THIS IS REALLY UNNERV-ING.

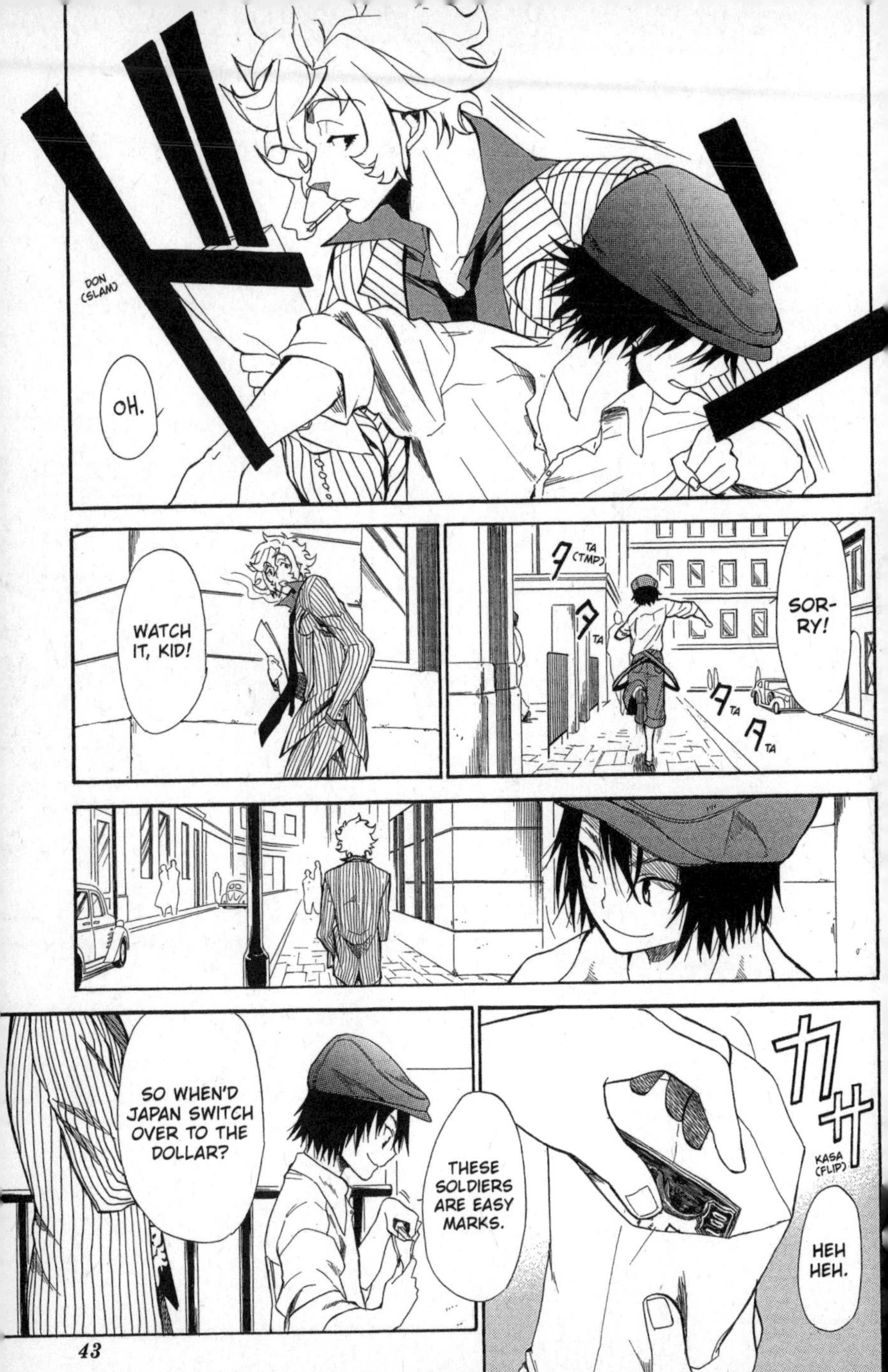
DON (SLAM)
OH.
SOR-RY!
TA (TMP)
TA
TA
TA
WATCH IT, KID!
KASA (FLIP)
HEH HEH.
THESE SOLDIERS ARE EASY MARKS.
SO WHEN'D JAPAN SWITCH OVER TO THE DOLLAR?

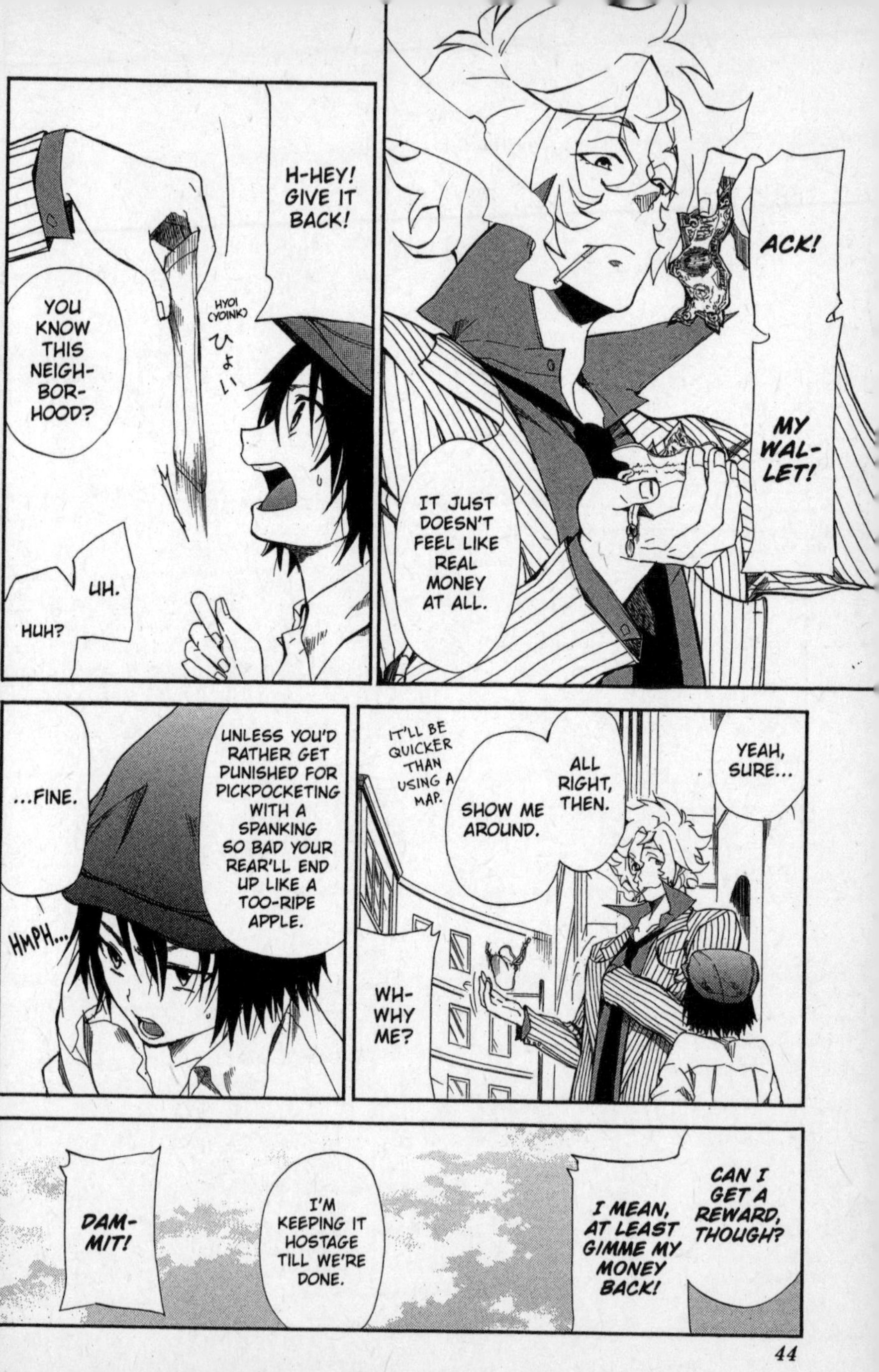
ACK!
MY WAL-LET!
IT JUST DOESN'T FEEL LIKE REAL MONEY AT ALL.
H-HEY! GIVE IT BACK!
HYOI (YOINK)
ひょい
YOU KNOW THIS NEIGH-BOR-HOOD?
UH.
HUH?
YEAH, SURE...
ALL RIGHT, THEN.
SHOW ME AROUND.
IT'LL BE QUICKER THAN USING A MAP.
WH-WHY ME?
UNLESS YOU'D RATHER GET PUNISHED FOR PICKPOCKETING WITH A SPANKING SO BAD YOUR REAR'LL END UP LIKE A TOO-RIPE APPLE.
...FINE.
HMPH...
CAN I GET A REWARD, THOUGH?
I MEAN, AT LEAST GIMME MY MONEY BACK!
I'M KEEPING IT HOSTAGE TILL WE'RE DONE.
DAM-MIT!

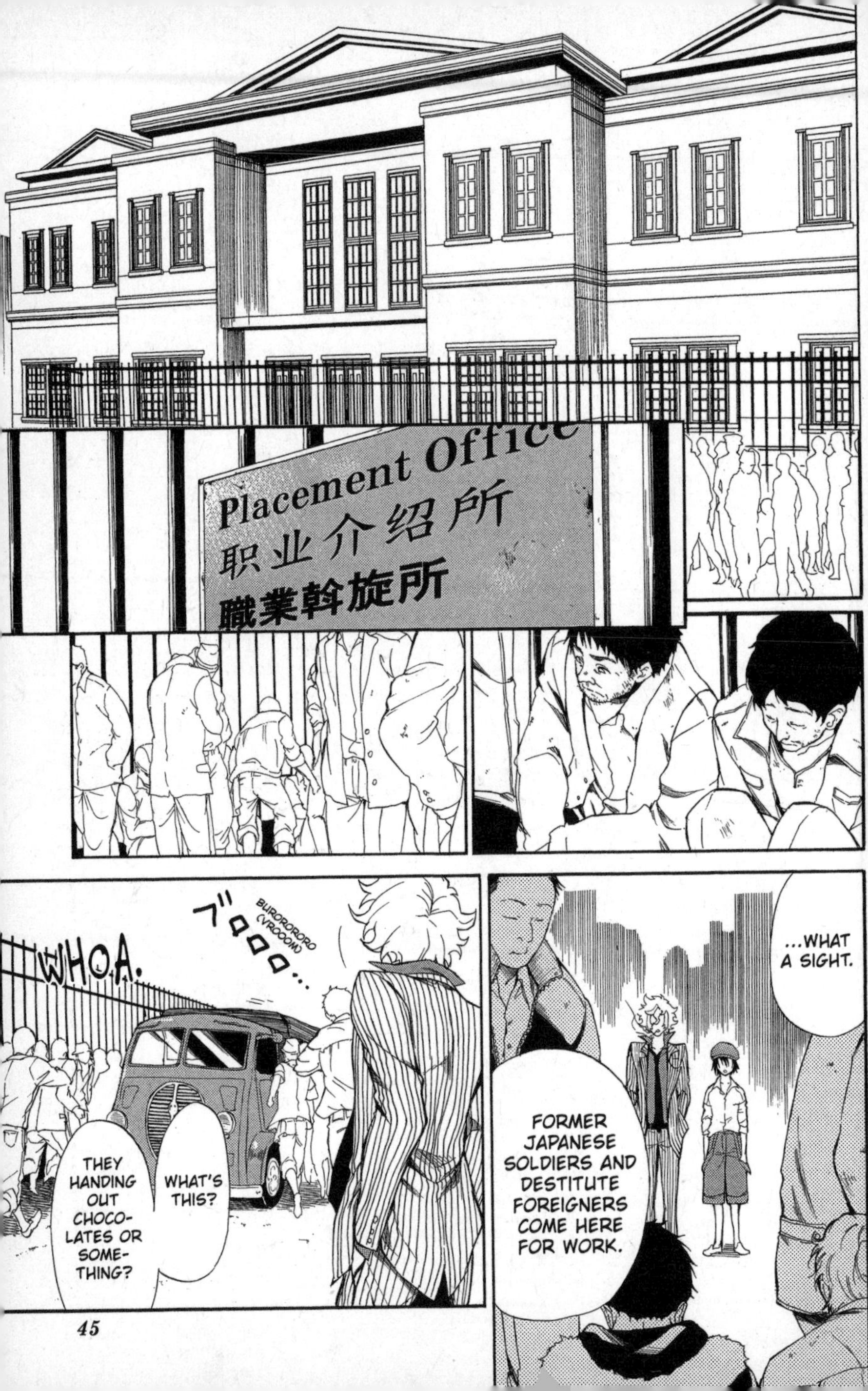
Placement Office
职业介绍所
職業斡旋所
...WHAT A SIGHT.
FORMER JAPANESE SOLDIERS AND DESTITUTE FOREIGNERS COME HERE FOR WORK.
ブロロロ...
BURORORO (VROOOM)
WHOA.
WHAT'S THIS?
THEY HANDING OUT CHOCO-LATES OR SOME-THING?

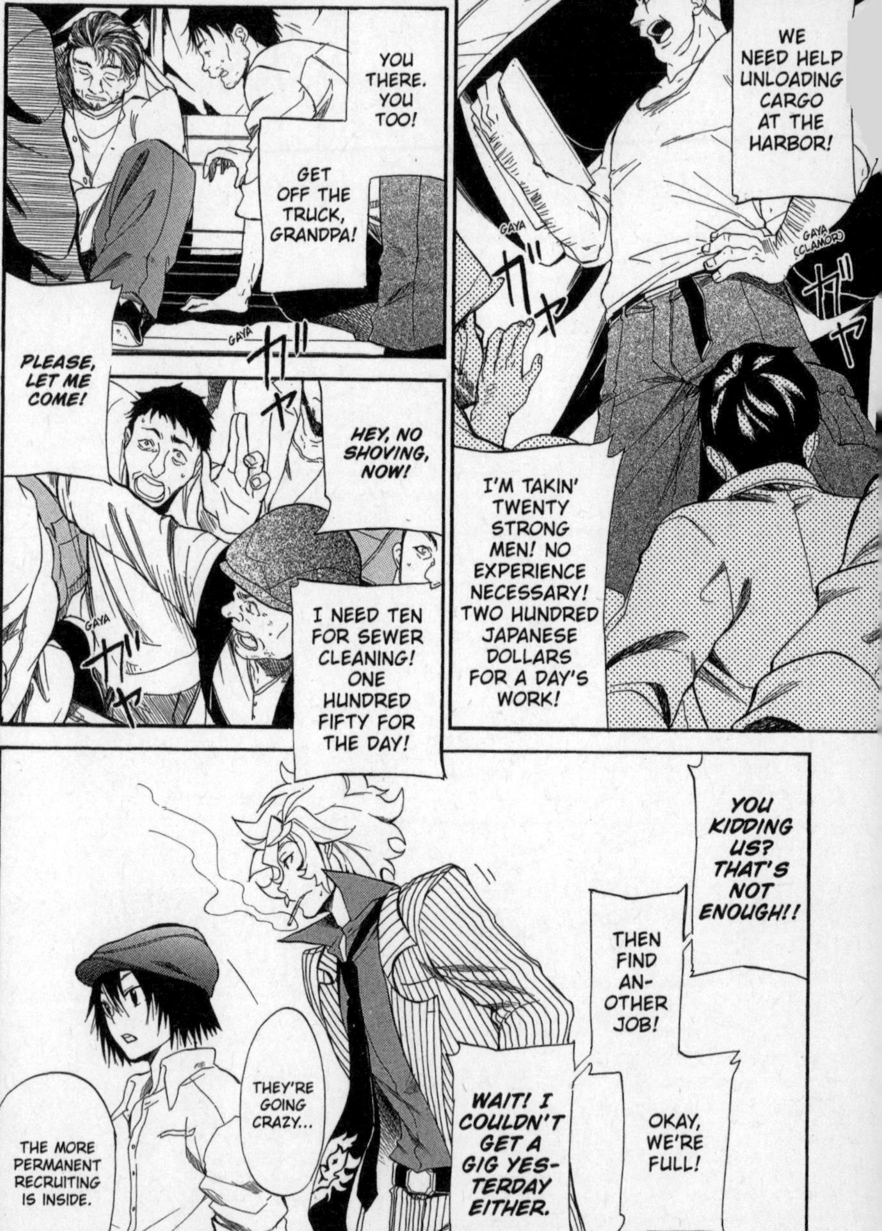
WE NEED HELP UNLOADING CARGO AT THE HARBOR!
GAYA (CLAMOR)
GAYA
I'M TAKIN' TWENTY STRONG MEN! NO EXPERIENCE NECESSARY! TWO HUNDRED JAPANESE DOLLARS FOR A DAY'S WORK!
YOU THERE. YOU TOO!
GET OFF THE TRUCK, GRANDPA!
GAYA
HEY, NO SHOVING, NOW!
PLEASE, LET ME COME!
GAYA
I NEED TEN FOR SEWER CLEANING! ONE HUNDRED FIFTY FOR THE DAY!
YOU KIDDING US? THAT'S NOT ENOUGH!!
THEN FIND AN-OTHER JOB!
OKAY, WE'RE FULL!
WAIT! I COULDN'T GET A GIG YES-TERDAY EITHER.
THEY'RE GOING CRAZY...
THE MORE PERMANENT RECRUITING IS INSIDE.

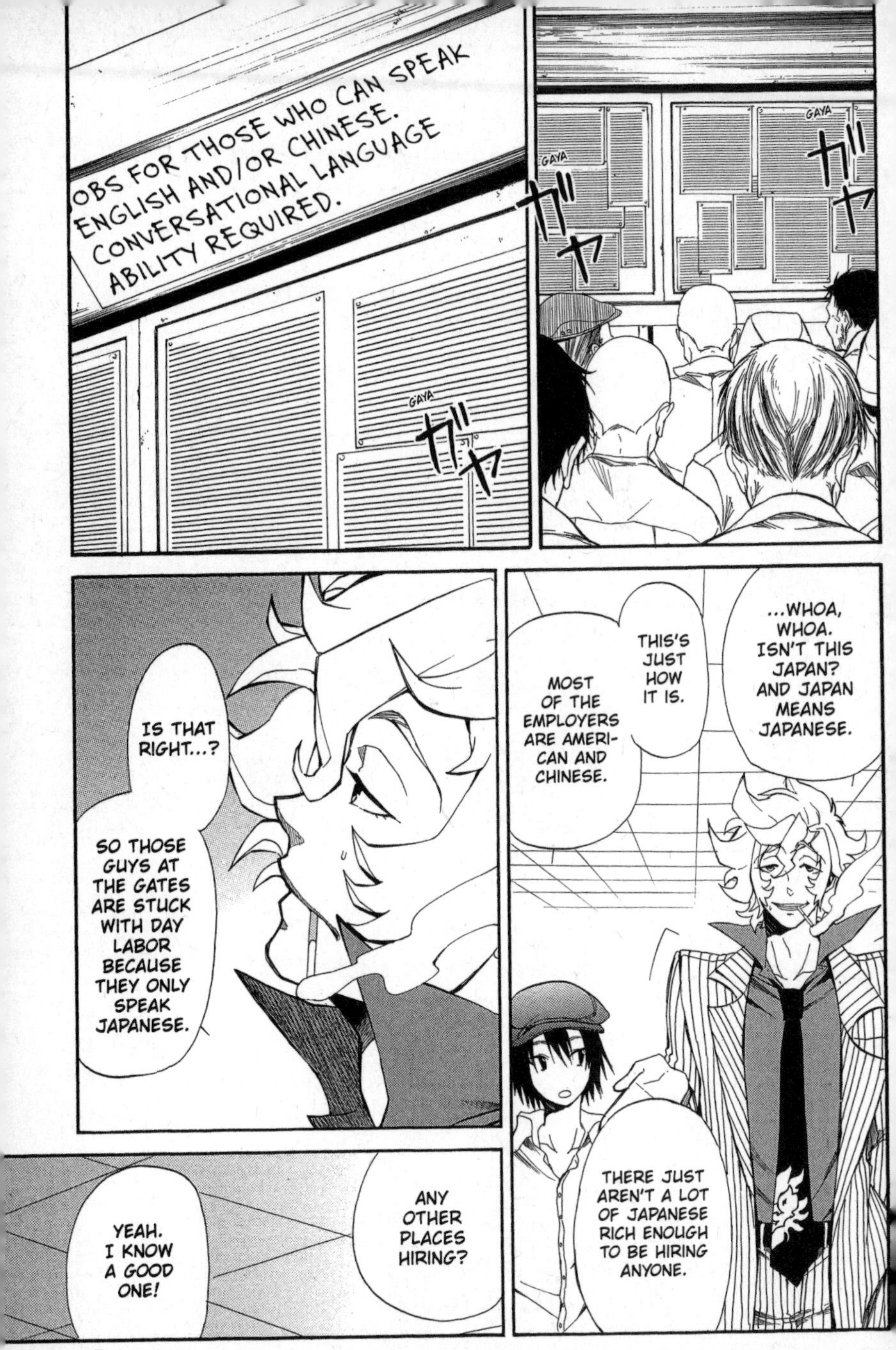
GAYA
GAYA
GAYA
OBS FOR THOSE WHO CAN SPEAK ENGLISH AND/OR CHINESE. CONVERSATIONAL LANGUAGE ABILITY REQUIRED.
GAYA
...WHOA, WHOA. ISN'T THIS JAPAN? AND JAPAN MEANS JAPANESE.
THIS'S JUST HOW IT IS.
MOST OF THE EMPLOYERS ARE AMERI-CAN AND CHINESE.
THERE JUST AREN'T A LOT OF JAPANESE RICH ENOUGH TO BE HIRING ANYONE.
IS THAT RIGHT...?
SO THOSE GUYS AT THE GATES ARE STUCK WITH DAY LABOR BECAUSE THEY ONLY SPEAK JAPANESE.
ANY OTHER PLACES HIRING?
YEAH. I KNOW A GOOD ONE!

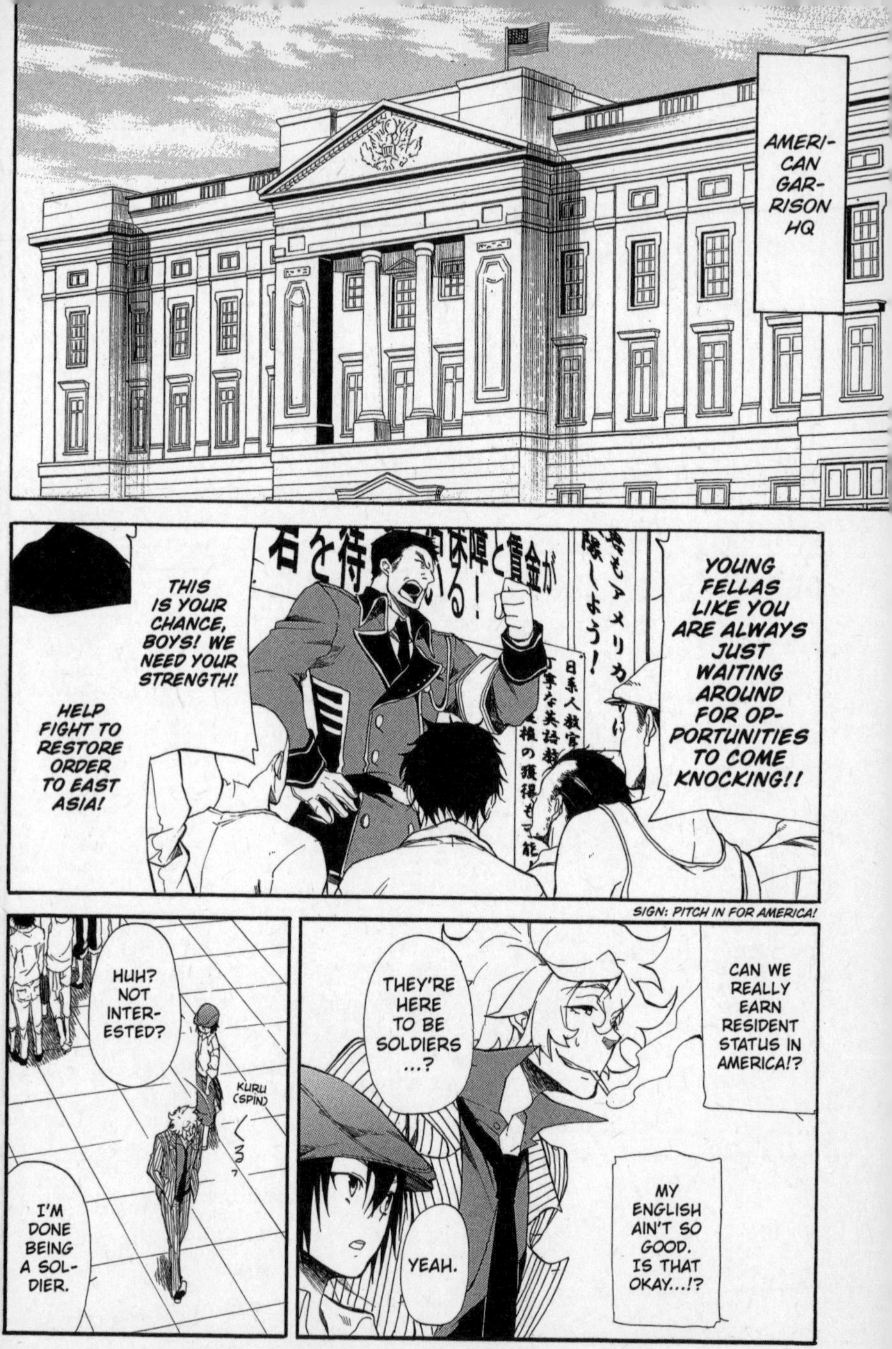
AMERICAN GARRISON HQ
YOUNG FELLAS LIKE YOU ARE ALWAYS JUST WAITING AROUND FOR OPPORTUNITIES TO COME KNOCKING!!
THIS IS YOUR CHANCE, BOYS! WE NEED YOUR STRENGTH!
HELP FIGHT TO RESTORE ORDER TO EAST ASIA!
SIGN: PITCH IN FOR AMERICA!
CAN WE REALLY EARN RESIDENT STATUS IN AMERICA!?
THEY'RE HERE TO BE SOLDIERS ...?
MY ENGLISH AIN'T SO GOOD. IS THAT OKAY...!?
YEAH.
HUH? NOT INTERESTED?
KURU (SPIN)
I'M DONE BEING A SOLDIER.

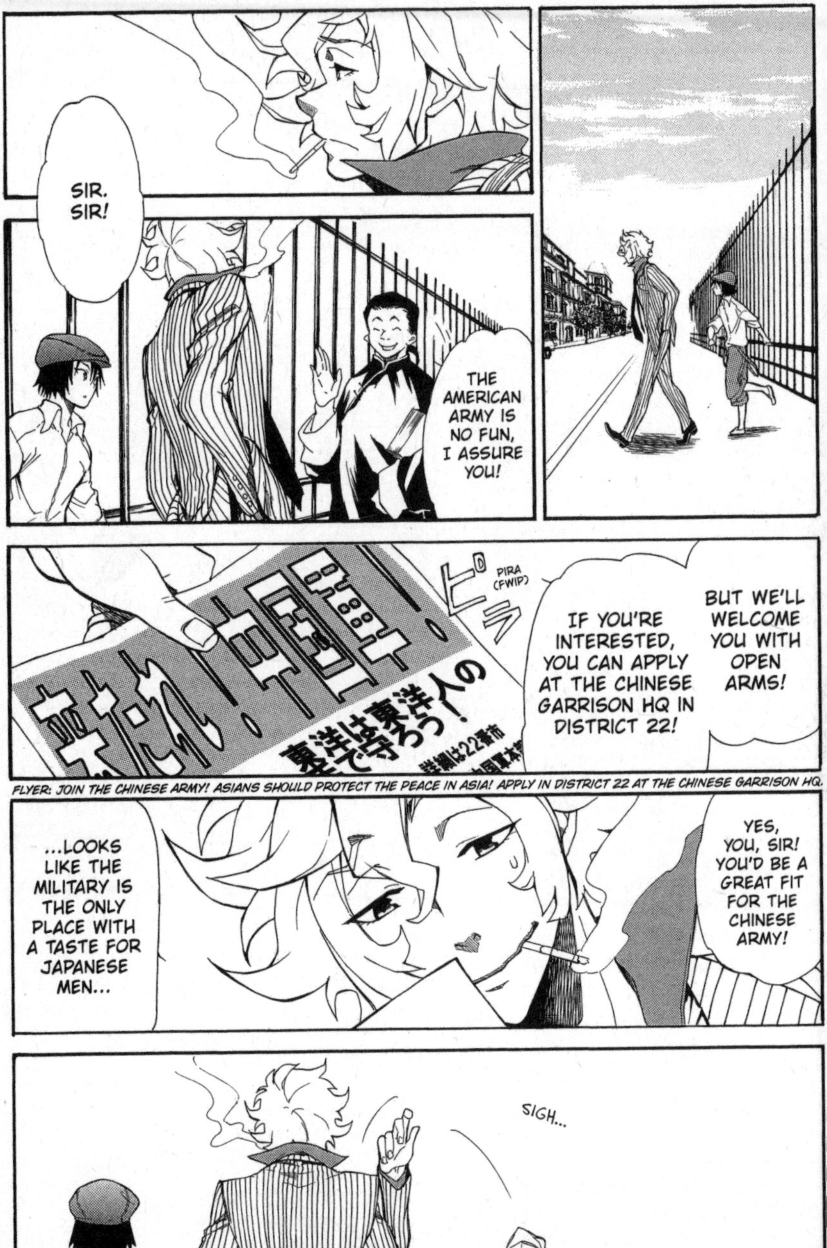
SIR. SIR!
THE AMERICAN ARMY IS NO FUN, I ASSURE YOU!
PIRA (FWIP)
BUT WE'LL WELCOME YOU WITH OPEN ARMS!
IF YOU'RE INTERESTED, YOU CAN APPLY AT THE CHINESE GARRISON HQ IN DISTRICT 22!
FLYER: JOIN THE CHINESE ARMY! ASIANS SHOULD PROTECT THE PEACE IN ASIA! APPLY IN DISTRICT 22 AT THE CHINESE GARRISON HQ.
YES, YOU, SIR! YOU'D BE A GREAT FIT FOR THE CHINESE ARMY!
...LOOKS LIKE THE MILITARY IS THE ONLY PLACE WITH A TASTE FOR JAPANESE MEN...
SIGH...

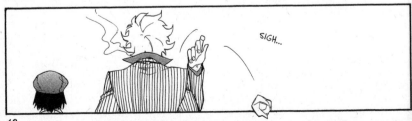

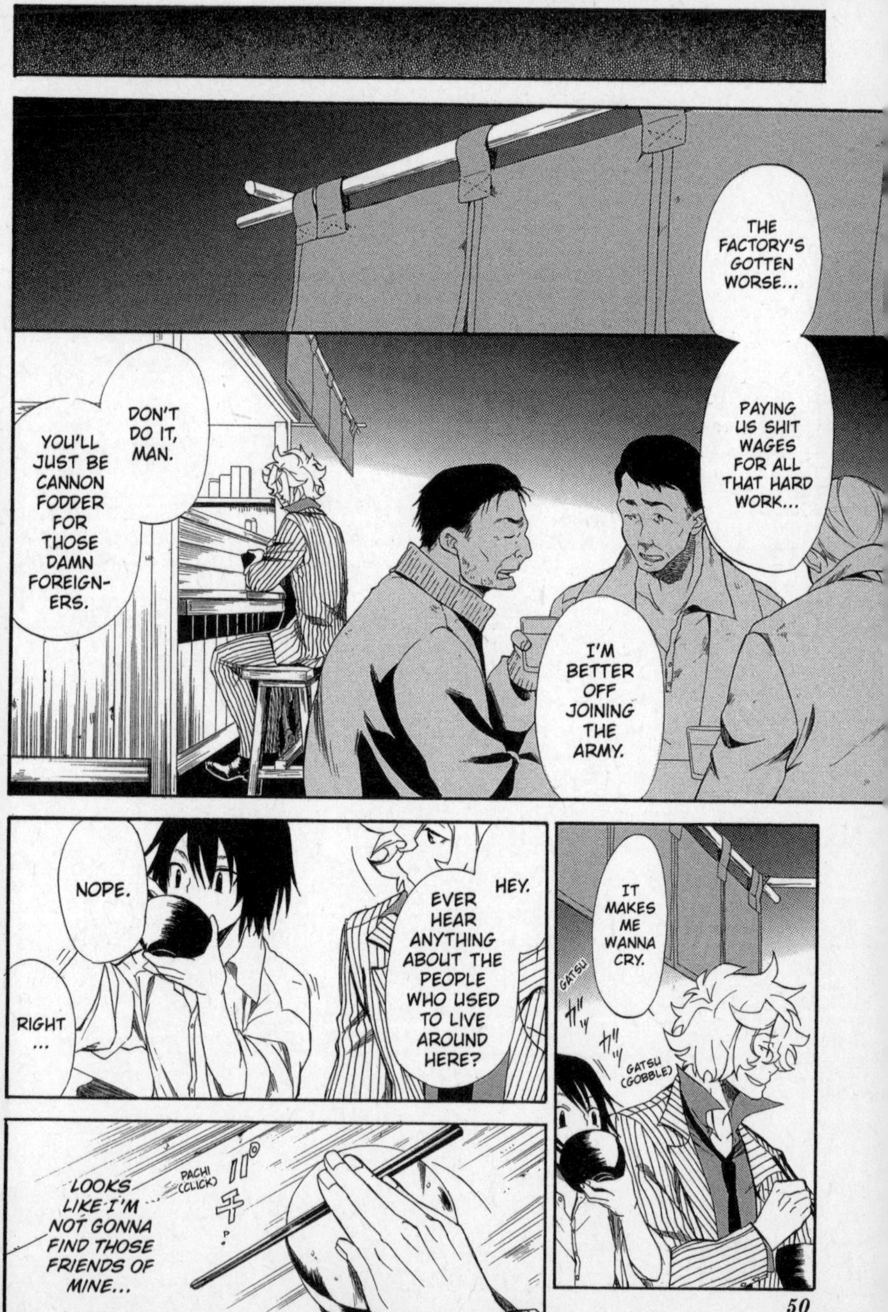
THE FACTORY'S GOTTEN WORSE...
PAYING US SHIT WAGES FOR ALL THAT HARD WORK...
I'M BETTER OFF JOINING THE ARMY.
DON'T DO IT, MAN.
YOU'LL JUST BE CANNON FODDER FOR THOSE DAMN FOREIGN-ERS.
IT MAKES ME WANNA CRY.
GATSU
GATSU (GOBBLE)
HEY.
EVER HEAR ANYTHING ABOUT THE PEOPLE WHO USED TO LIVE AROUND HERE?
NOPE.
RIGHT...
PACHI (CLICK)
LOOKS LIKE I'M NOT GONNA FIND THOSE FRIENDS OF MINE...

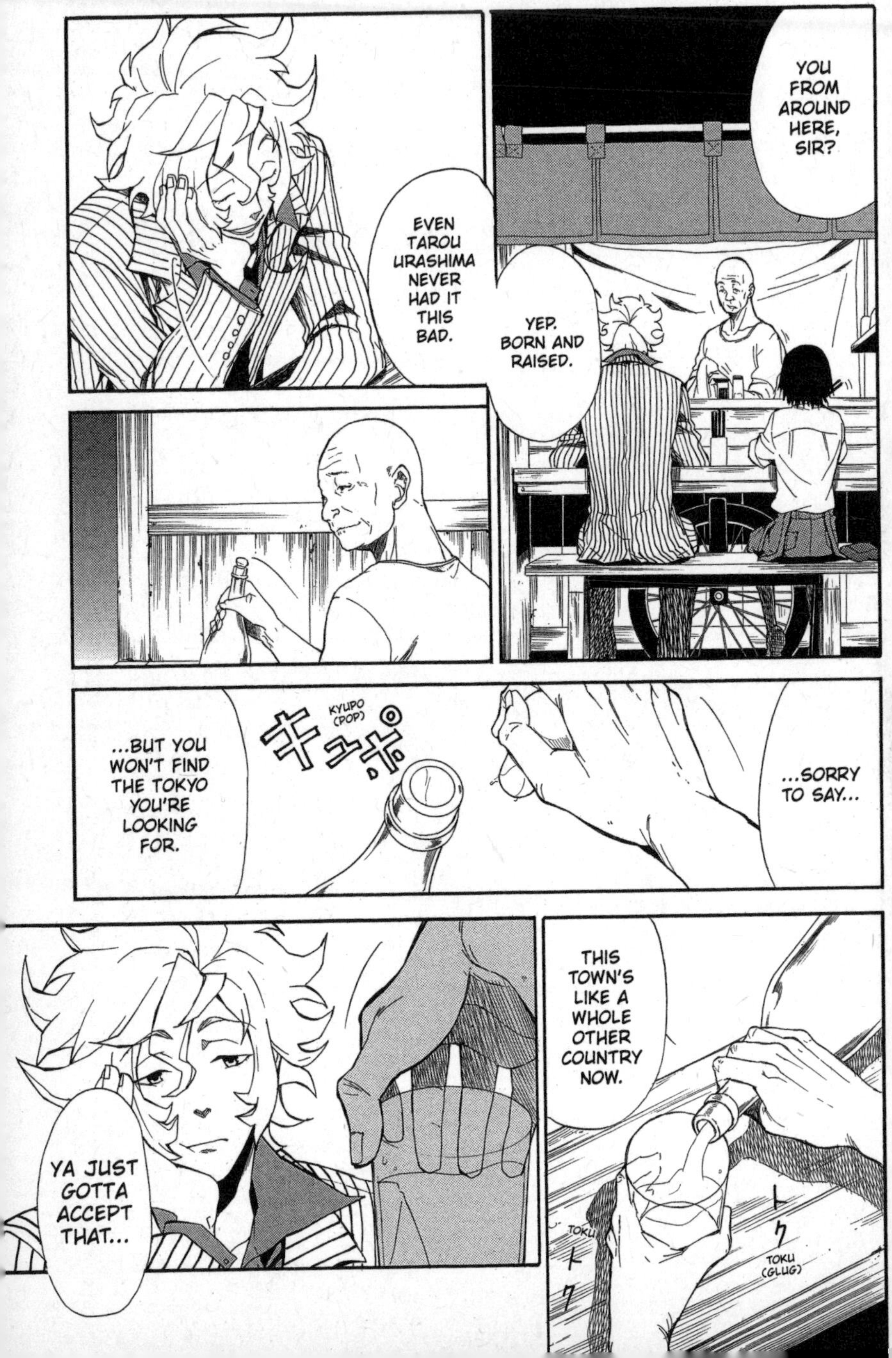
YOU FROM AROUND HERE, SIR?
YEP. BORN AND RAISED.
EVEN TAROU URASHIMA NEVER HAD IT THIS BAD.
...SORRY TO SAY...
キュポ
KYUPO (POP)
...BUT YOU WON'T FIND THE TOKYO YOU'RE LOOKING FOR.
THIS TOWN'S LIKE A WHOLE OTHER COUNTRY NOW.
トク
TOKU (GLUG)
トク
TOKU
YA JUST GOTTA ACCEPT THAT...

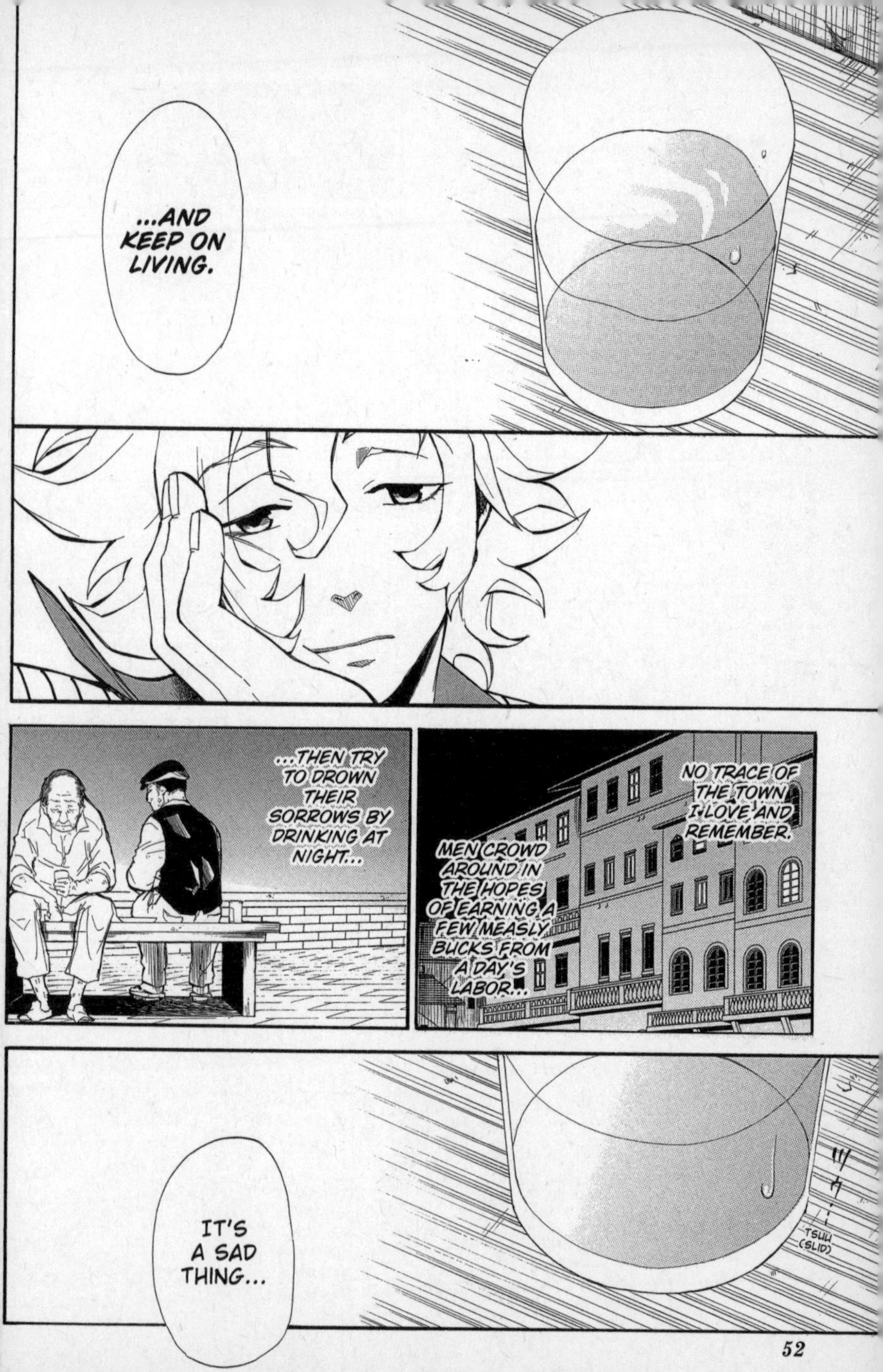
...AND KEEP ON LIVING.
NO TRACE OF THE TOWN I LOVE AND REMEMBER.
MEN CROWD AROUND IN THE HOPES OF EARNING A FEW MEASLY BUCKS FROM A DAY'S LABOR...
...THEN TRY TO DROWN THEIR SORROWS BY DRINKING AT NIGHT...
TSUU (SLID)
IT'S A SAD THING...

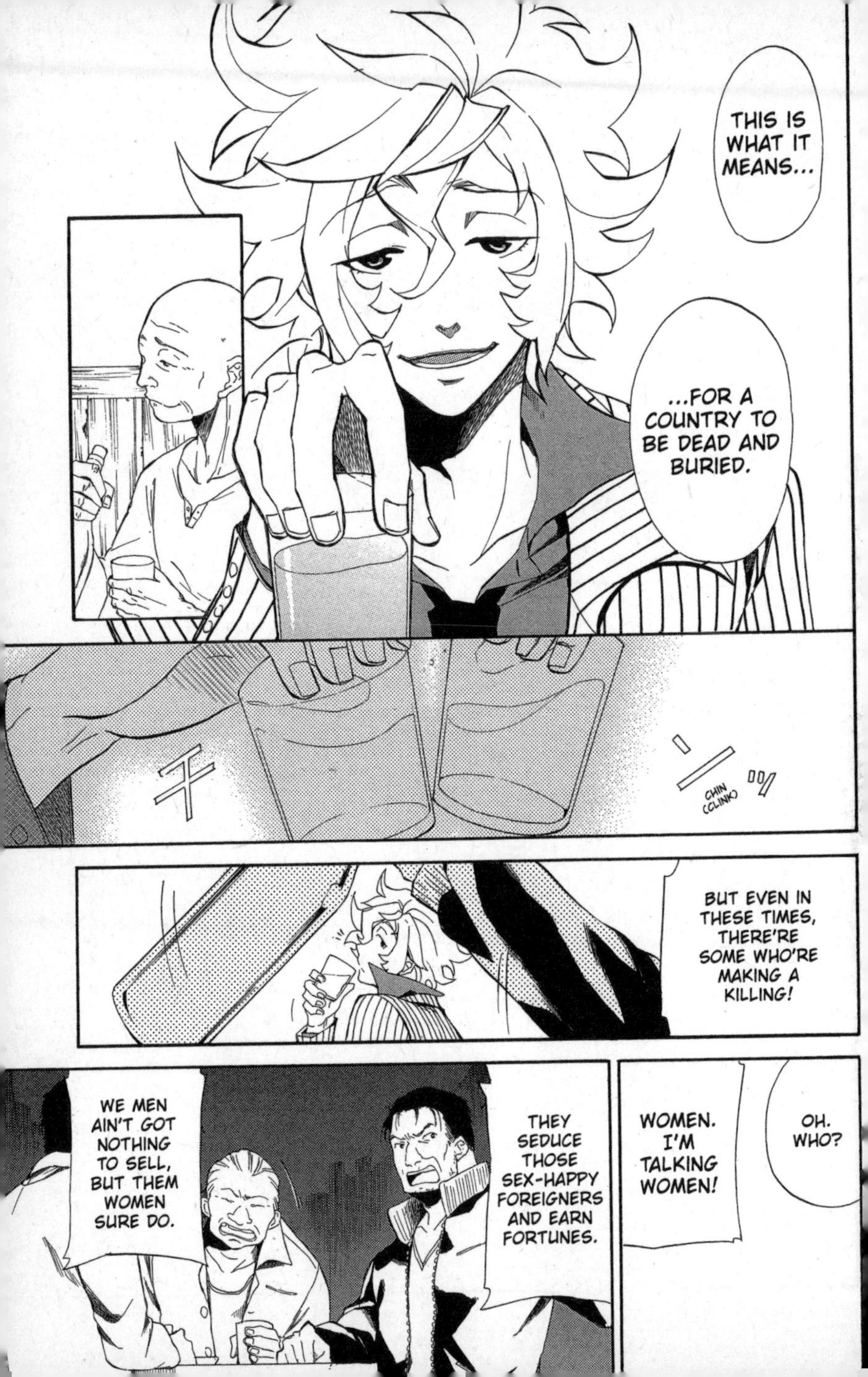
THIS IS WHAT IT MEANS...
...FOR A COUNTRY TO BE DEAD AND BURIED.
CHIN (CLINK)
BUT EVEN IN THESE TIMES, THERE'RE SOME WHO'RE MAKING A KILLING!
OH. WHO?
WOMEN. I'M TALKING WOMEN!
THEY SEDUCE THOSE SEX-HAPPY FOREIGNERS AND EARN FORTUNES.
WE MEN AIN'T GOT NOTHING TO SELL, BUT THEM WOMEN SURE DO.

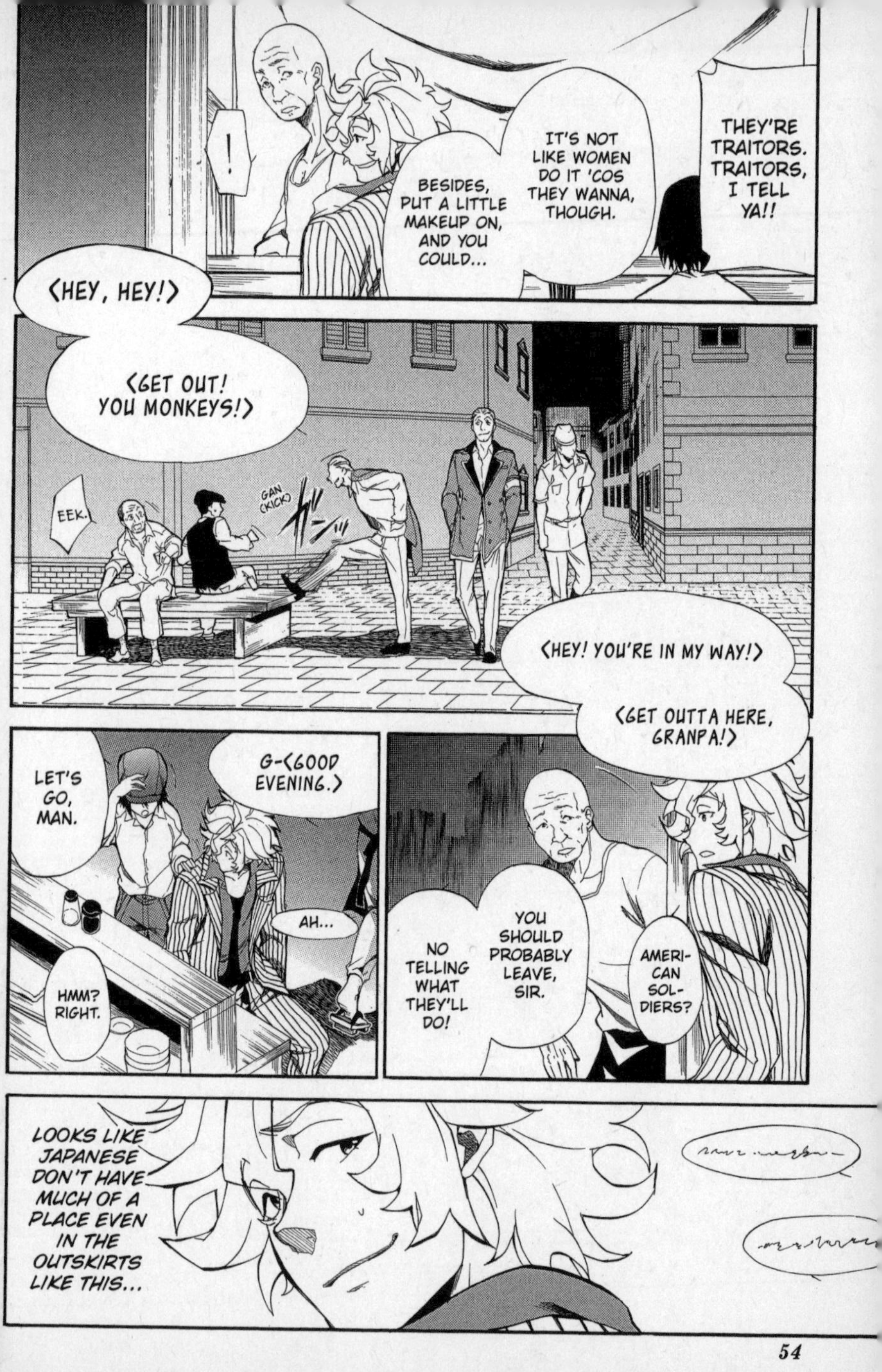
THEY'RE TRAITORS. TRAITORS, I TELL YA!!
IT'S NOT LIKE WOMEN DO IT 'COS THEY WANNA, THOUGH.
BESIDES, PUT A LITTLE MAKEUP ON, AND YOU COULD...
!
<HEY, HEY!>
<GET OUT! YOU MONKEYS!>
GAN (KICK)
EEK.
<HEY! YOU'RE IN MY WAY!>
<GET OUTTA HERE, GRANPA!>
AMERI-CAN SOL-DIERS?
YOU SHOULD PROBABLY LEAVE, SIR.
NO TELLING WHAT THEY'LL DO!
G-<GOOD EVENING.>
LET'S GO, MAN.
AH...
HMM? RIGHT.
LOOKS LIKE JAPANESE DON'T HAVE MUCH OF A PLACE EVEN IN THE OUTSKIRTS LIKE THIS...

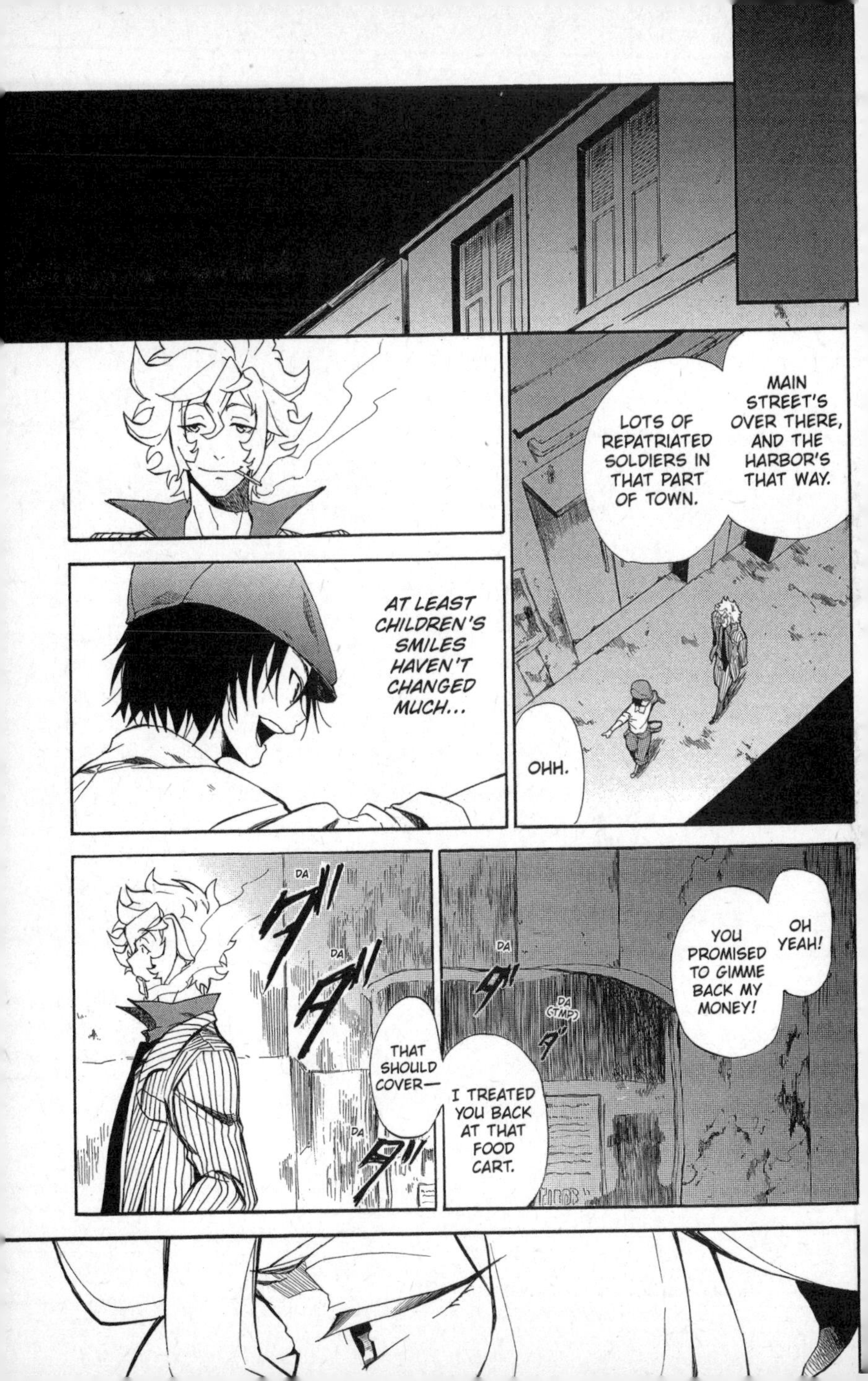
MAIN STREET'S OVER THERE, AND THE HARBOR'S THAT WAY.
LOTS OF REPATRIATED SOLDIERS IN THAT PART OF TOWN.
OHH.
AT LEAST CHILDREN'S SMILES HAVEN'T CHANGED MUCH...
OH YEAH!
YOU PROMISED TO GIMME BACK MY MONEY!
DA
DA (TMP)
I TREATED YOU BACK AT THAT FOOD CART.
THAT SHOULD COVER—
DA
DA
DA

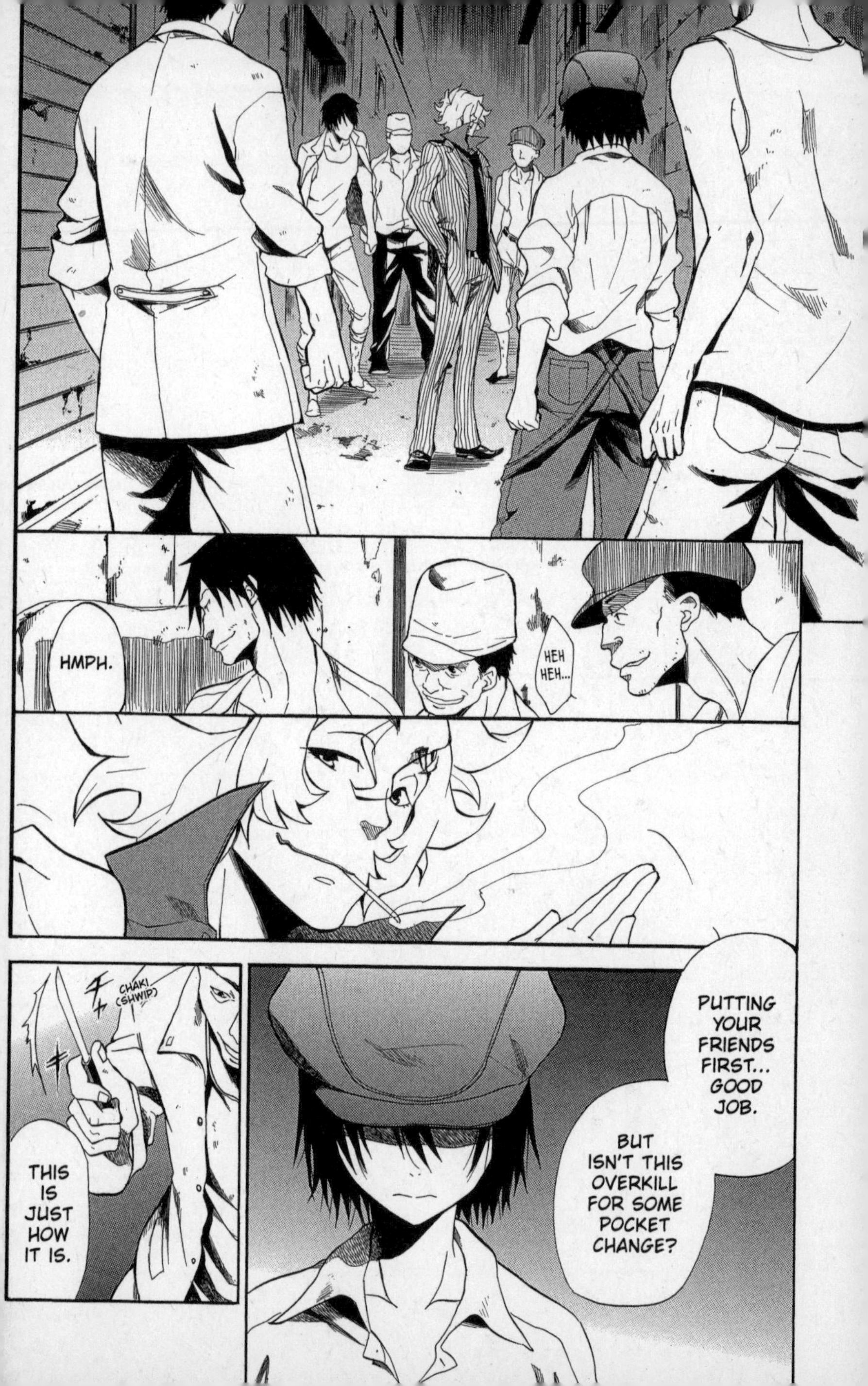
HEH HEH...
HMPH.
PUTTING YOUR FRIENDS FIRST... GOOD JOB.
BUT ISN'T THIS OVERKILL FOR SOME POCKET CHANGE?
CHAKI (SHWIP)
THIS IS JUST HOW IT IS.

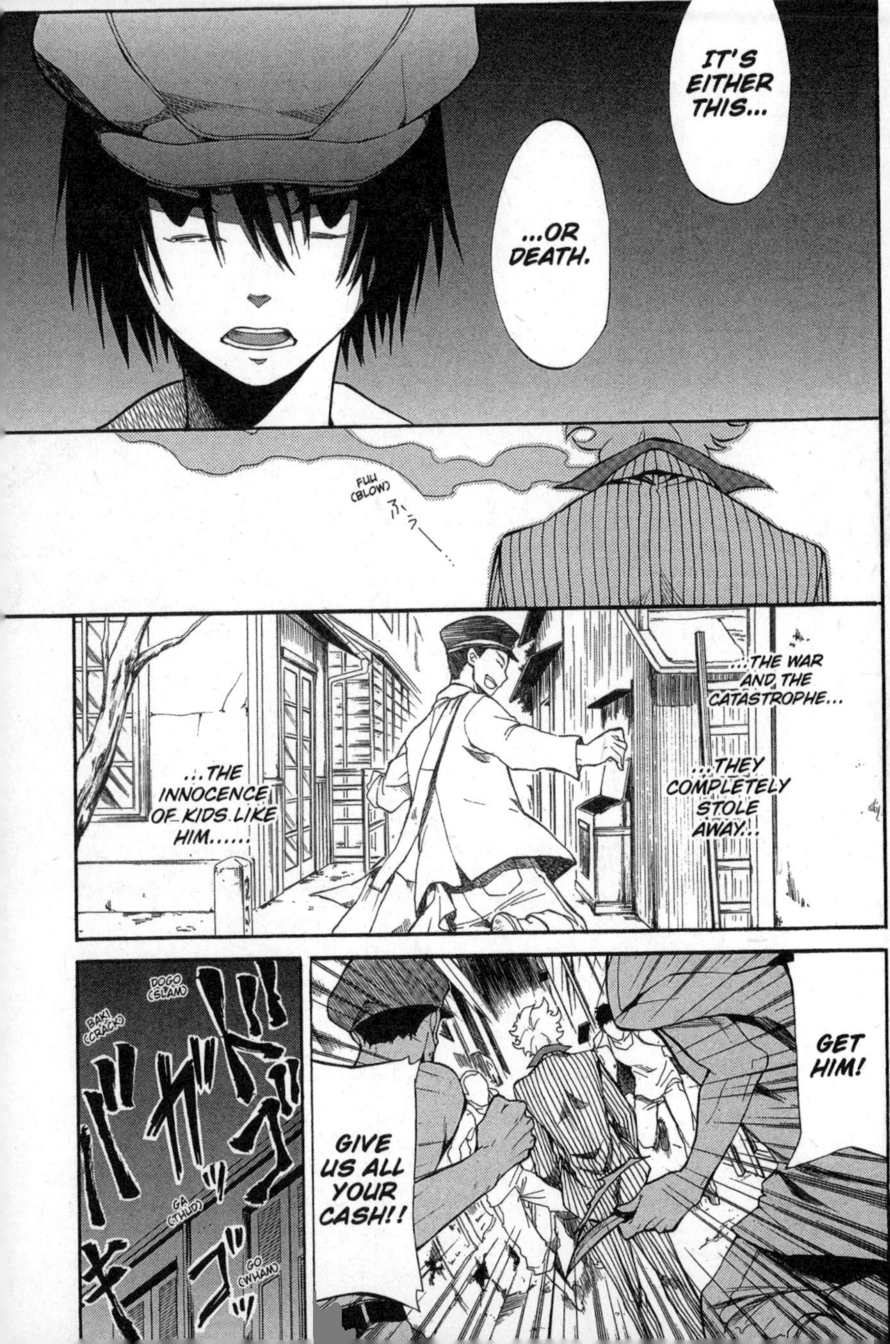
IT'S EITHER THIS...
...OR DEATH.
FUU (BLOW)
ふう——…
...THE WAR AND THE CATASTROPHE...
...THEY COMPLETELY STOLE AWAY...
...THE INNOCENCE OF KIDS LIKE HIM......
GET HIM!
GIVE US ALL YOUR CASH!!
DOGO (SLAM)
BAKI (CRACK)
GA (THUD)
GO (WHAM)
バキッ ドゴッ ガッ ゴッ

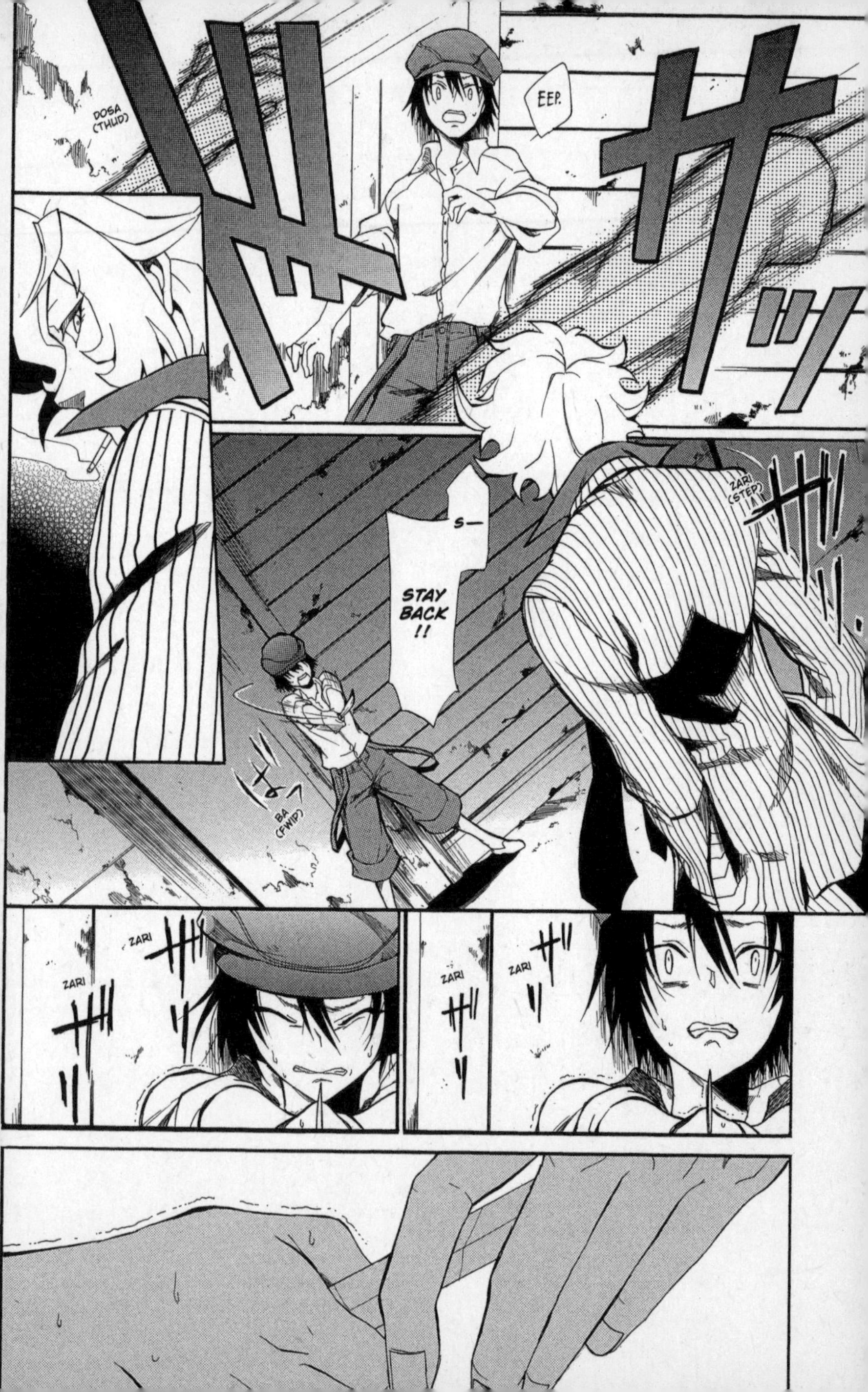
EEP.
DOSA (THUD)
ZARI (STEP)
S—
STAY BACK!!
BA (FWIP)
ZARI
ZARI
ZARI
ZARI

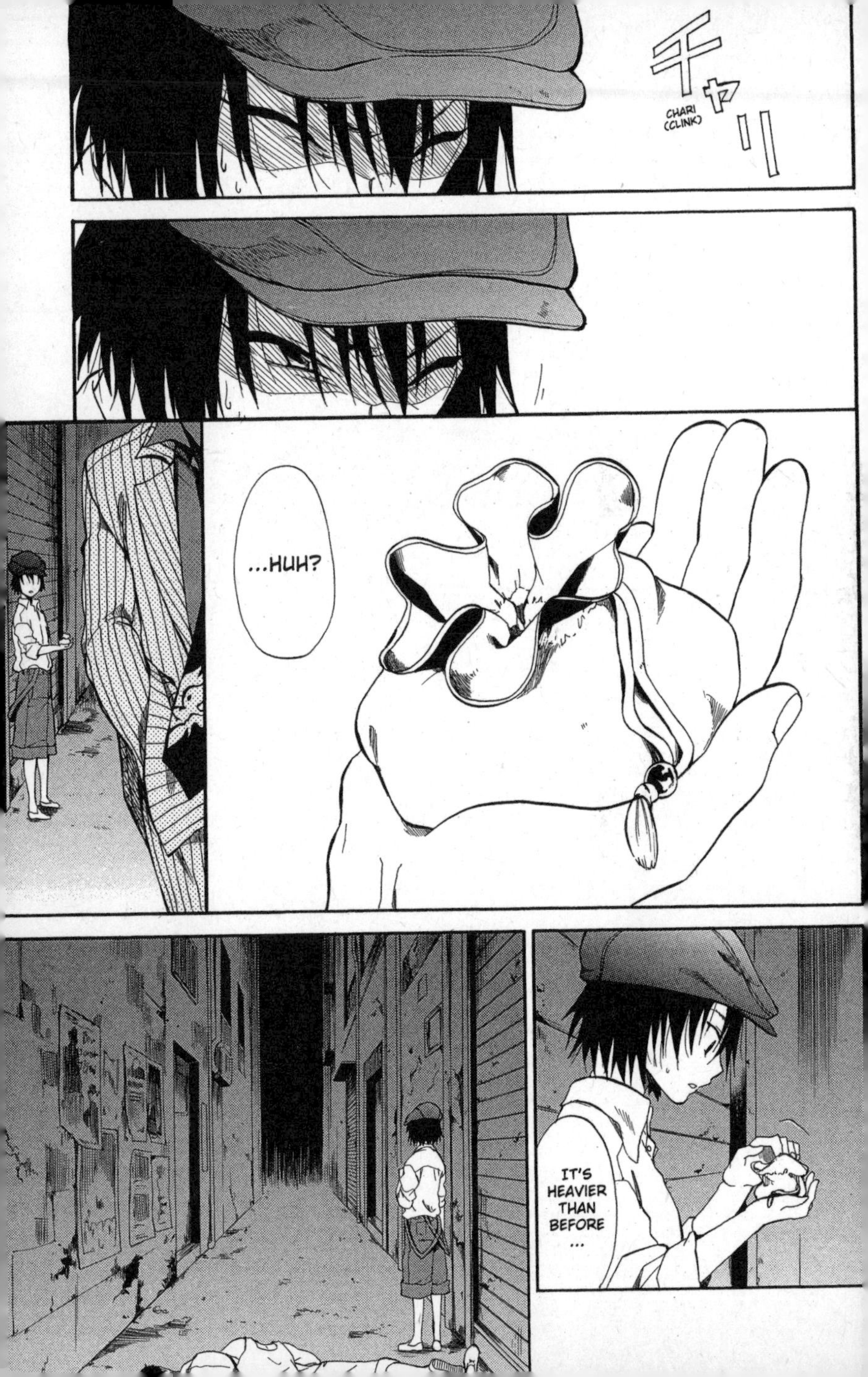
チャリ
CHARI (CLINK)
...HUH?
IT'S HEAVIER THAN BEFORE ...

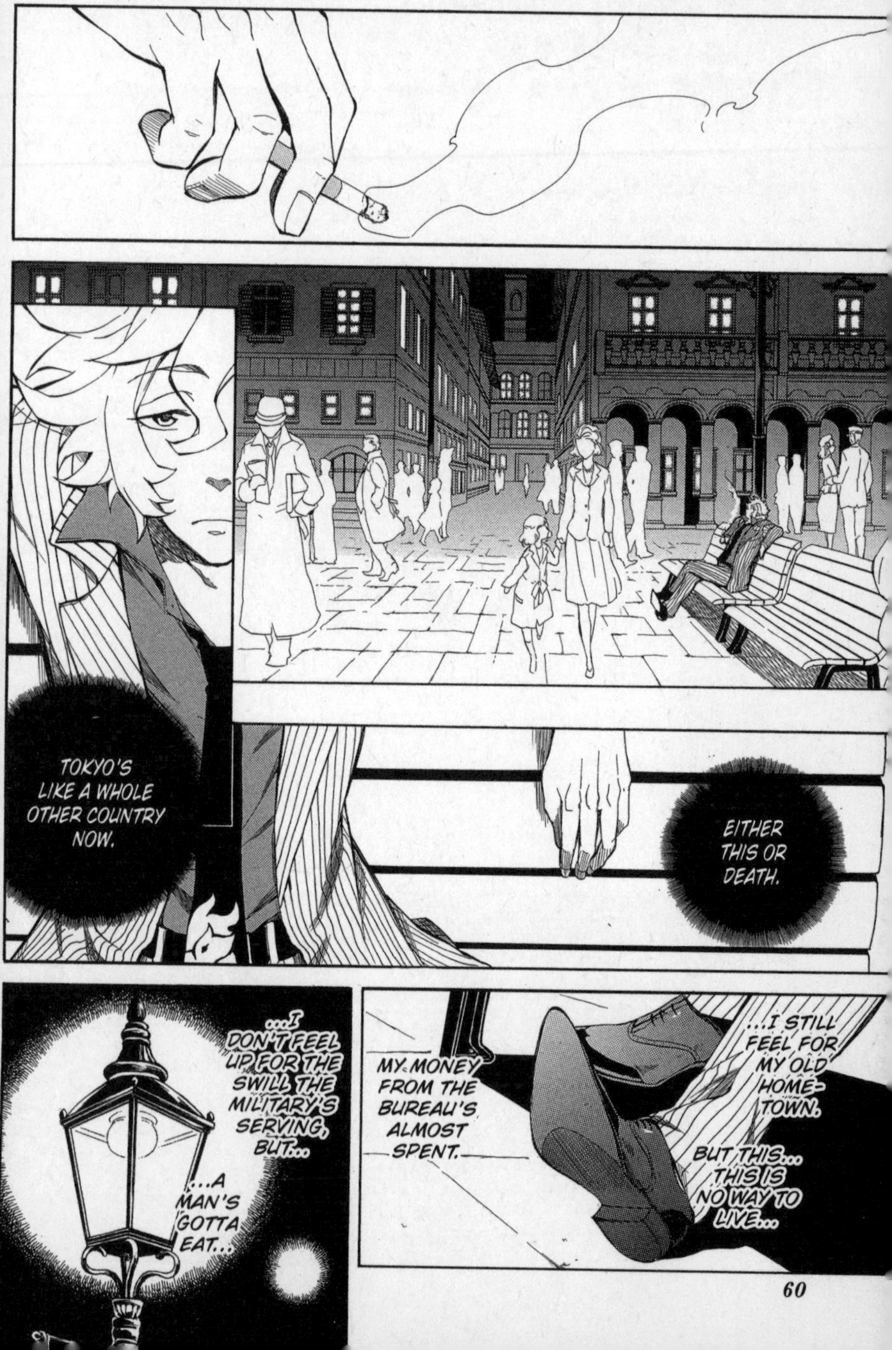
EITHER THIS OR DEATH.
TOKYO'S LIKE A WHOLE OTHER COUNTRY NOW.
...I STILL FEEL FOR MY OLD HOME-TOWN.
MY MONEY FROM THE BUREAU'S ALMOST SPENT.
BUT THIS... THIS IS NO WAY TO LIVE...
...I DON'T FEEL UP FOR THE SWILL THE MILITARY'S SERVING, BUT...
...A MAN'S GOTTA EAT...

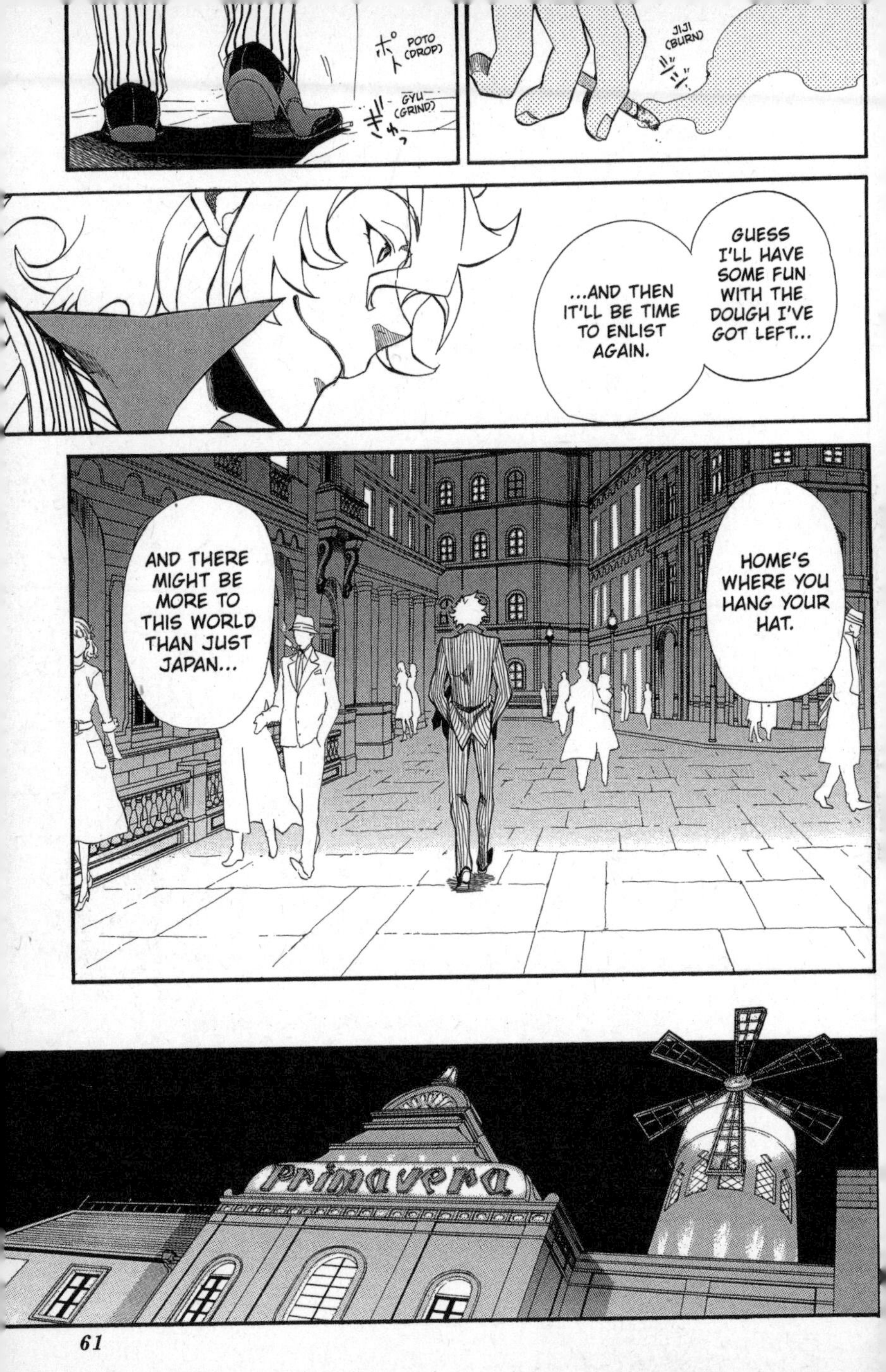
ジジ JIJI (BURN)
ポト POTO (DROP)
ぎゅっ GYU (GRIND)
GUESS I'LL HAVE SOME FUN WITH THE DOUGH I'VE GOT LEFT...
...AND THEN IT'LL BE TIME TO ENLIST AGAIN.
HOME'S WHERE YOU HANG YOUR HAT.
AND THERE MIGHT BE MORE TO THIS WORLD THAN JUST JAPAN...
Primavera

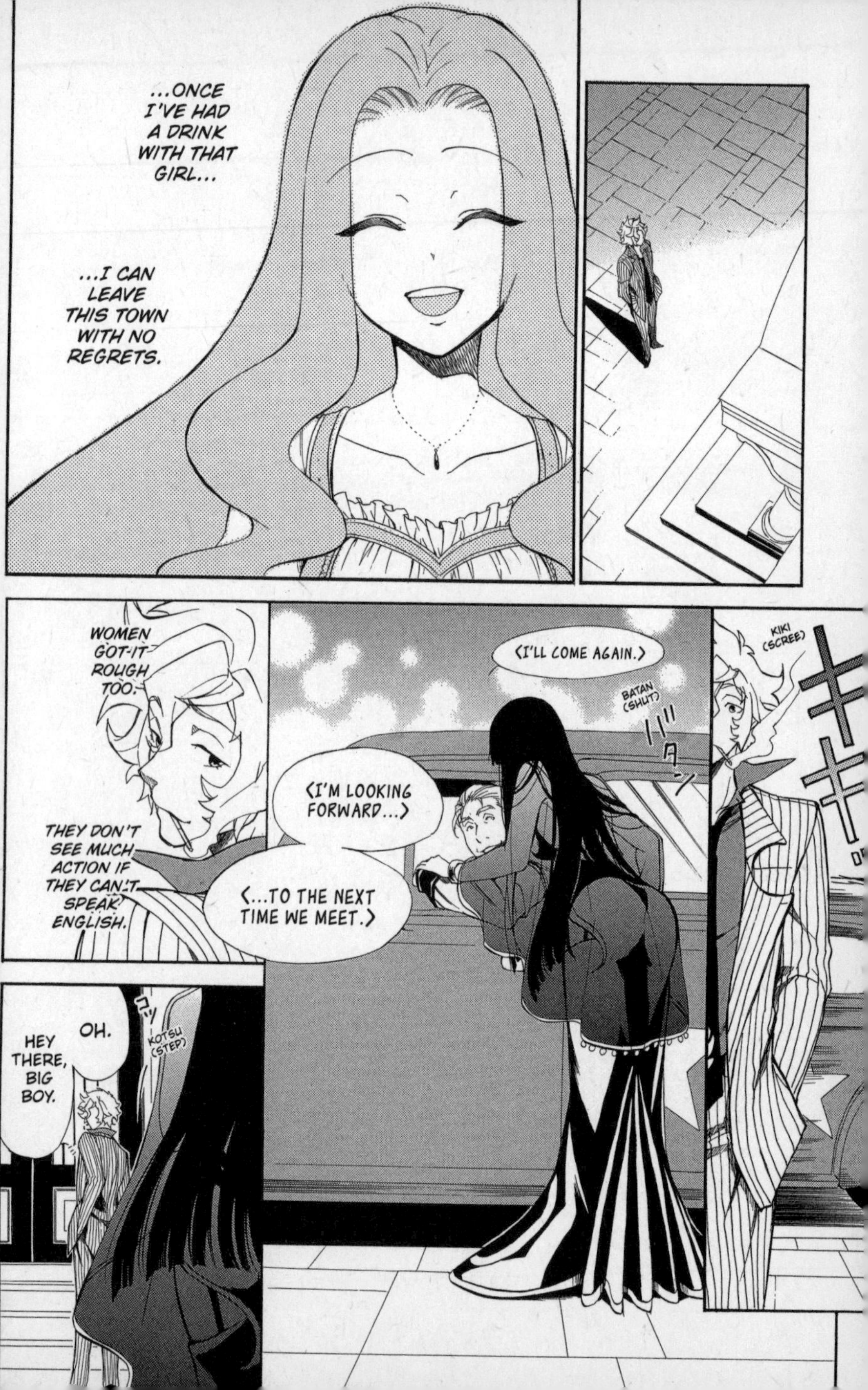
...ONCE I'VE HAD A DRINK WITH THAT GIRL...
...I CAN LEAVE THIS TOWN WITH NO REGRETS.
KIKI (SCREE)
〈I'LL COME AGAIN.〉
BATAN (SHUT)
〈I'M LOOKING FORWARD...〉
〈...TO THE NEXT TIME WE MEET.〉
WOMEN GOT IT ROUGH TOO.
THEY DON'T SEE MUCH ACTION IF THEY CAN'T SPEAK ENGLISH.
KOTSU (STEP)
OH.
HEY THERE, BIG BOY.

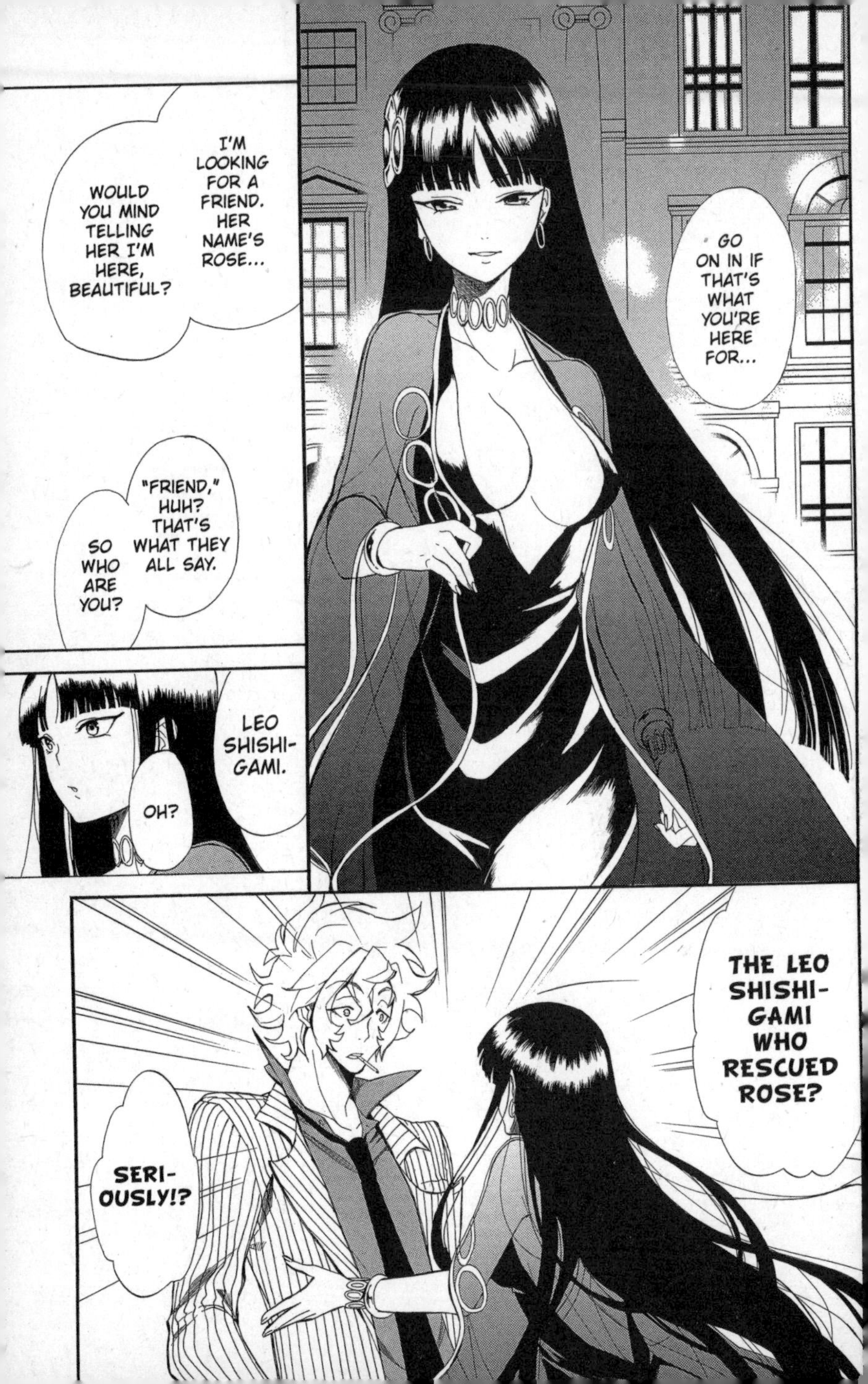
GO ON IN IF THAT'S WHAT YOU'RE HERE FOR...
I'M LOOKING FOR A FRIEND. HER NAME'S ROSE...
WOULD YOU MIND TELLING HER I'M HERE, BEAUTIFUL?
"FRIEND," HUH? THAT'S WHAT THEY ALL SAY.
SO WHO ARE YOU?
LEO SHISHI-GAMI.
OH?
THE LEO SHISHI-GAMI WHO RESCUED ROSE?
SERI-OUSLY!?

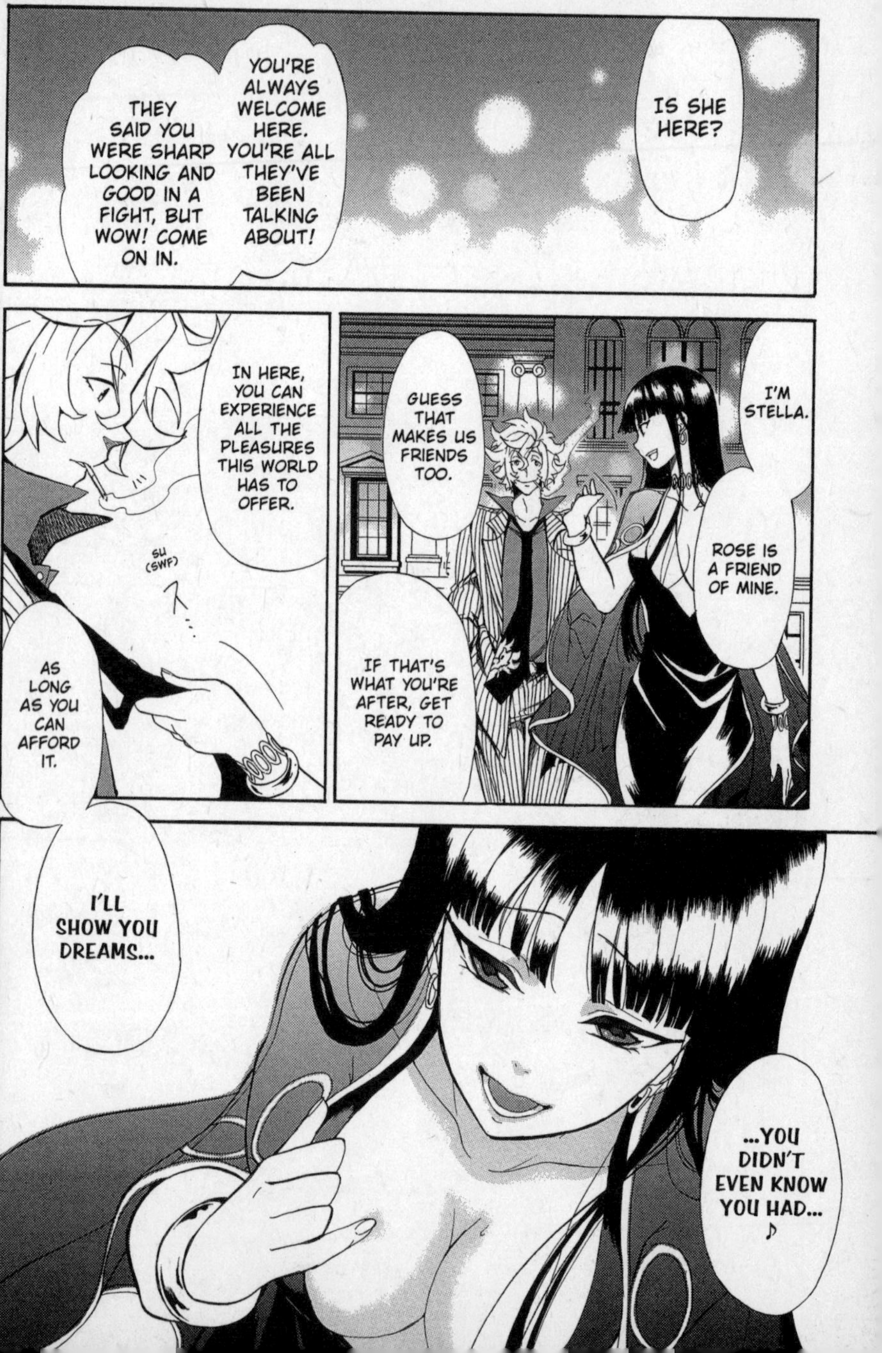
IS SHE HERE?
YOU'RE ALWAYS WELCOME HERE. YOU'RE ALL THEY'VE BEEN TALKING ABOUT!
THEY SAID YOU WERE SHARP LOOKING AND GOOD IN A FIGHT, BUT WOW! COME ON IN.
I'M STELLA.
ROSE IS A FRIEND OF MINE.
GUESS THAT MAKES US FRIENDS TOO.
IF THAT'S WHAT YOU'RE AFTER, GET READY TO PAY UP.
IN HERE, YOU CAN EXPERIENCE ALL THE PLEASURES THIS WORLD HAS TO OFFER.
SU (SWF)
AS LONG AS YOU CAN AFFORD IT.
I'LL SHOW YOU DREAMS...
...YOU DIDN'T EVEN KNOW YOU HAD... ♪

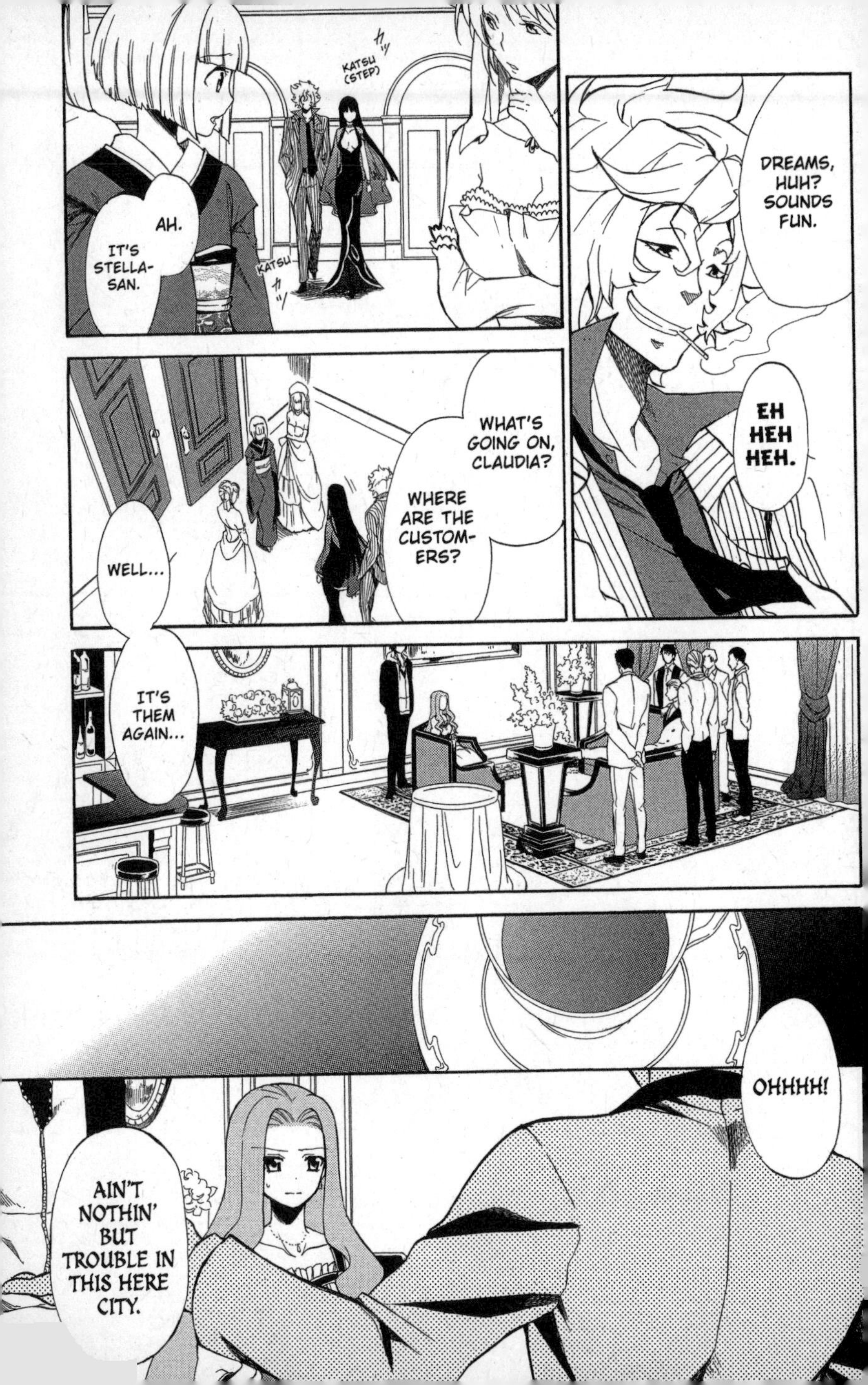
DREAMS, HUH? SOUNDS FUN.
EH HEH HEH.
KATSU (STEP)
KATSU
AH.
IT'S STELLA-SAN.
WHAT'S GOING ON, CLAUDIA?
WHERE ARE THE CUSTOM-ERS?
WELL...
IT'S THEM AGAIN...
OHHHH!
AIN'T NOTHIN' BUT TROUBLE IN THIS HERE CITY.

ROSE GUNS DAYS

Season 1

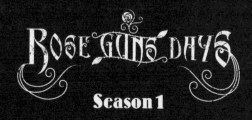

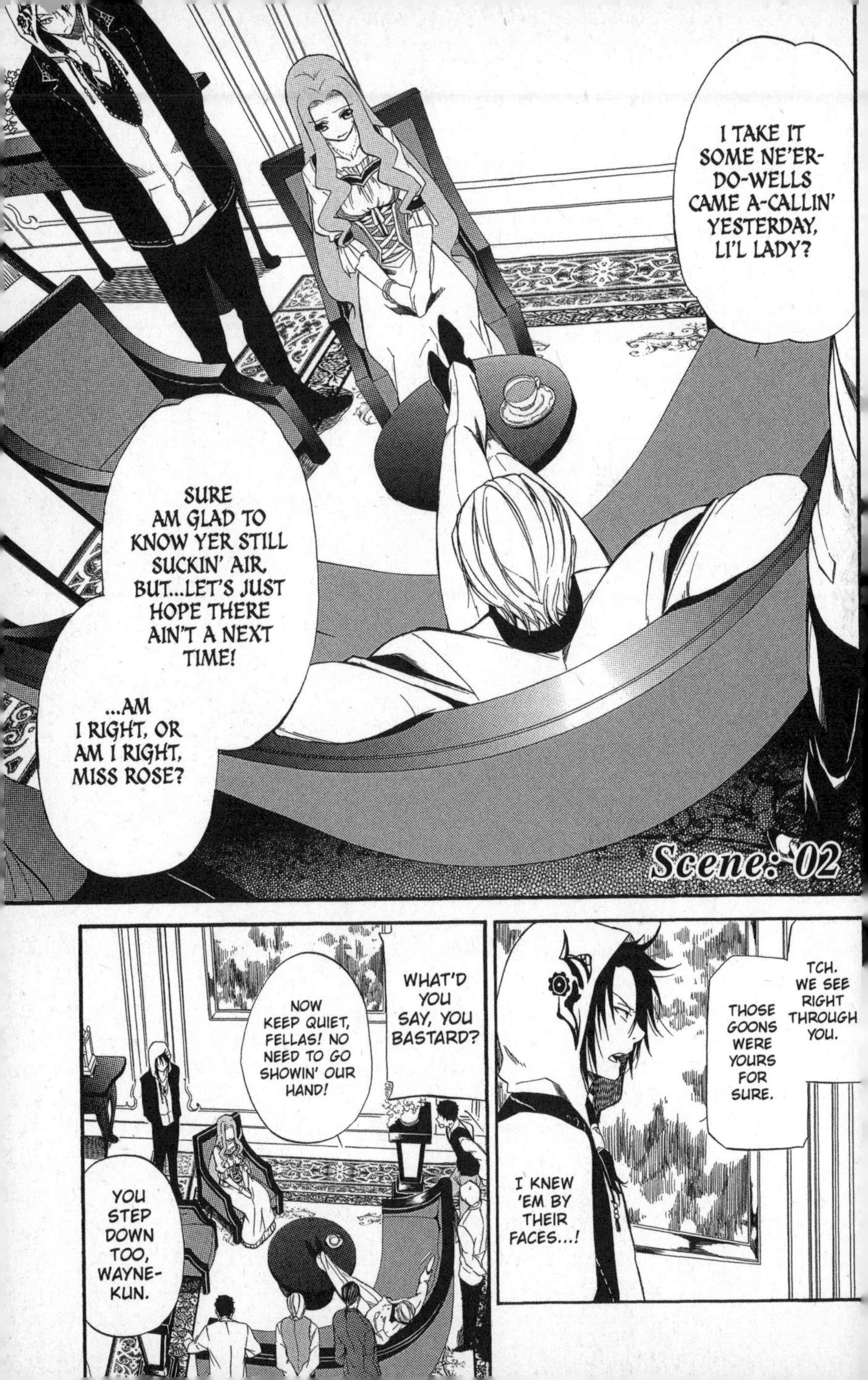
I TAKE IT SOME NE'ER-DO-WELLS CAME A-CALLIN' YESTERDAY, LI'L LADY?
SURE AM GLAD TO KNOW YER STILL SUCKIN' AIR, BUT...LET'S JUST HOPE THERE AIN'T A NEXT TIME!
...AM I RIGHT, OR AM I RIGHT, MISS ROSE?
Scene: 02
TCH. WE SEE RIGHT THROUGH YOU.
THOSE GOONS WERE YOURS FOR SURE.
I KNEW 'EM BY THEIR FACES...!
WHAT'D YOU SAY, YOU BASTARD?
NOW KEEP QUIET, FELLAS! NO NEED TO GO SHOWIN' OUR HAND!
YOU STEP DOWN TOO, WAYNE-KUN.

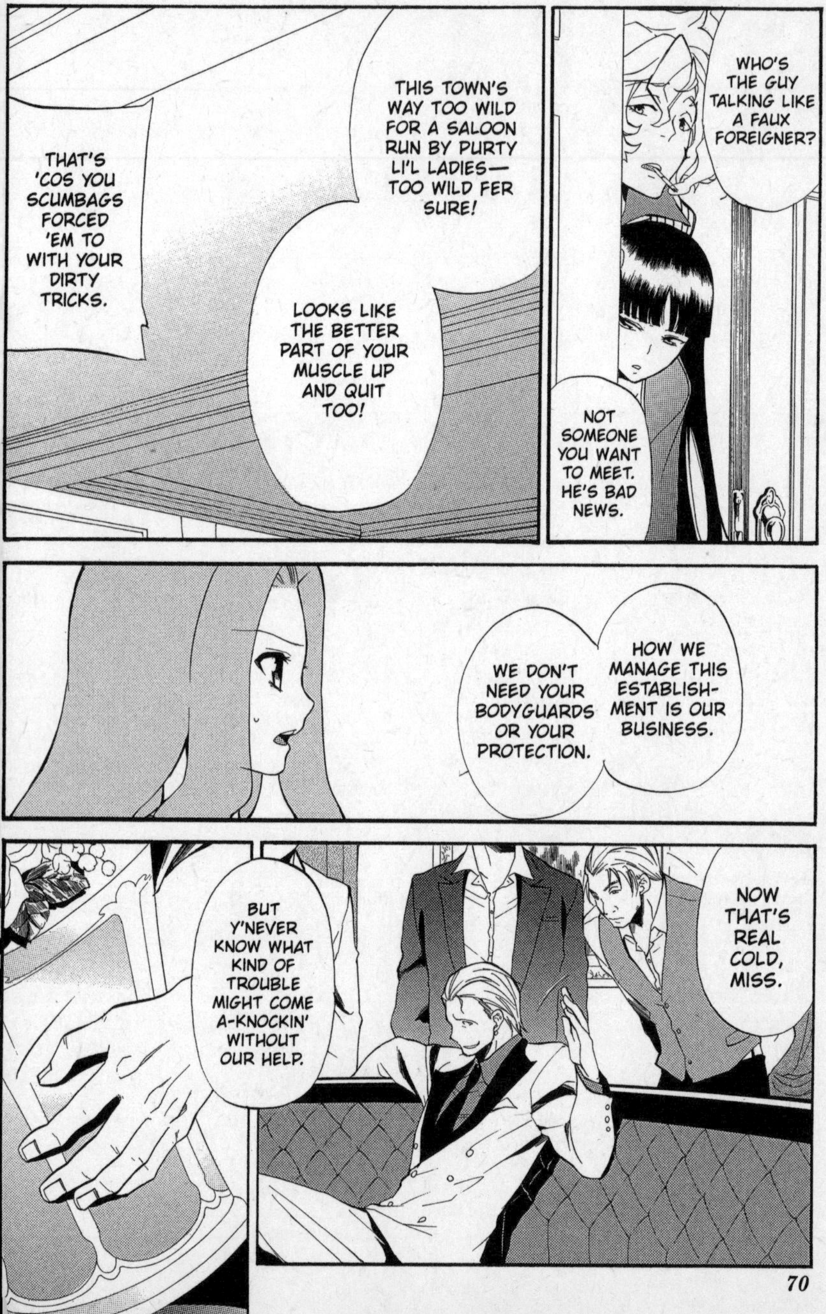
WHO'S THE GUY TALKING LIKE A FAUX FOREIGNER?
NOT SOMEONE YOU WANT TO MEET. HE'S BAD NEWS.
THIS TOWN'S WAY TOO WILD FOR A SALOON RUN BY PURTY LI'L LADIES— TOO WILD FER SURE!
LOOKS LIKE THE BETTER PART OF YOUR MUSCLE UP AND QUIT TOO!
THAT'S 'COS YOU SCUMBAGS FORCED 'EM TO WITH YOUR DIRTY TRICKS.
HOW WE MANAGE THIS ESTABLISH- MENT IS OUR BUSINESS.
WE DON'T NEED YOUR BODYGUARDS OR YOUR PROTECTION.
NOW THAT'S REAL COLD, MISS.
BUT Y'NEVER KNOW WHAT KIND OF TROUBLE MIGHT COME A-KNOCKIN' WITHOUT OUR HELP.

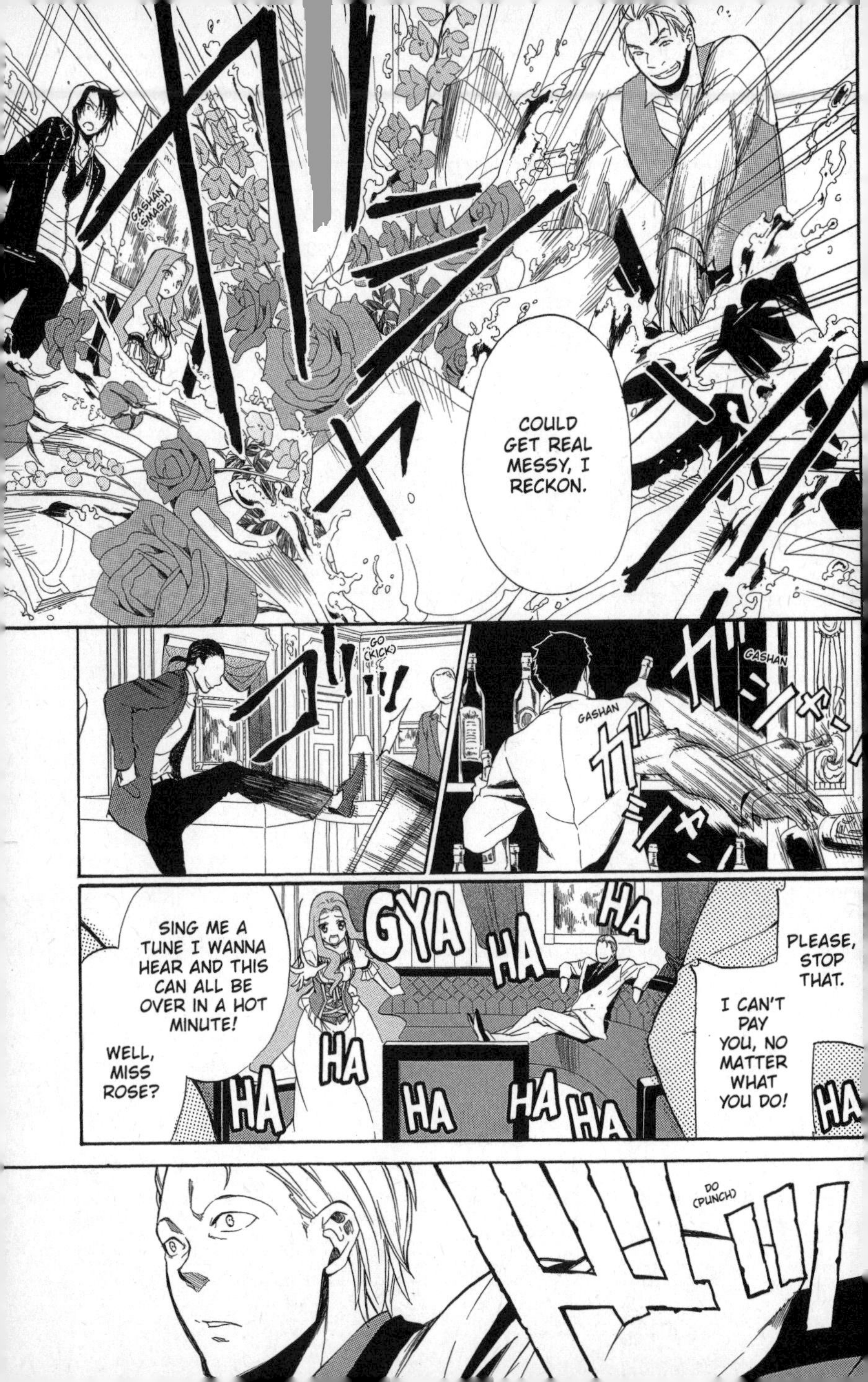
COULD GET REAL MESSY, I RECKON.
GASHAN (SMASH)
GASHAN
GASHAN
GO (KICK)
PLEASE, STOP THAT.
I CAN'T PAY YOU, NO MATTER WHAT YOU DO!
HA
GYA HA HA HA HA HA HA HA HA
SING ME A TUNE I WANNA HEAR AND THIS CAN ALL BE OVER IN A HOT MINUTE!
WELL, MISS ROSE?
DO (PUNCH)

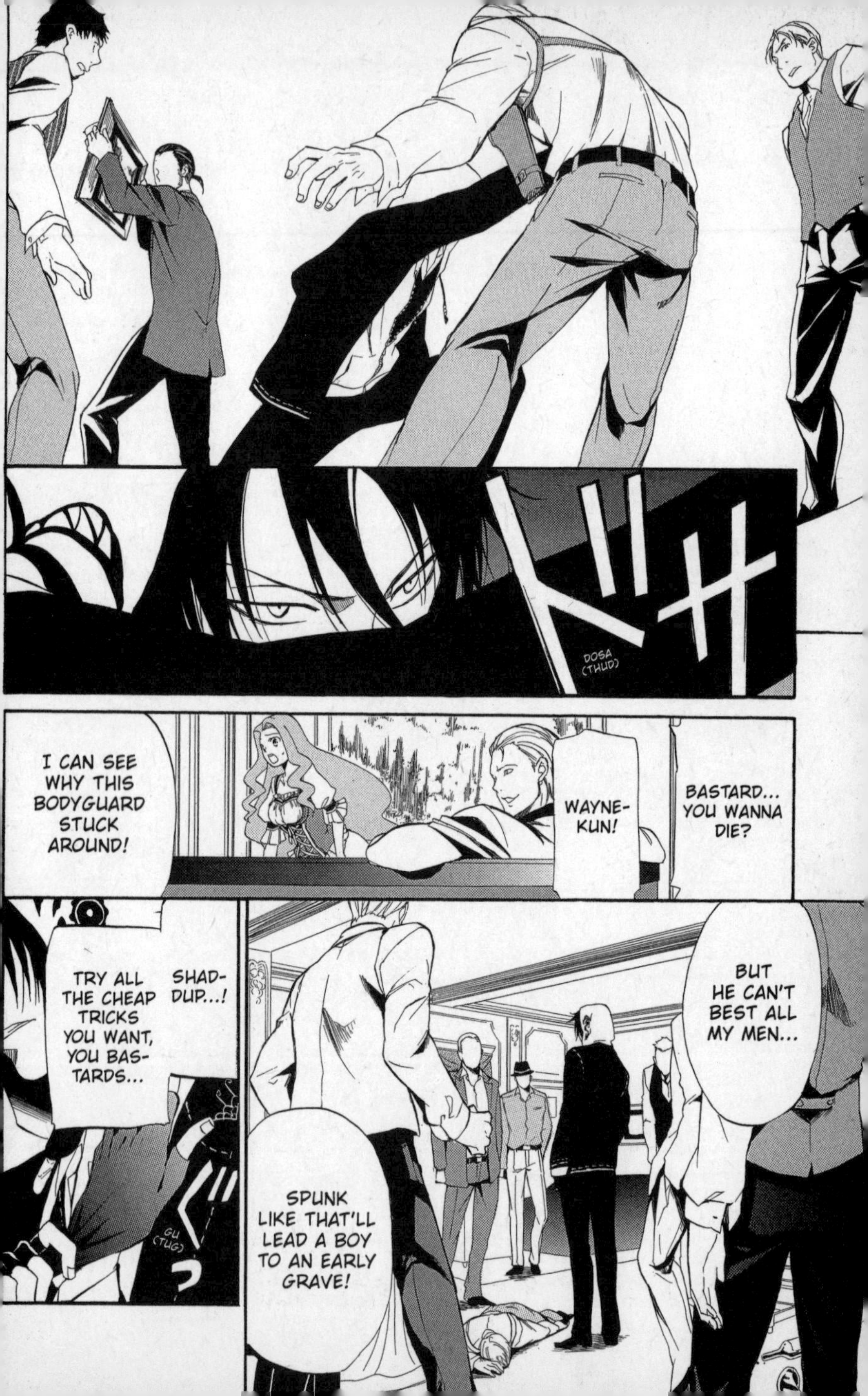
DOSA (THUD)
BASTARD... YOU WANNA DIE?
WAYNE-KUN!
I CAN SEE WHY THIS BODYGUARD STUCK AROUND!
BUT HE CAN'T BEST ALL MY MEN...
SPUNK LIKE THAT'LL LEAD A BOY TO AN EARLY GRAVE!
SHAD-DUP...!
TRY ALL THE CHEAP TRICKS YOU WANT, YOU BAS-TARDS...
GU (TUG)

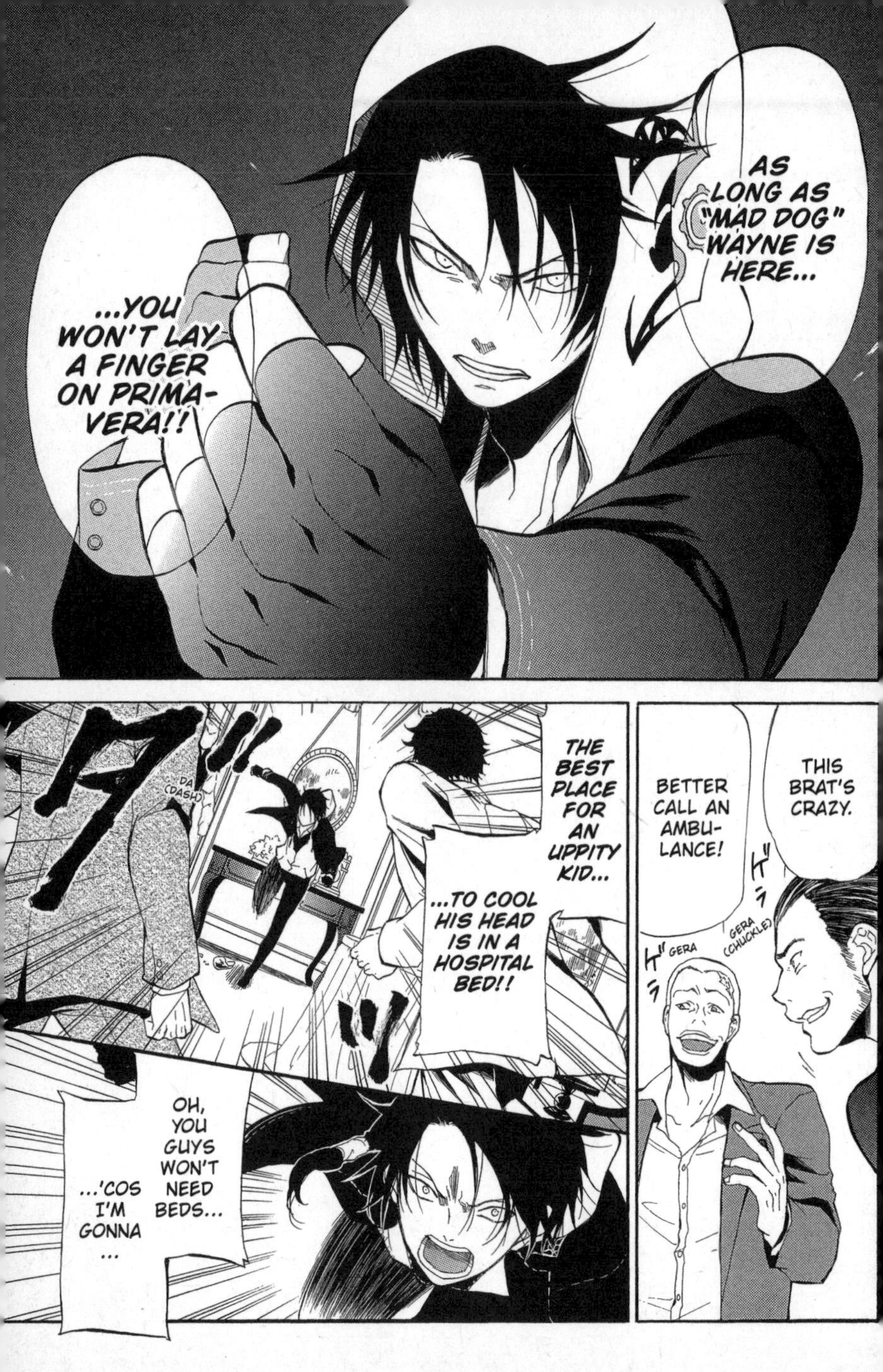
AS LONG AS "MAD DOG" WAYNE IS HERE...
...YOU WON'T LAY A FINGER ON PRIMA-VERA!!
THIS BRAT'S CRAZY.
BETTER CALL AN AMBU-LANCE!
GERA (CHUCKLE)
GERA
THE BEST PLACE FOR AN UPPITY KID...
...TO COOL HIS HEAD IS IN A HOSPITAL BED!!
DA (DASH)
OH, YOU GUYS WON'T NEED BEDS...
...'COS I'M GONNA ...

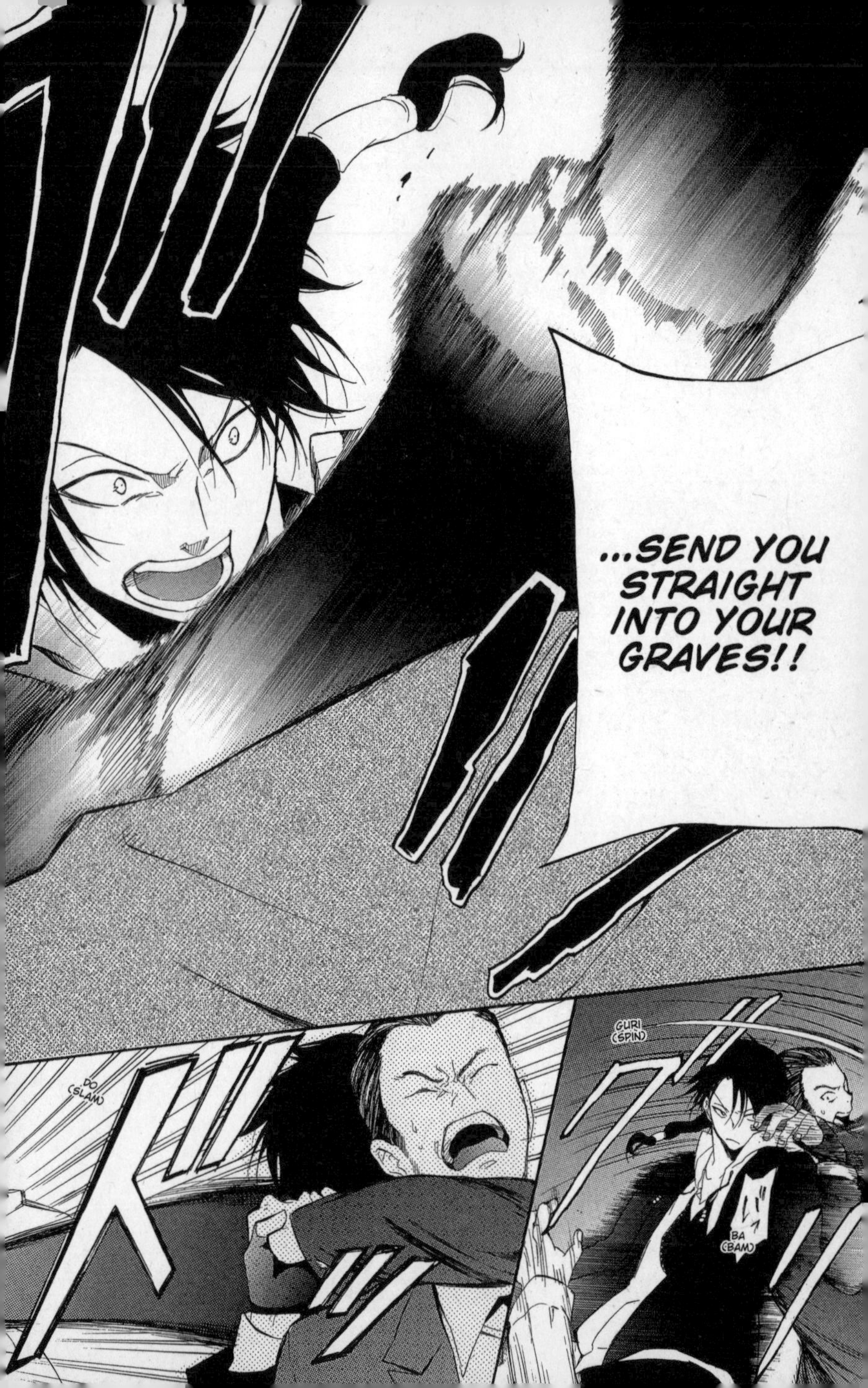
...SEND YOU STRAIGHT INTO YOUR GRAVES!!
GURI (SPIN)
BA (BAM)
DO (SLAM)

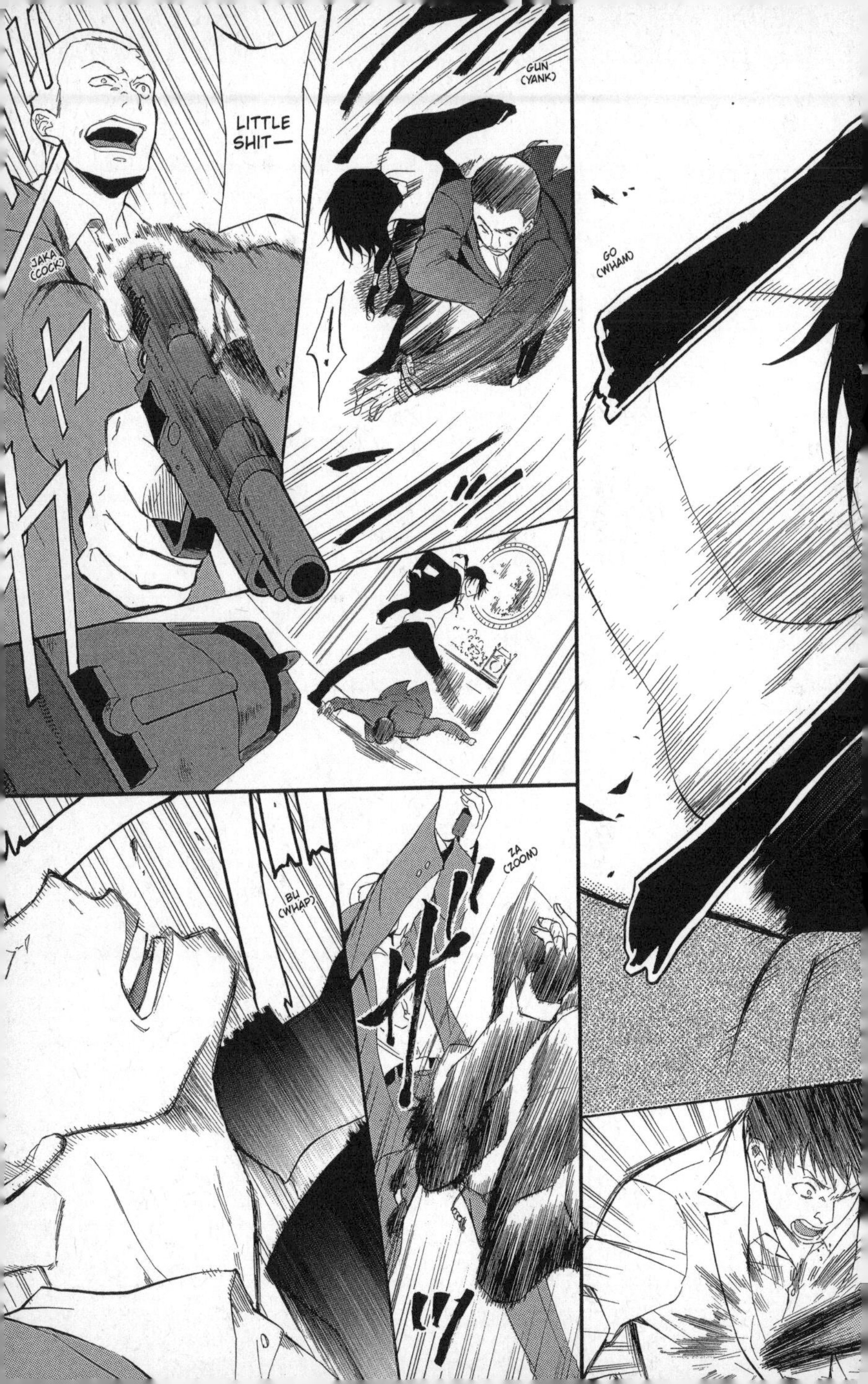

GO (WHAM)
GUN (YANK)
LITTLE SHIT—
JAKA (COCK)
ZA (ZOOM)
BU (WHAP)

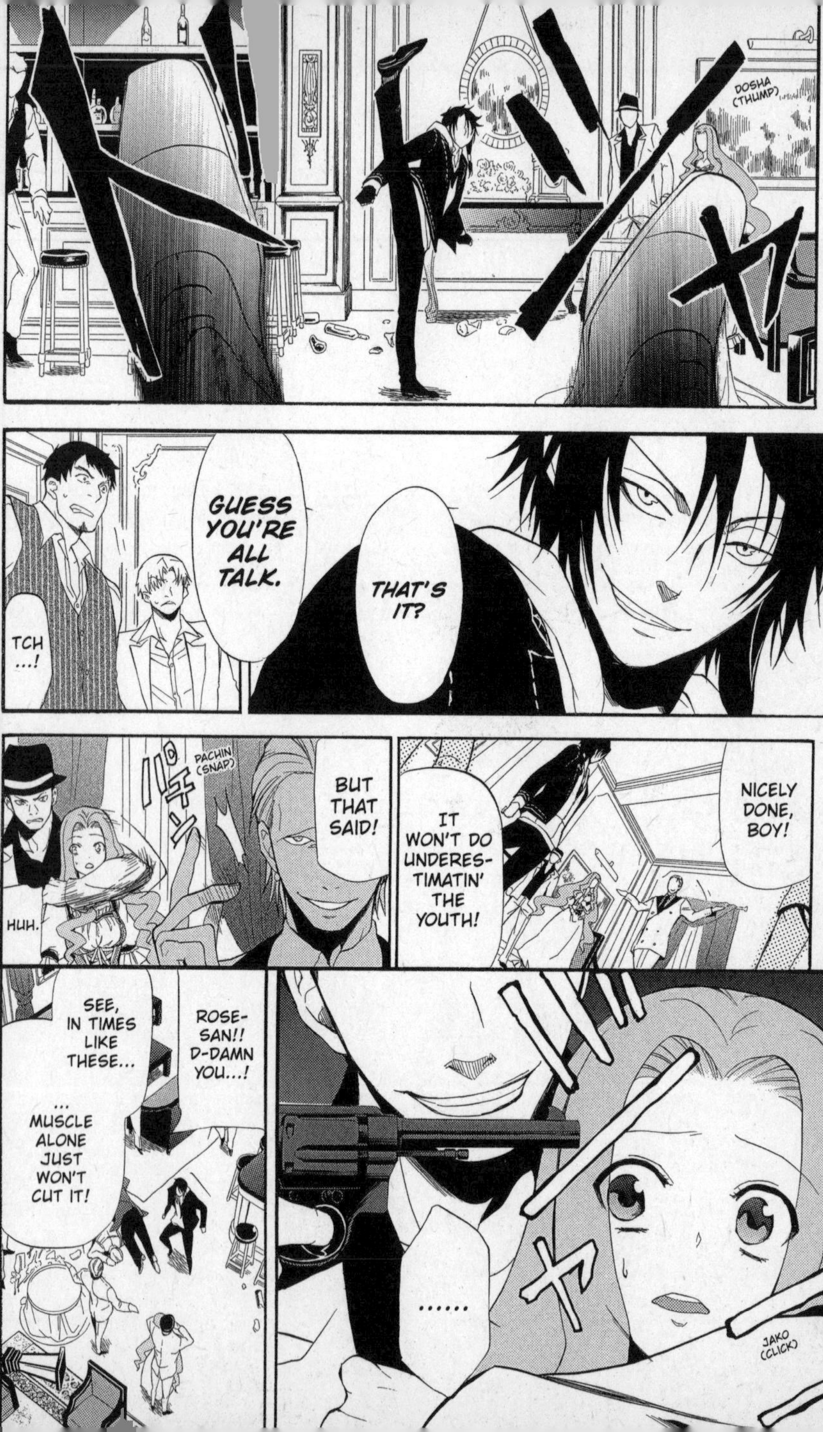
DOSHA (THUMP)
THAT'S IT?
GUESS YOU'RE ALL TALK.
TCH ...!
NICELY DONE, BOY!
IT WON'T DO UNDERES-TIMATIN' THE YOUTH!
BUT THAT SAID!
PACHIN (SNAP)
HUH.
......
JAKO (CLICK)
ROSE-SAN!! D-DAMN YOU...!
SEE, IN TIMES LIKE THESE...
... MUSCLE ALONE JUST WON'T CUT IT!

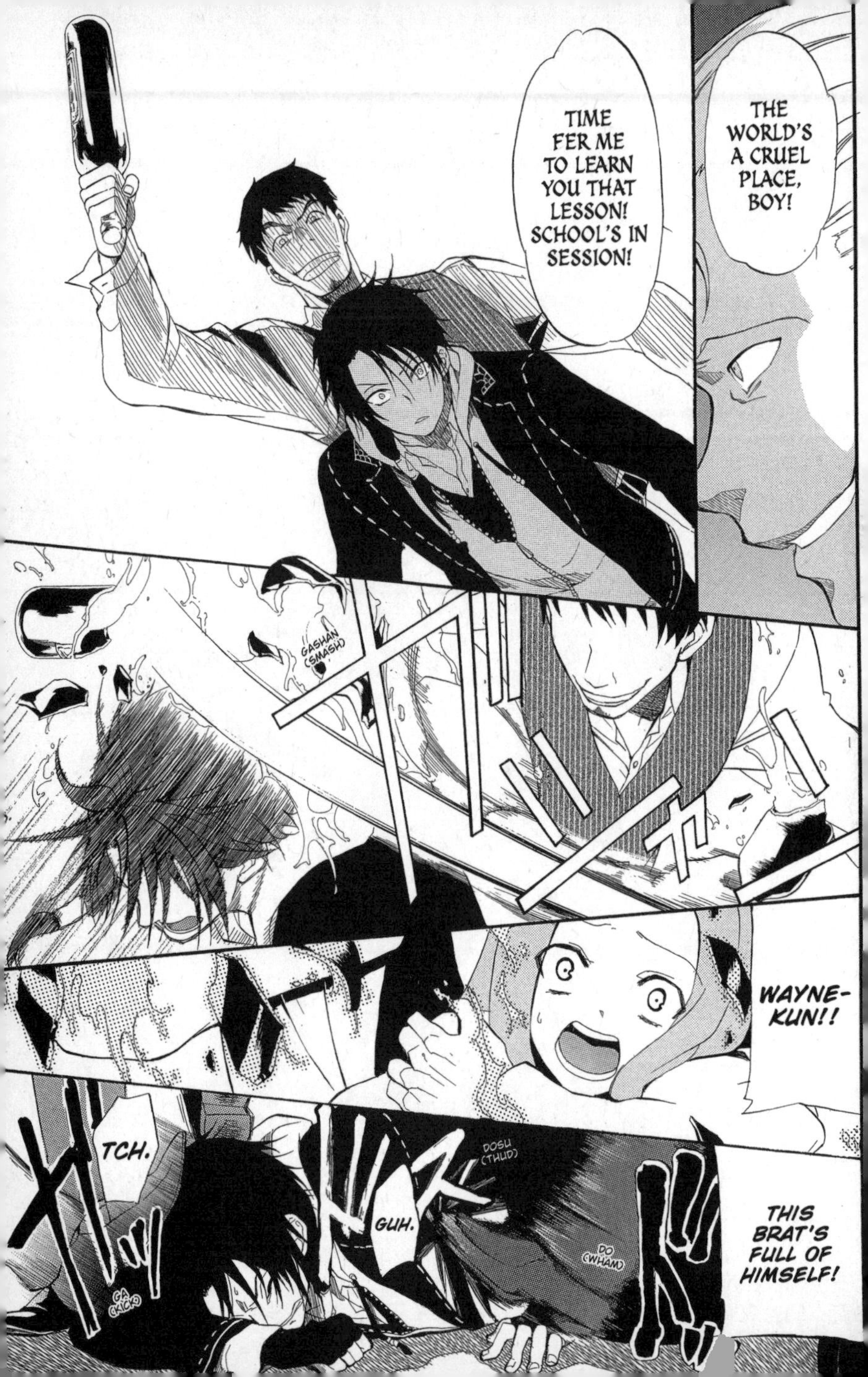
THE WORLD'S A CRUEL PLACE, BOY!
TIME FER ME TO LEARN YOU THAT LESSON! SCHOOL'S IN SESSION!
GASHAN (SMASH)
WAYNE-KUN!!
THIS BRAT'S FULL OF HIMSELF!
DOSU (THUD)
DO (WHAM)
GUH.
TCH.
GA (KICK)

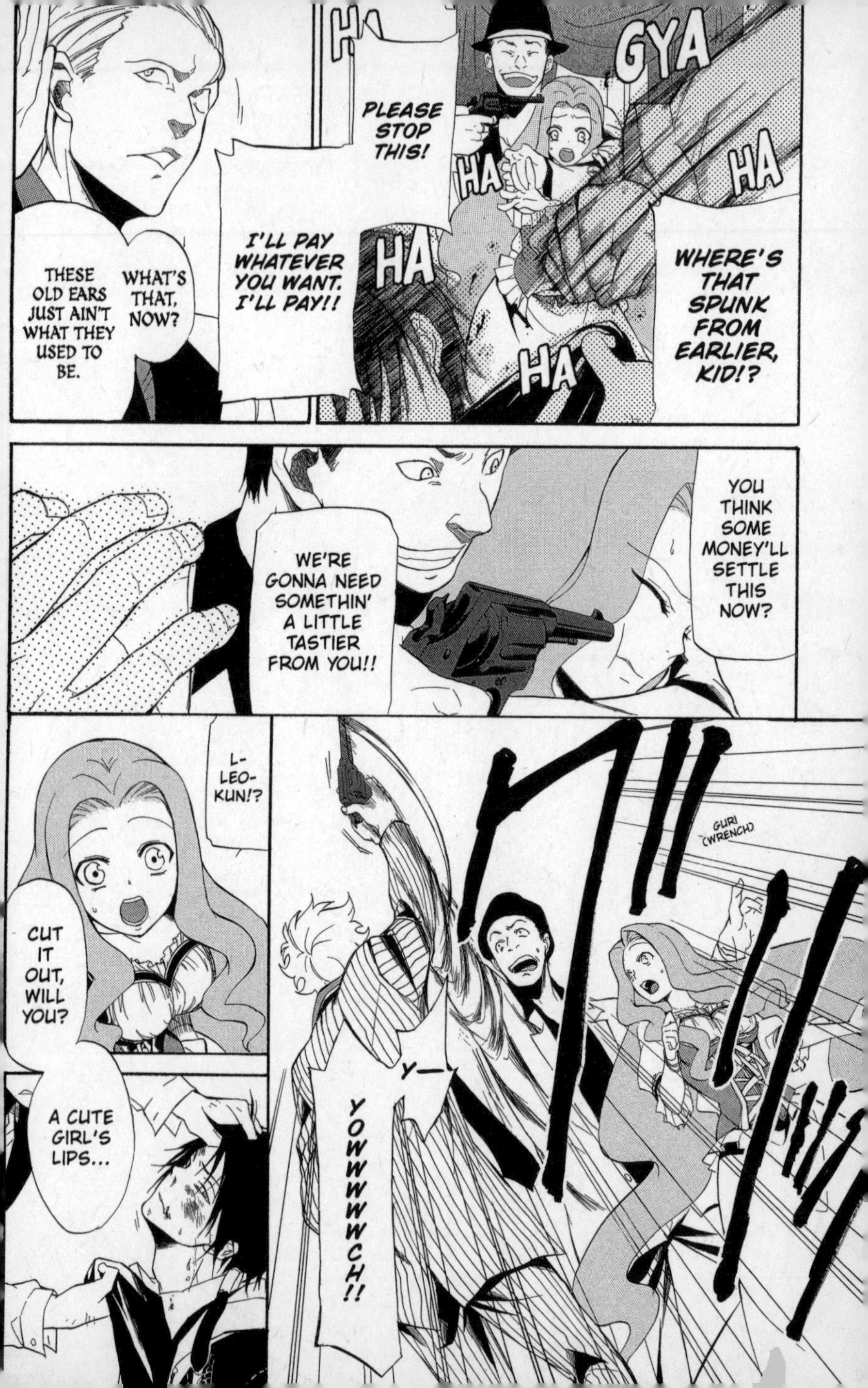
GYA
PLEASE STOP THIS!
HA
HA
WHERE'S THAT SPUNK FROM EARLIER, KID!?
I'LL PAY WHATEVER YOU WANT. I'LL PAY!!
HA
HA
WHAT'S THAT, NOW?
THESE OLD EARS JUST AIN'T WHAT THEY USED TO BE.
YOU THINK SOME MONEY'LL SETTLE THIS NOW?
WE'RE GONNA NEED SOMETHIN' A LITTLE TASTIER FROM YOU!!
GURI (WRENCH)
Y—
YOWWWWWWCH!!
L-LEO-KUN!?
CUT IT OUT, WILL YOU?
A CUTE GIRL'S LIPS...

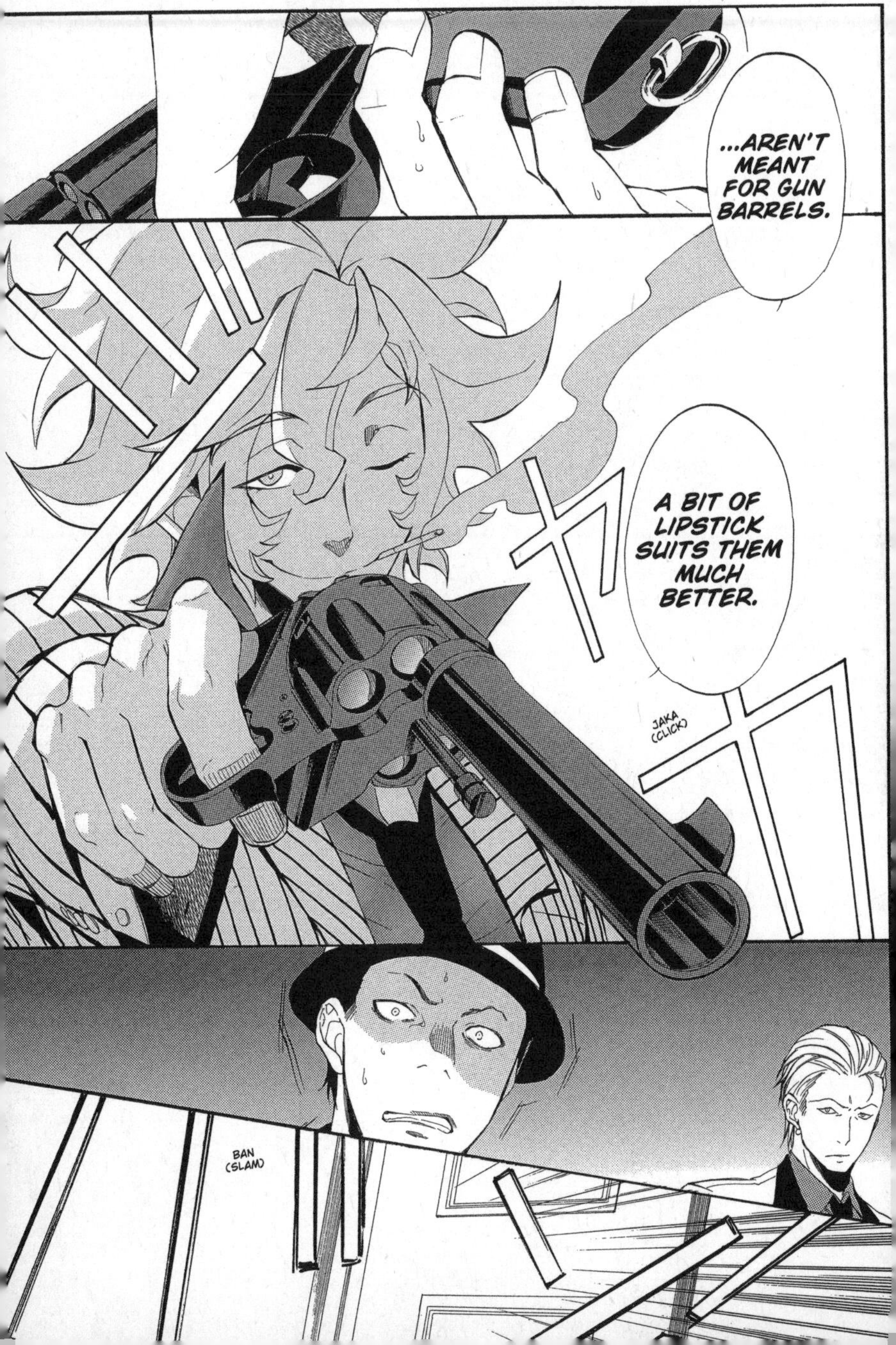
...AREN'T MEANT FOR GUN BARRELS.
A BIT OF LIPSTICK SUITS THEM MUCH BETTER.
JAKA (CLICK)
BAN (SLAM)

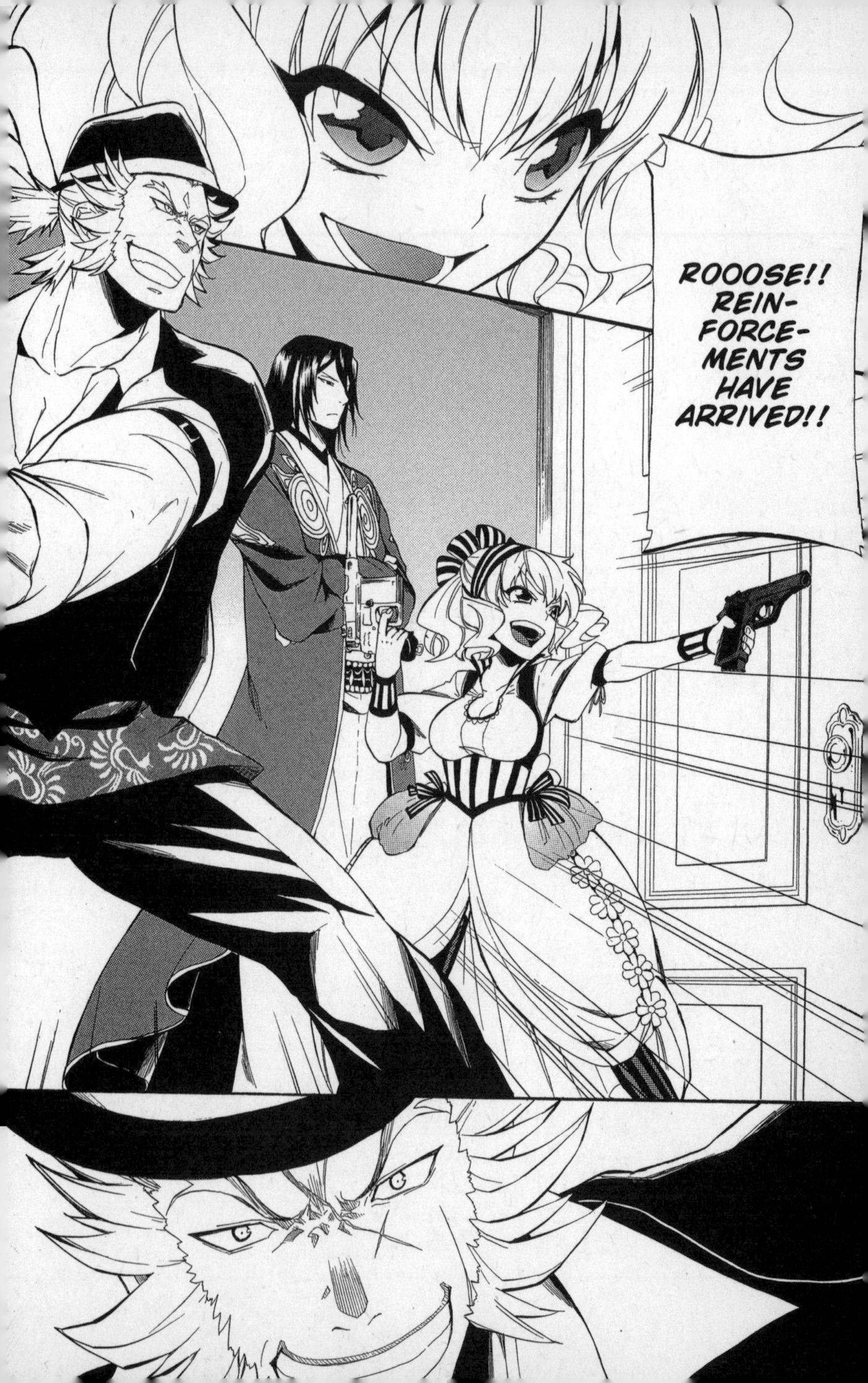
ROOOSE!! REIN-FORCE-MENTS HAVE ARRIVED!!

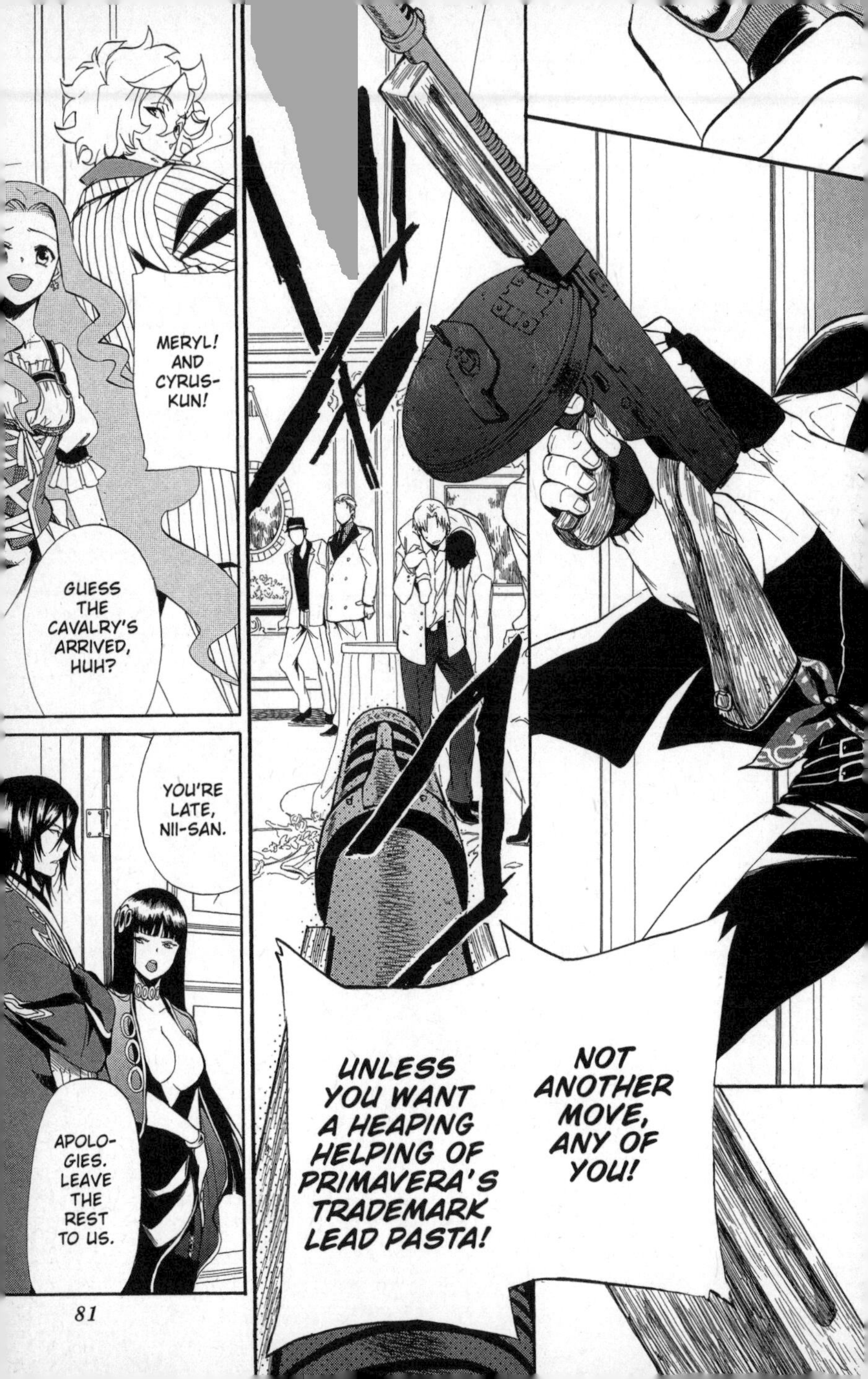
NOT ANOTHER MOVE, ANY OF YOU!
UNLESS YOU WANT A HEAPING HELPING OF PRIMAVERA'S TRADEMARK LEAD PASTA!
MERYL! AND CYRUS-KUN!
GUESS THE CAVALRY'S ARRIVED, HUH?
YOU'RE LATE, NII-SAN.
APOLOGIES. LEAVE THE REST TO US.

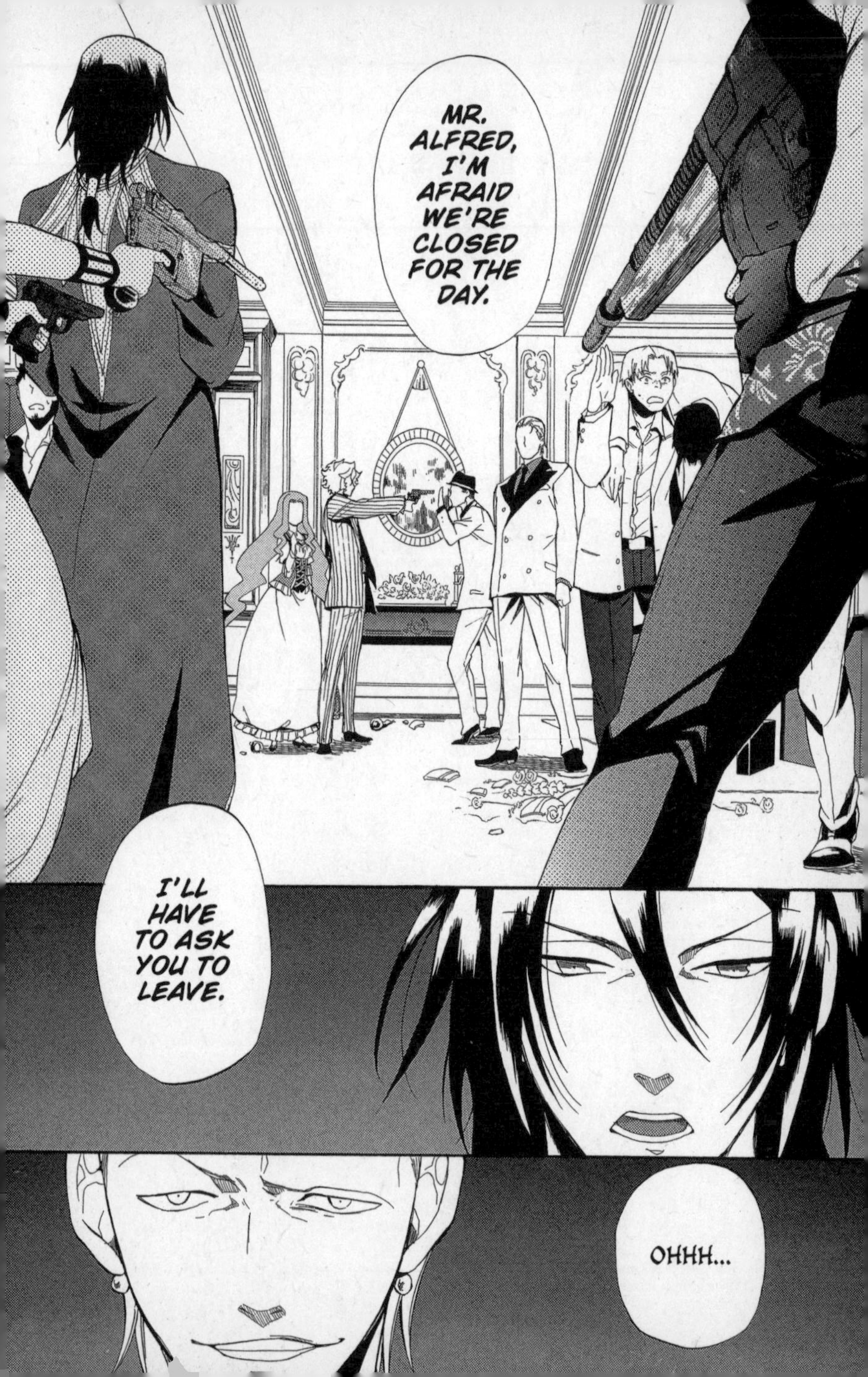
MR. ALFRED, I'M AFRAID WE'RE CLOSED FOR THE DAY.
I'LL HAVE TO ASK YOU TO LEAVE.
OHHH...

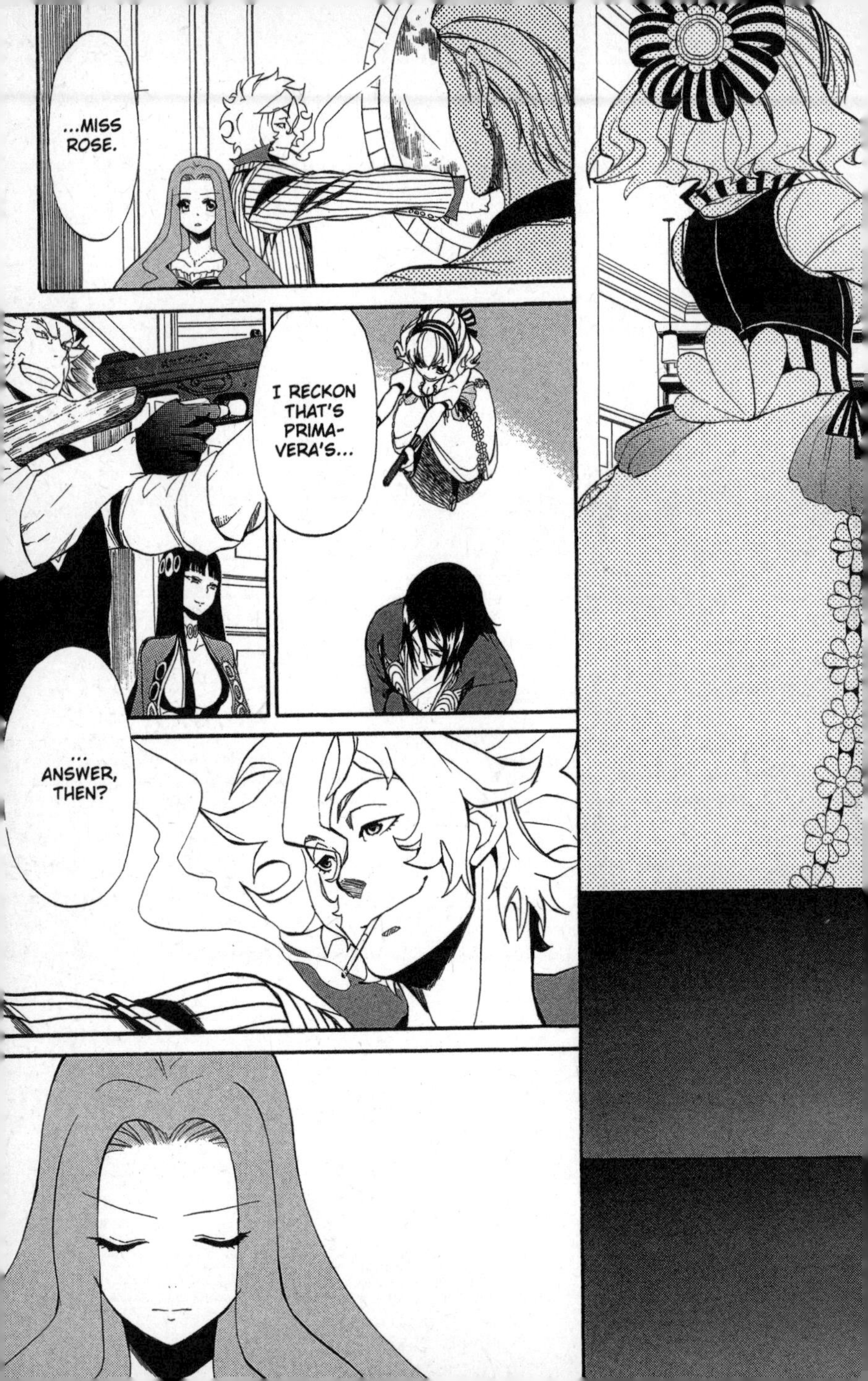
...MISS ROSE.
I RECKON THAT'S PRIMA-VERA'S...
... ANSWER, THEN?

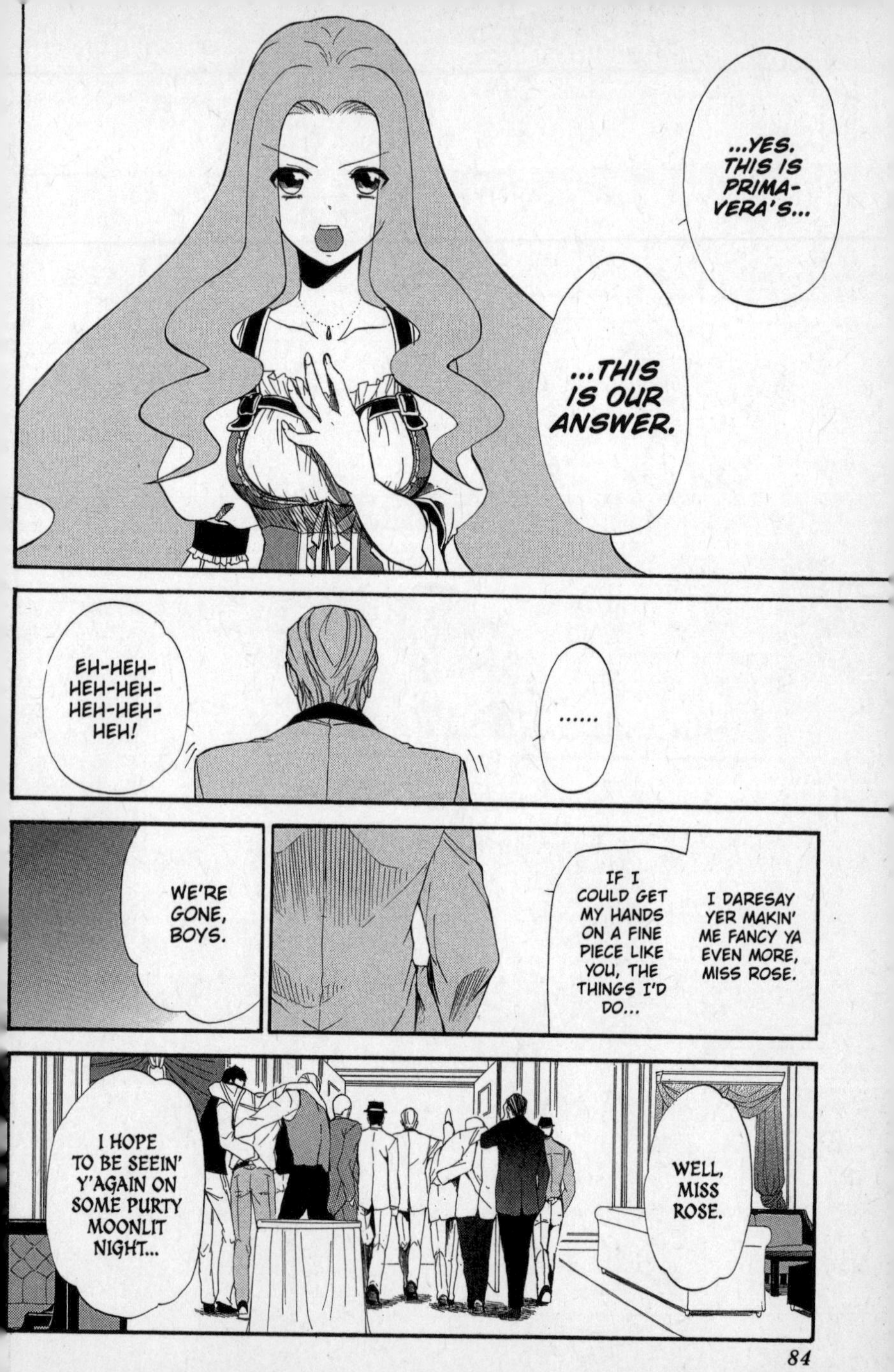
...YES. THIS IS PRIMAVERA'S...
...THIS IS OUR ANSWER.
......
EH-HEH-HEH-HEH-HEH-HEH-HEH!
I DARESAY YER MAKIN' ME FANCY YA EVEN MORE, MISS ROSE.
IF I COULD GET MY HANDS ON A FINE PIECE LIKE YOU, THE THINGS I'D DO...
WE'RE GONE, BOYS.
WELL, MISS ROSE.
I HOPE TO BE SEEIN' Y'AGAIN ON SOME PURTY MOONLIT NIGHT...

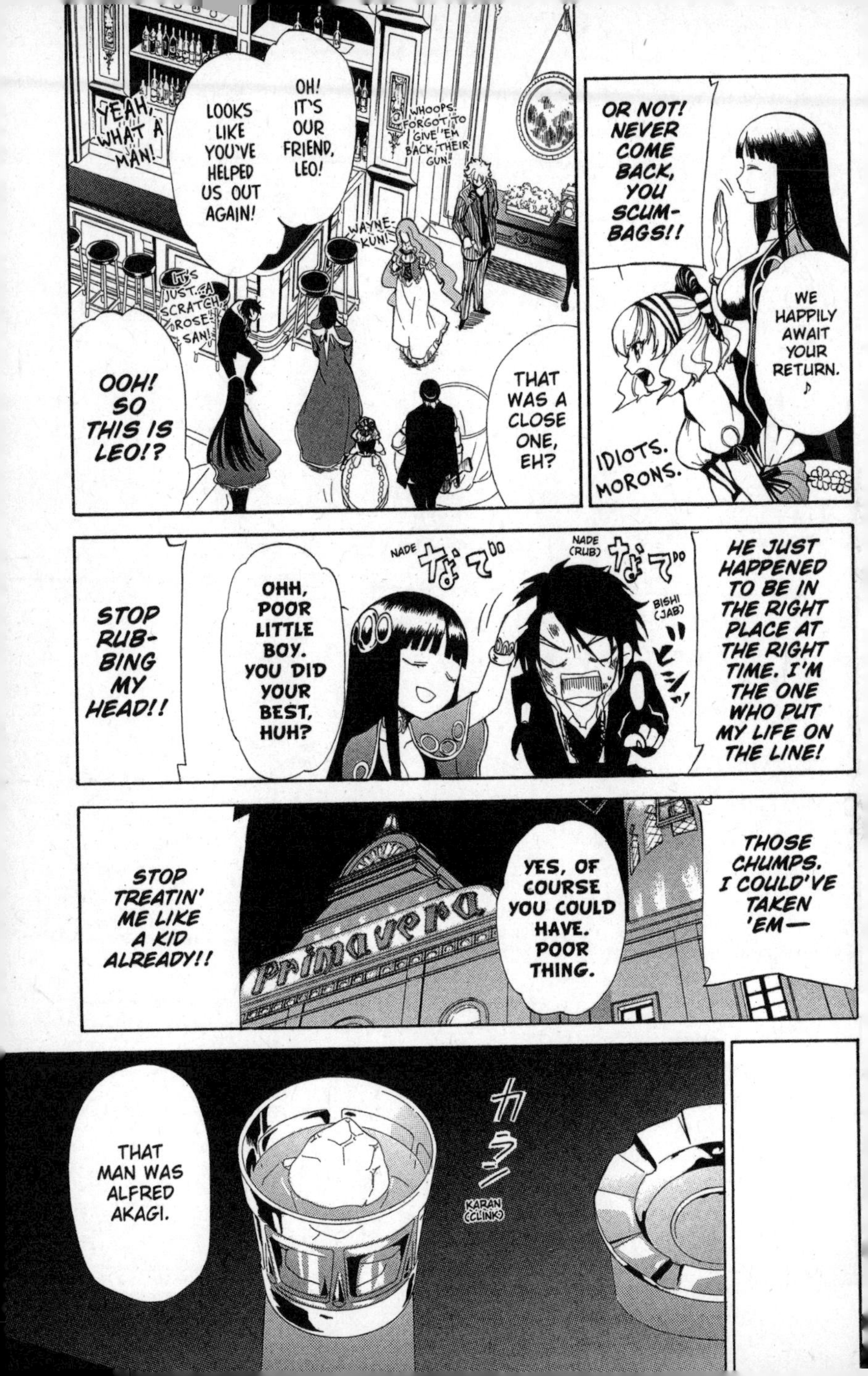
WE HAPPILY AWAIT YOUR RETURN. ♪
OR NOT! NEVER COME BACK, YOU SCUMBAGS!!
IDIOTS. MORONS.
OH! IT'S OUR FRIEND, LEO!
WHOOPS! FORGOT TO GIVE 'EM BACK THEIR GUN!
LOOKS LIKE YOU'VE HELPED US OUT AGAIN!
YEAH, WHAT A MAN!
WAYNE-KUN!
THAT WAS A CLOSE ONE, EH?
IT'S JUST...A SCRATCH, ROSE-SAN!
OOH! SO THIS IS LEO!?
HE JUST HAPPENED TO BE IN THE RIGHT PLACE AT THE RIGHT TIME. I'M THE ONE WHO PUT MY LIFE ON THE LINE!
なで NADE (RUB)
BISHI (JAB)
OHH, POOR LITTLE BOY. YOU DID YOUR BEST, HUH?
なで NADE
STOP RUBBING MY HEAD!!
THOSE CHUMPS. I COULD'VE TAKEN 'EM—
Primavera
YES, OF COURSE YOU COULD HAVE. POOR THING.
STOP TREATIN' ME LIKE A KID ALREADY!!
カラン KARAN (CLINK)
THAT MAN WAS ALFRED AKAGI.

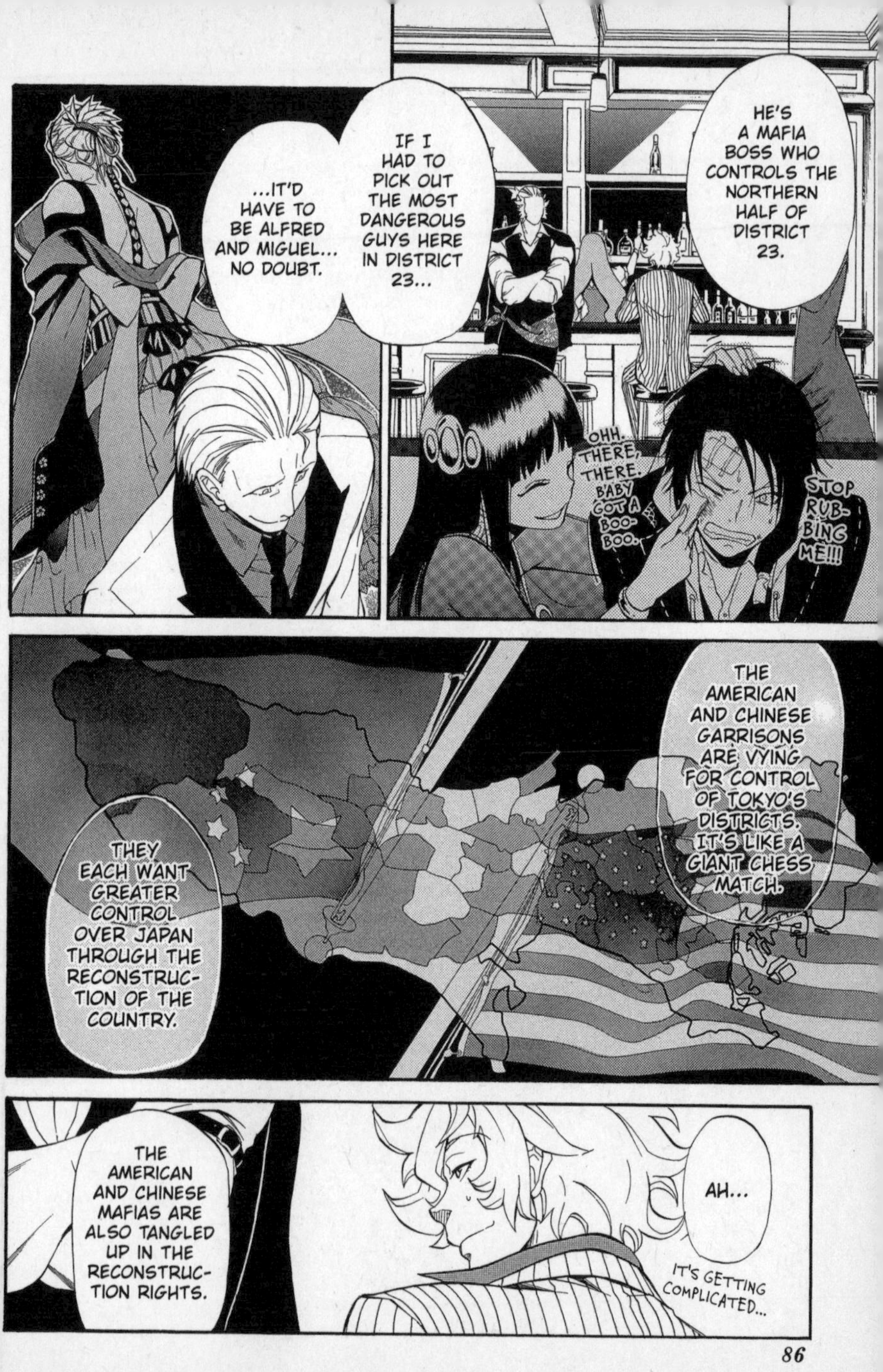
HE'S A MAFIA BOSS WHO CONTROLS THE NORTHERN HALF OF DISTRICT 23.
STOP RUB-BING ME!!!
OHH. THERE, THERE. BABY GOT A BOO-BOO.
IF I HAD TO PICK OUT THE MOST DANGEROUS GUYS HERE IN DISTRICT 23...
...IT'D HAVE TO BE ALFRED AND MIGUEL... NO DOUBT.
THE AMERICAN AND CHINESE GARRISONS ARE VYING FOR CONTROL OF TOKYO'S DISTRICTS. IT'S LIKE A GIANT CHESS MATCH.
THEY EACH WANT GREATER CONTROL OVER JAPAN THROUGH THE RECONSTRUC-TION OF THE COUNTRY.
AH...
IT'S GETTING COMPLICATED...
THE AMERICAN AND CHINESE MAFIAS ARE ALSO TANGLED UP IN THE RECONSTRUC-TION RIGHTS.

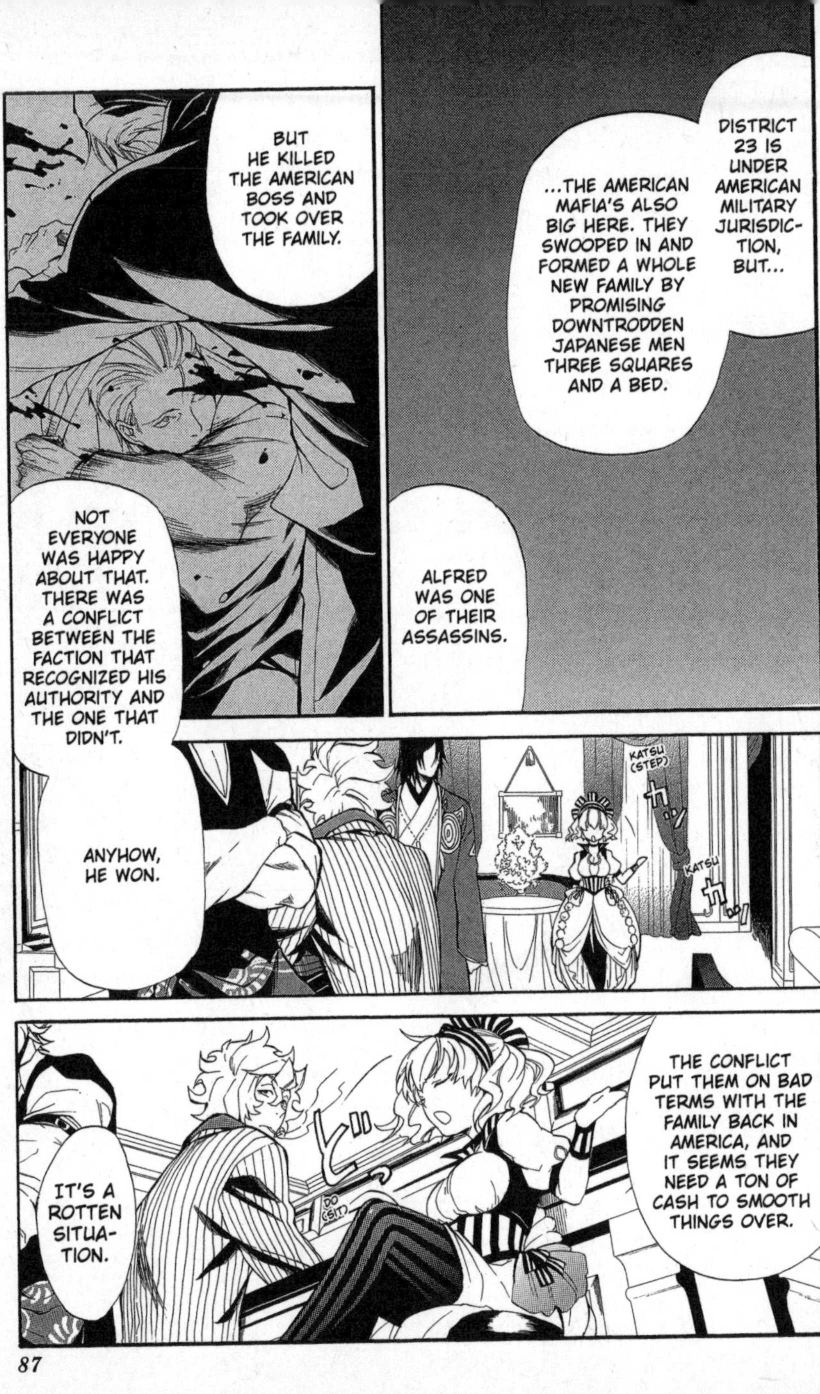
DISTRICT 23 IS UNDER AMERICAN MILITARY JURISDICTION, BUT...
...THE AMERICAN MAFIA'S ALSO BIG HERE. THEY SWOOPED IN AND FORMED A WHOLE NEW FAMILY BY PROMISING DOWNTRODDEN JAPANESE MEN THREE SQUARES AND A BED.
ALFRED WAS ONE OF THEIR ASSASSINS.
BUT HE KILLED THE AMERICAN BOSS AND TOOK OVER THE FAMILY.
NOT EVERYONE WAS HAPPY ABOUT THAT. THERE WAS A CONFLICT BETWEEN THE FACTION THAT RECOGNIZED HIS AUTHORITY AND THE ONE THAT DIDN'T.
KATSU (STEP)
KATSU
ANYHOW, HE WON.
THE CONFLICT PUT THEM ON BAD TERMS WITH THE FAMILY BACK IN AMERICA, AND IT SEEMS THEY NEED A TON OF CASH TO SMOOTH THINGS OVER.
DO (SIT)
IT'S A ROTTEN SITUATION.

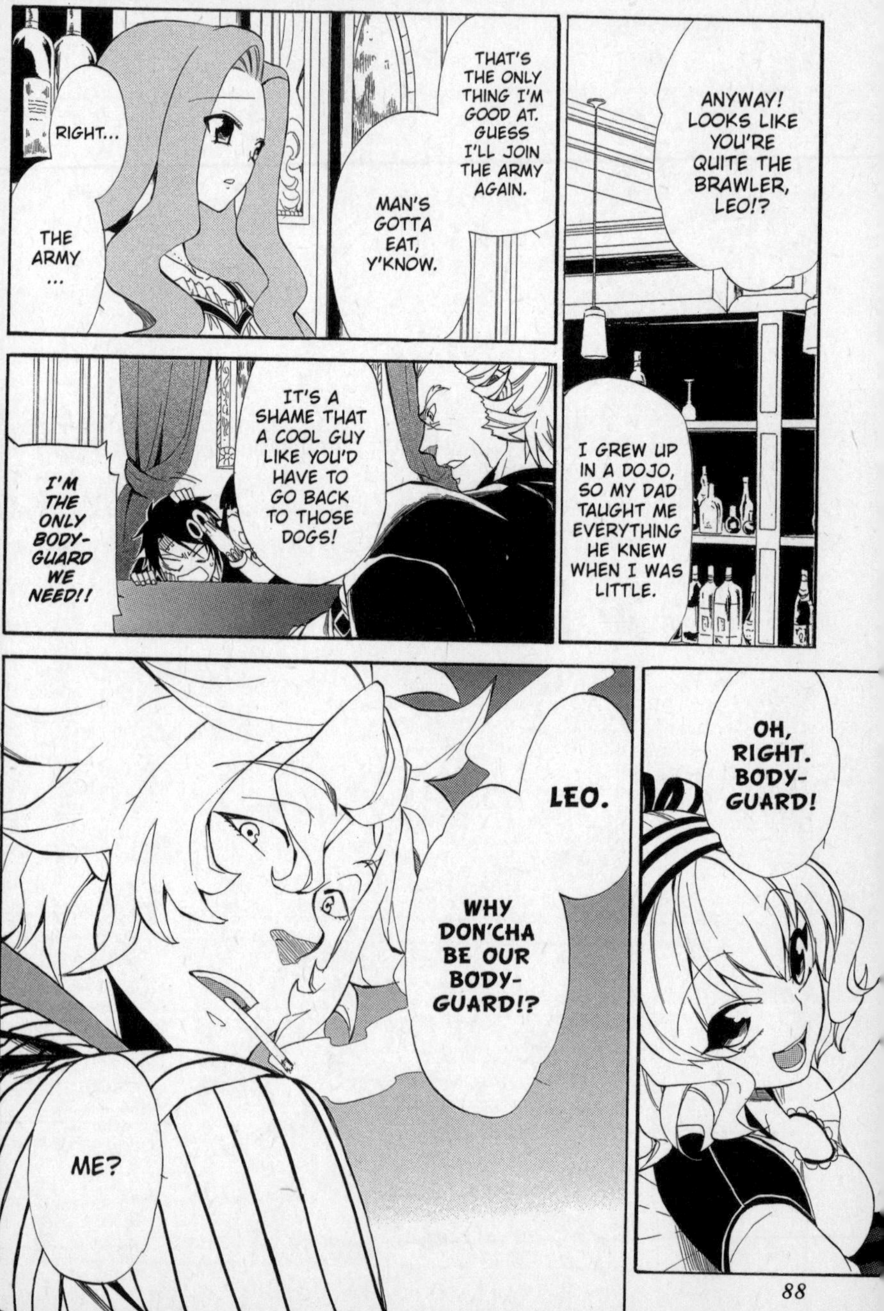
ANYWAY! LOOKS LIKE YOU'RE QUITE THE BRAWLER, LEO!?
I GREW UP IN A DOJO, SO MY DAD TAUGHT ME EVERYTHING HE KNEW WHEN I WAS LITTLE.
THAT'S THE ONLY THING I'M GOOD AT. GUESS I'LL JOIN THE ARMY AGAIN.
MAN'S GOTTA EAT, Y'KNOW.
RIGHT...
THE ARMY...
IT'S A SHAME THAT A COOL GUY LIKE YOU'D HAVE TO GO BACK TO THOSE DOGS!
I'M THE ONLY BODY-GUARD WE NEED!!
OH, RIGHT. BODY-GUARD!
LEO.
WHY DON'CHA BE OUR BODY-GUARD!?
ME?

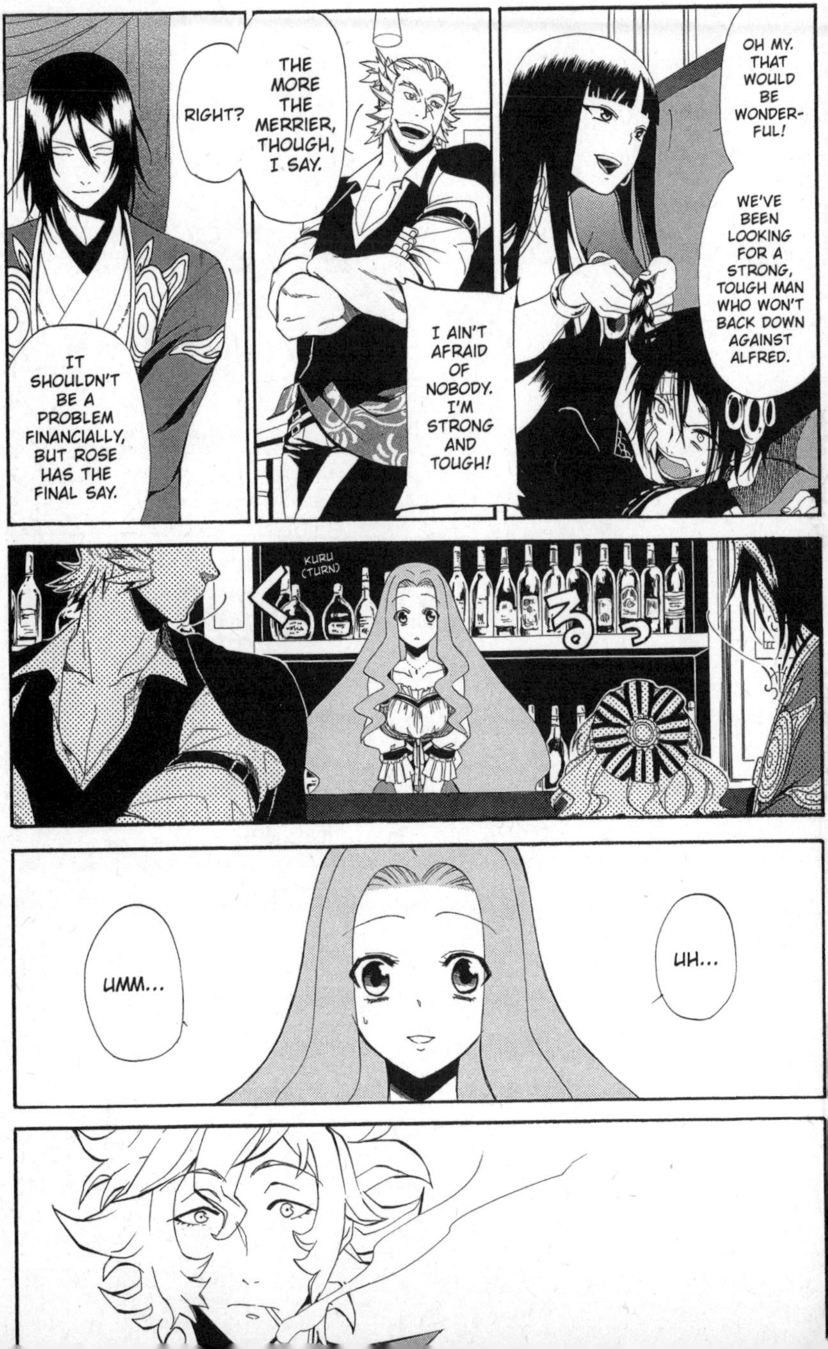
OH MY. THAT WOULD BE WONDERFUL!
WE'VE BEEN LOOKING FOR A STRONG, TOUGH MAN WHO WON'T BACK DOWN AGAINST ALFRED.
I AIN'T AFRAID OF NOBODY. I'M STRONG AND TOUGH!
THE MORE THE MERRIER, THOUGH, I SAY.
RIGHT?
IT SHOULDN'T BE A PROBLEM FINANCIALLY, BUT ROSE HAS THE FINAL SAY.
KURU (TURN)
UH...
UMM...

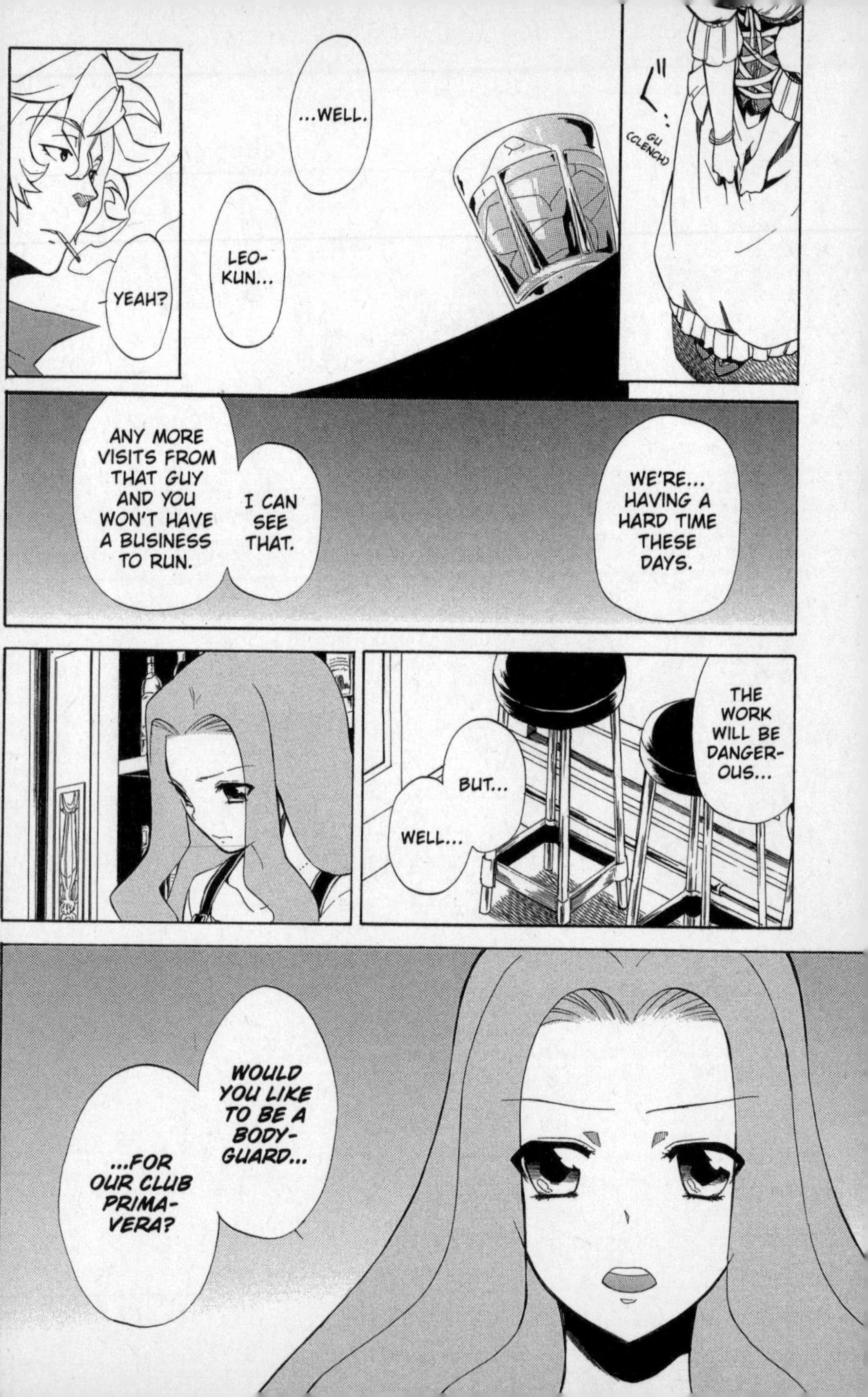
GU (CLENCH)
...WELL.
LEO-KUN...
YEAH?
WE'RE... HAVING A HARD TIME THESE DAYS.
I CAN SEE THAT.
ANY MORE VISITS FROM THAT GUY AND YOU WON'T HAVE A BUSINESS TO RUN.
THE WORK WILL BE DANGER-OUS...
BUT...
WELL...
WOULD YOU LIKE TO BE A BODY-GUARD...
...FOR OUR CLUB PRIMA-VERA?

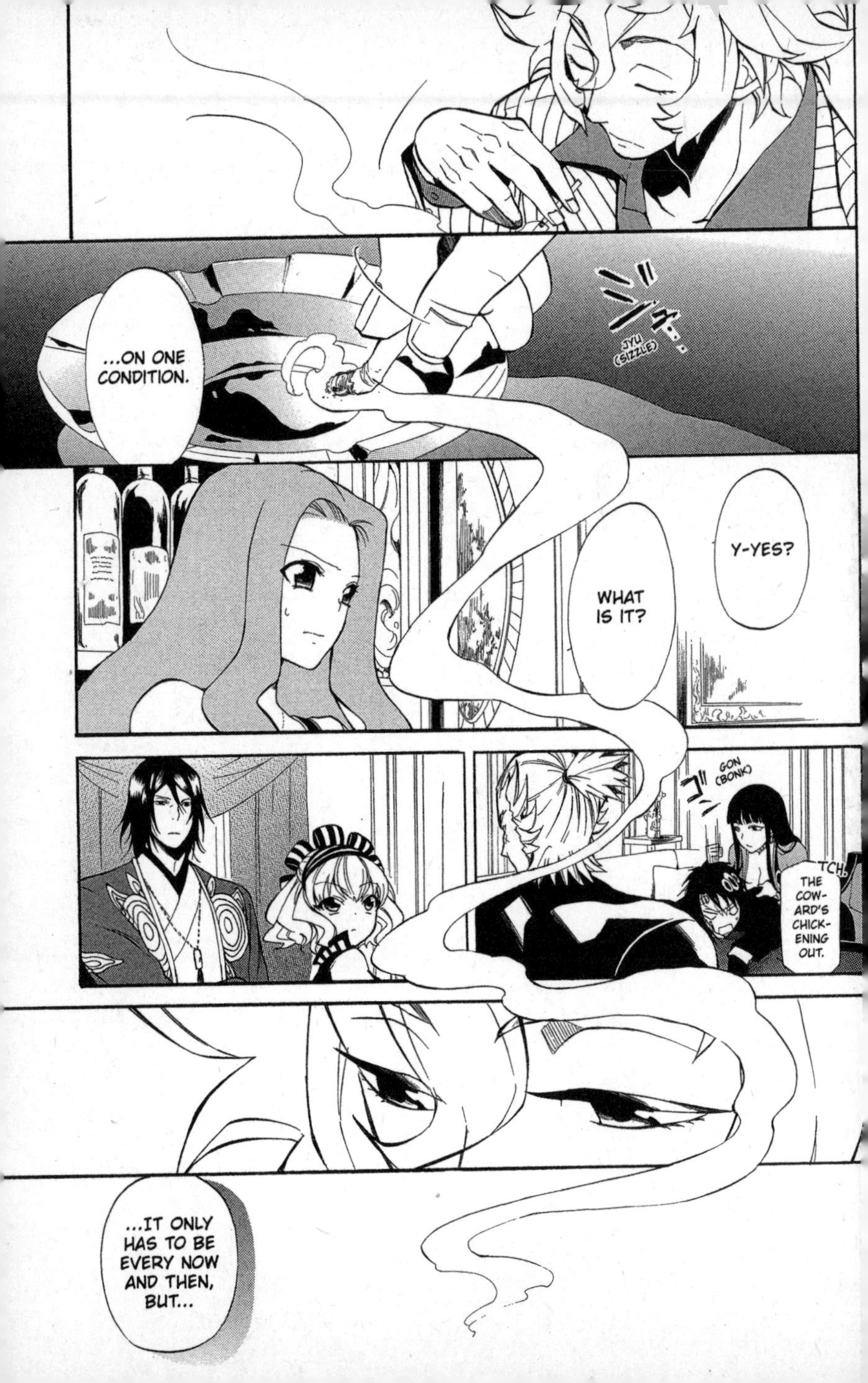
JYU (SIZZLE)
...ON ONE CONDITION.
Y-YES?
WHAT IS IT?
TCH.
THE COW-ARD'S CHICK-ENING OUT.
GON (BONK)
...IT ONLY HAS TO BE EVERY NOW AND THEN, BUT...

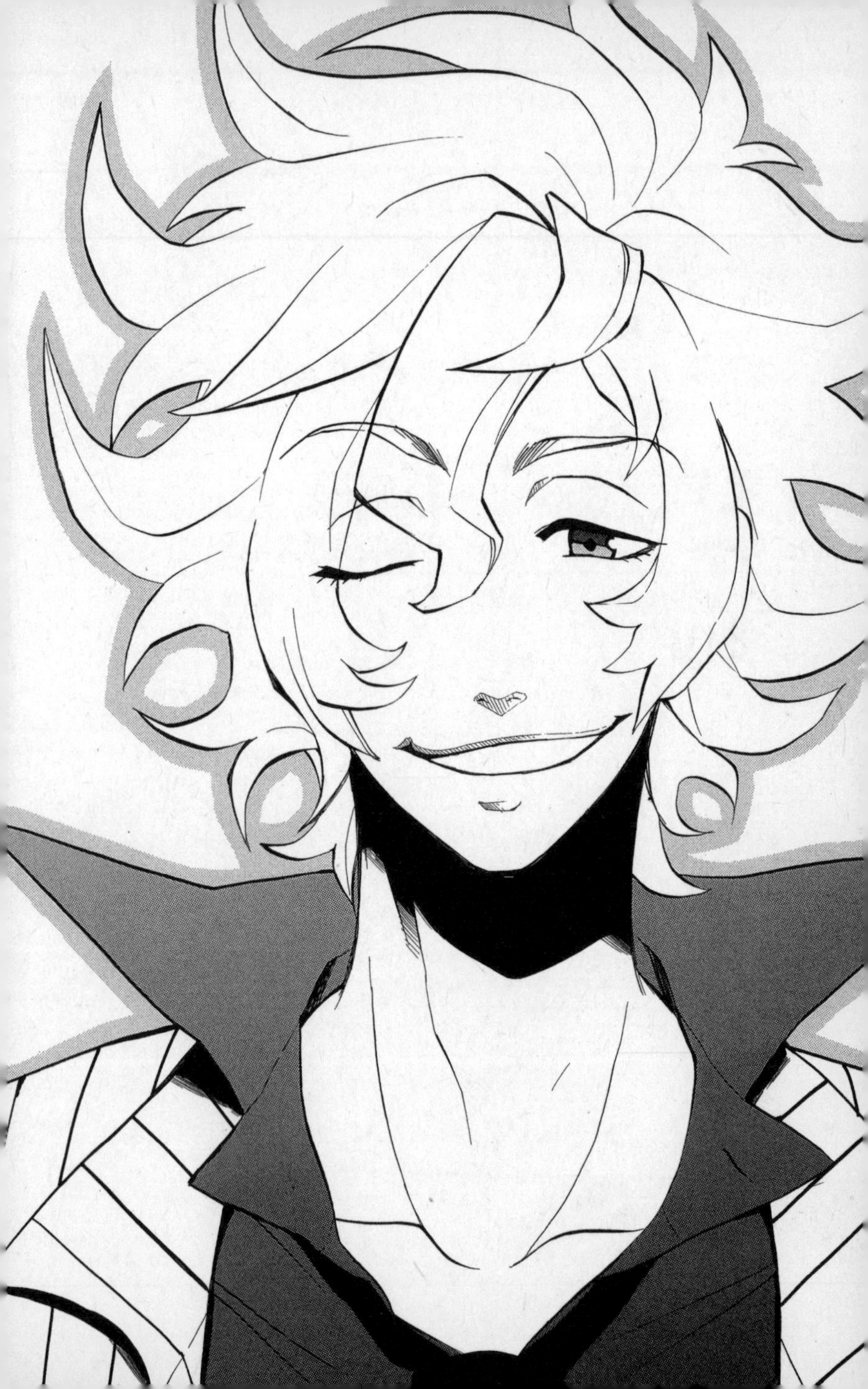

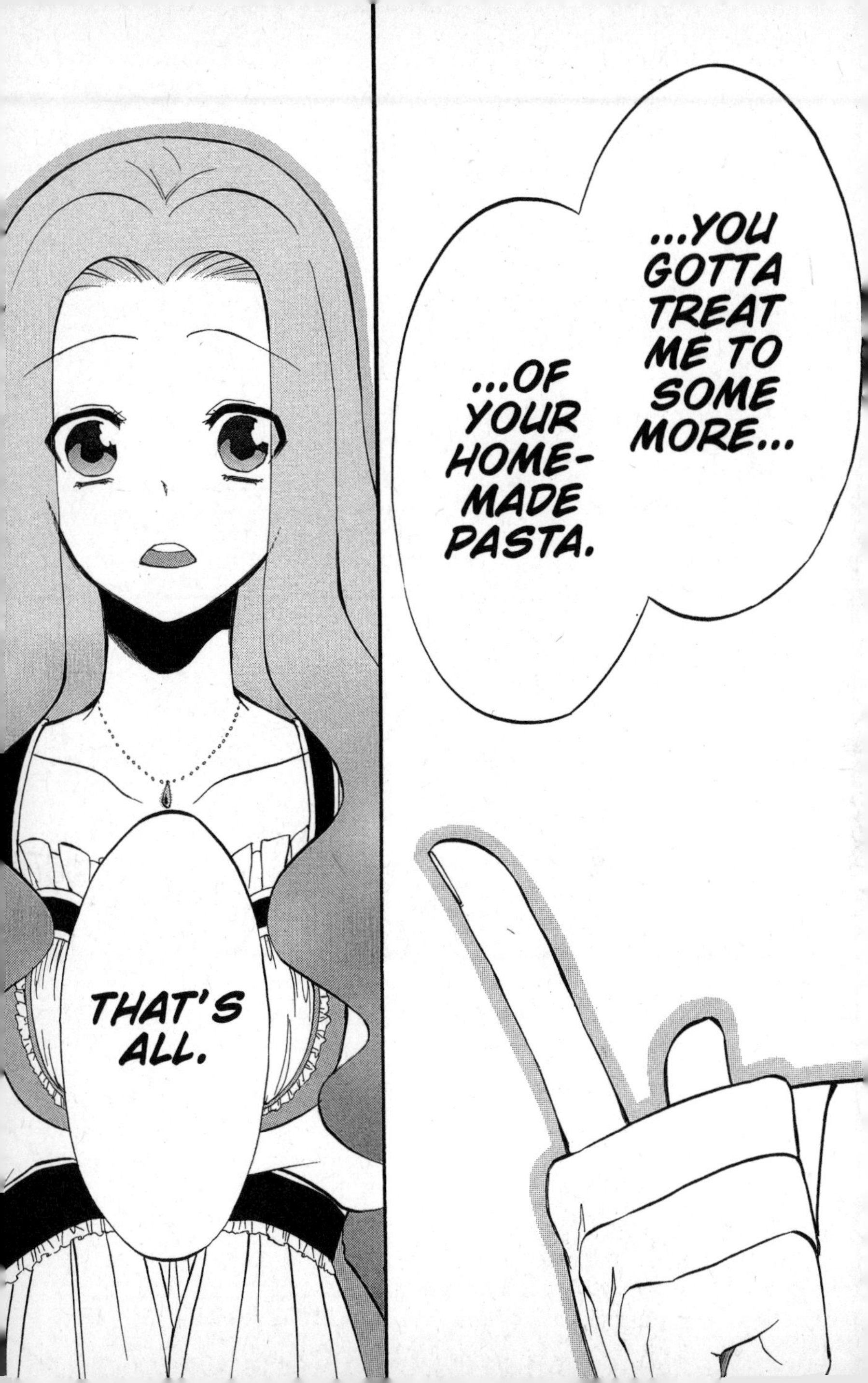
...YOU GOTTA TREAT ME TO SOME MORE...
...OF YOUR HOME-MADE PASTA.
THAT'S ALL.

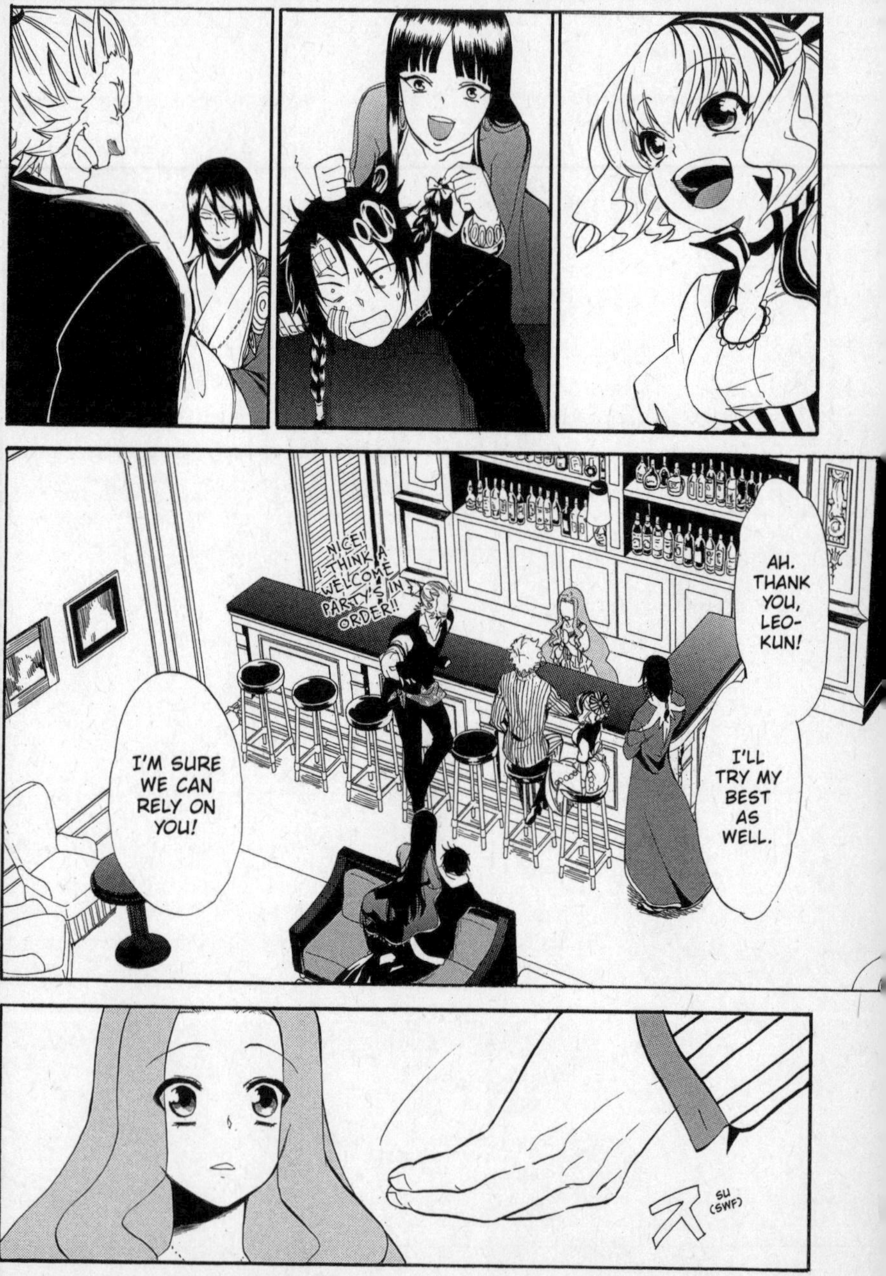
AH. THANK YOU, LEO-KUN!
I'LL TRY MY BEST AS WELL.
NICE! I THINK A WELCOME PARTY'S IN ORDER!!
I'M SURE WE CAN RELY ON YOU!
ス
SU (SWF)

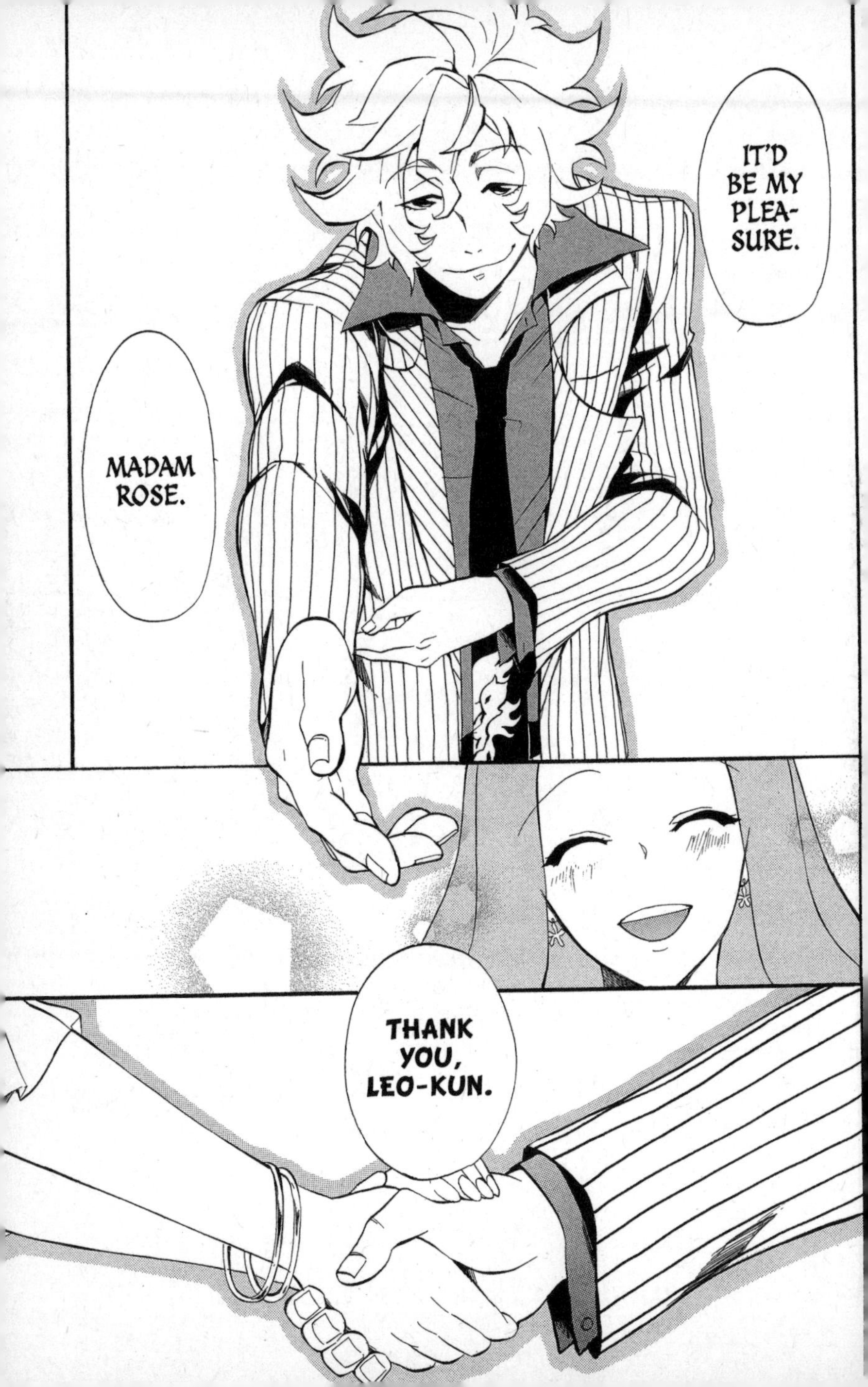
IT'D BE MY PLEA-SURE.
MADAM ROSE.
THANK YOU, LEO-KUN.

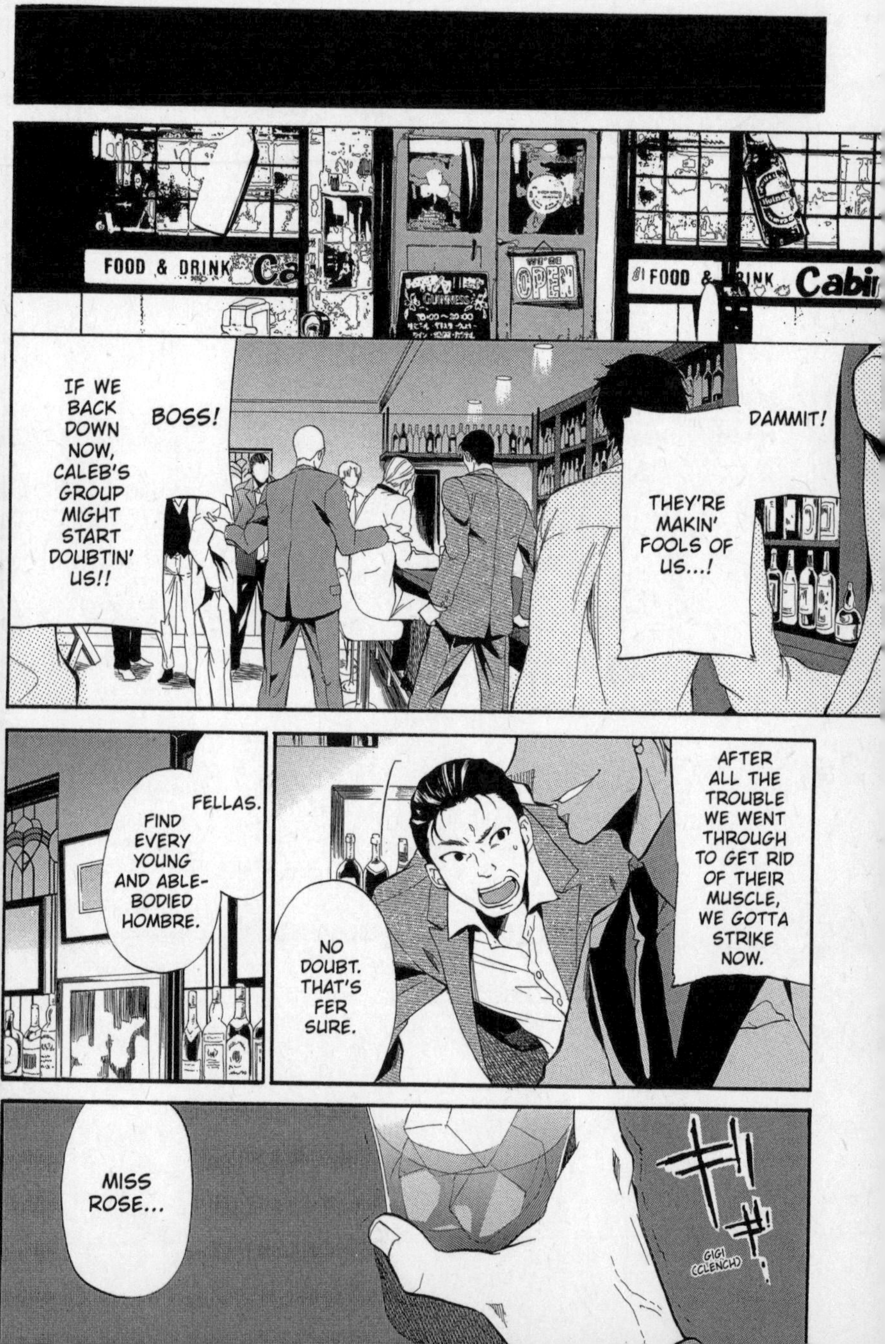
FOOD & DRINK Cabi
OPEN
GUINNESS
FOOD & DRINK
DAMMIT!
THEY'RE MAKIN' FOOLS OF US...!
BOSS!
IF WE BACK DOWN NOW, CALEB'S GROUP MIGHT START DOUBTIN' US!!
AFTER ALL THE TROUBLE WE WENT THROUGH TO GET RID OF THEIR MUSCLE, WE GOTTA STRIKE NOW.
NO DOUBT. THAT'S FER SURE.
FELLAS.
FIND EVERY YOUNG AND ABLE-BODIED HOMBRE.
GIGI (CLENCH)
MISS ROSE...

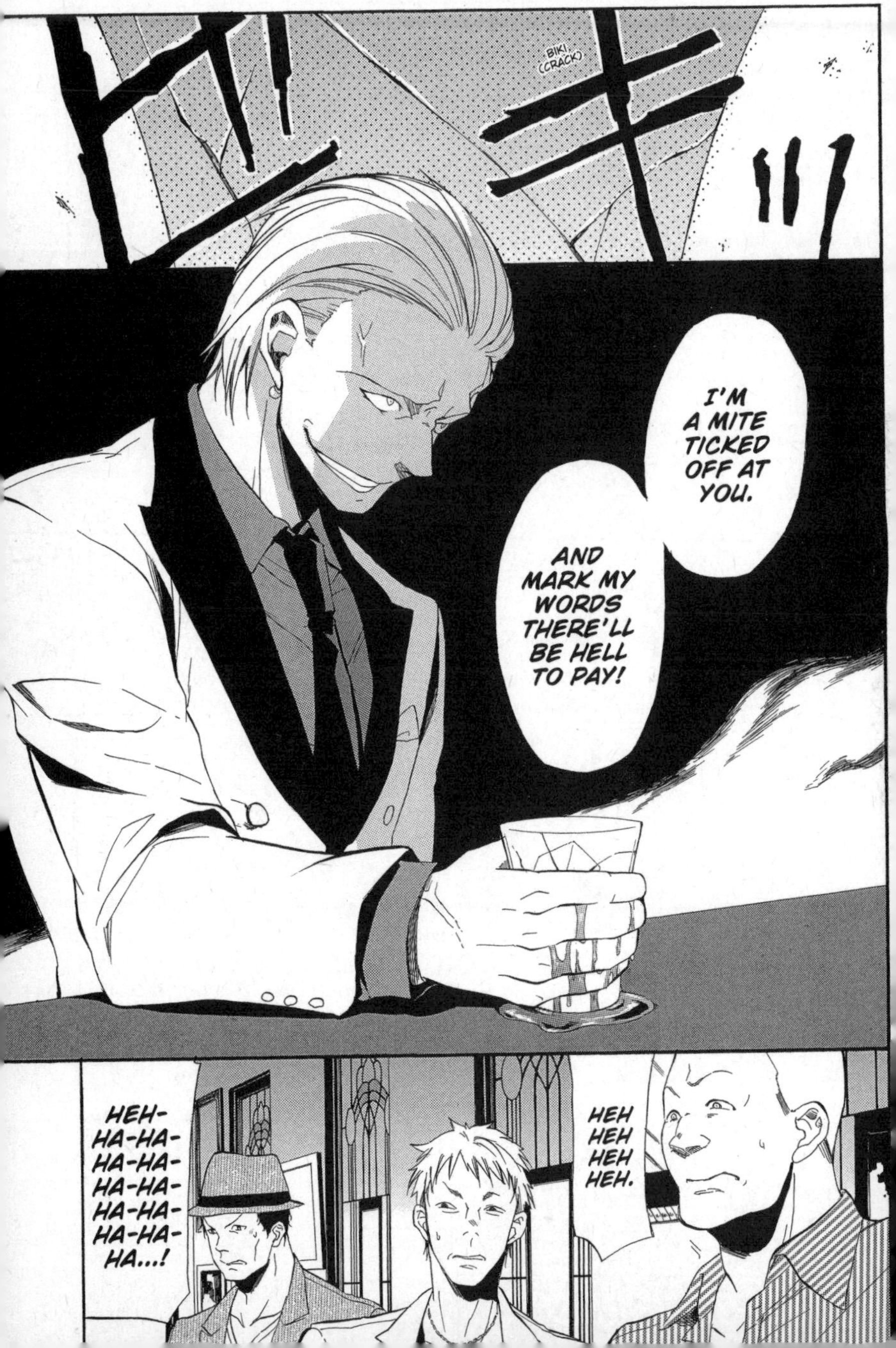
BIKI (CRACK)
I'M A MITE TICKED OFF AT YOU.
AND MARK MY WORDS THERE'LL BE HELL TO PAY!
HEH HEH HEH HEH.
HEH-HA-HA-HA-HA-HA-HA-HA-HA-HA-HA-HA...!

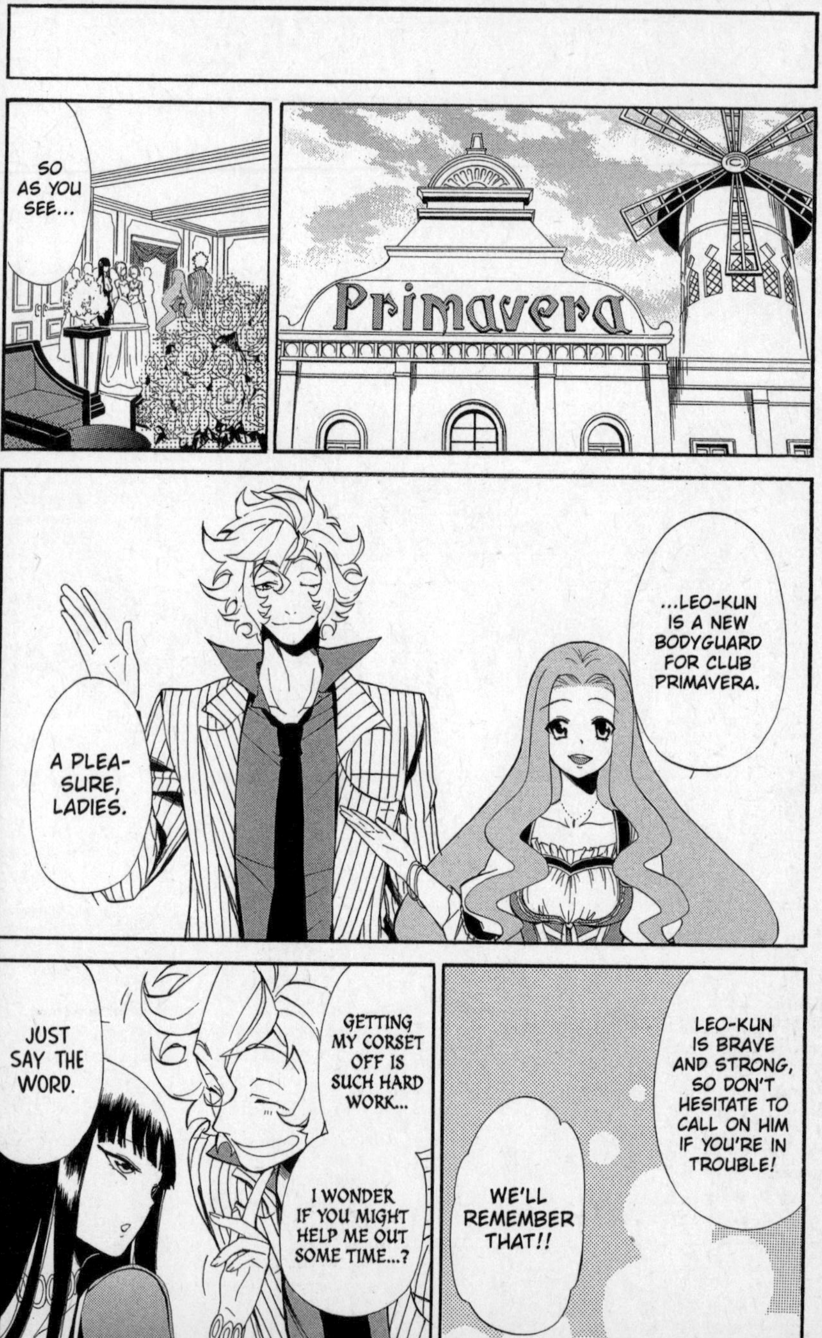

Primavera
SO AS YOU SEE...
...LEO-KUN IS A NEW BODYGUARD FOR CLUB PRIMAVERA.
A PLEA-SURE, LADIES.
LEO-KUN IS BRAVE AND STRONG, SO DON'T HESITATE TO CALL ON HIM IF YOU'RE IN TROUBLE!
WE'LL REMEMBER THAT!!
GETTING MY CORSET OFF IS SUCH HARD WORK...
I WONDER IF YOU MIGHT HELP ME OUT SOME TIME...?
JUST SAY THE WORD.

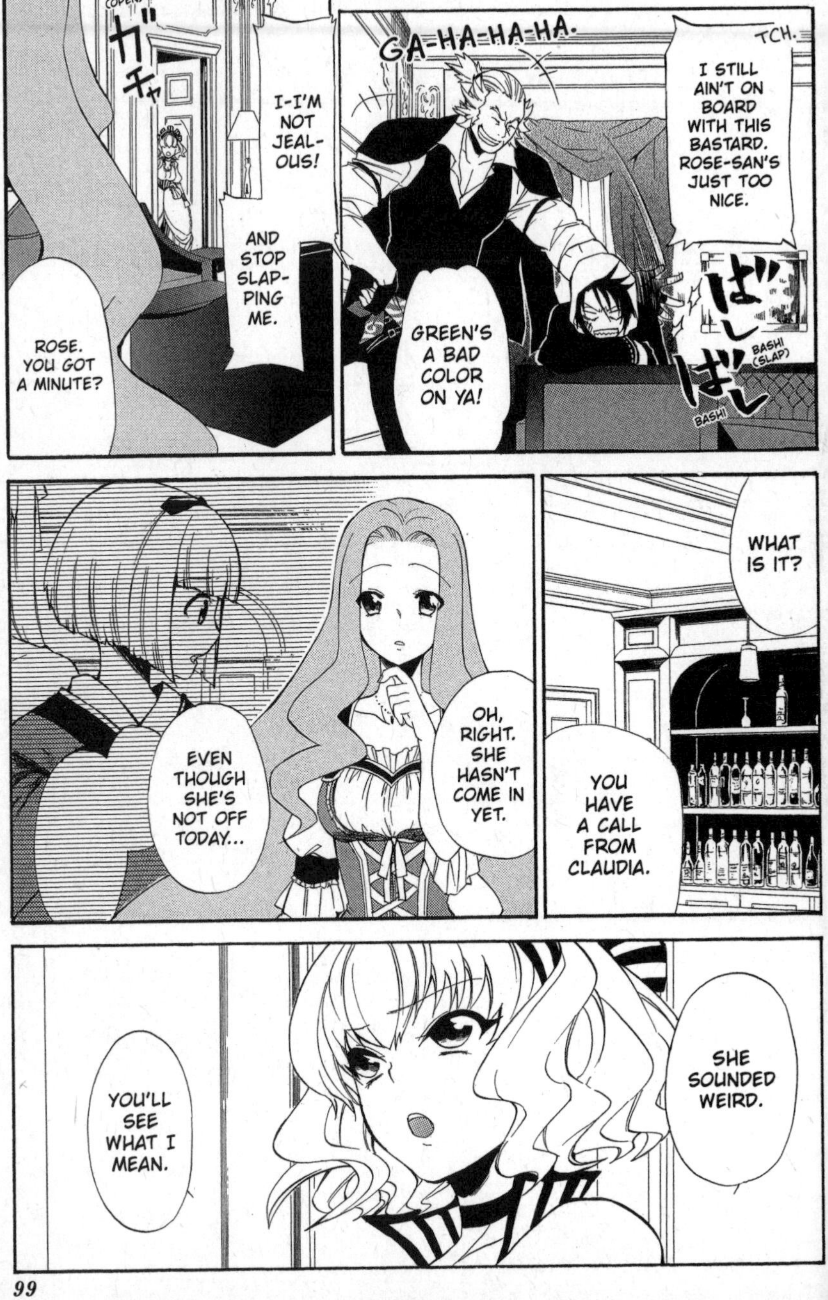
TCH.
I STILL AIN'T ON BOARD WITH THIS BASTARD. ROSE-SAN'S JUST TOO NICE.
GA-HA-HA-HA.
ばしばし
BASHI (SLAP)
BASHI
GREEN'S A BAD COLOR ON YA!
I-I'M NOT JEAL-OUS!
AND STOP SLAP-PING ME.
ガチャ
GACHA (OPEN)
ROSE. YOU GOT A MINUTE?
WHAT IS IT?
YOU HAVE A CALL FROM CLAUDIA.
OH, RIGHT. SHE HASN'T COME IN YET.
EVEN THOUGH SHE'S NOT OFF TODAY...
SHE SOUNDED WEIRD.
YOU'LL SEE WHAT I MEAN.

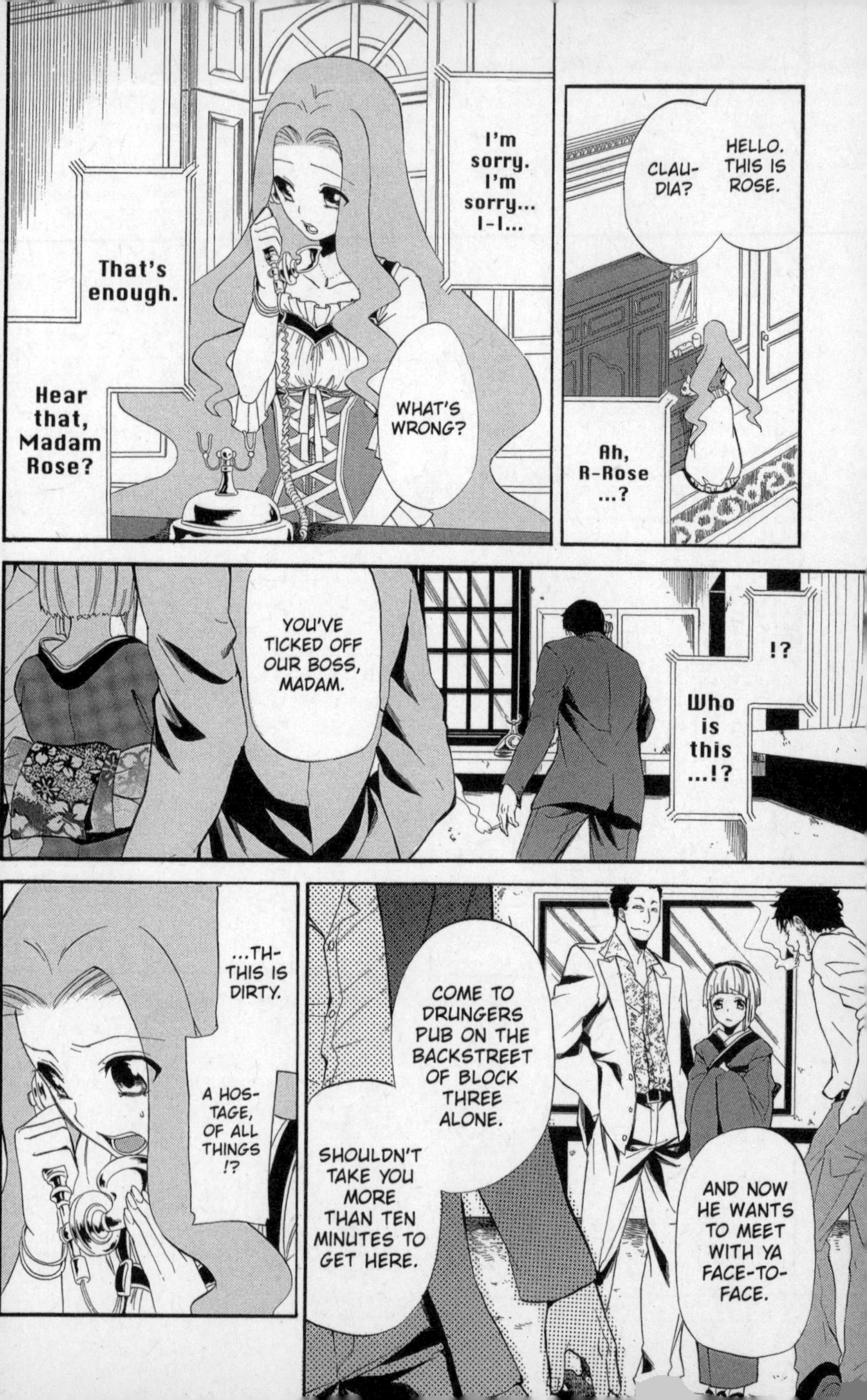
HELLO. THIS IS ROSE.
CLAU-DIA?
Ah, R-Rose ...?
WHAT'S WRONG?
I'm sorry. I'm sorry... I-I...
That's enough.
Hear that, Madam Rose?
!?
Who is this ...!?
YOU'VE TICKED OFF OUR BOSS, MADAM.
AND NOW HE WANTS TO MEET WITH YA FACE-TO-FACE.
COME TO DRUNGERS PUB ON THE BACKSTREET OF BLOCK THREE ALONE.
SHOULDN'T TAKE YOU MORE THAN TEN MINUTES TO GET HERE.
...TH-THIS IS DIRTY.
A HOS-TAGE, OF ALL THINGS !?

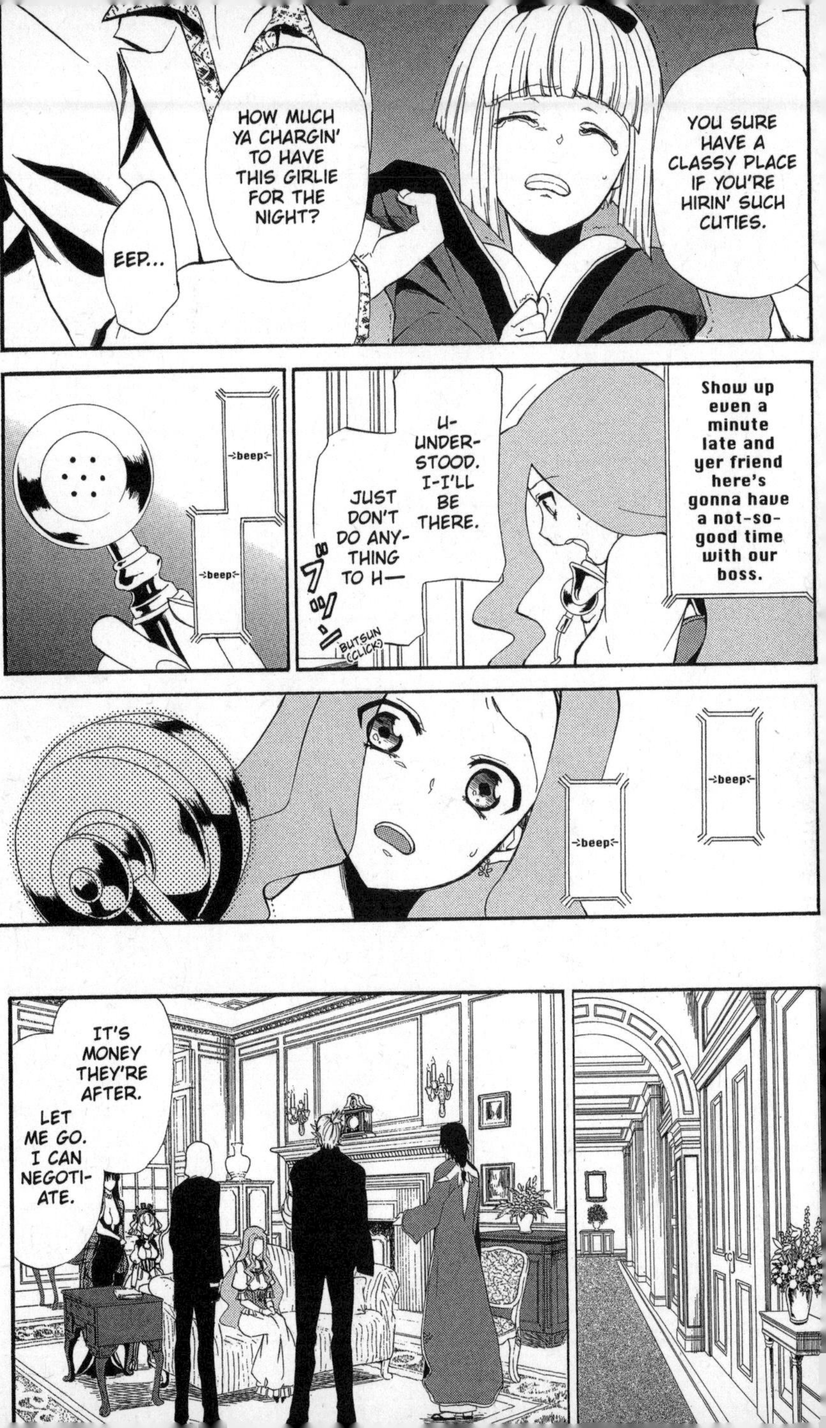
YOU SURE HAVE A CLASSY PLACE IF YOU'RE HIRIN' SUCH CUTIES.
HOW MUCH YA CHARGIN' TO HAVE THIS GIRLIE FOR THE NIGHT?
EEP...
Show up even a minute late and yer friend here's gonna have a not-so-good time with our boss.
U-UNDERSTOOD. I-I'LL BE THERE.
JUST DON'T DO ANY-THING TO H—
BUTSUN (CLICK)
beep
beep
beep
beep
IT'S MONEY THEY'RE AFTER.
LET ME GO. I CAN NEGOTI-ATE.

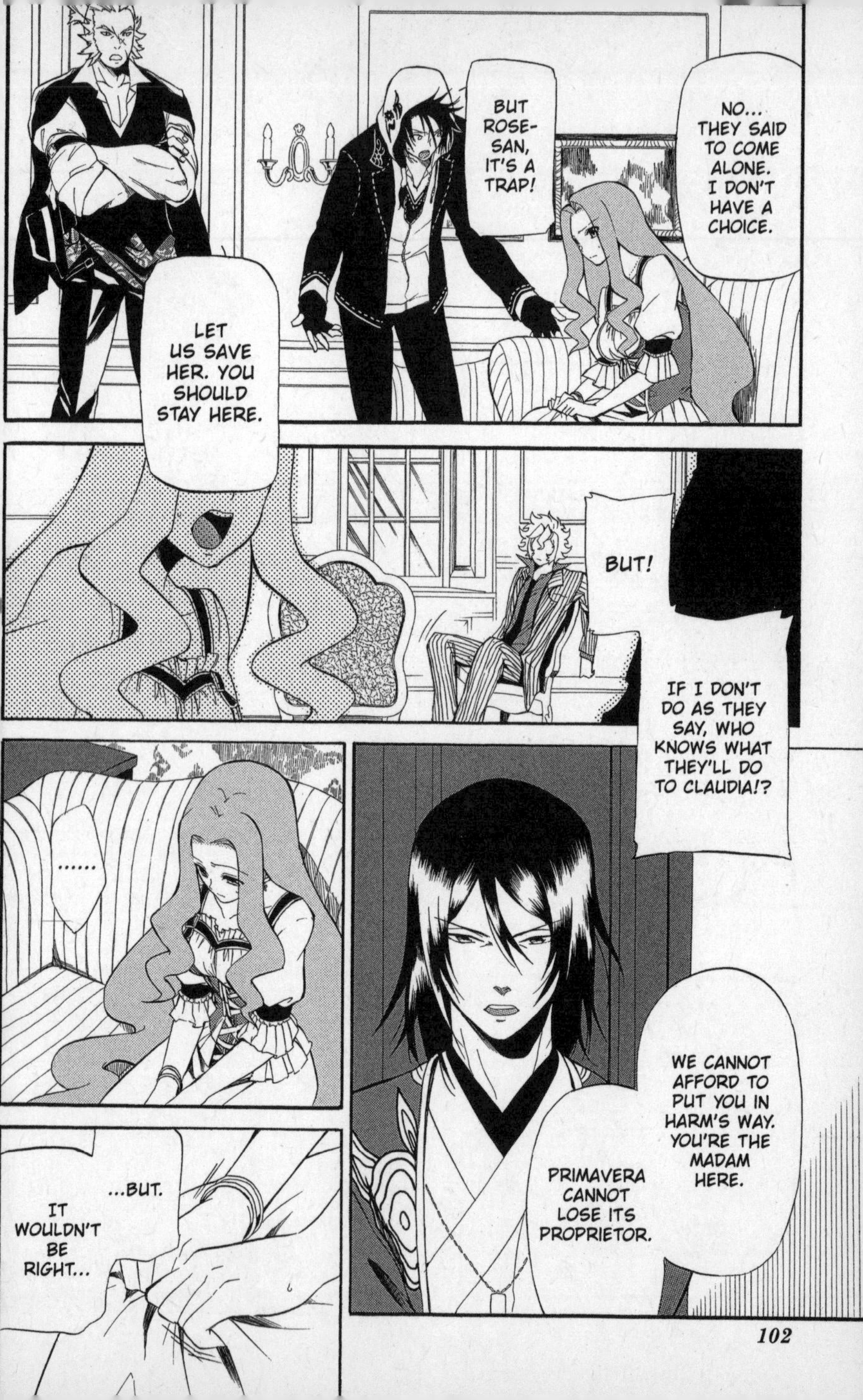
NO... THEY SAID TO COME ALONE. I DON'T HAVE A CHOICE.
BUT ROSE-SAN, IT'S A TRAP!
LET US SAVE HER. YOU SHOULD STAY HERE.
BUT!
IF I DON'T DO AS THEY SAY, WHO KNOWS WHAT THEY'LL DO TO CLAUDIA!?
WE CANNOT AFFORD TO PUT YOU IN HARM'S WAY. YOU'RE THE MADAM HERE.
PRIMAVERA CANNOT LOSE ITS PROPRIETOR.
......
...BUT.
IT WOULDN'T BE RIGHT...

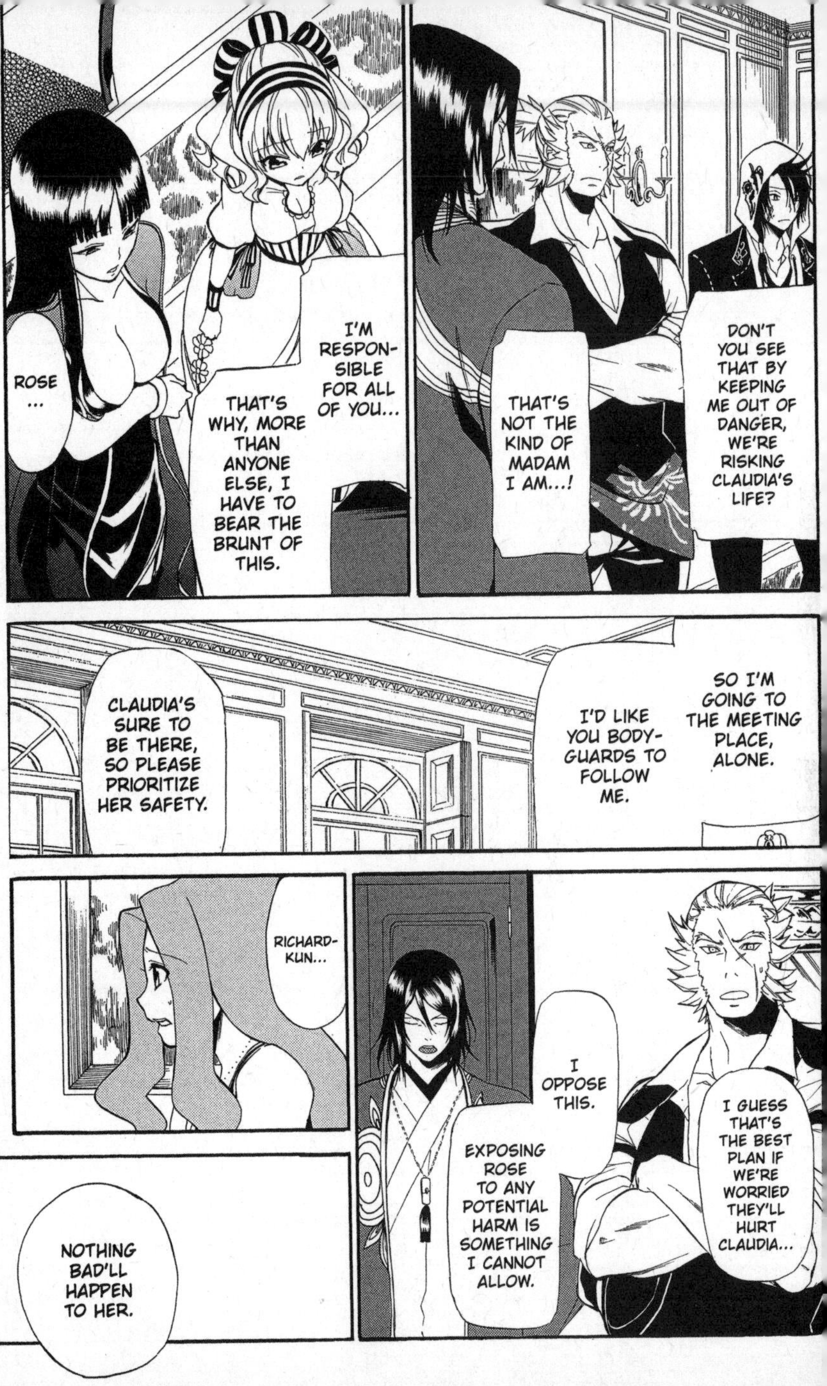

DON'T YOU SEE THAT BY KEEPING ME OUT OF DANGER, WE'RE RISKING CLAUDIA'S LIFE?
THAT'S NOT THE KIND OF MADAM I AM...!
I'M RESPONSIBLE FOR ALL OF YOU...
THAT'S WHY, MORE THAN ANYONE ELSE, I HAVE TO BEAR THE BRUNT OF THIS.
ROSE...
SO I'M GOING TO THE MEETING PLACE, ALONE.
I'D LIKE YOU BODYGUARDS TO FOLLOW ME.
CLAUDIA'S SURE TO BE THERE, SO PLEASE PRIORITIZE HER SAFETY.
I GUESS THAT'S THE BEST PLAN IF WE'RE WORRIED THEY'LL HURT CLAUDIA...
I OPPOSE THIS.
EXPOSING ROSE TO ANY POTENTIAL HARM IS SOMETHING I CANNOT ALLOW.
RICHARD-KUN...
NOTHING BAD'LL HAPPEN TO HER.

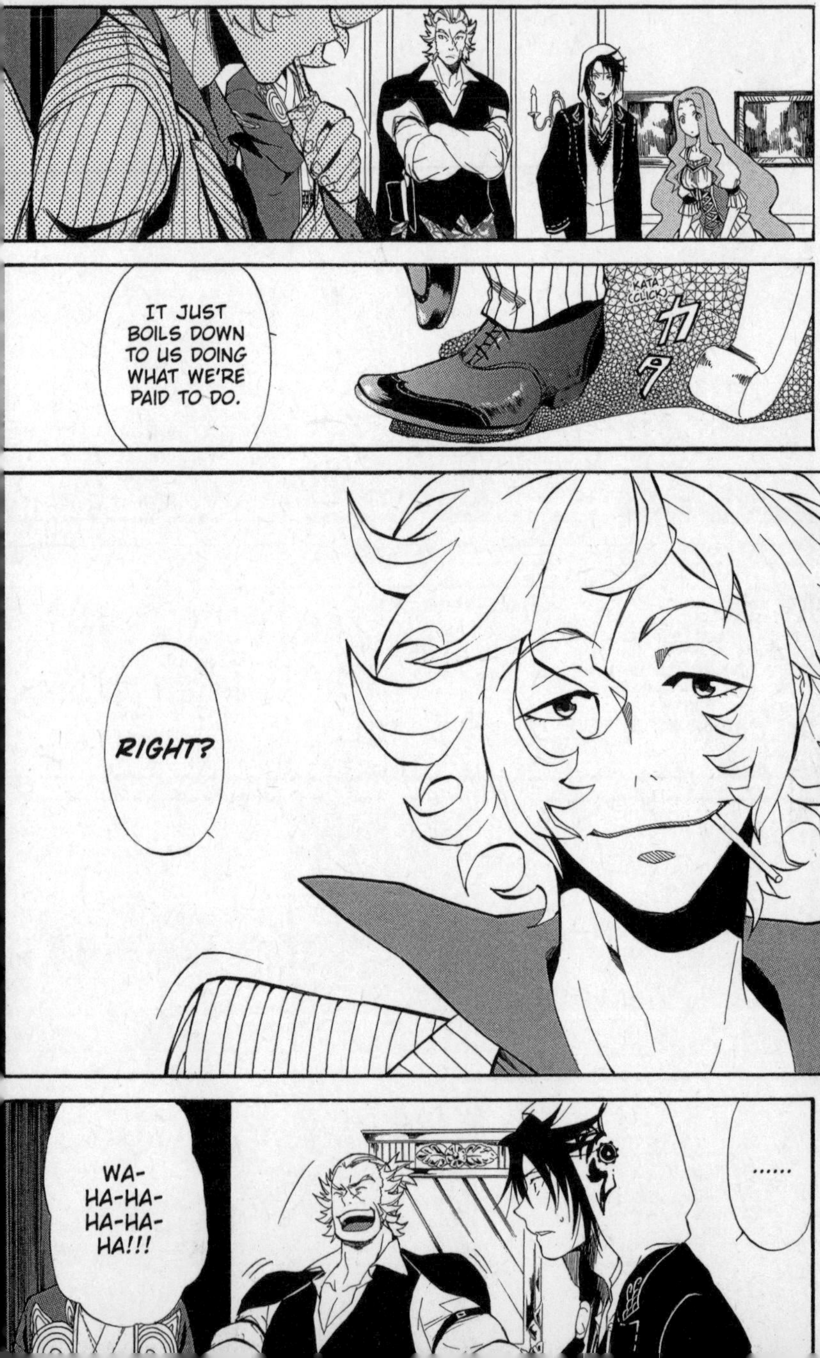
KATA (CLICK)
カタ
IT JUST BOILS DOWN TO US DOING WHAT WE'RE PAID TO DO.
RIGHT?
......
WA-HA-HA-HA-HA-HA!!!

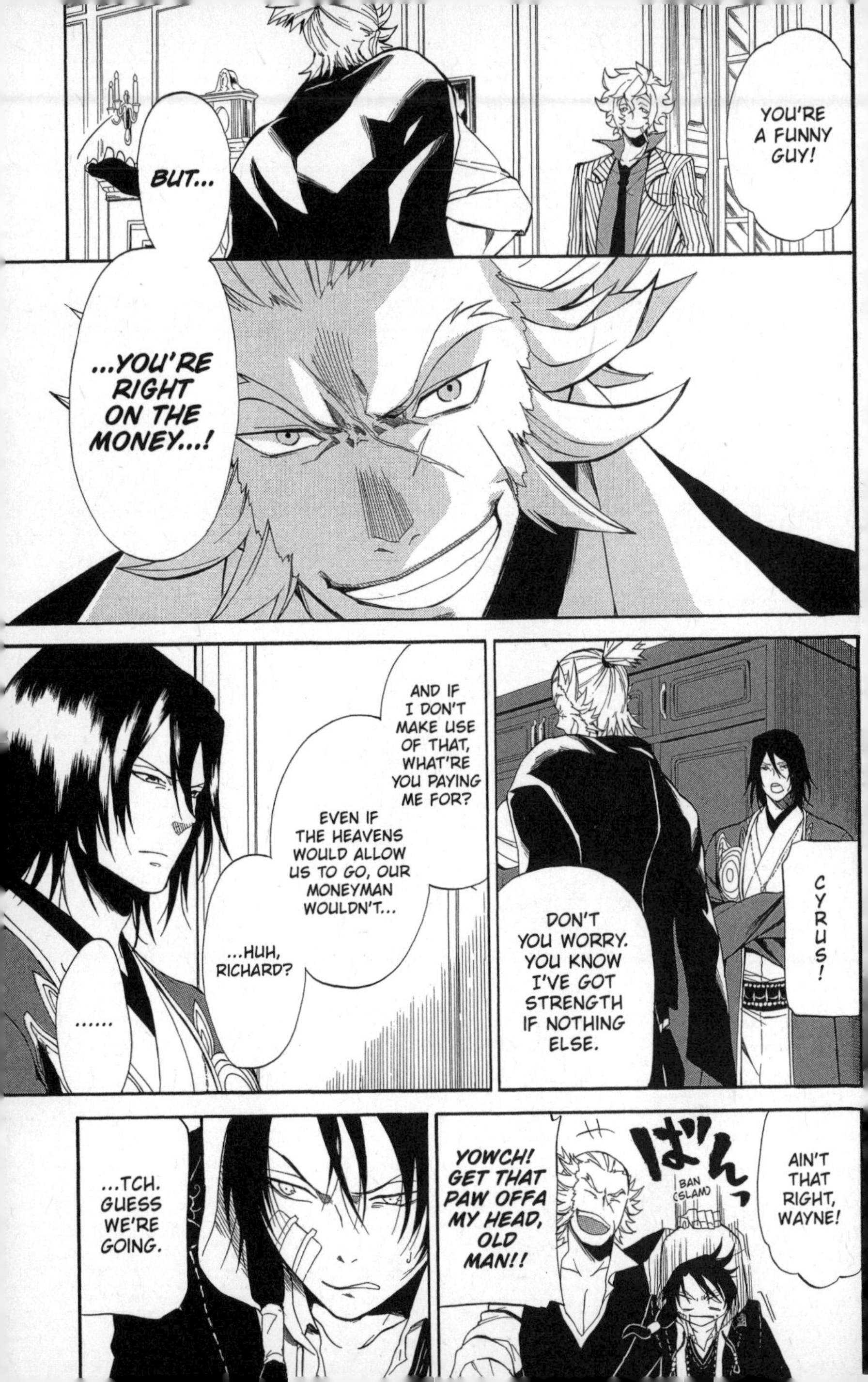
YOU'RE A FUNNY GUY!
BUT...
...YOU'RE RIGHT ON THE MONEY...!
CYRUS!
DON'T YOU WORRY. YOU KNOW I'VE GOT STRENGTH IF NOTHING ELSE.
AND IF I DON'T MAKE USE OF THAT, WHAT'RE YOU PAYING ME FOR?
EVEN IF THE HEAVENS WOULD ALLOW US TO GO, OUR MONEYMAN WOULDN'T...
...HUH, RICHARD?
......
AIN'T THAT RIGHT, WAYNE!
BAN (SLAM)
YOWCH! GET THAT PAW OFFA MY HEAD, OLD MAN!!
...TCH. GUESS WE'RE GOING.

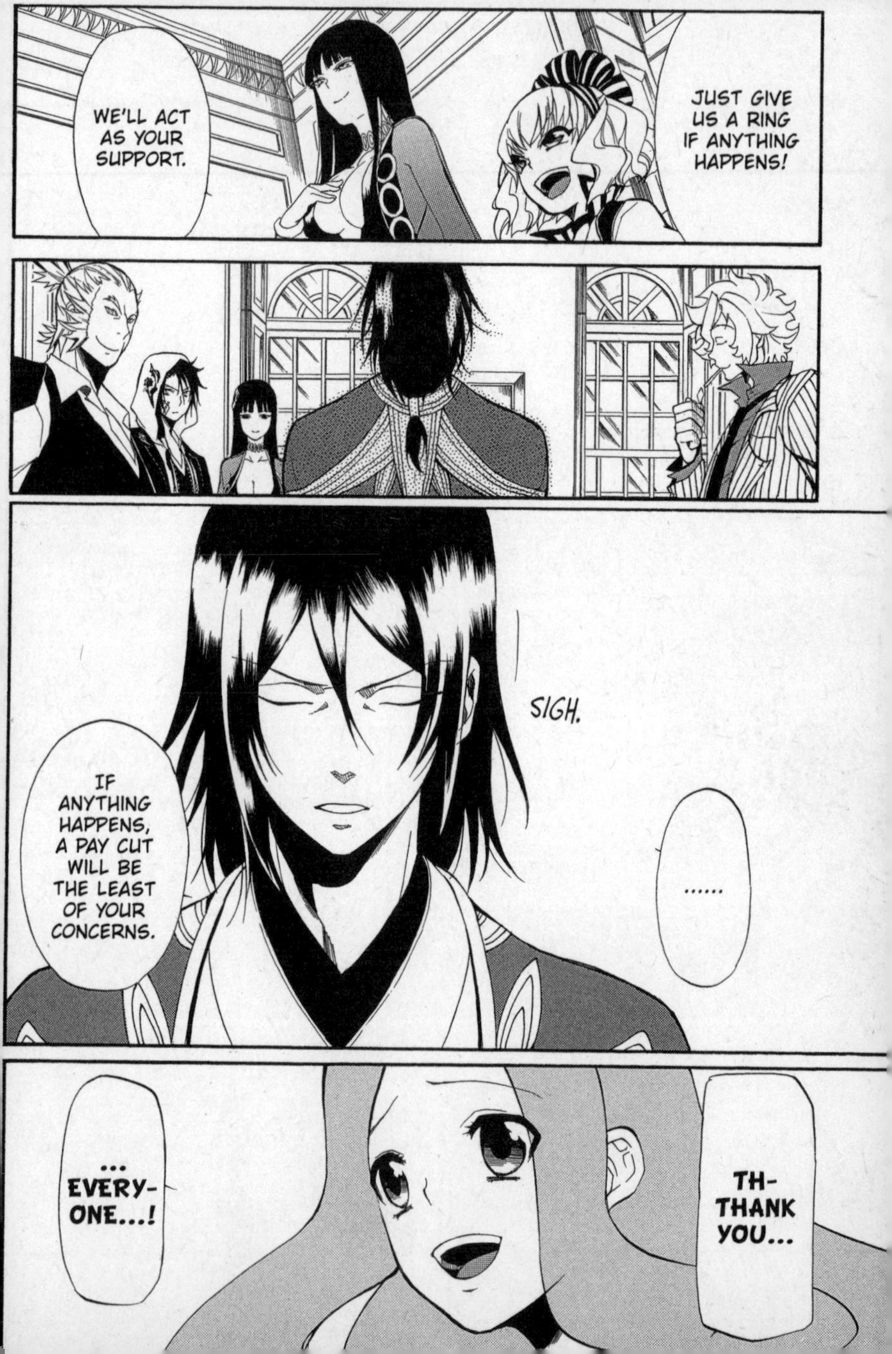
JUST GIVE US A RING IF ANYTHING HAPPENS!
WE'LL ACT AS YOUR SUPPORT.
SIGH.
......
IF ANYTHING HAPPENS, A PAY CUT WILL BE THE LEAST OF YOUR CONCERNS.
TH-THANK YOU...
...EVERY-ONE...!

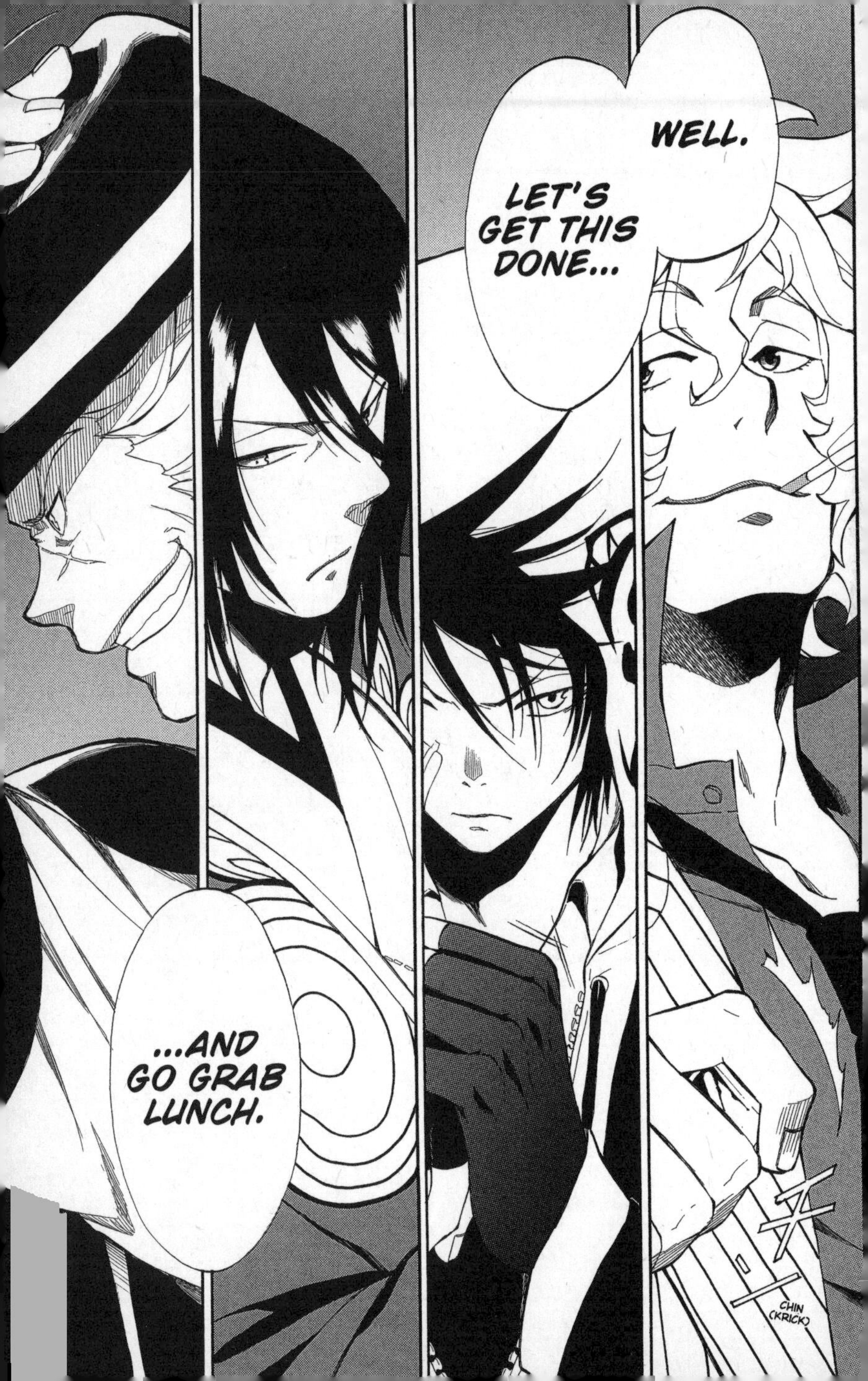
WELL.
LET'S GET THIS DONE...
CHIN (KRICK)
...AND GO GRAB LUNCH.

ROSE GUNS DAYS

Season 1

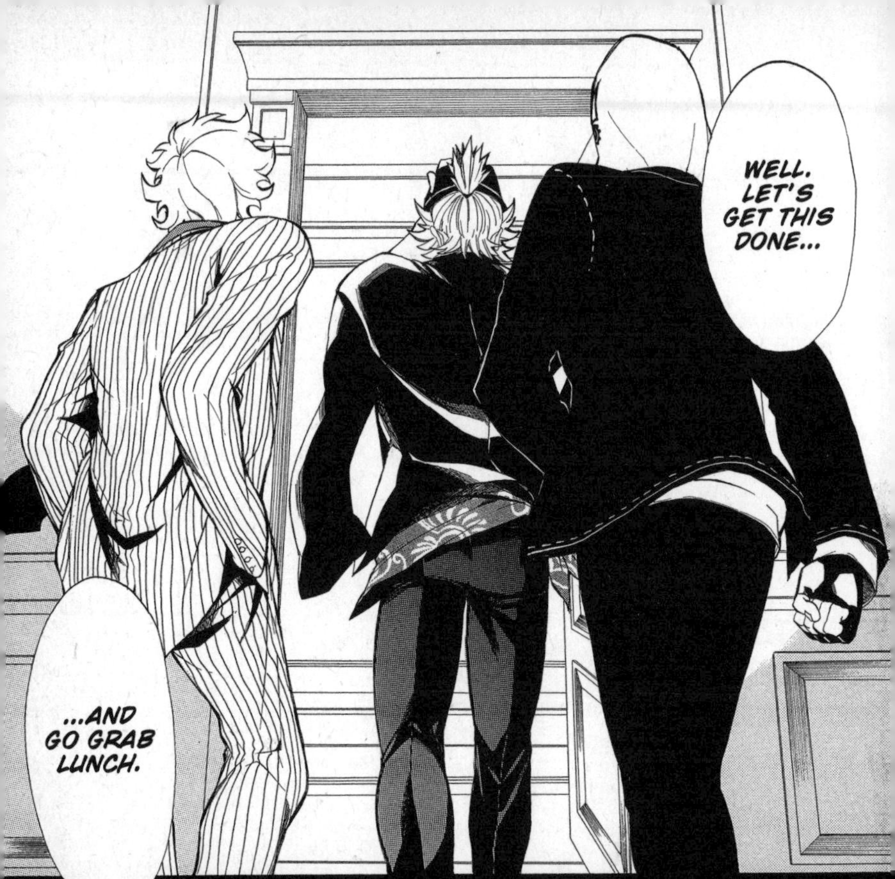
WELL. LET'S GET THIS DONE...
...AND GO GRAB LUNCH.

Scene: 03

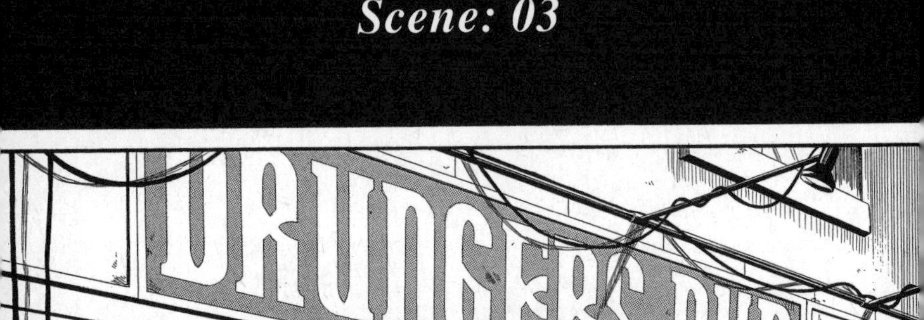
DRUNGERS PU

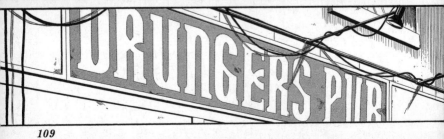

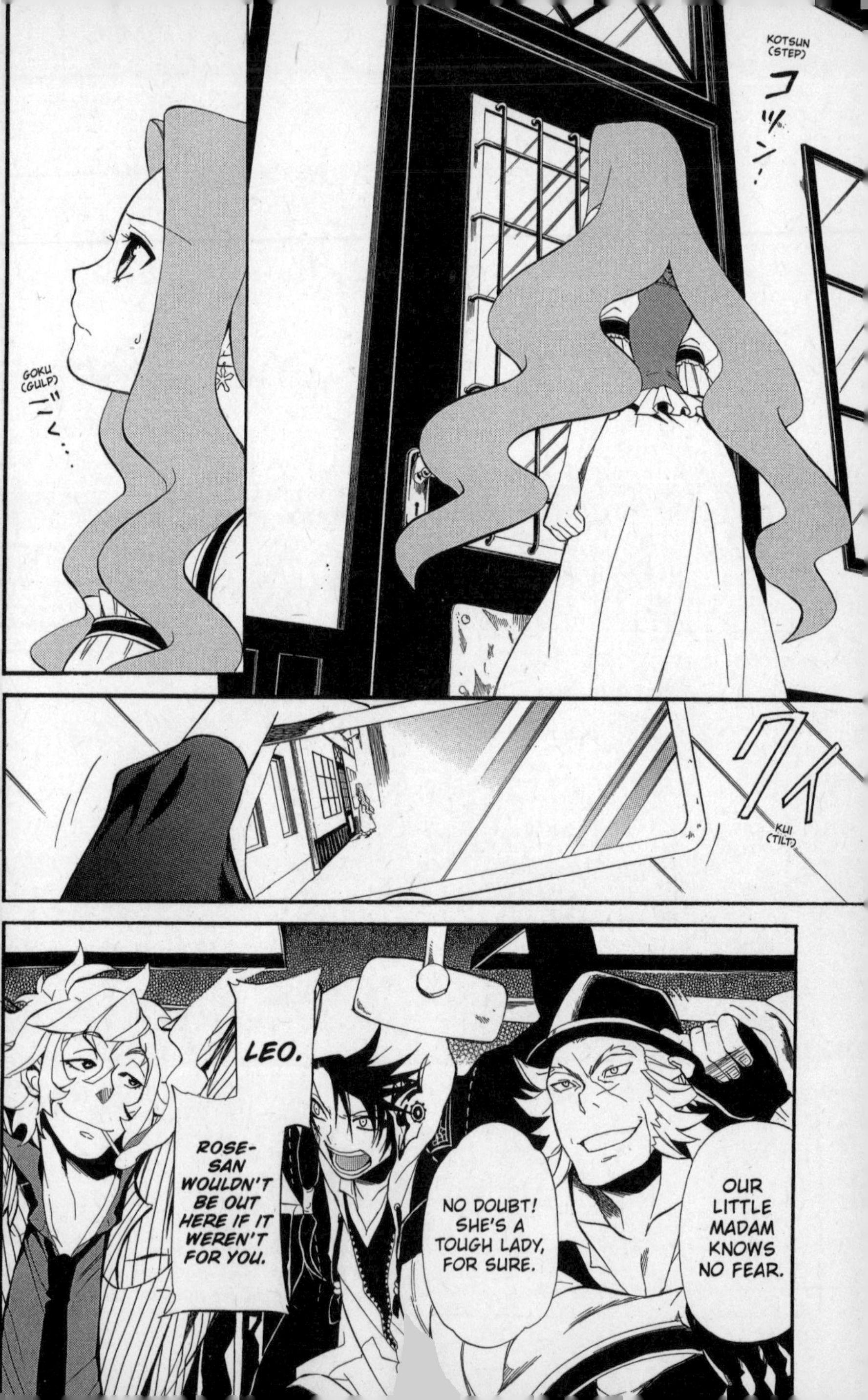
KOTSUN (STEP)
コツン！
GOKU (GULP)
クイ
KUI (TILT)
OUR LITTLE MADAM KNOWS NO FEAR.
NO DOUBT! SHE'S A TOUGH LADY, FOR SURE.
LEO.
ROSE-SAN WOULDN'T BE OUT HERE IF IT WEREN'T FOR YOU.

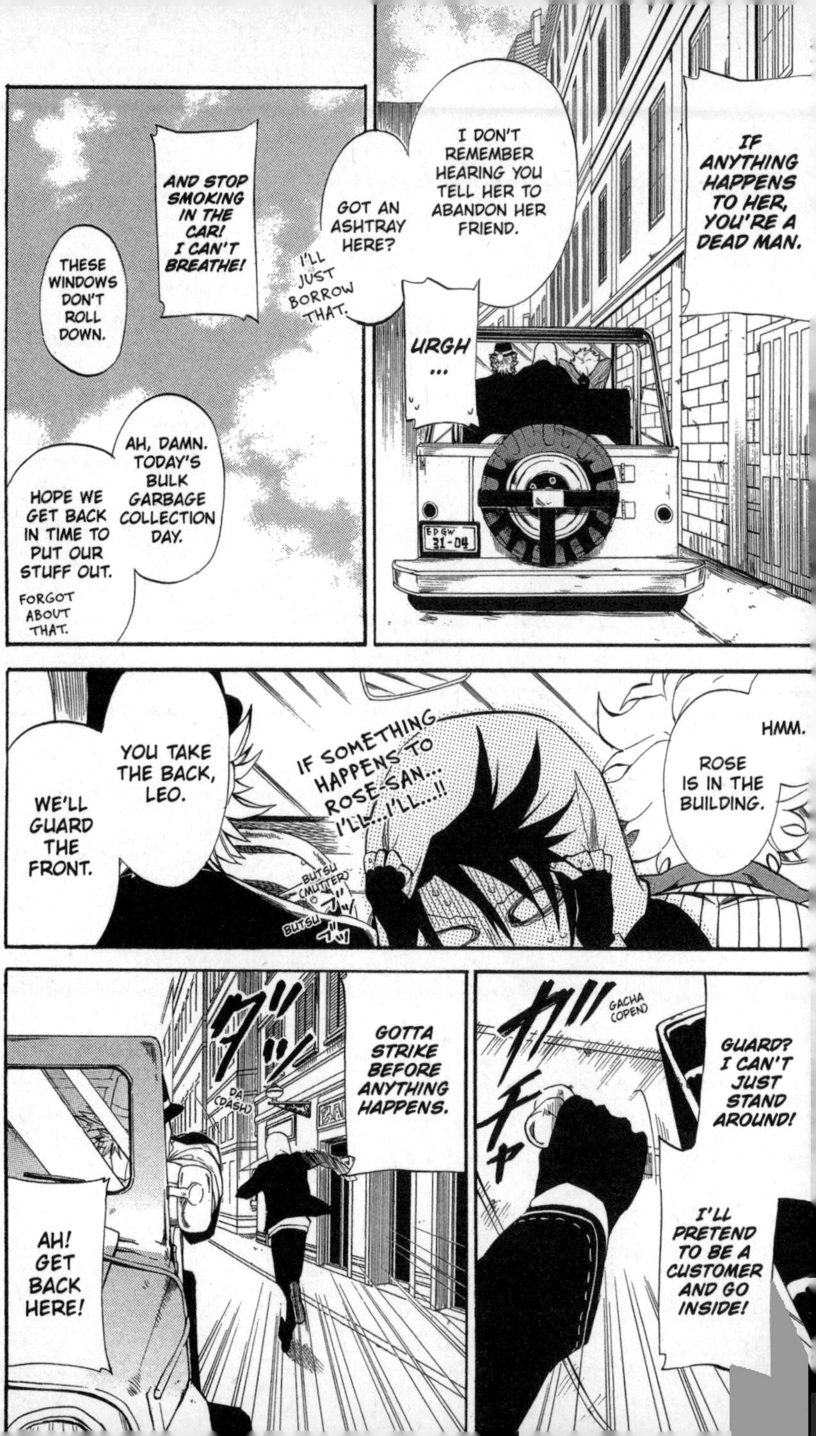
IF ANYTHING HAPPENS TO HER, YOU'RE A DEAD MAN.
I DON'T REMEMBER HEARING YOU TELL HER TO ABANDON HER FRIEND.
URGH...
GOT AN ASHTRAY HERE?
I'LL JUST BORROW THAT.
AND STOP SMOKING IN THE CAR! I CAN'T BREATHE!
THESE WINDOWS DON'T ROLL DOWN.
AH, DAMN. TODAY'S BULK GARBAGE COLLECTION DAY.
HOPE WE GET BACK IN TIME TO PUT OUR STUFF OUT.
FORGOT ABOUT THAT.
HMM.
ROSE IS IN THE BUILDING.
IF SOMETHING HAPPENS TO ROSE-SAN... I'LL...I'LL...!!
BUTSU (MUTTER)
BUTSU
YOU TAKE THE BACK, LEO.
WE'LL GUARD THE FRONT.
GACHA (OPEN)
GUARD? I CAN'T JUST STAND AROUND!
I'LL PRETEND TO BE A CUSTOMER AND GO INSIDE!
GOTTA STRIKE BEFORE ANYTHING HAPPENS.
DA (DASH)
AH! GET BACK HERE!

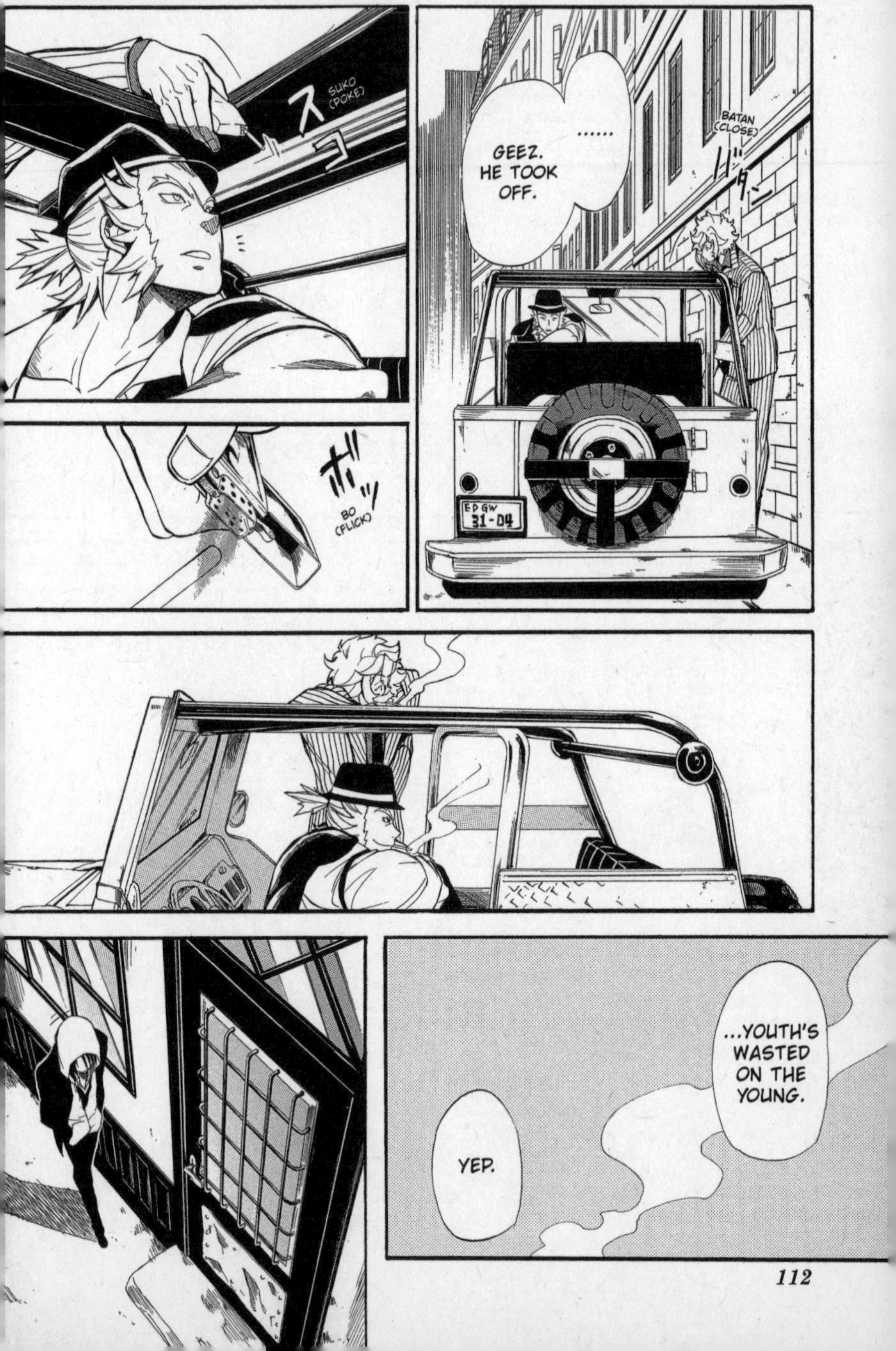
BATAN (CLOSE)
......
GEEZ. HE TOOK OFF.
SUKO (POKE)
BO (FLICK)
...YOUTH'S WASTED ON THE YOUNG.
YEP.

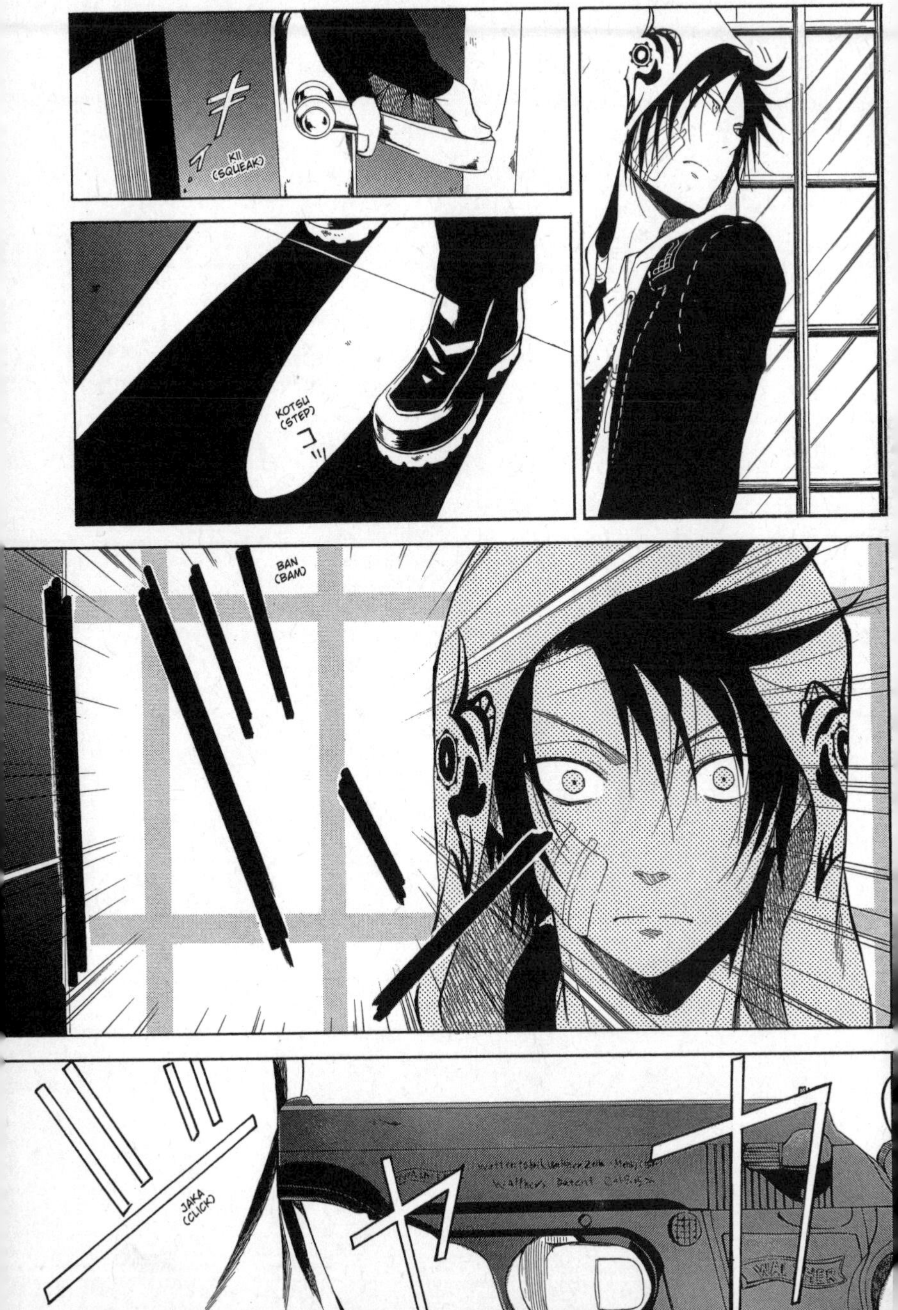
KII (SQUEAK)
KOTSU (STEP)
BAN (BAM)
JAKA (CLICK)

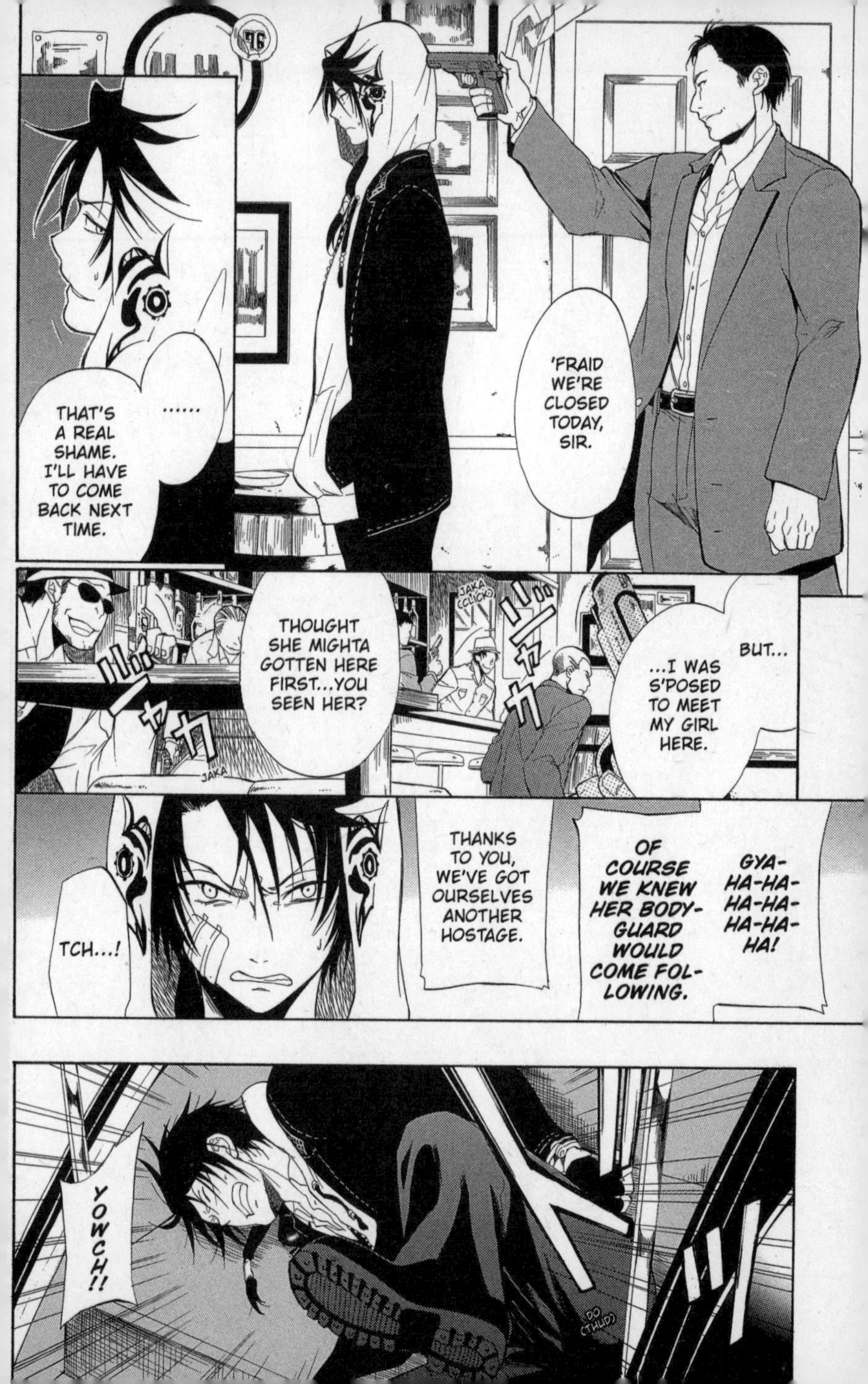
76
'FRAID WE'RE CLOSED TODAY, SIR.
......
THAT'S A REAL SHAME. I'LL HAVE TO COME BACK NEXT TIME.
BUT...
...I WAS S'POSED TO MEET MY GIRL HERE.
JAKA (CLICK)
THOUGHT SHE MIGHTA GOTTEN HERE FIRST...YOU SEEN HER?
JAKA
GYA-HA-HA-HA-HA-HA-HA-HA!
OF COURSE WE KNEW HER BODY-GUARD WOULD COME FOL-LOWING.
THANKS TO YOU, WE'VE GOT OURSELVES ANOTHER HOSTAGE.
TCH...!
YOWCH!!
DO (THUD)

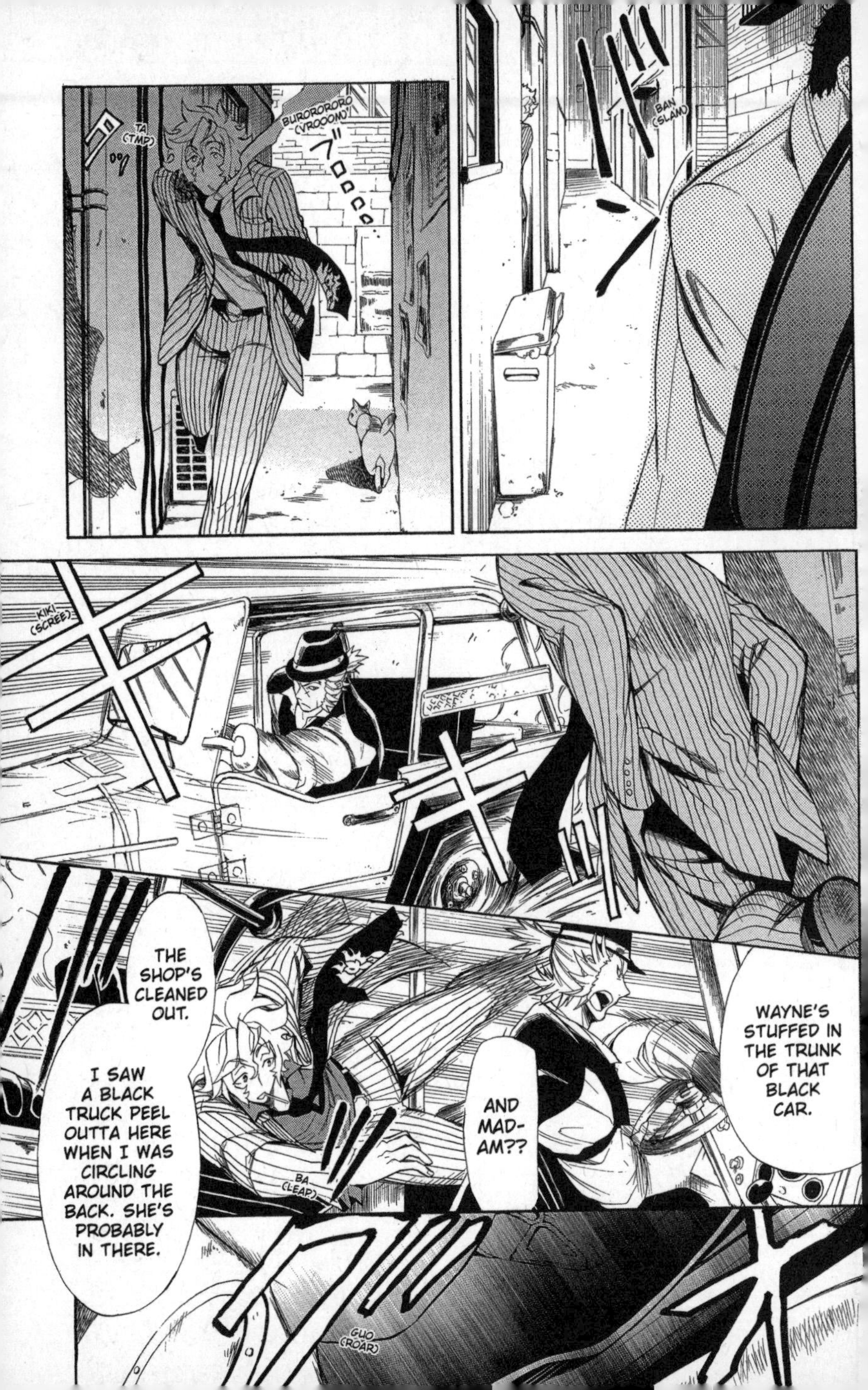
BAN (SLAM)
TA (TMP)
BURORORORO (VROOOM)
KIKI (SCREE)
WAYNE'S STUFFED IN THE TRUNK OF THAT BLACK CAR.
AND MAD-AM??
THE SHOP'S CLEANED OUT.
I SAW A BLACK TRUCK PEEL OUTTA HERE WHEN I WAS CIRCLING AROUND THE BACK. SHE'S PROBABLY IN THERE.
BA (LEAP)
GUO (ROAR)

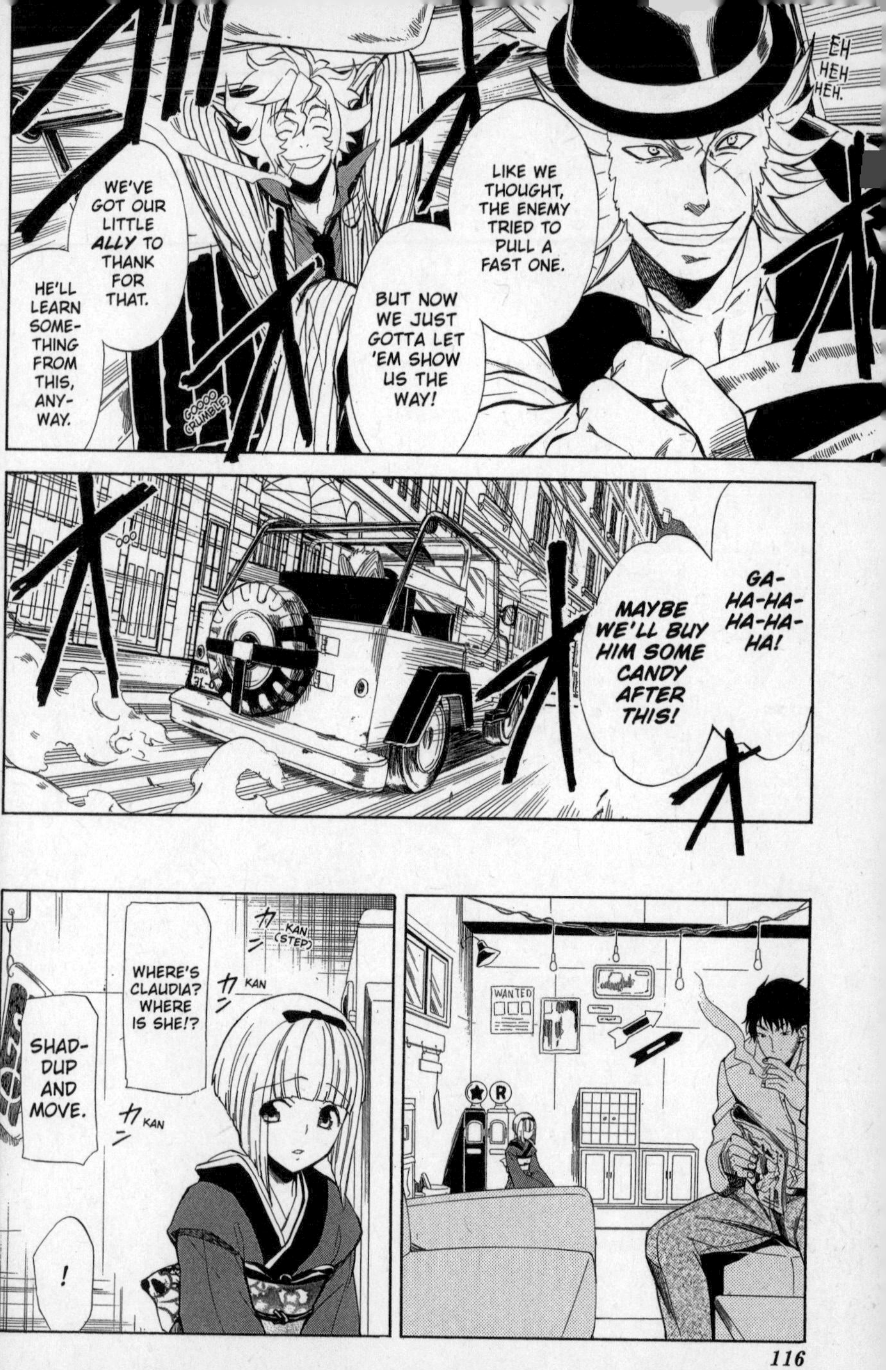
EH HEH HEH.
LIKE WE THOUGHT, THE ENEMY TRIED TO PULL A FAST ONE.
BUT NOW WE JUST GOTTA LET 'EM SHOW US THE WAY!
WE'VE GOT OUR LITTLE ALLY TO THANK FOR THAT.
HE'LL LEARN SOME-THING FROM THIS, ANY-WAY.
GOOOO (RUMBLE)
GA-HA-HA-HA-HA-HA!
MAYBE WE'LL BUY HIM SOME CANDY AFTER THIS!
WANTED
KAN (STEP)
KAN
WHERE'S CLAUDIA? WHERE IS SHE!?
SHAD-DUP AND MOVE.
KAN
!

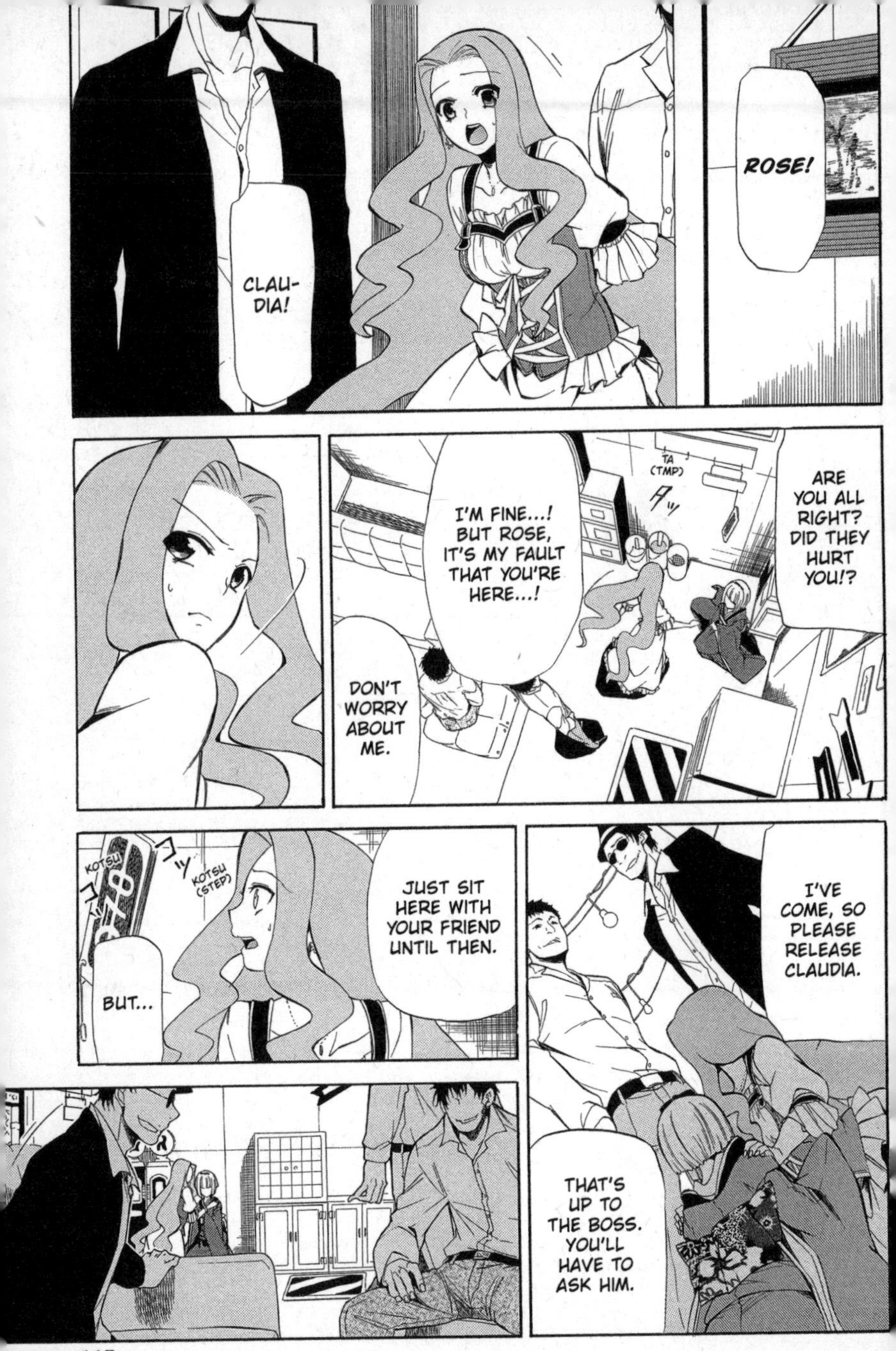
ROSE!
CLAU-DIA!
ARE YOU ALL RIGHT? DID THEY HURT YOU!?
TA (TMP)
I'M FINE...! BUT ROSE, IT'S MY FAULT THAT YOU'RE HERE...!
DON'T WORRY ABOUT ME.
I'VE COME, SO PLEASE RELEASE CLAUDIA.
THAT'S UP TO THE BOSS. YOU'LL HAVE TO ASK HIM.
JUST SIT HERE WITH YOUR FRIEND UNTIL THEN.
KOTSU
KOTSU (STEP)
BUT...

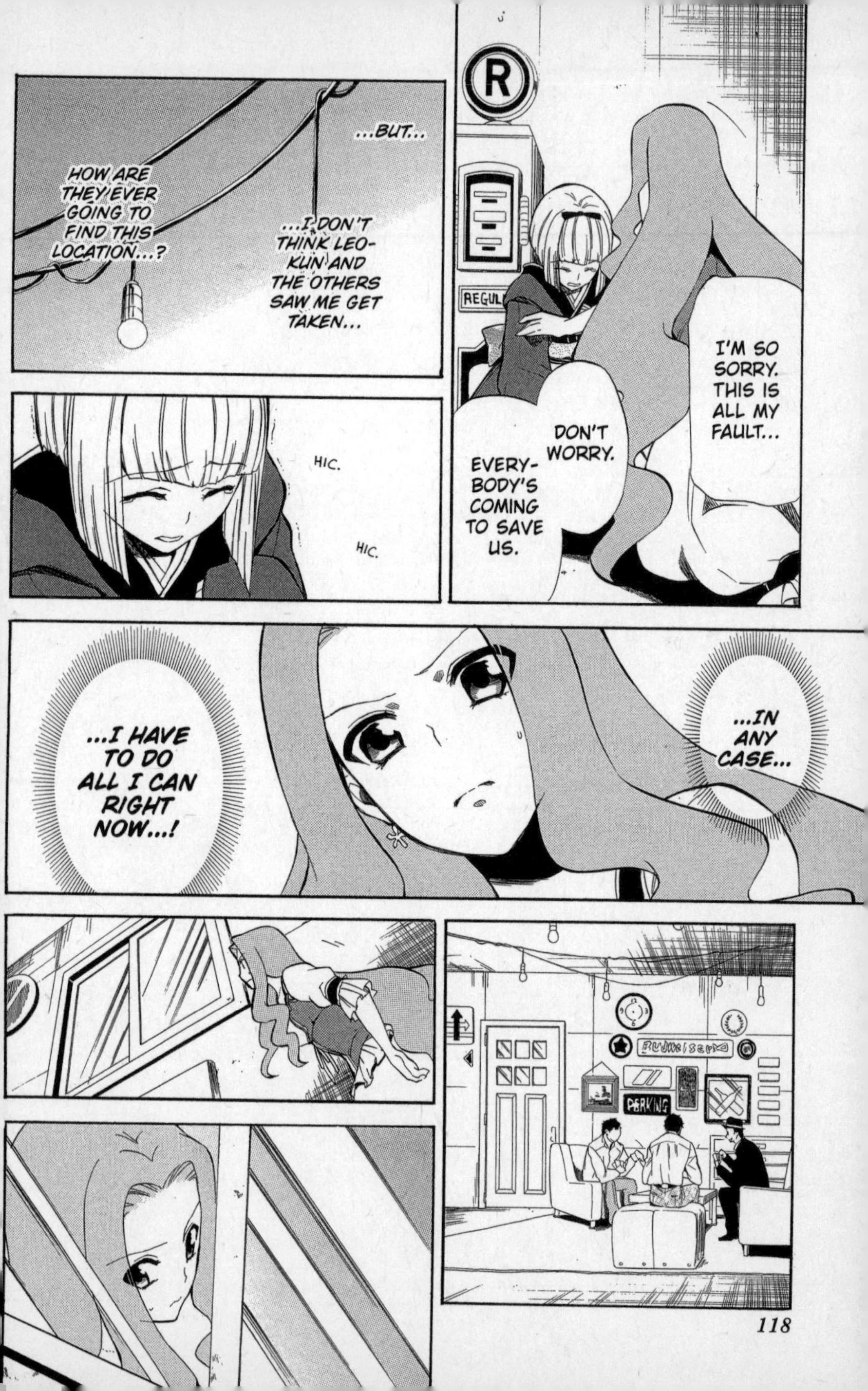
I'M SO SORRY. THIS IS ALL MY FAULT...
DON'T WORRY.
EVERY-BODY'S COMING TO SAVE US.
...BUT...
...I DON'T THINK LEO-KUN AND THE OTHERS SAW ME GET TAKEN...
HOW ARE THEY EVER GOING TO FIND THIS LOCATION...?
HIC.
HIC.
...IN ANY CASE...
...I HAVE TO DO ALL I CAN RIGHT NOW...!
PARKING

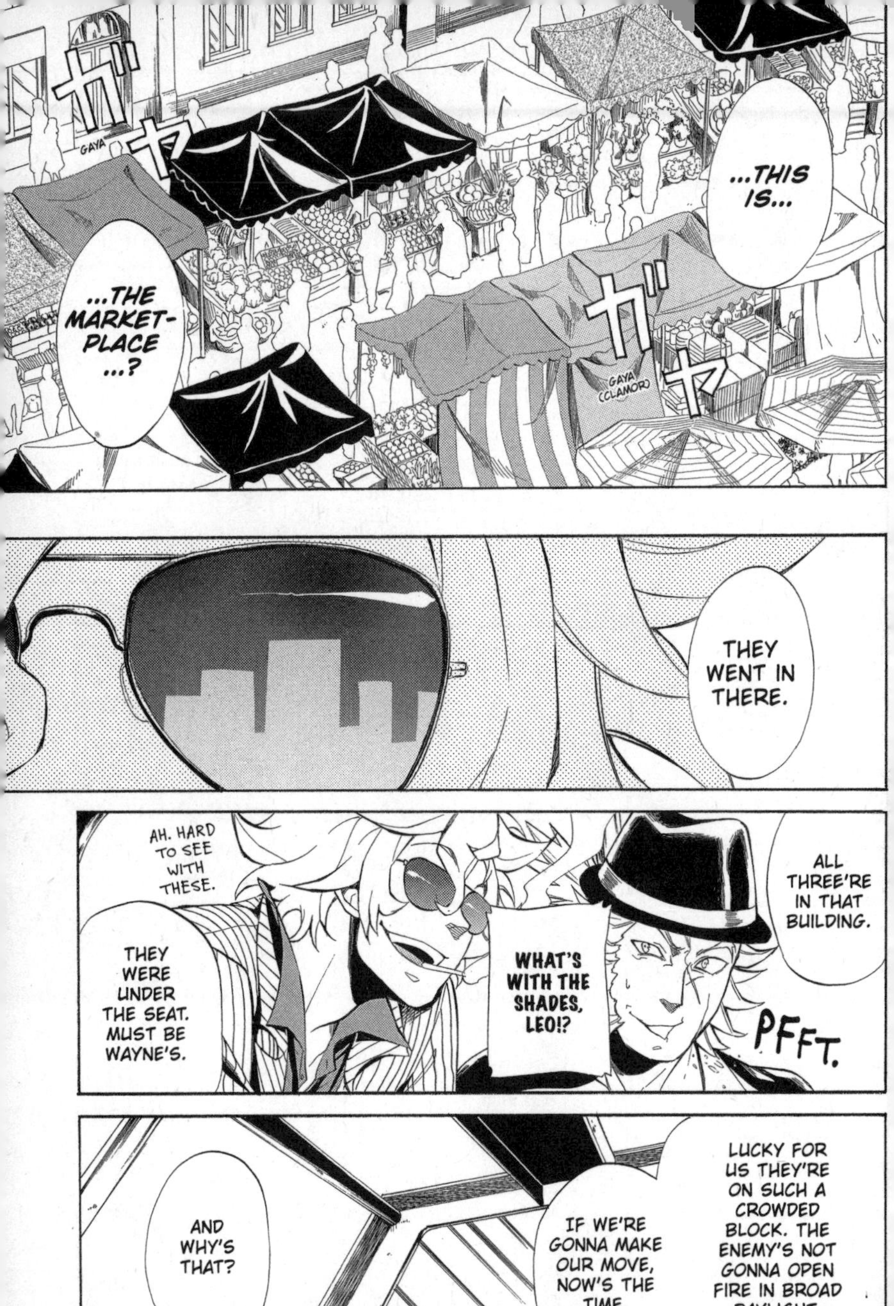
ガヤ
GAYA
...THIS IS...
ガヤ
GAYA (CLAMOR)
...THE MARKET-PLACE ...?
THEY WENT IN THERE.
ALL THREE'RE IN THAT BUILDING.
PFFT.
WHAT'S WITH THE SHADES, LEO!?
AH. HARD TO SEE WITH THESE.
THEY WERE UNDER THE SEAT. MUST BE WAYNE'S.
LUCKY FOR US THEY'RE ON SUCH A CROWDED BLOCK. THE ENEMY'S NOT GONNA OPEN FIRE IN BROAD DAYLIGHT.
IF WE'RE GONNA MAKE OUR MOVE, NOW'S THE TIME.
AND WHY'S THAT?

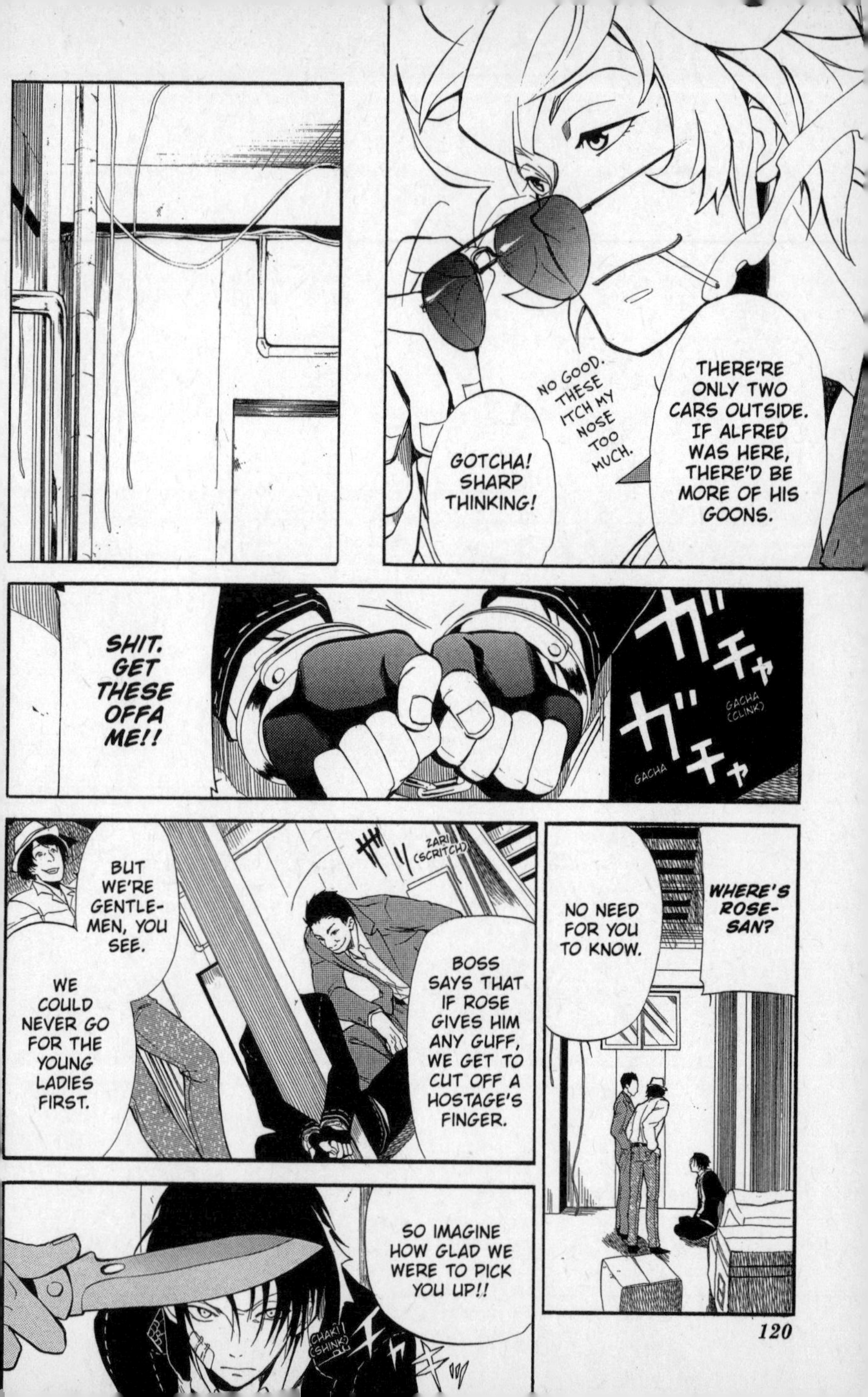
THERE'RE ONLY TWO CARS OUTSIDE. IF ALFRED WAS HERE, THERE'D BE MORE OF HIS GOONS.
NO GOOD. THESE ITCH MY NOSE TOO MUCH.
GOTCHA! SHARP THINKING!
ガチャ
GACHA (CLINK)
ガチャ
GACHA
SHIT. GET THESE OFFA ME!!
WHERE'S ROSE-SAN?
NO NEED FOR YOU TO KNOW.
ザリ
ZARI (SCRITCH)
BOSS SAYS THAT IF ROSE GIVES HIM ANY GUFF, WE GET TO CUT OFF A HOSTAGE'S FINGER.
BUT WE'RE GENTLEMEN, YOU SEE.
WE COULD NEVER GO FOR THE YOUNG LADIES FIRST.
SO IMAGINE HOW GLAD WE WERE TO PICK YOU UP!!
CHAKI (SHINK)

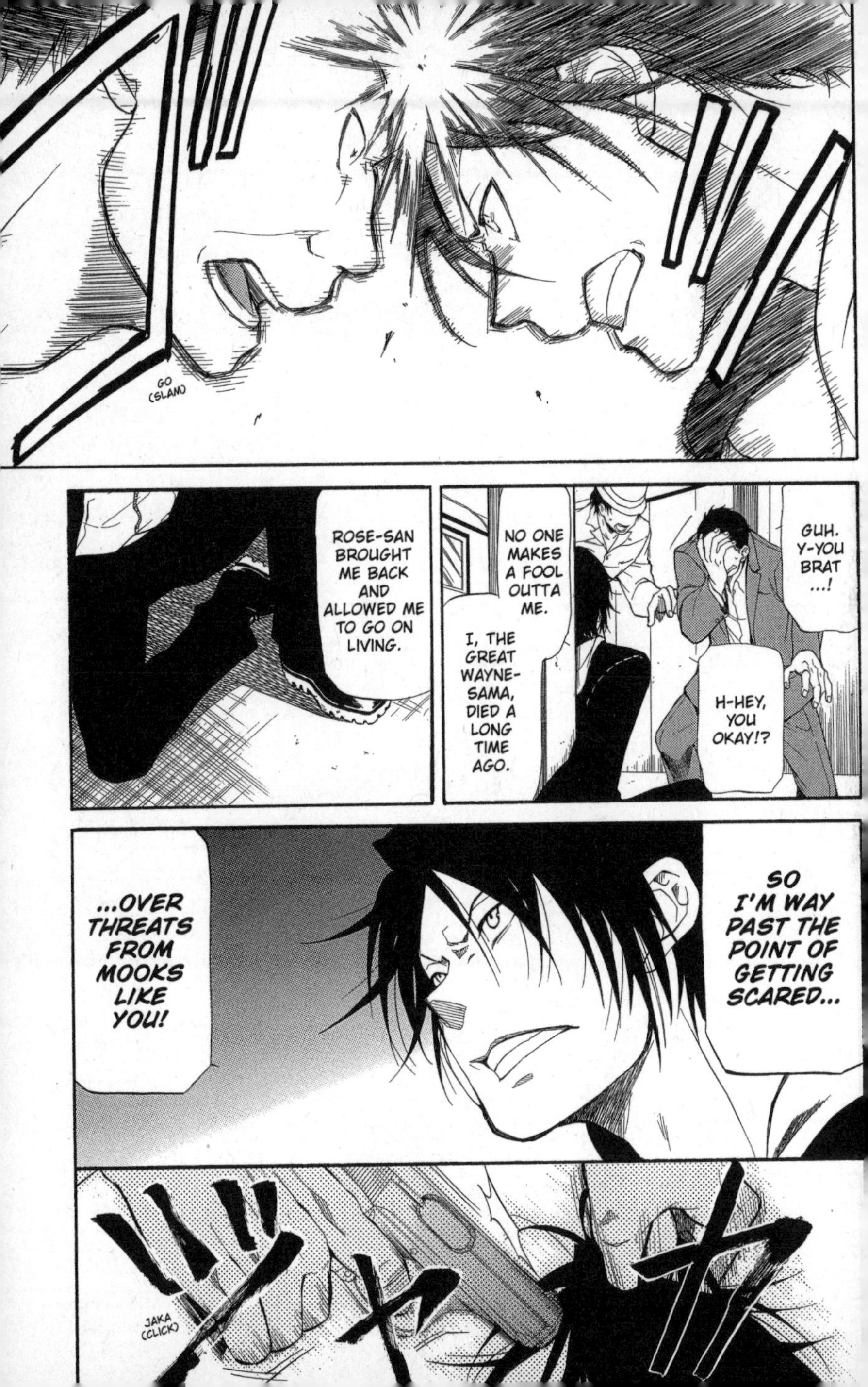
GO (SLAM)
GUH. Y-YOU BRAT ...!
H-HEY, YOU OKAY!?
NO ONE MAKES A FOOL OUTTA ME.
I, THE GREAT WAYNE-SAMA, DIED A LONG TIME AGO.
ROSE-SAN BROUGHT ME BACK AND ALLOWED ME TO GO ON LIVING.
SO I'M WAY PAST THE POINT OF GETTING SCARED...
...OVER THREATS FROM MOOKS LIKE YOU!
JAKA (CLICK)

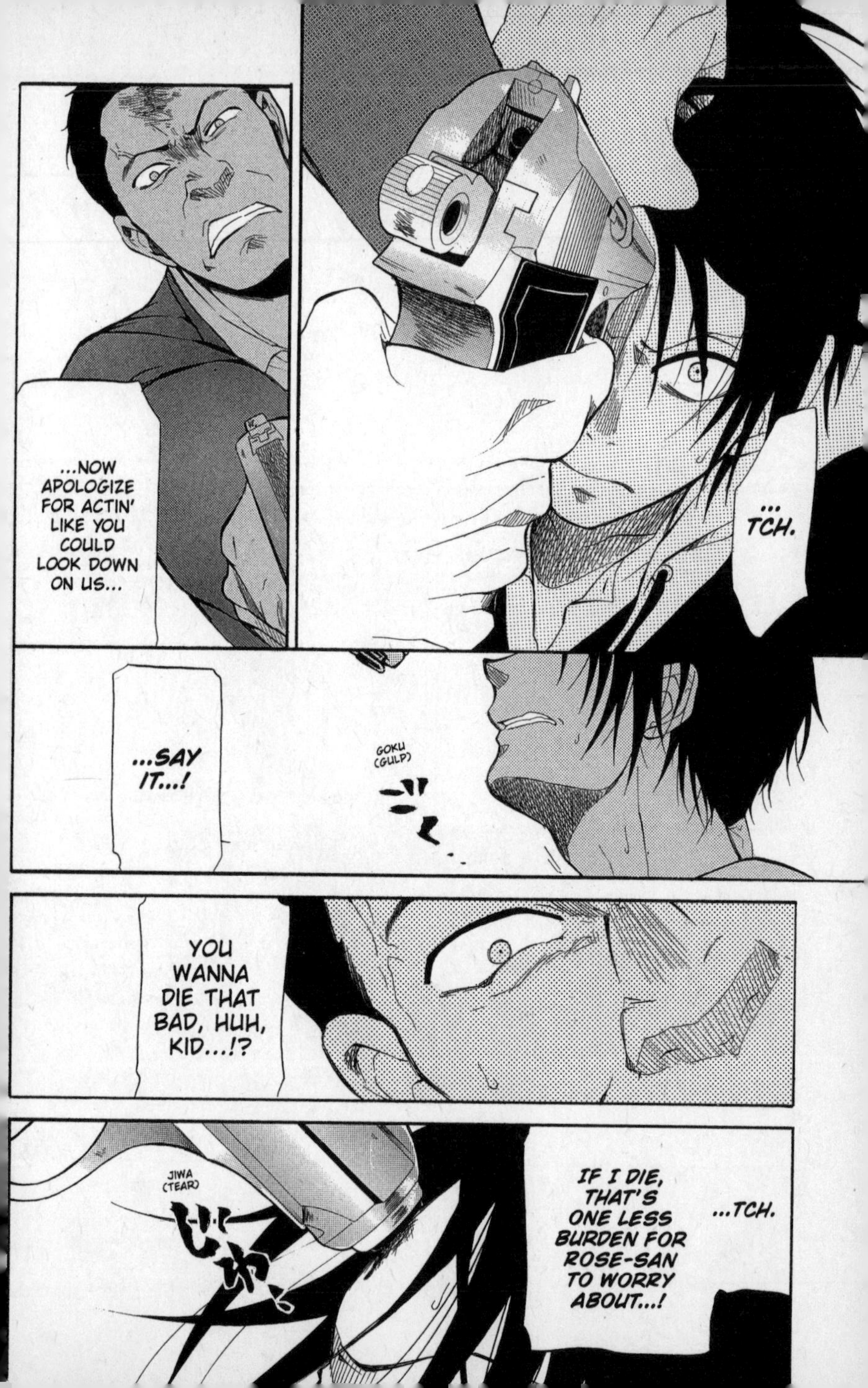
...
TCH.
...NOW APOLOGIZE FOR ACTIN' LIKE YOU COULD LOOK DOWN ON US...
GOKU (GULP)
...SAY IT...!
YOU WANNA DIE THAT BAD, HUH, KID...!?
...TCH.
IF I DIE, THAT'S ONE LESS BURDEN FOR ROSE-SAN TO WORRY ABOUT...!
JIWA (TEAR)

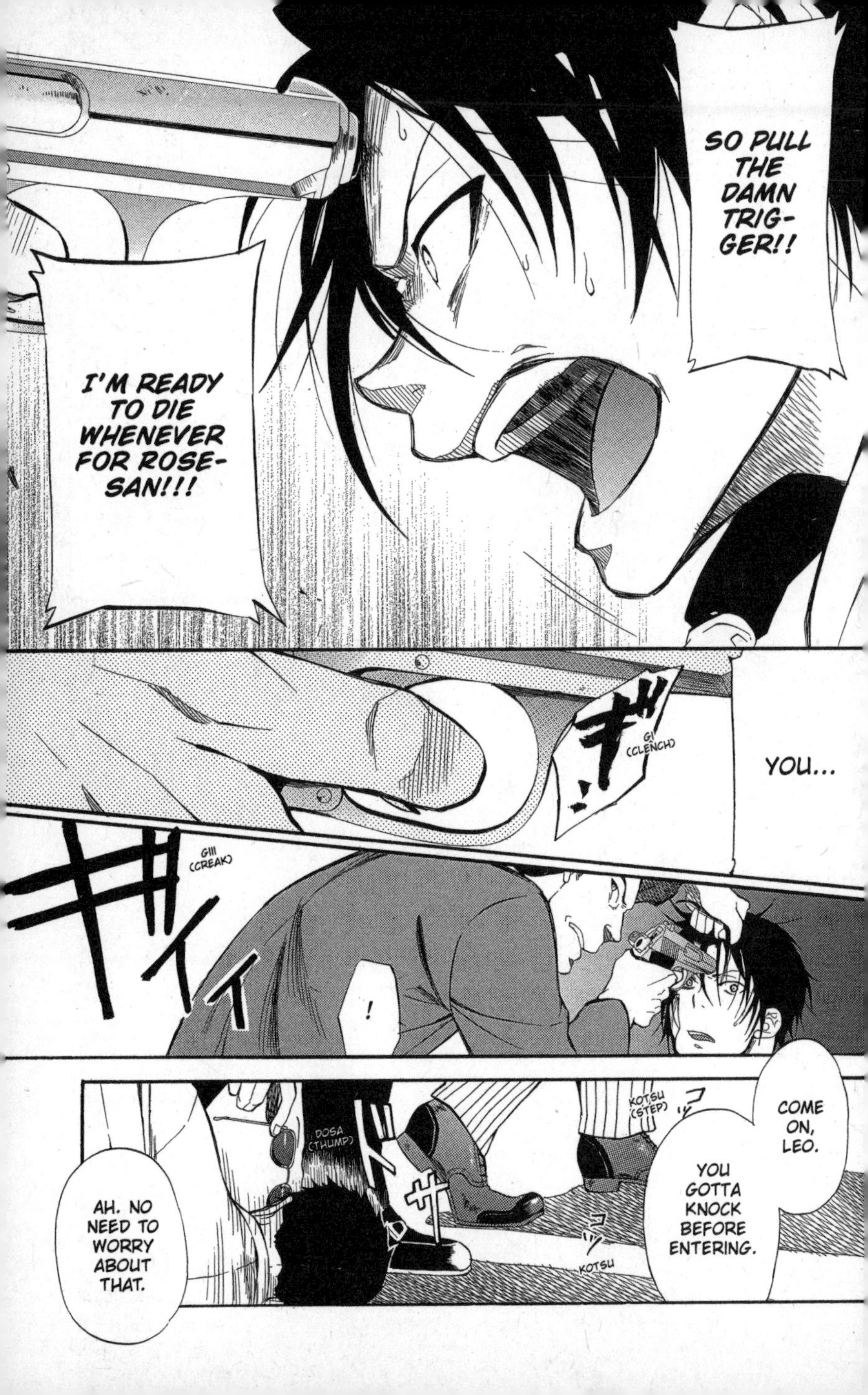
SO PULL THE DAMN TRIG-GER!!
I'M READY TO DIE WHENEVER FOR ROSE-SAN!!!
YOU...
GI (CLENCH)
GIII (CREAK)
!
COME ON, LEO.
YOU GOTTA KNOCK BEFORE ENTERING.
KOTSU (STEP)
KOTSU
DOSA (THUMP)
AH. NO NEED TO WORRY ABOUT THAT.

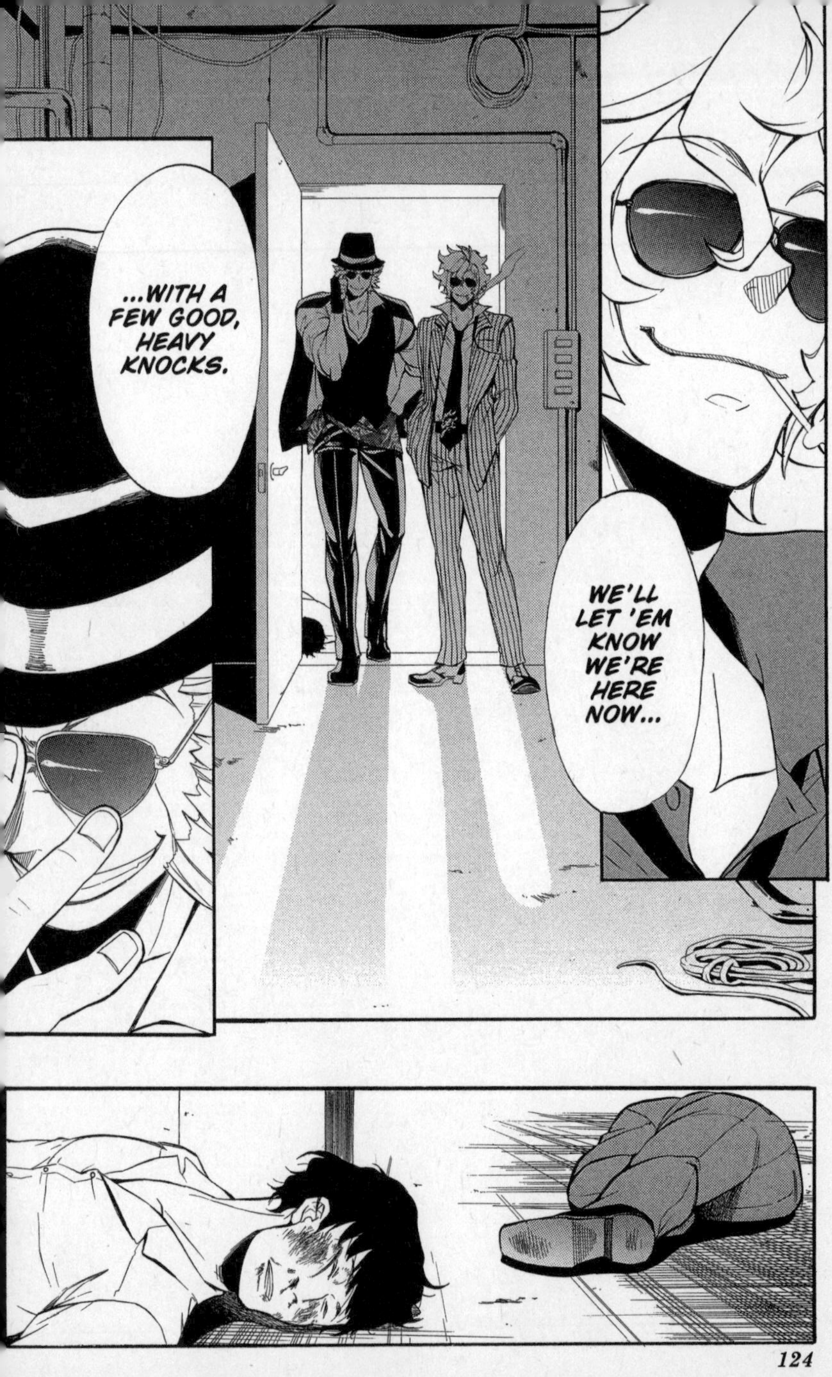
WE'LL LET 'EM KNOW WE'RE HERE NOW...
...WITH A FEW GOOD, HEAVY KNOCKS.

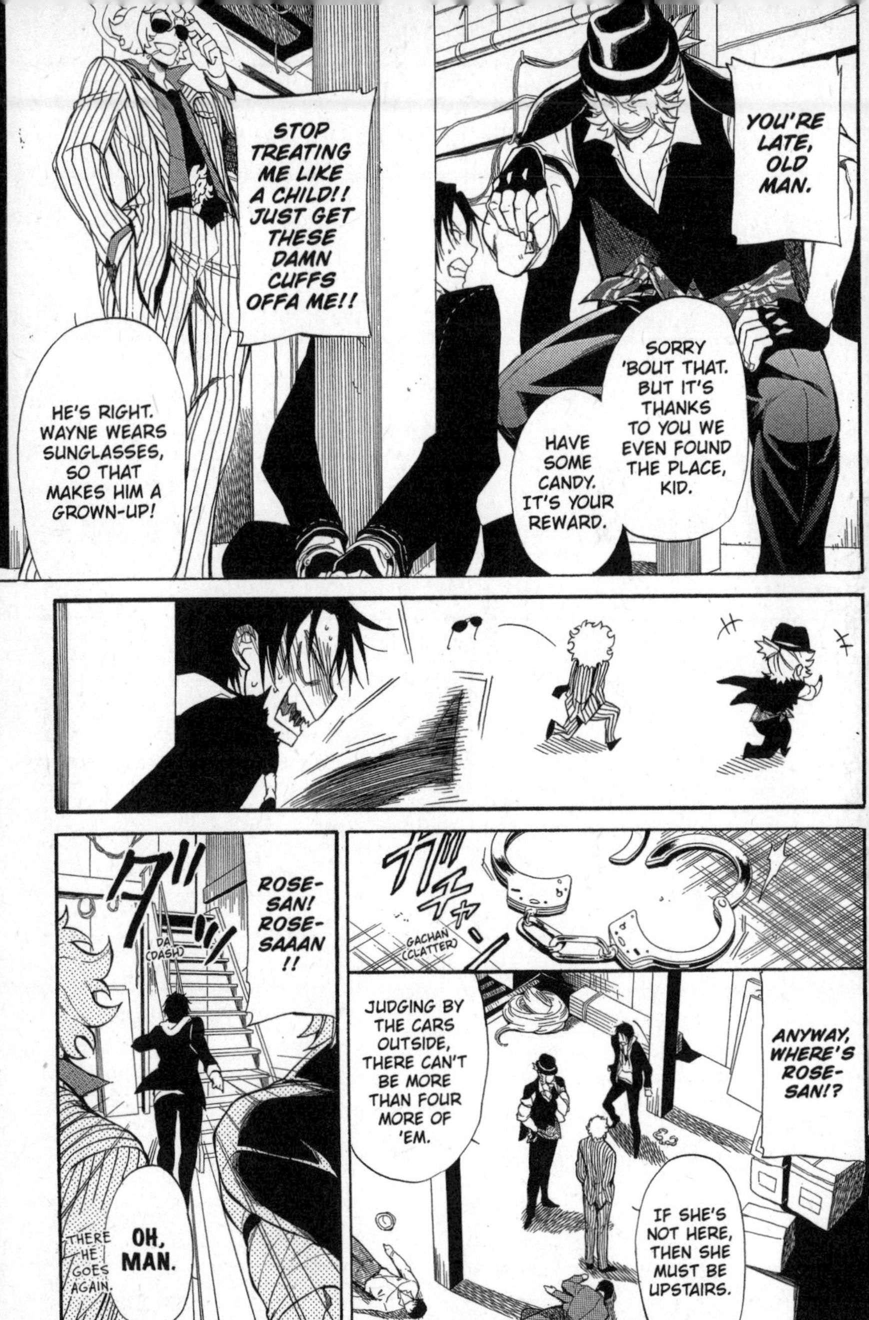
YOU'RE LATE, OLD MAN.
SORRY 'BOUT THAT. BUT IT'S THANKS TO YOU WE EVEN FOUND THE PLACE, KID.
HAVE SOME CANDY. IT'S YOUR REWARD.
STOP TREATING ME LIKE A CHILD!! JUST GET THESE DAMN CUFFS OFFA ME!!
HE'S RIGHT. WAYNE WEARS SUNGLASSES, SO THAT MAKES HIM A GROWN-UP!
GACHAN (CLATTER)
ANYWAY, WHERE'S ROSE-SAN!?
IF SHE'S NOT HERE, THEN SHE MUST BE UPSTAIRS.
JUDGING BY THE CARS OUTSIDE, THERE CAN'T BE MORE THAN FOUR MORE OF 'EM.
ROSE-SAN! ROSE-SAAAN!!
DA (DASH)
OH, MAN.
THERE HE GOES AGAIN.

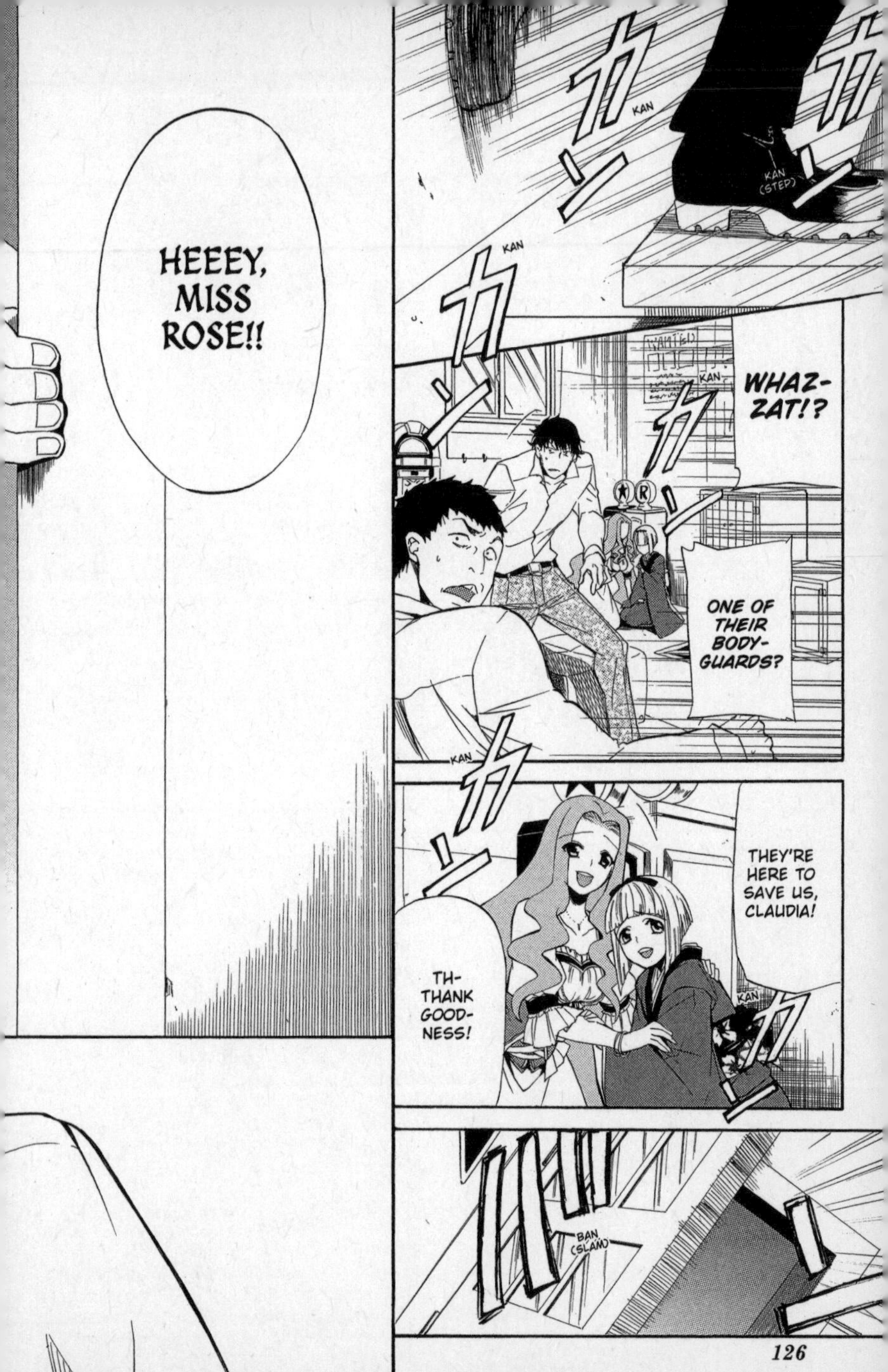
KAN
(STEP)
KAN
KAN
WHAZ-
ZAT!?
KAN
ONE OF
THEIR
BODY-
GUARDS?
KAN
THEY'RE
HERE TO
SAVE US,
CLAUDIA!
KAN
TH-
THANK
GOOD-
NESS!
BAN
(SLAM)
HEEEY,
MISS
ROSE!!

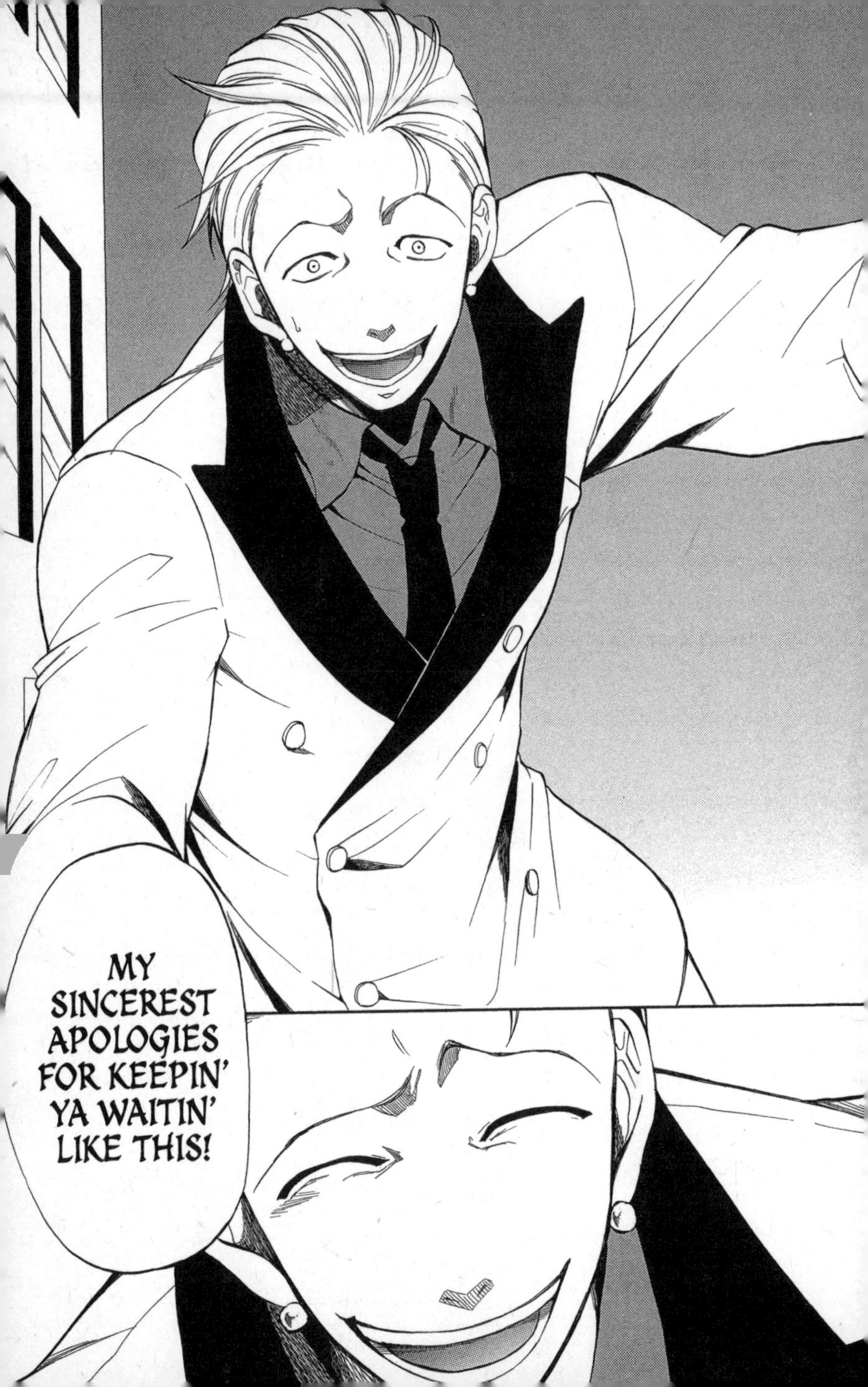
MY SINCEREST APOLOGIES FOR KEEPIN' YA WAITIN' LIKE THIS!

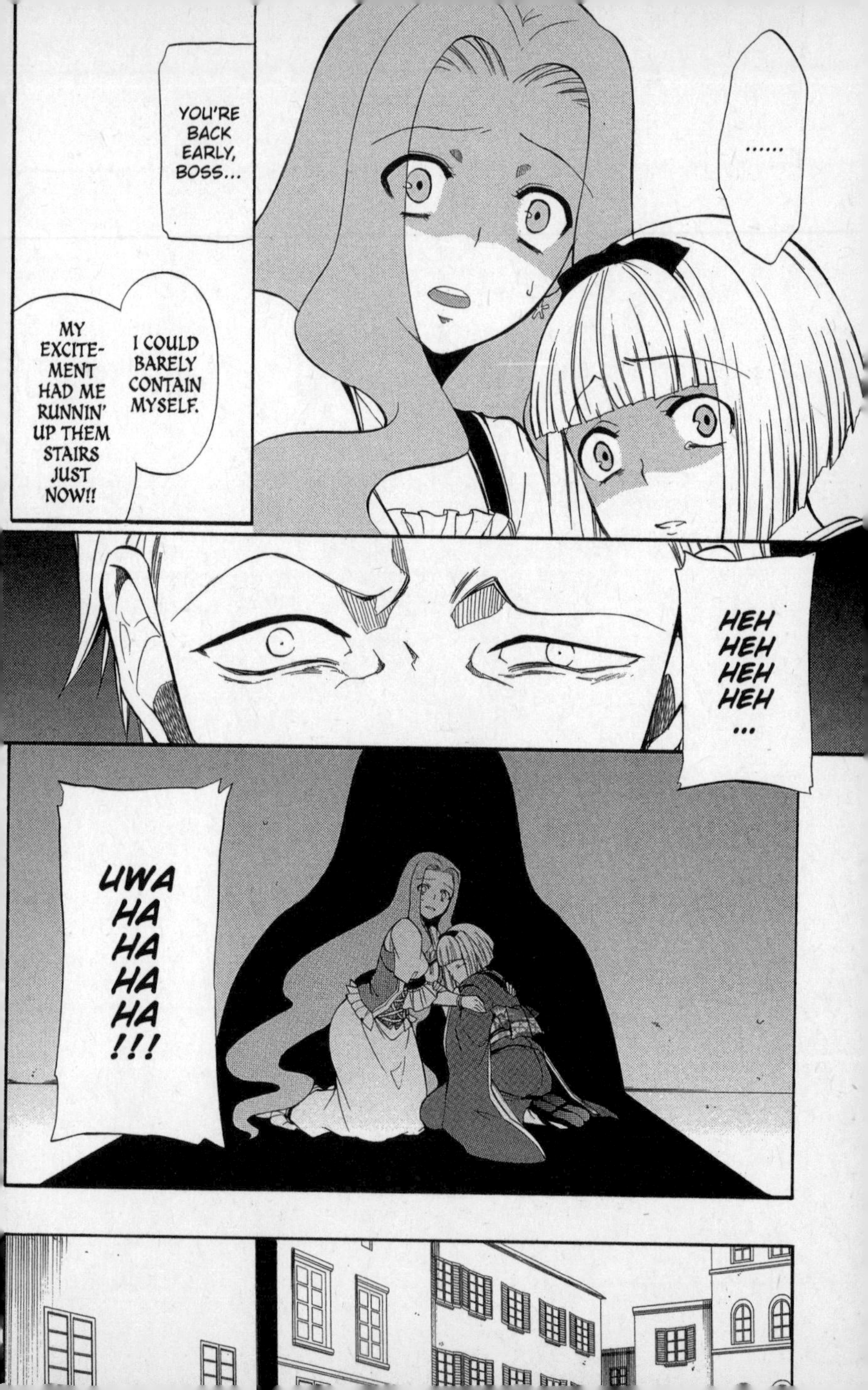
......
YOU'RE BACK EARLY, BOSS...
I COULD BARELY CONTAIN MYSELF.
MY EXCITEMENT HAD ME RUNNIN' UP THEM STAIRS JUST NOW!!
HEH HEH HEH HEH...
UWA HA HA HA HA HA!!!

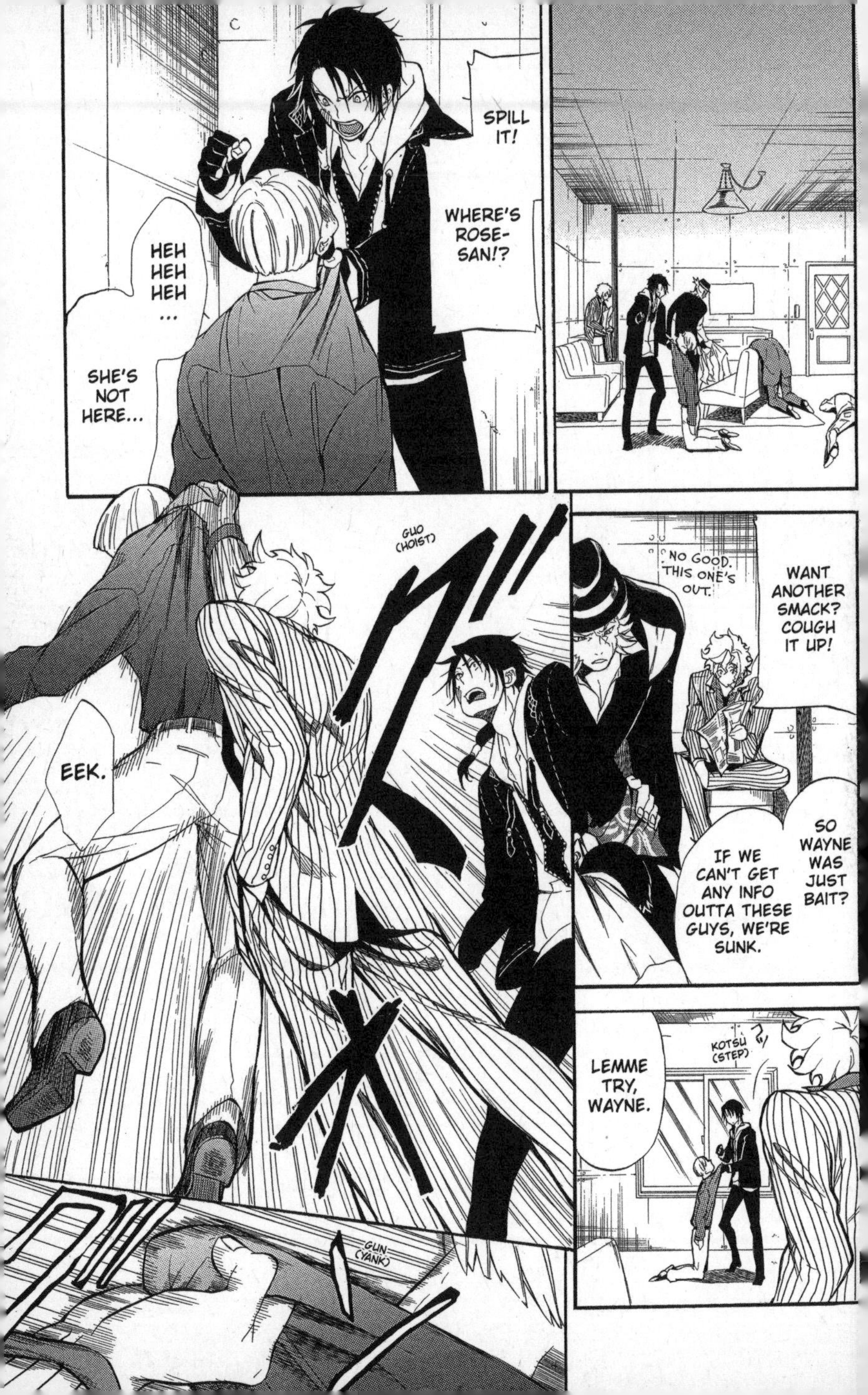
SPILL IT!
WHERE'S ROSE-SAN!?
HEH HEH HEH...
SHE'S NOT HERE...
WANT ANOTHER SMACK? COUGH IT UP!
NO GOOD. THIS ONE'S OUT.
SO WAYNE WAS JUST BAIT?
IF WE CAN'T GET ANY INFO OUTTA THESE GUYS, WE'RE SUNK.
KOTSU (STEP)
LEMME TRY, WAYNE.
GUO (HOIST)
EEK.
GUN (YANK)

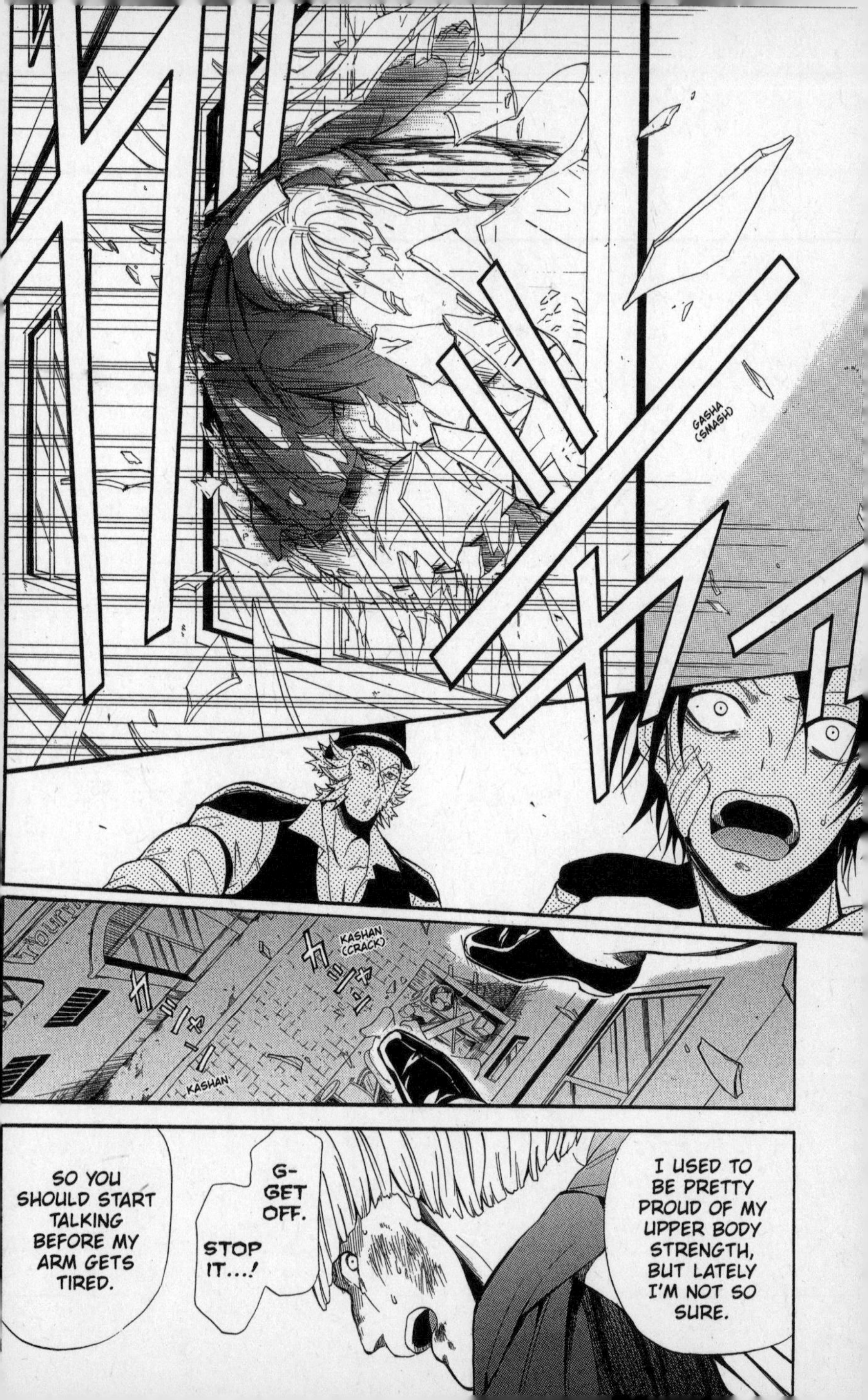
GASHA (SMASH)
KASHAN (CRACK)
KASHAN
I USED TO BE PRETTY PROUD OF MY UPPER BODY STRENGTH, BUT LATELY I'M NOT SO SURE.
G-GET OFF.
STOP IT...!
SO YOU SHOULD START TALKING BEFORE MY ARM GETS TIRED.

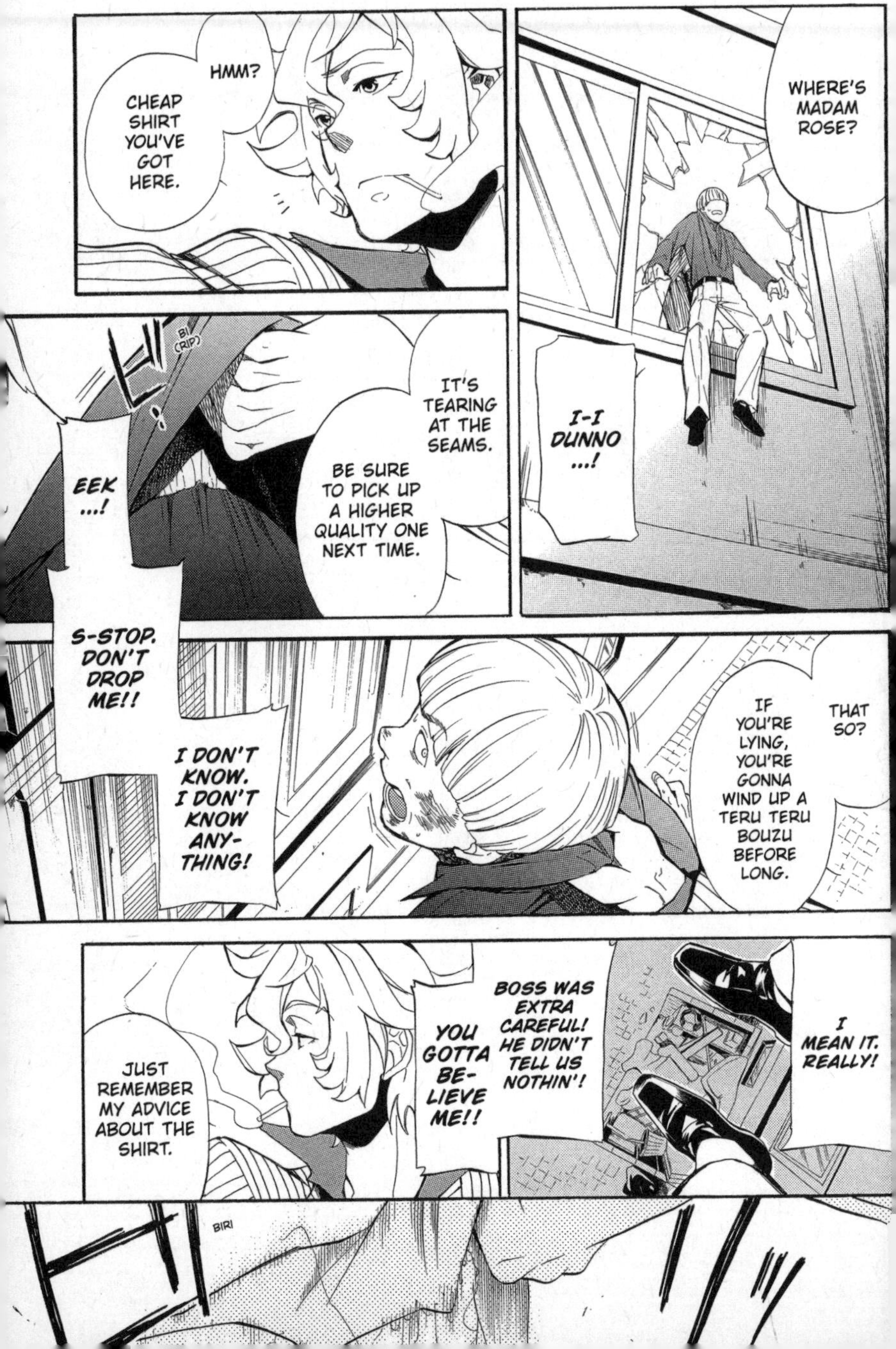
WHERE'S MADAM ROSE?
I-I DUNNO ...!
HMM?
CHEAP SHIRT YOU'VE GOT HERE.
BI (RIP)
IT'S TEARING AT THE SEAMS.
BE SURE TO PICK UP A HIGHER QUALITY ONE NEXT TIME.
EEK ...!
THAT SO?
IF YOU'RE LYING, YOU'RE GONNA WIND UP A TERU TERU BOUZU BEFORE LONG.
S-STOP. DON'T DROP ME!!
I DON'T KNOW. I DON'T KNOW ANY-THING!
I MEAN IT. REALLY!
BOSS WAS EXTRA CAREFUL! HE DIDN'T TELL US NOTHIN'!
YOU GOTTA BE-LIEVE ME!!
JUST REMEMBER MY ADVICE ABOUT THE SHIRT.
BIRI

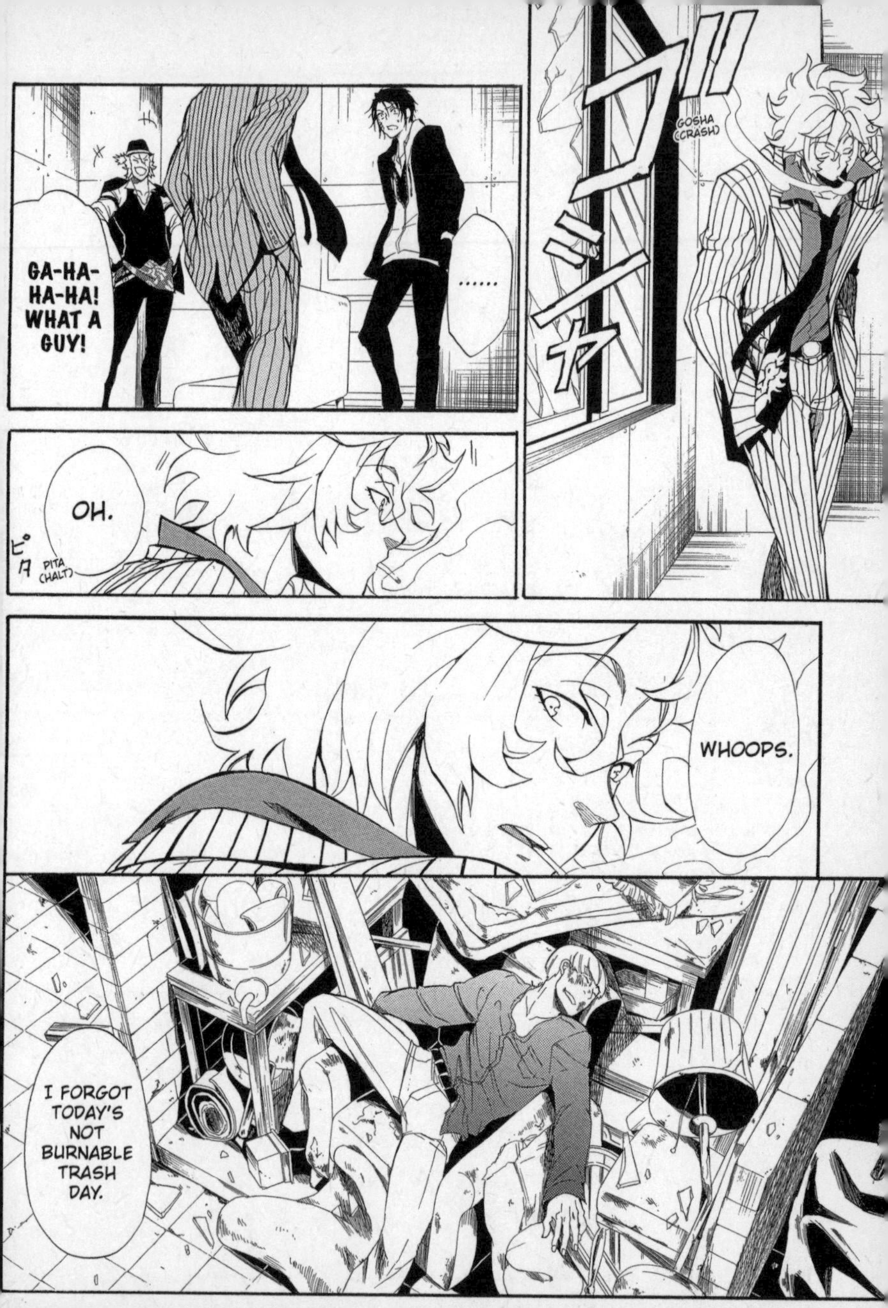
ゴシャ
GOSHA (CRASH)
......
GA-HA-HA-HA! WHAT A GUY!
OH.
ピタ
PITA (HALT)
WHOOPS.
I FORGOT TODAY'S NOT BURNABLE TRASH DAY.

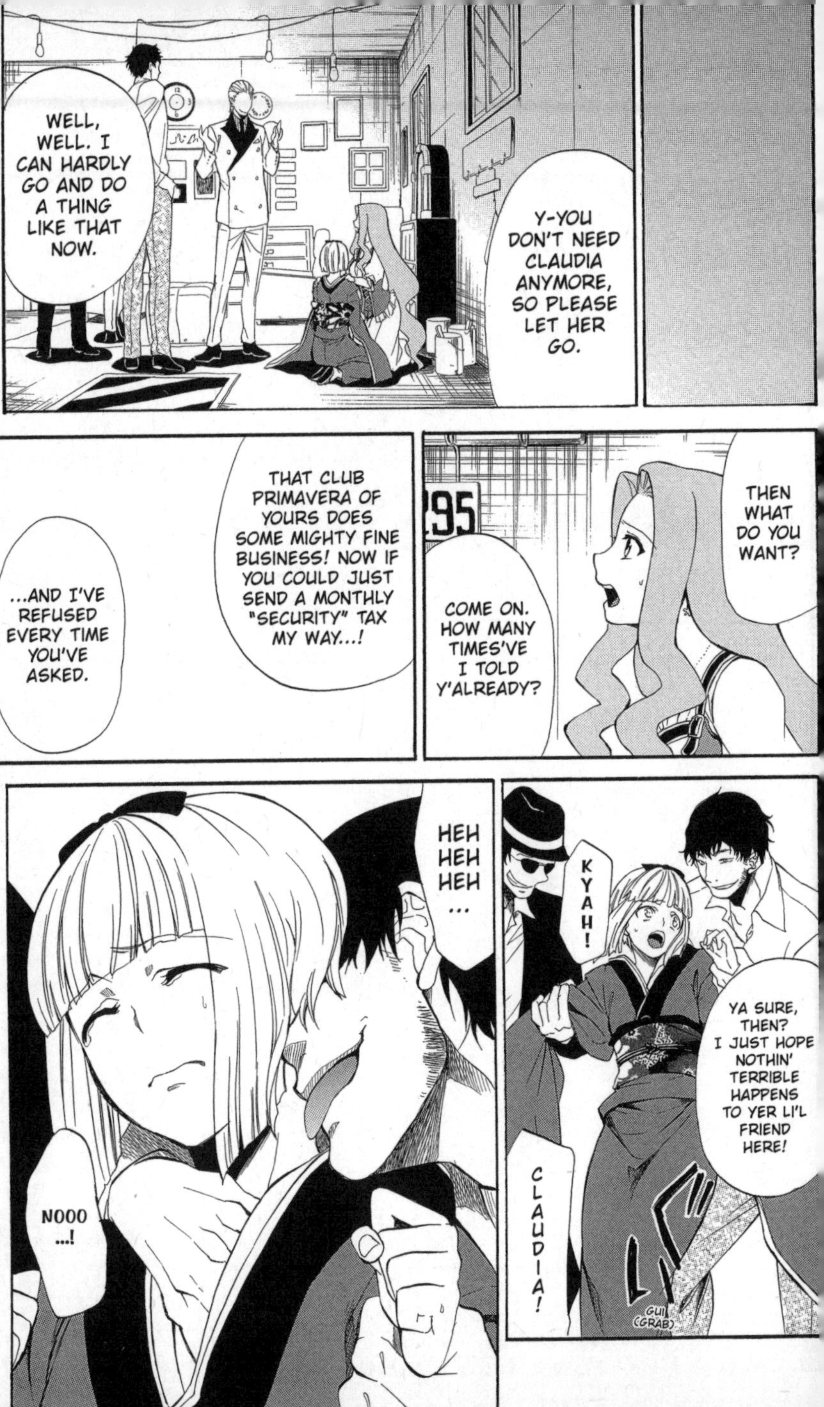
Y-YOU DON'T NEED CLAUDIA ANYMORE, SO PLEASE LET HER GO.
WELL, WELL. I CAN HARDLY GO AND DO A THING LIKE THAT NOW.
THEN WHAT DO YOU WANT?
COME ON. HOW MANY TIMES'VE I TOLD Y'ALREADY?
THAT CLUB PRIMAVERA OF YOURS DOES SOME MIGHTY FINE BUSINESS! NOW IF YOU COULD JUST SEND A MONTHLY "SECURITY" TAX MY WAY...!
...AND I'VE REFUSED EVERY TIME YOU'VE ASKED.
KYAH!
YA SURE, THEN? I JUST HOPE NOTHIN' TERRIBLE HAPPENS TO YER LI'L FRIEND HERE!
CLAUDIA!
GUI (GRAB)
HEH HEH HEH ...
NOOO ...!

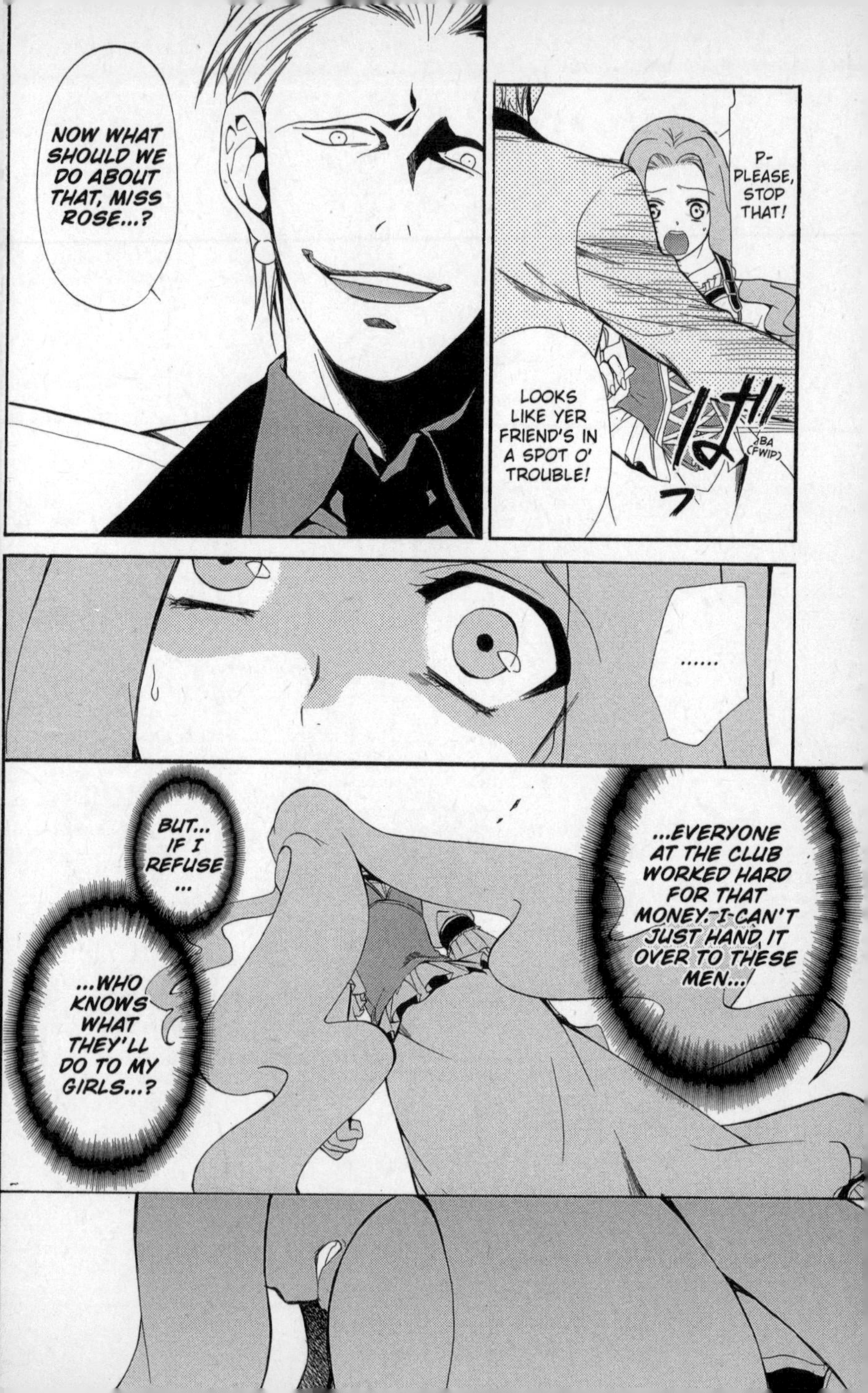
P-PLEASE, STOP THAT!
LOOKS LIKE YER FRIEND'S IN A SPOT O' TROUBLE!
ばっ
BA (FWIP)
NOW WHAT SHOULD WE DO ABOUT THAT, MISS ROSE...?
......
...EVERYONE AT THE CLUB WORKED HARD FOR THAT MONEY. I CAN'T JUST HAND IT OVER TO THESE MEN...
BUT... IF I REFUSE...
...WHO KNOWS WHAT THEY'LL DO TO MY GIRLS...?

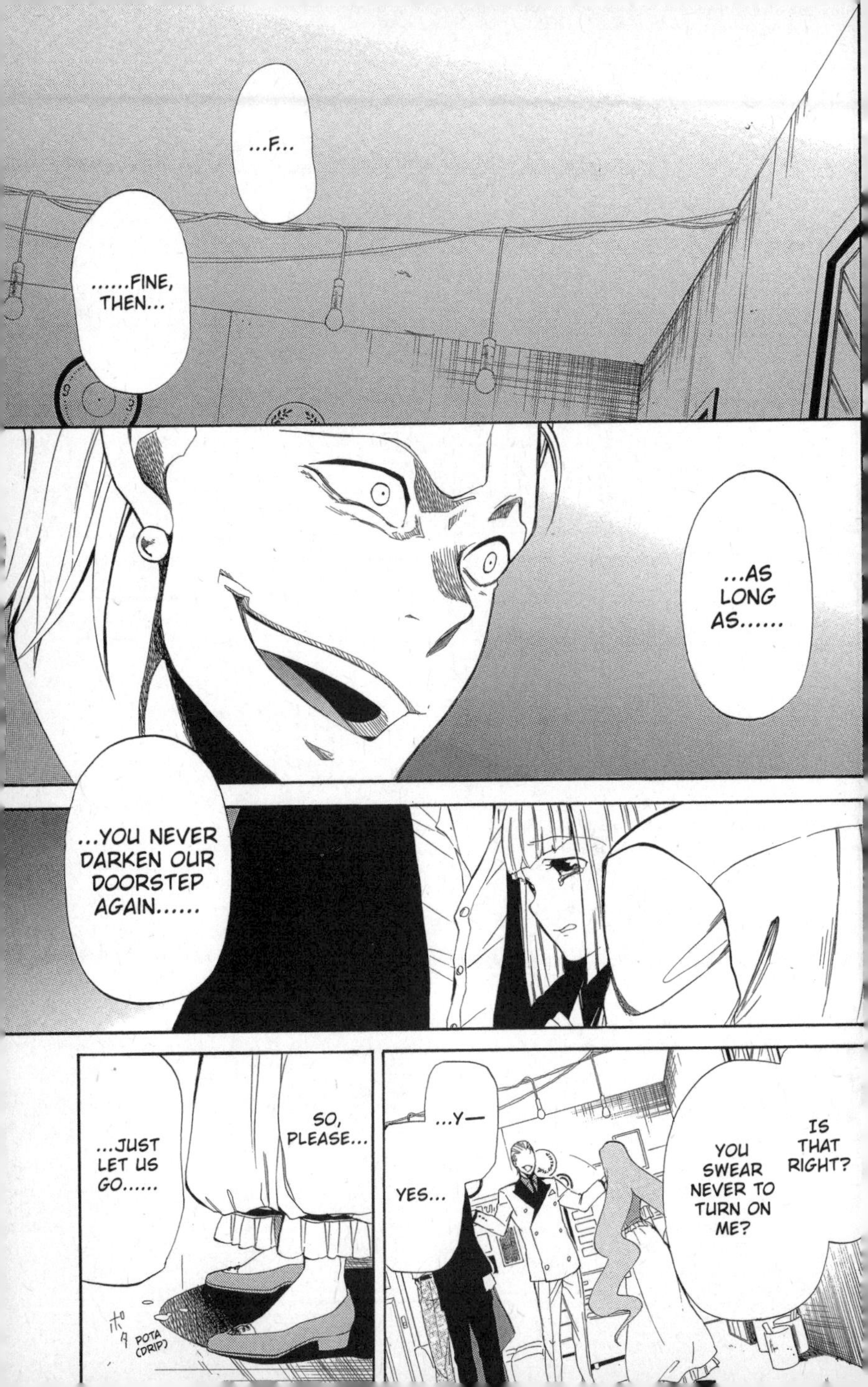
...F...
......FINE, THEN...
...AS LONG AS......
...YOU NEVER DARKEN OUR DOORSTEP AGAIN......
IS THAT RIGHT?
YOU SWEAR NEVER TO TURN ON ME?
...Y—
YES...
SO, PLEASE...
...JUST LET US GO......
ポタ POTA (DRIP)

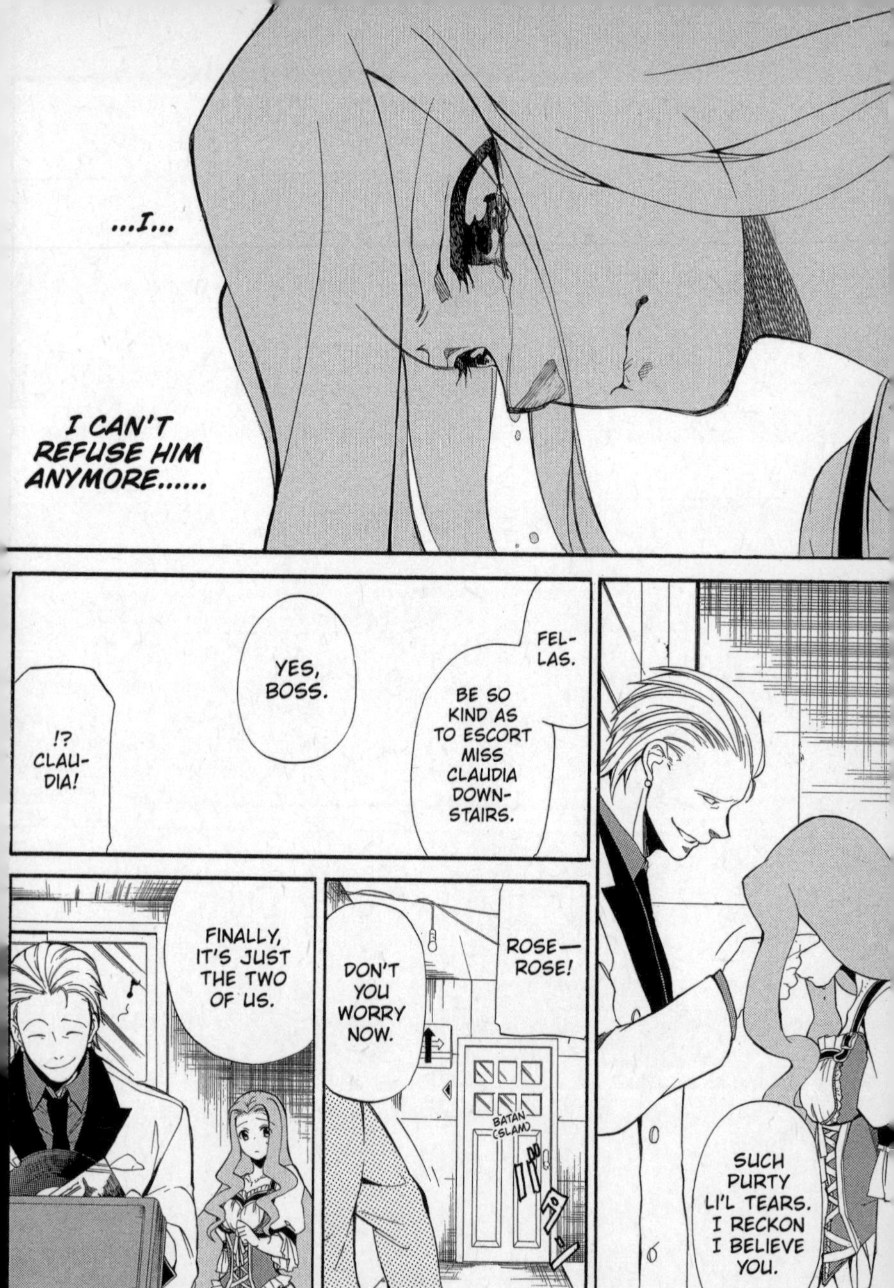
...I...
I CAN'T REFUSE HIM ANYMORE......
SUCH PURTY LI'L TEARS. I RECKON I BELIEVE YOU.
FEL-LAS.
BE SO KIND AS TO ESCORT MISS CLAUDIA DOWN-STAIRS.
YES, BOSS.
!? CLAU-DIA!
ROSE—ROSE!
DON'T YOU WORRY NOW.
BATAN (SLAM)
FINALLY, IT'S JUST THE TWO OF US.

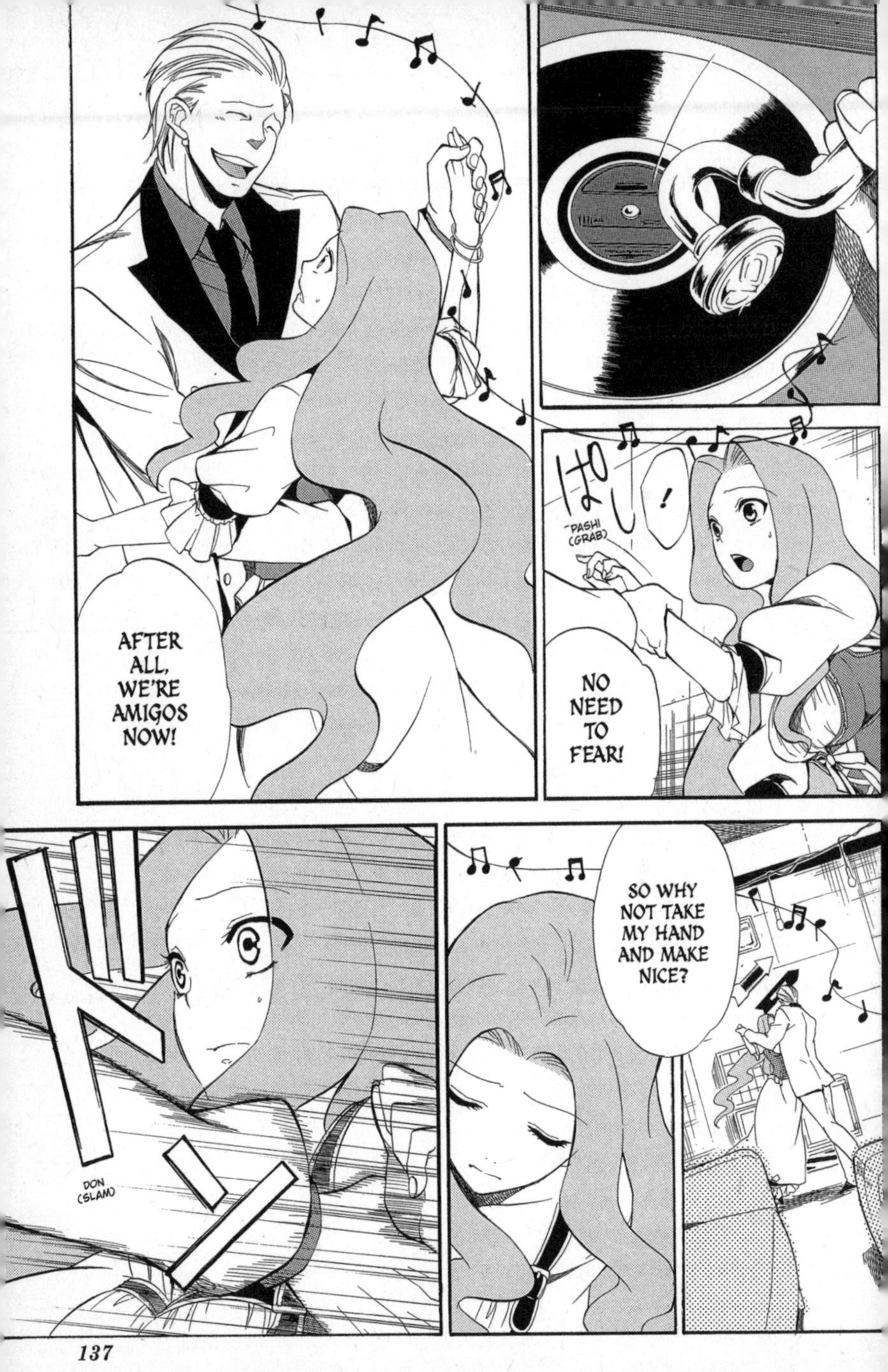
ぱし
PASHI (GRAB)
!
NO NEED TO FEAR!
AFTER ALL, WE'RE AMIGOS NOW!
SO WHY NOT TAKE MY HAND AND MAKE NICE?
ドン
DON (SLAM)

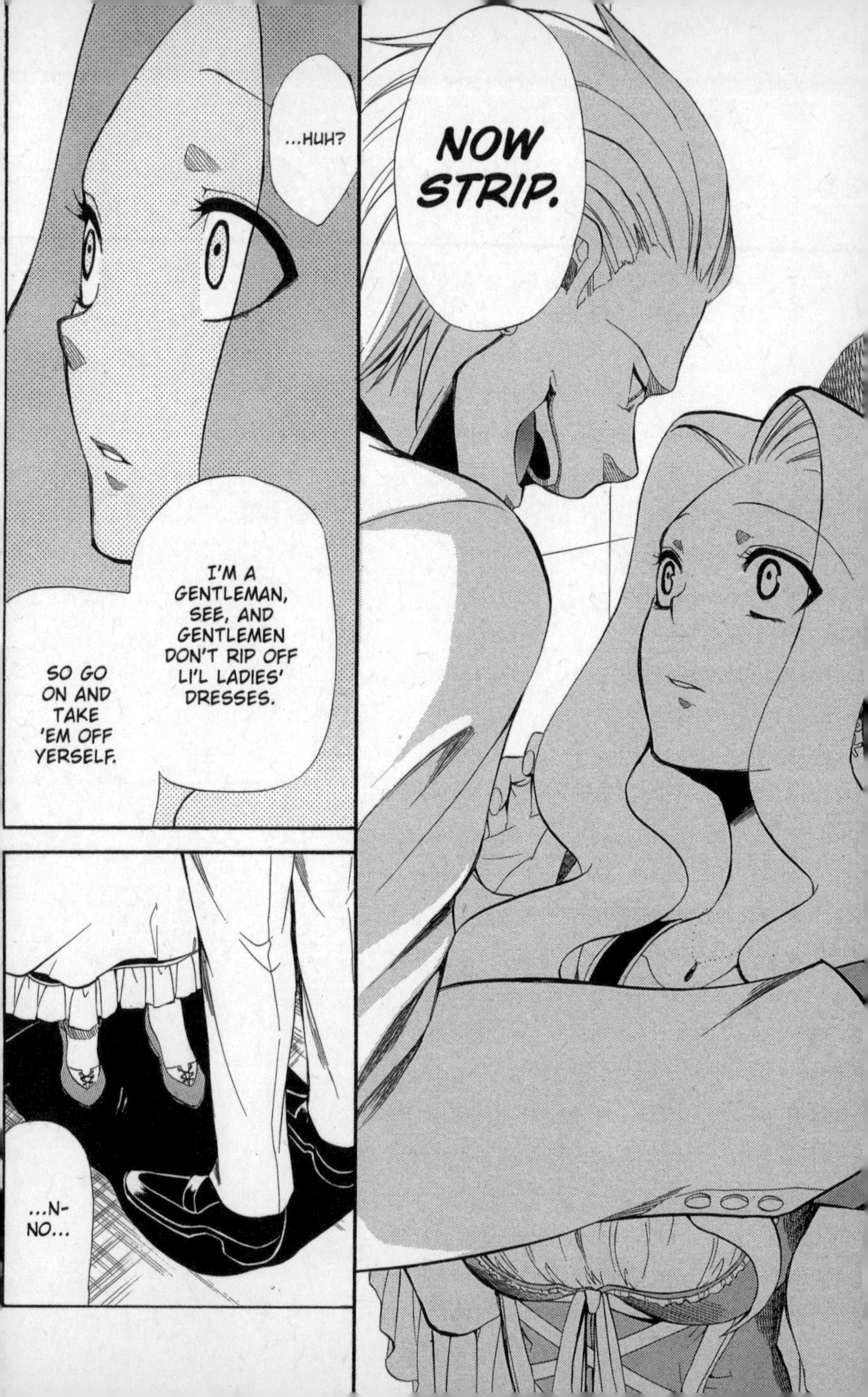
NOW STRIP.
...HUH?
I'M A GENTLEMAN, SEE, AND GENTLEMEN DON'T RIP OFF LI'L LADIES' DRESSES.
SO GO ON AND TAKE 'EM OFF YERSELF.
...N-NO...

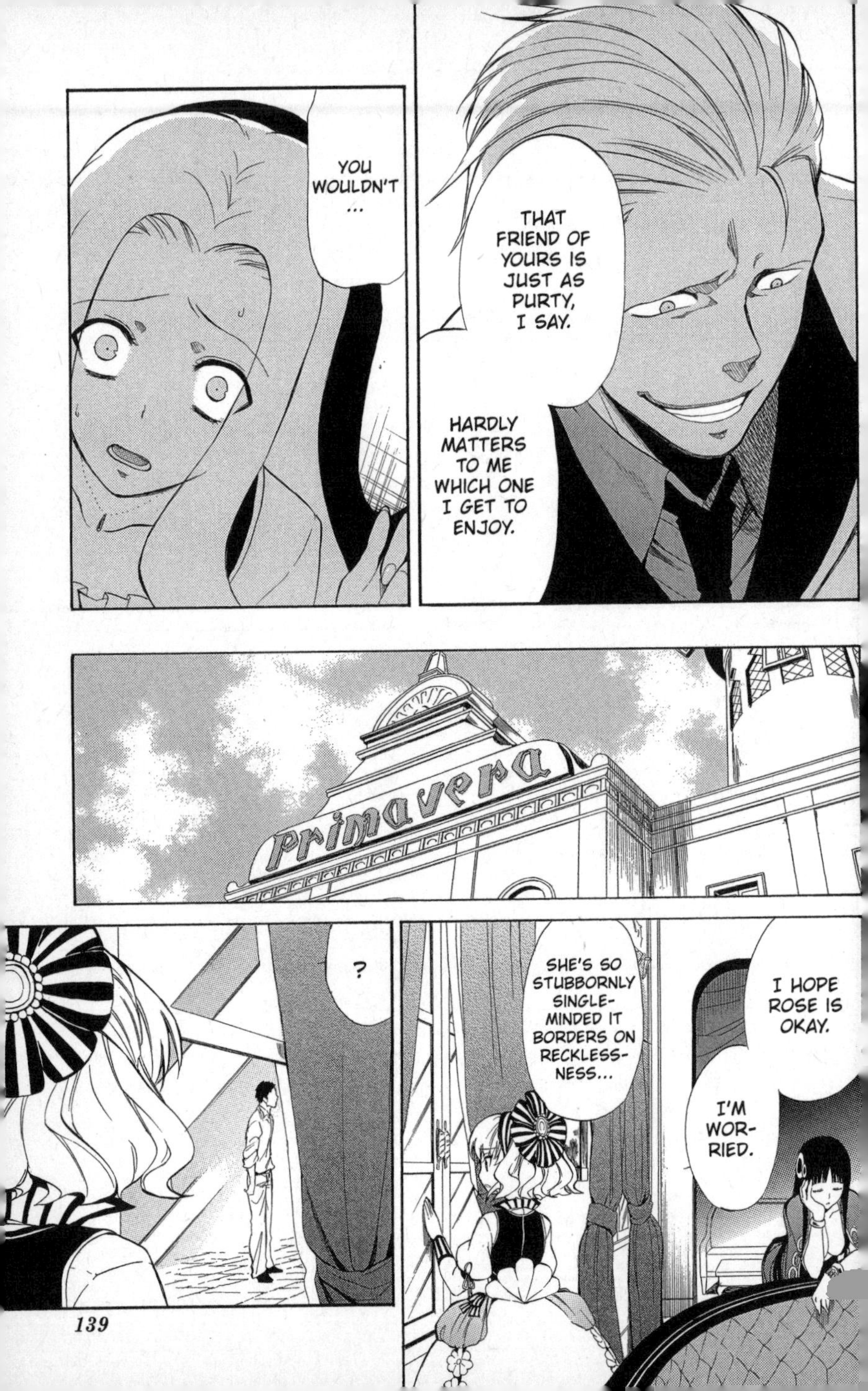
THAT FRIEND OF YOURS IS JUST AS PURTY, I SAY.
HARDLY MATTERS TO ME WHICH ONE I GET TO ENJOY.
YOU WOULDN'T ...
Primavera
I HOPE ROSE IS OKAY.
I'M WOR-RIED.
SHE'S SO STUBBORNLY SINGLE-MINDED IT BORDERS ON RECKLESS-NESS...
?

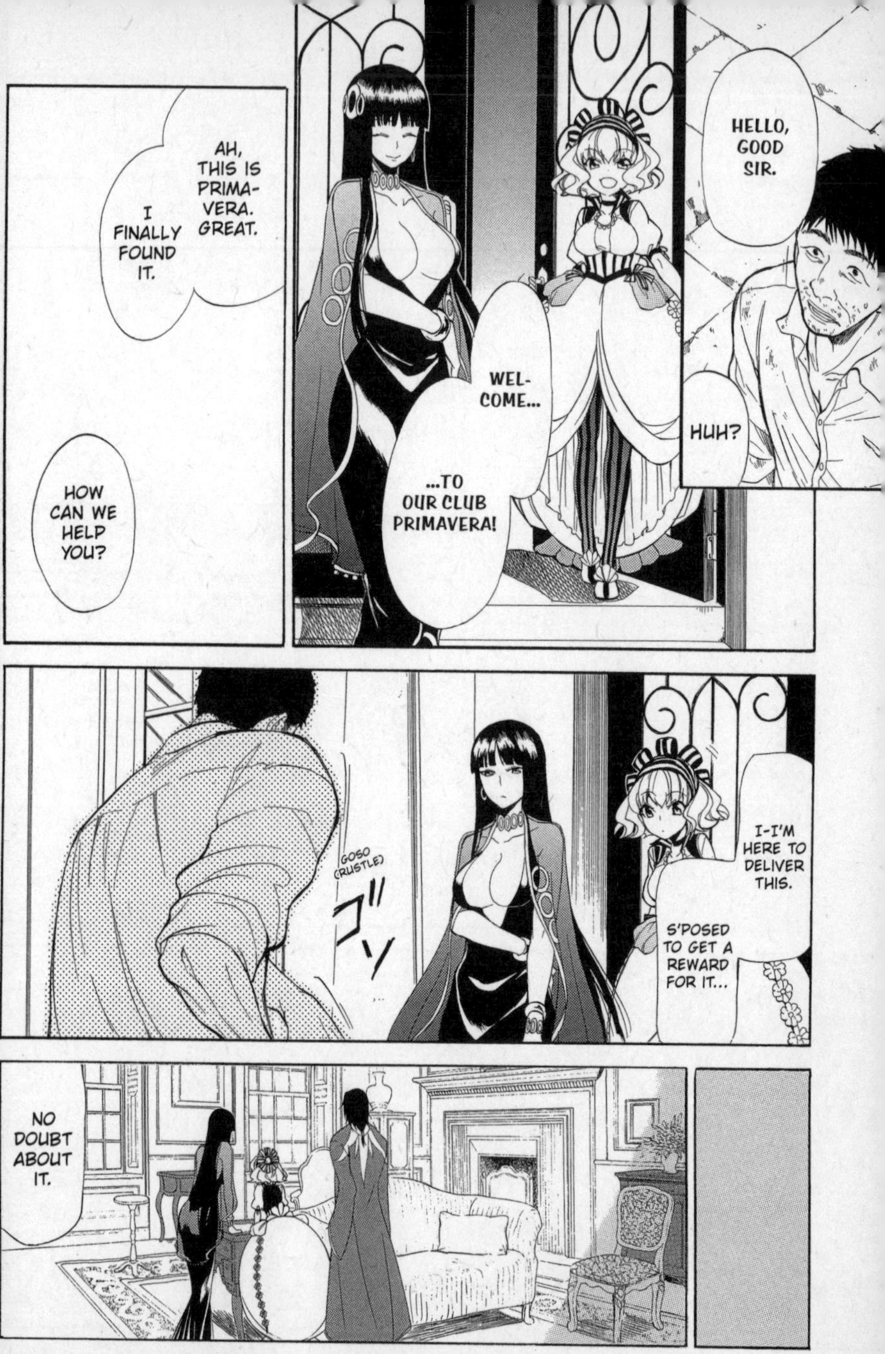
HELLO, GOOD SIR.
HUH?
WEL-COME...
...TO OUR CLUB PRIMAVERA!
AH, THIS IS PRIMA-VERA. GREAT.
I FINALLY FOUND IT.
HOW CAN WE HELP YOU?
I-I'M HERE TO DELIVER THIS.
S'POSED TO GET A REWARD FOR IT...
ゴソ
GOSO (RUSTLE)
NO DOUBT ABOUT IT.

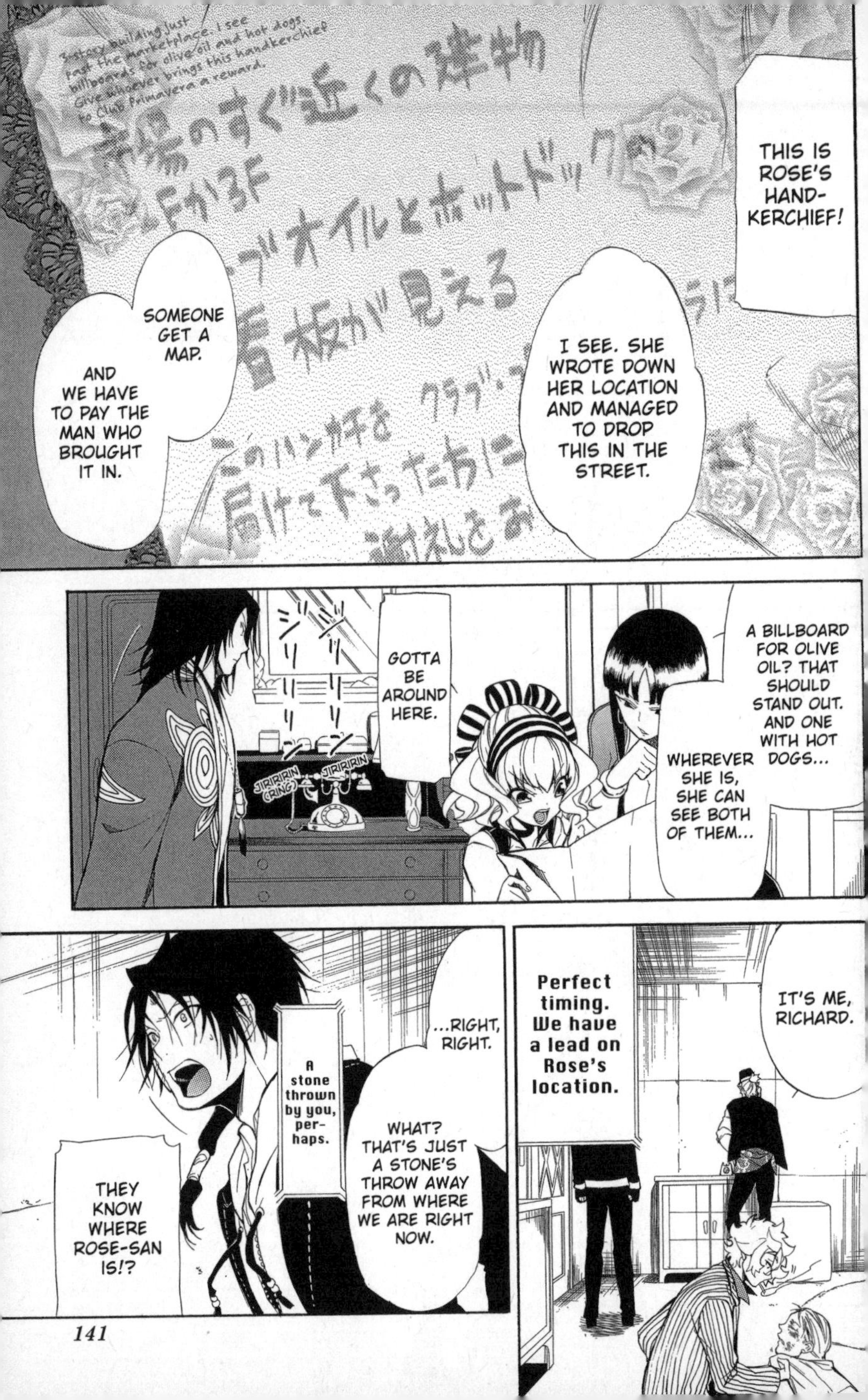
3-story building just past the marketplace. I see billboards for olive oil and hot dogs. Give whoever brings this handkerchief to Club Primavera a reward.
THIS IS ROSE'S HAND-KERCHIEF!
I SEE. SHE WROTE DOWN HER LOCATION AND MANAGED TO DROP THIS IN THE STREET.
SOMEONE GET A MAP.
AND WE HAVE TO PAY THE MAN WHO BROUGHT IT IN.
A BILLBOARD FOR OLIVE OIL? THAT SHOULD STAND OUT. AND ONE WITH HOT DOGS...
WHEREVER SHE IS, SHE CAN SEE BOTH OF THEM...
GOTTA BE AROUND HERE.
JIRIRIRIN
JIRIRIRIN (RING)
IT'S ME, RICHARD.
Perfect timing. We have a lead on Rose's location.
...RIGHT, RIGHT.
WHAT? THAT'S JUST A STONE'S THROW AWAY FROM WHERE WE ARE RIGHT NOW.
A stone thrown by you, per-haps.
THEY KNOW WHERE ROSE-SAN IS!?

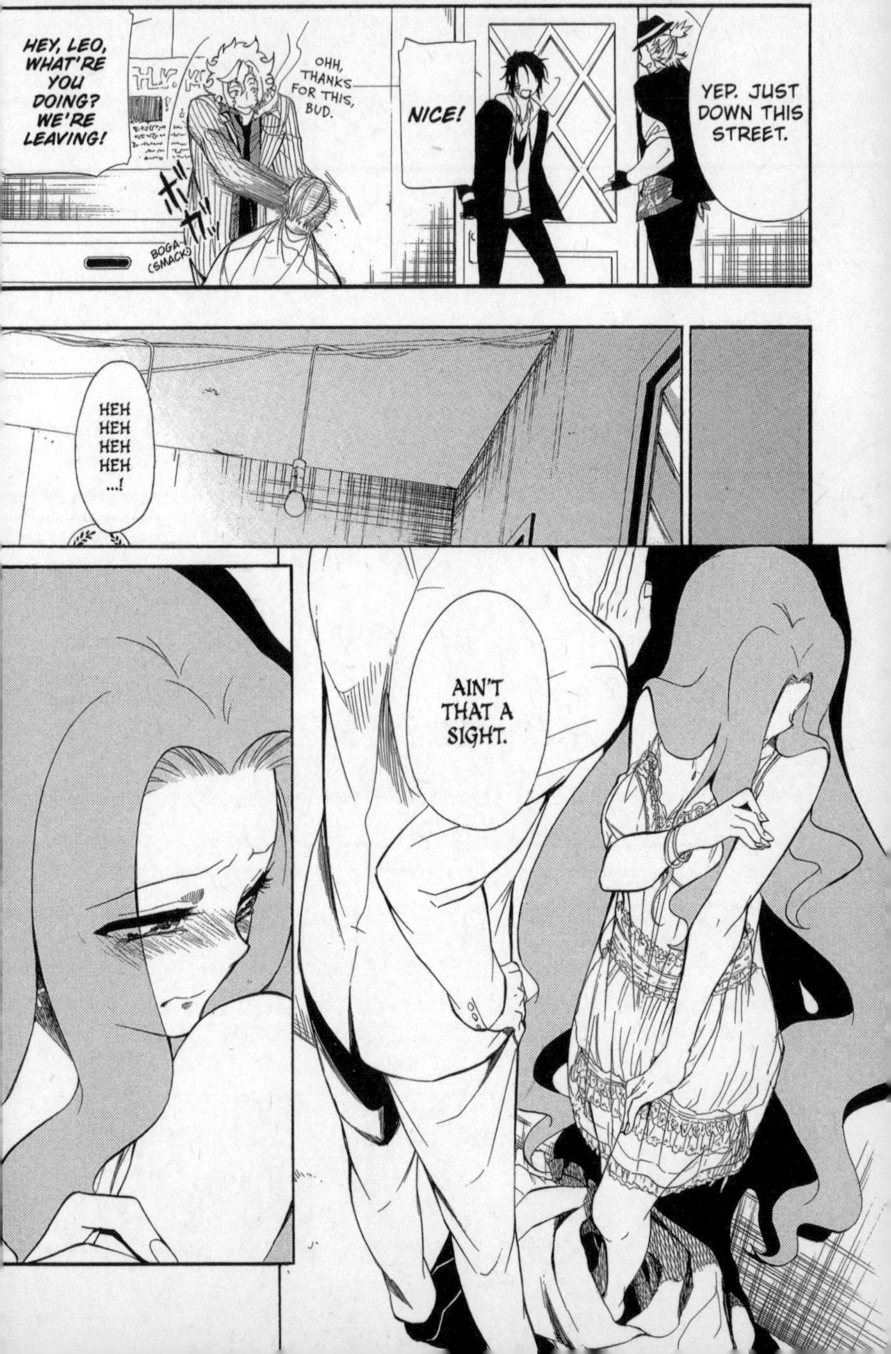
YEP. JUST DOWN THIS STREET.
NICE!
OHH, THANKS FOR THIS, BUD.
HEY, LEO, WHAT'RE YOU DOING? WE'RE LEAVING!
BOGA (SMACK)
HEH HEH HEH HEH ...!
AIN'T THAT A SIGHT.

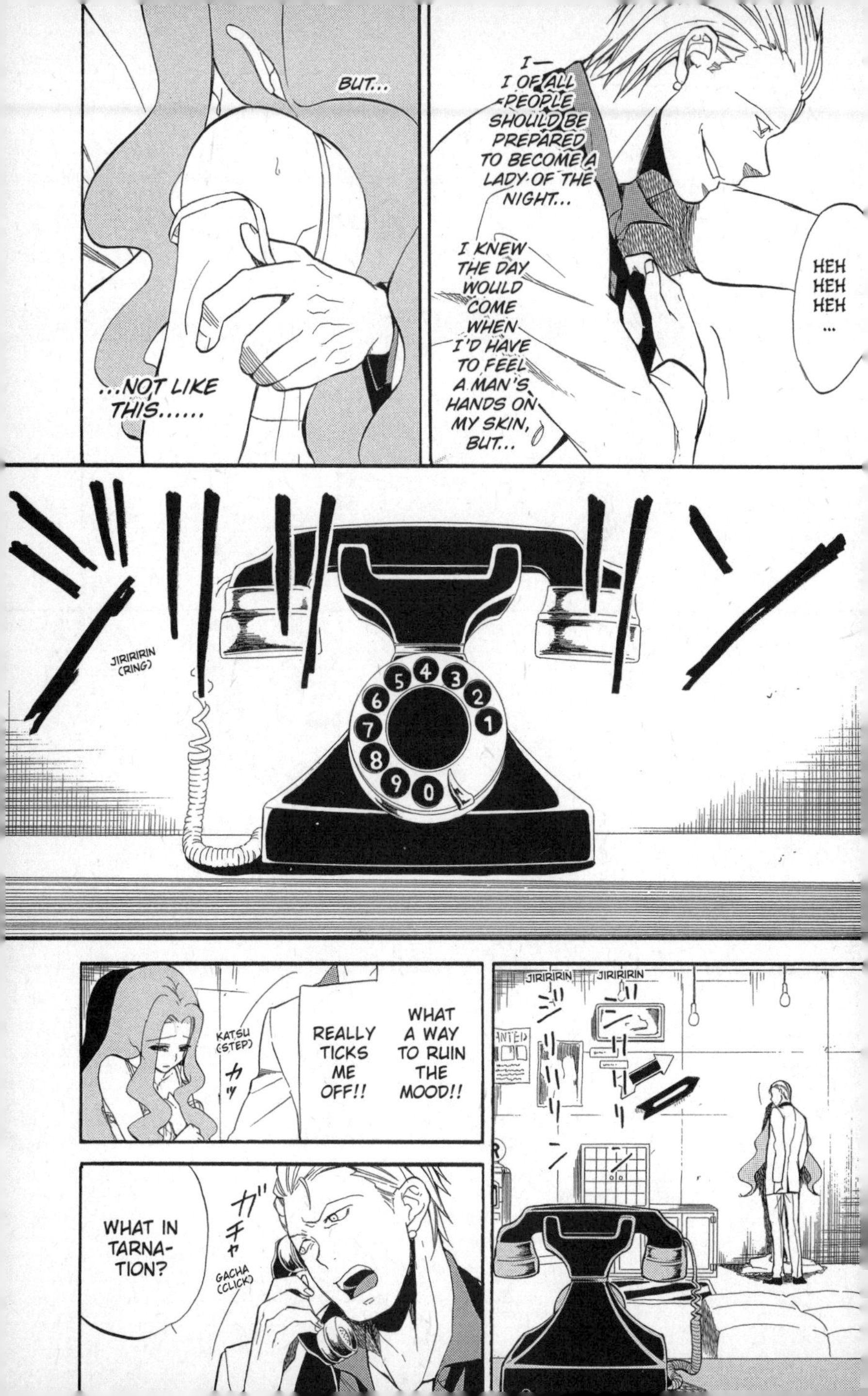
I— I OF ALL PEOPLE SHOULD BE PREPARED TO BECOME A LADY OF THE NIGHT...
HEH HEH HEH ...
I KNEW THE DAY WOULD COME WHEN I'D HAVE TO FEEL A MAN'S HANDS ON MY SKIN, BUT...
BUT...
...NOT LIKE THIS......
JIRIRIRIN (RING)
JIRIRIRIN
JIRIRIRIN
WHAT A WAY TO RUIN THE MOOD!!
REALLY TICKS ME OFF!!
KATSU (STEP)
GACHA (CLICK)
WHAT IN TARNATION?

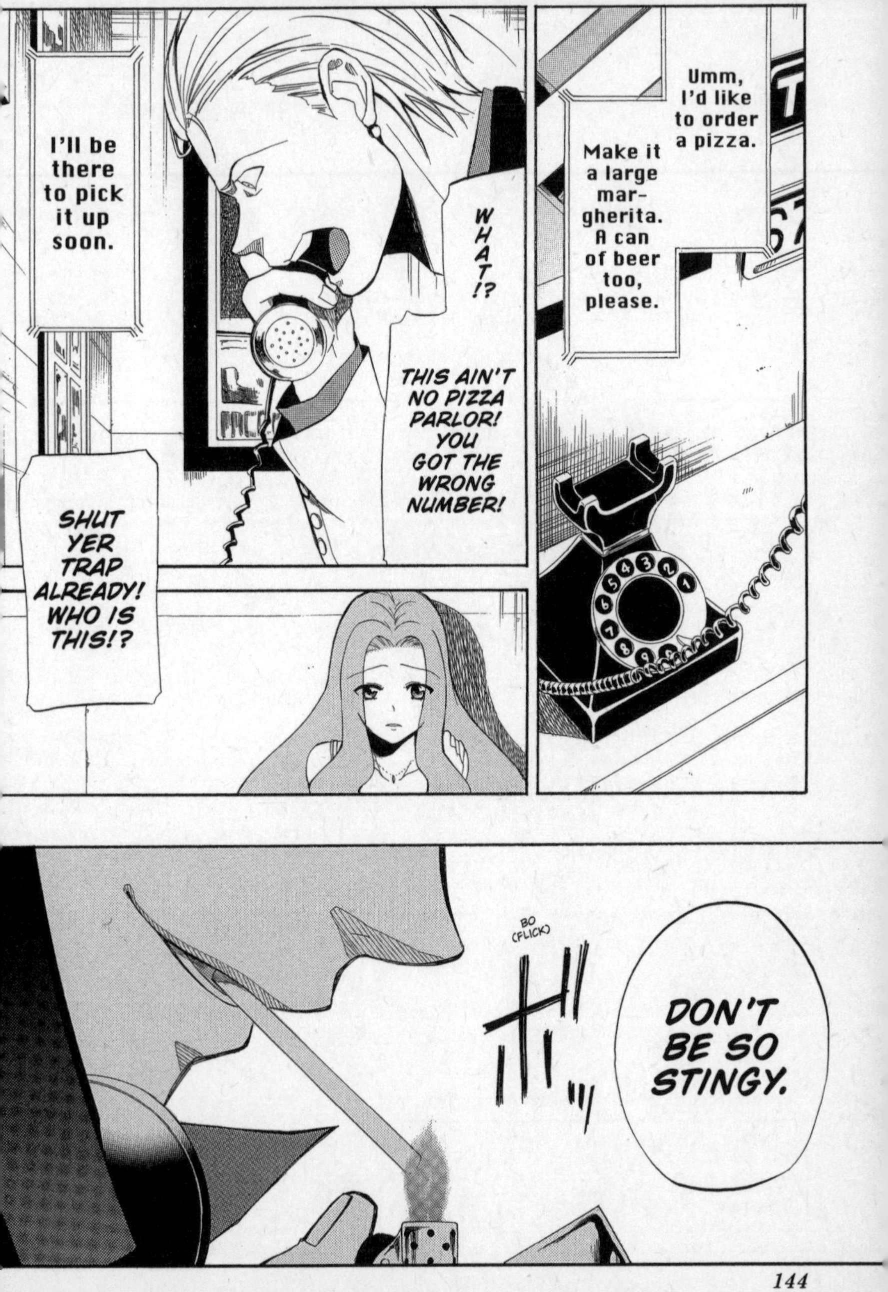
Umm, I'd like to order a pizza.
Make it a large mar-gherita. A can of beer too, please.
WHAT!?
THIS AIN'T NO PIZZA PARLOR! YOU GOT THE WRONG NUMBER!
I'll be there to pick it up soon.
SHUT YER TRAP ALREADY! WHO IS THIS!?
DON'T BE SO STINGY.
BO (FLICK)

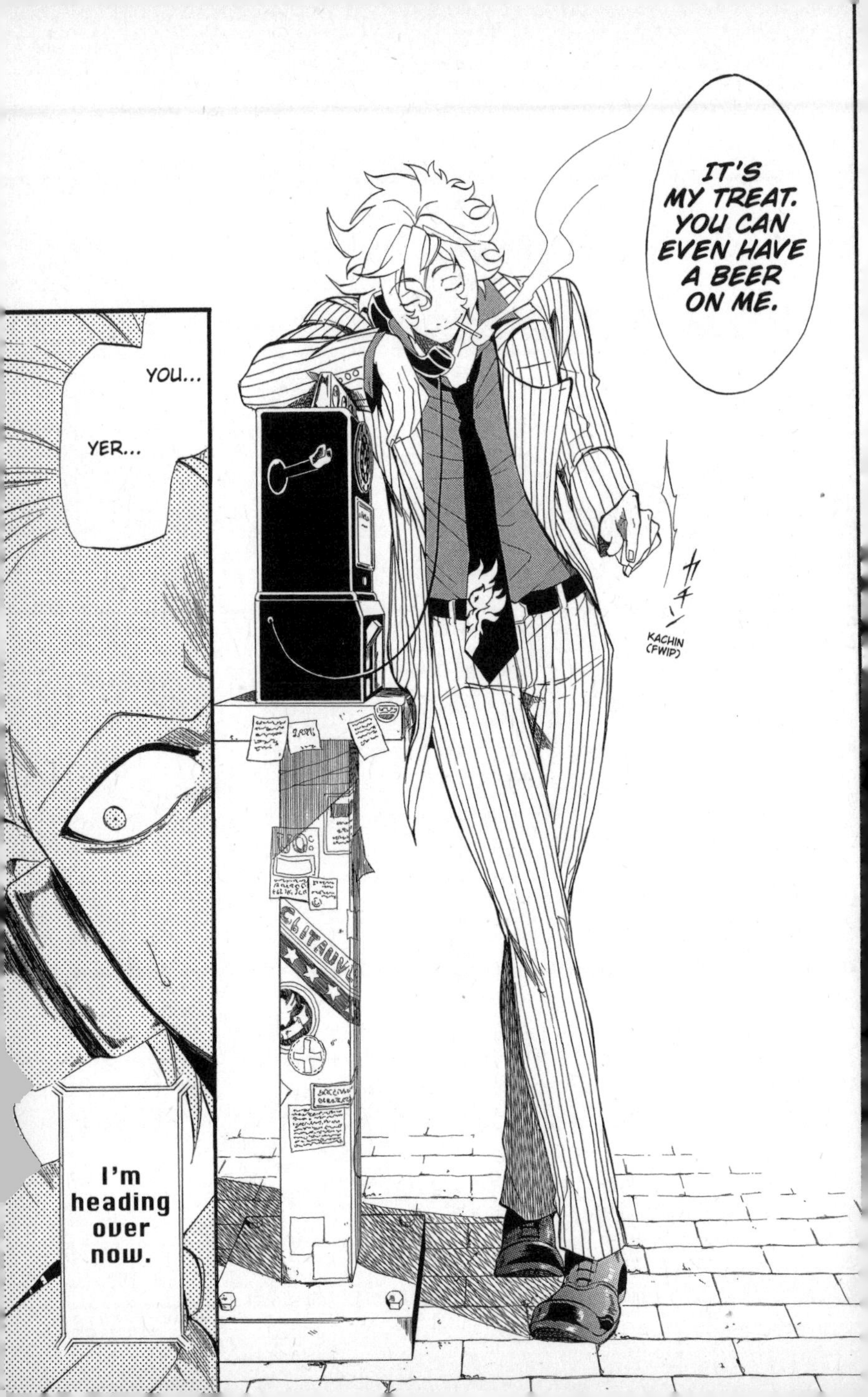
IT'S MY TREAT. YOU CAN EVEN HAVE A BEER ON ME.
カチン
KACHIN (FWIP)
YOU...
YER...
I'm heading over now.

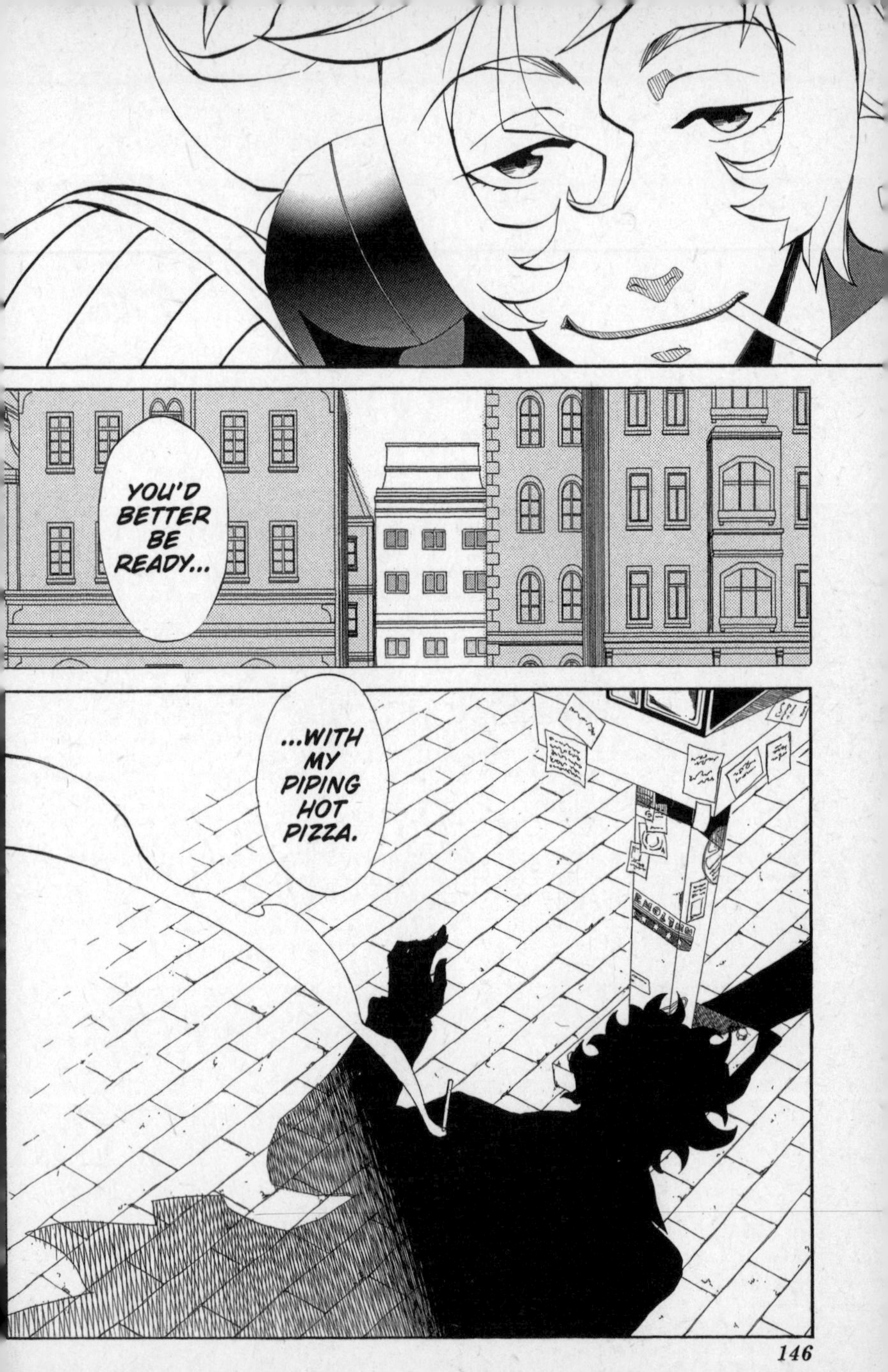
YOU'D BETTER BE READY...
...WITH MY PIPING HOT PIZZA.

TRANSLATION NOTES

COMMON HONORIFICS

no honorific: Indicates familiarity or closeness; if used without permission or reason, addressing someone in this manner would constitute an insult.

-san: The Japanese equivalent of Mr./Mrs./Miss. If a situation calls for politeness, this is the fail-safe honorific.

-sama: Conveys great respect; may also indicate that the social status of the speaker is lower than that of the addressee.

-kun: Used most often when referring to boys, this indicates affection or familiarity. Occasionally used by older men among their peers, but it may also be used by anyone referring to a person of lower standing.

-chan: An affectionate honorific indicating familiarity used mostly in reference to girls; also used in reference to cute persons or animals of either gender.

-senpai: A suffix used to address upperclassmen or more experienced coworkers.

PAGE 51

Tarou Urashima is the titular hero of a Japanese Rip Van Winkle-esque folktale. Tarou Urashima visits a magical underwater kingdom for three days, but when he returns home, three hundred years have passed.

PAGE 131

Teru teru bouzu are small white dolls made of paper or cloth that are hung by strings around their necks. They're meant to bring good weather.

PAGE 132

In Japan, ordinary garbage is sorted into "burnable" and "non-burnable," with each having different collection days. There are also days for recyclables as well as large, bulky items like furniture.

ROSE GUNS DAYS
Season 1

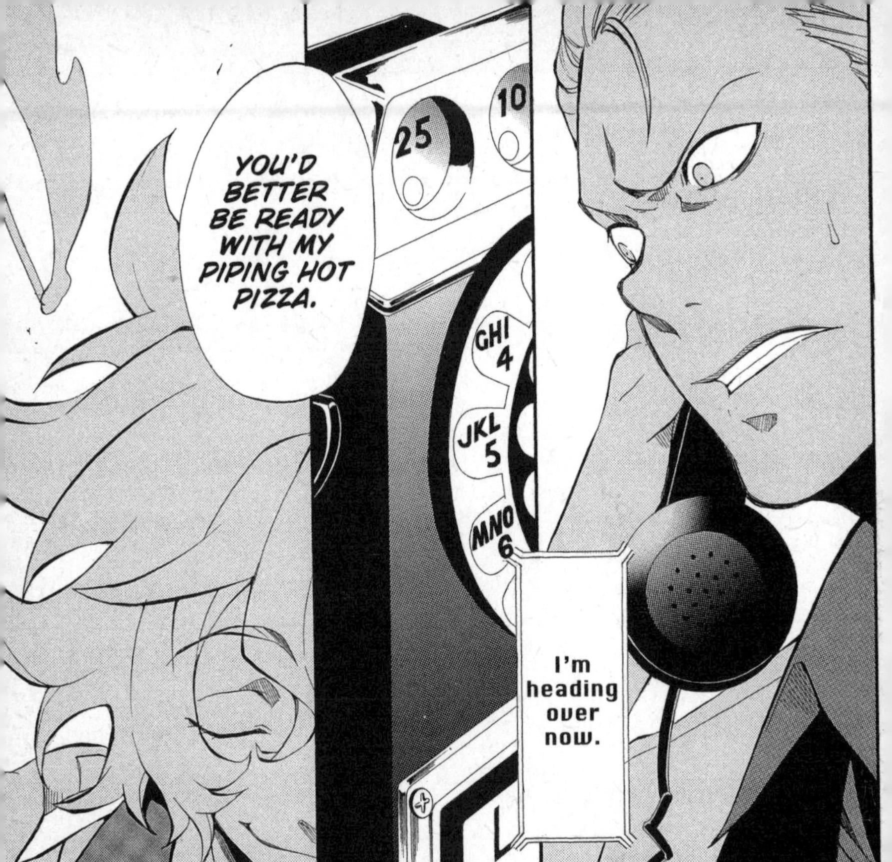
I'm heading over now.
YOU'D BETTER BE READY WITH MY PIPING HOT PIZZA.
10
25
GHI 4
JKL 5
MNO 6

Scene: 04

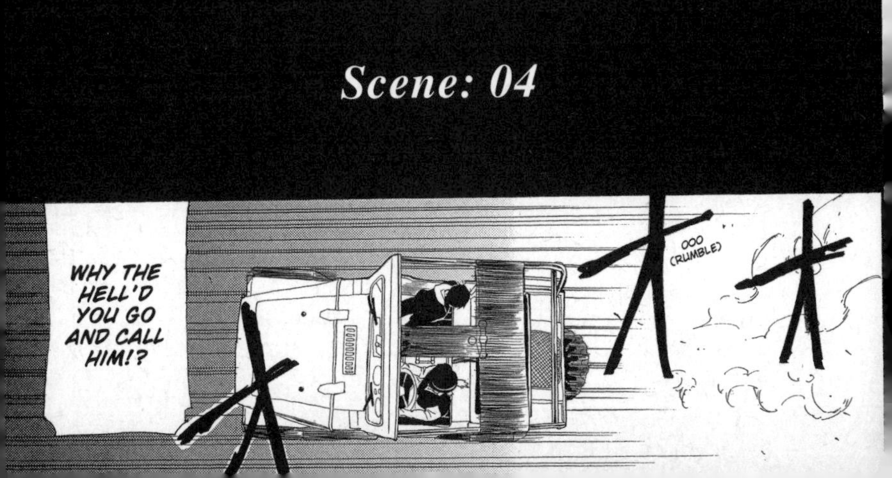
OOO (RUMBLE)
WHY THE HELL'D YOU GO AND CALL HIM!?

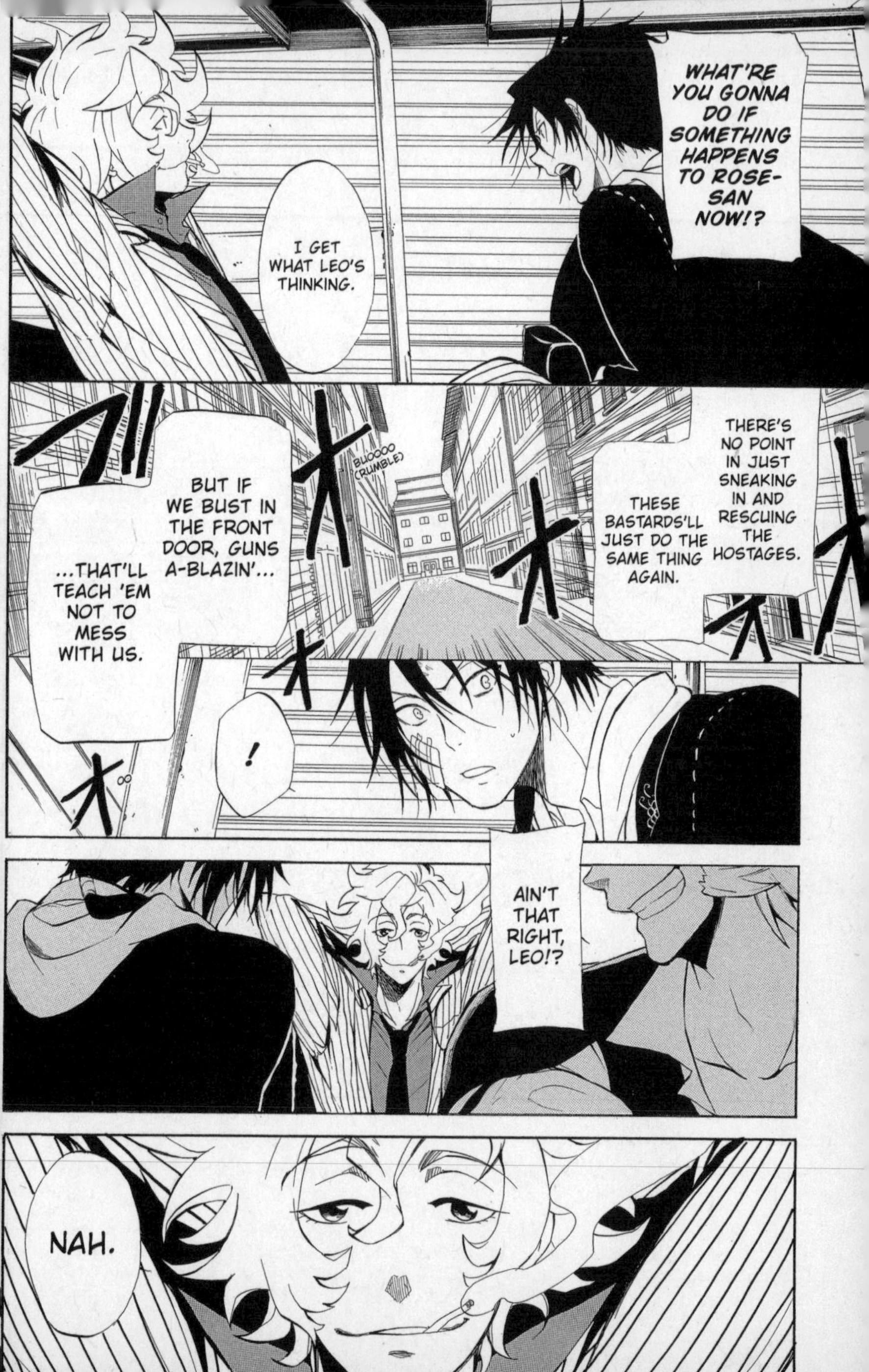
WHAT'RE YOU GONNA DO IF SOMETHING HAPPENS TO ROSE-SAN NOW!?
I GET WHAT LEO'S THINKING.
THERE'S NO POINT IN JUST SNEAKING IN AND RESCUING THE HOSTAGES.
THESE BASTARDS'LL JUST DO THE SAME THING AGAIN.
BUOOOO (RUMBLE)
BUT IF WE BUST IN THE FRONT DOOR, GUNS A-BLAZIN'...
...THAT'LL TEACH 'EM NOT TO MESS WITH US.
!
AIN'T THAT RIGHT, LEO!?
NAH.

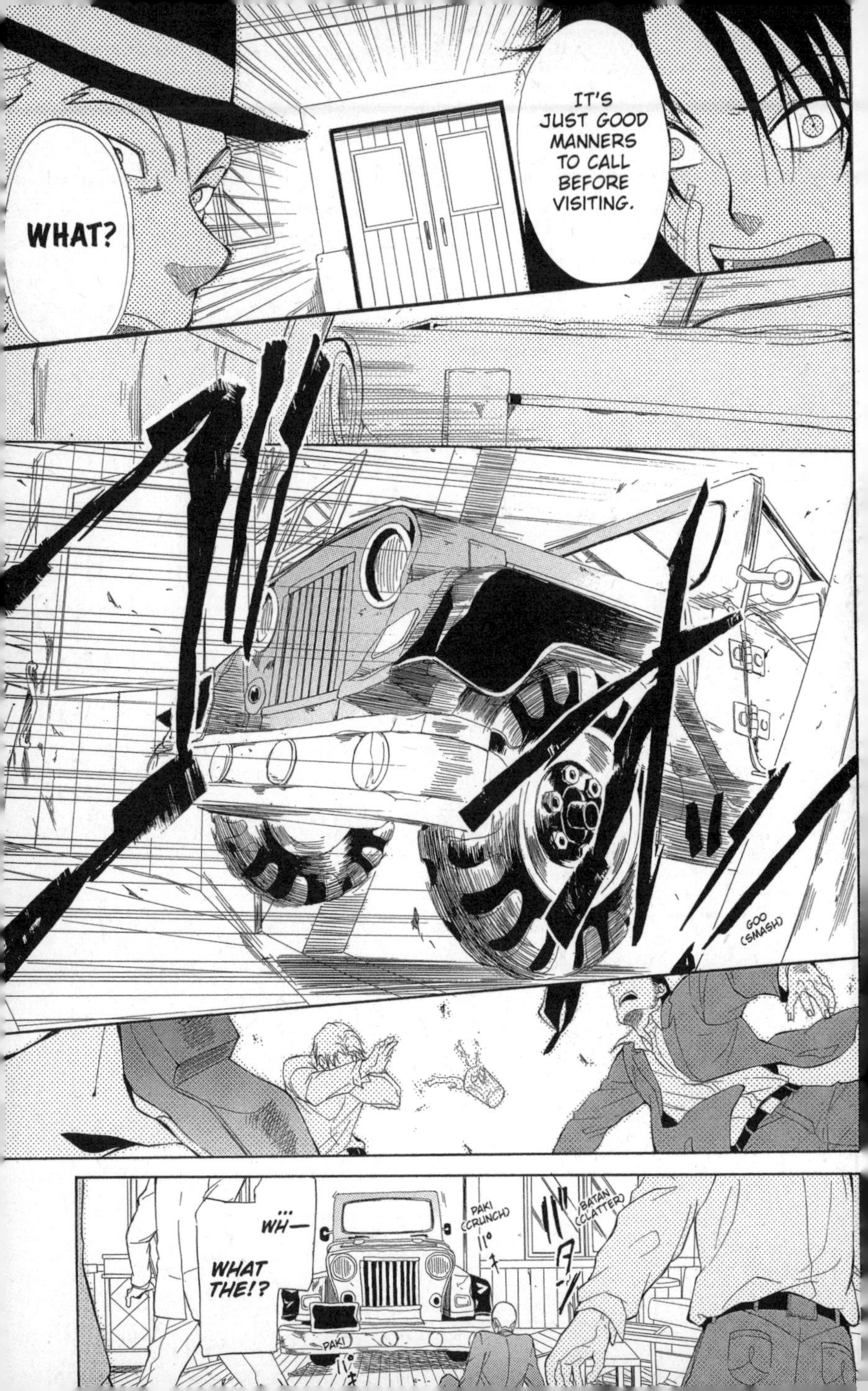
IT'S JUST GOOD MANNERS TO CALL BEFORE VISITING.
WHAT?
GOO (SMASH)
BATAN (CLATTER)
PAKI (CRUNCH)
WH—
WHAT THE!?
PAKI

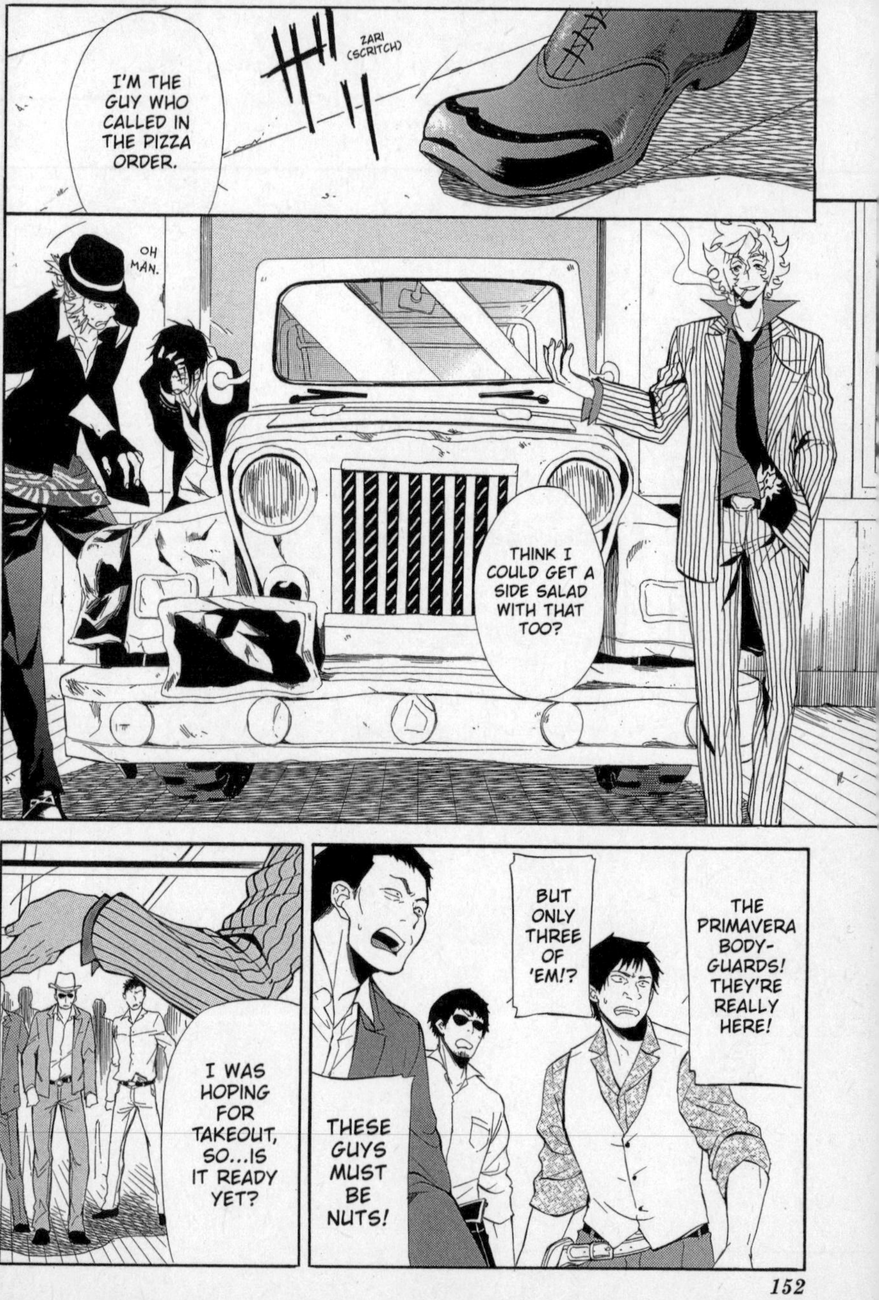
ZARI (SCRITCH)
I'M THE GUY WHO CALLED IN THE PIZZA ORDER.
THINK I COULD GET A SIDE SALAD WITH THAT TOO?
OH MAN.
THE PRIMAVERA BODY-GUARDS! THEY'RE REALLY HERE!
BUT ONLY THREE OF 'EM!?
THESE GUYS MUST BE NUTS!
I WAS HOPING FOR TAKEOUT, SO...IS IT READY YET?

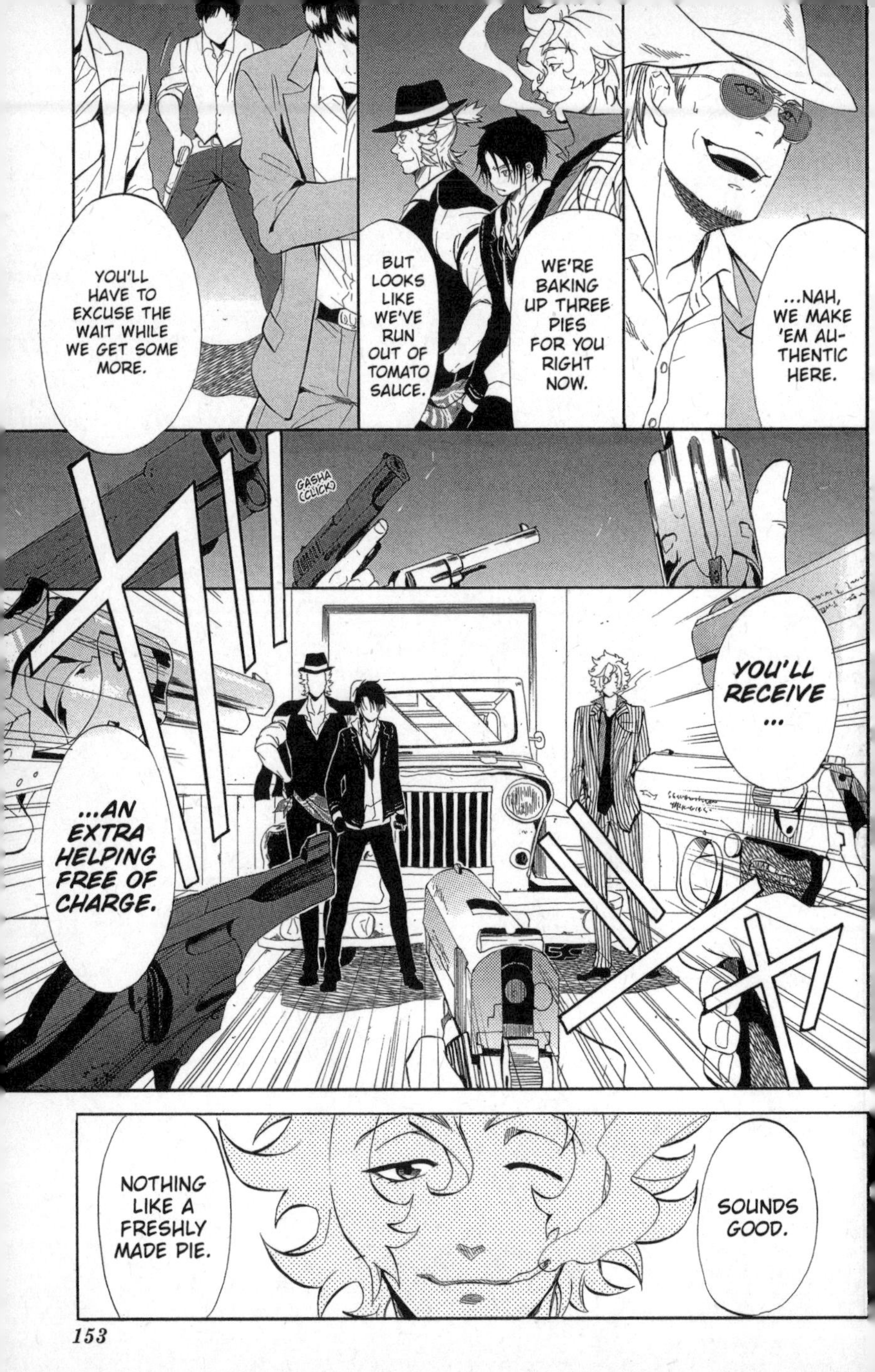
...NAH, WE MAKE 'EM AUTHENTIC HERE.
WE'RE BAKING UP THREE PIES FOR YOU RIGHT NOW.
BUT LOOKS LIKE WE'VE RUN OUT OF TOMATO SAUCE.
YOU'LL HAVE TO EXCUSE THE WAIT WHILE WE GET SOME MORE.
GASHA (CLICK)
YOU'LL RECEIVE ...
...AN EXTRA HELPING FREE OF CHARGE.
SOUNDS GOOD.
NOTHING LIKE A FRESHLY MADE PIE.

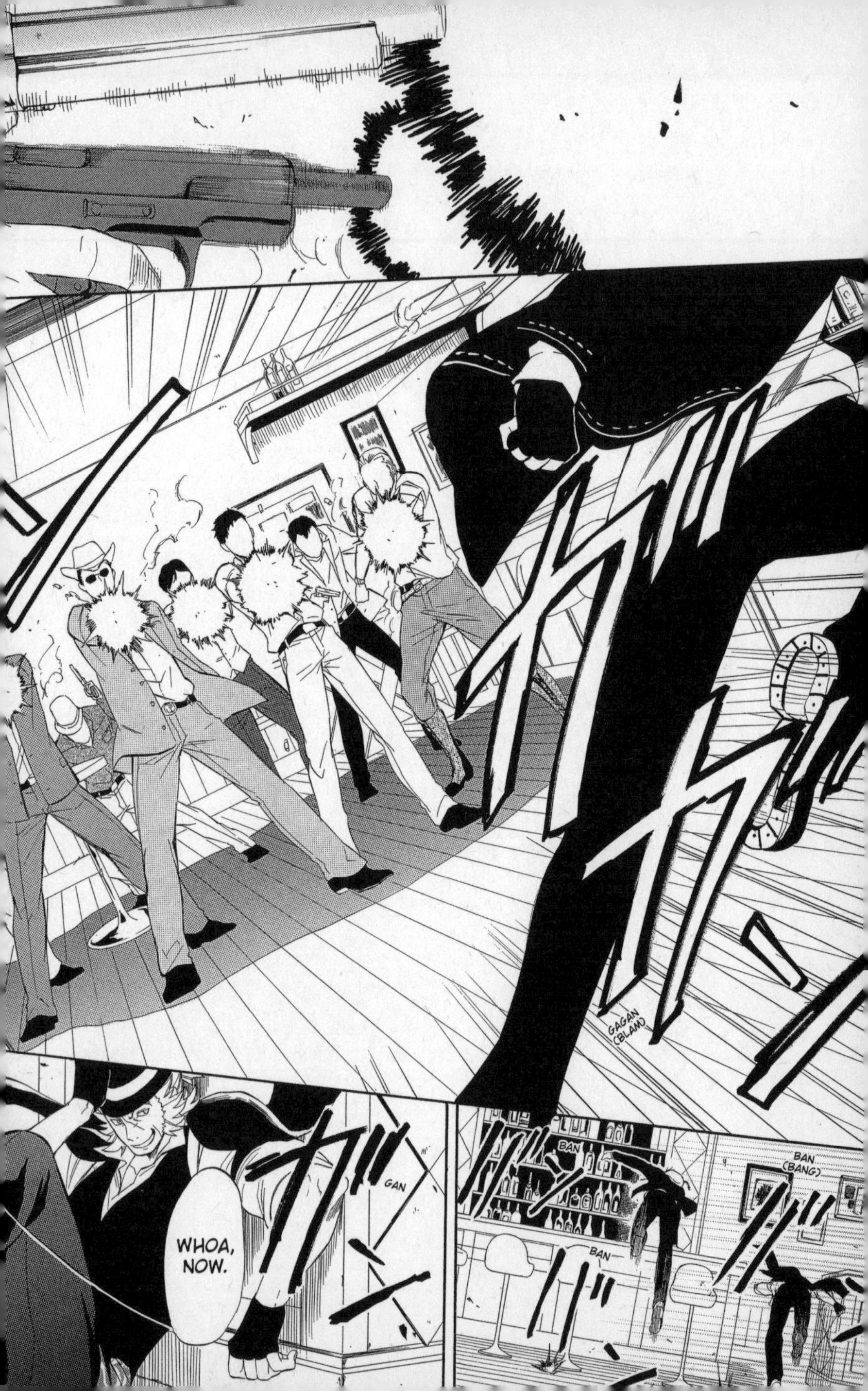
GAGAN (BLAM)
WHOA, NOW.
GAN
BAN (BANG)
BAN
BAN

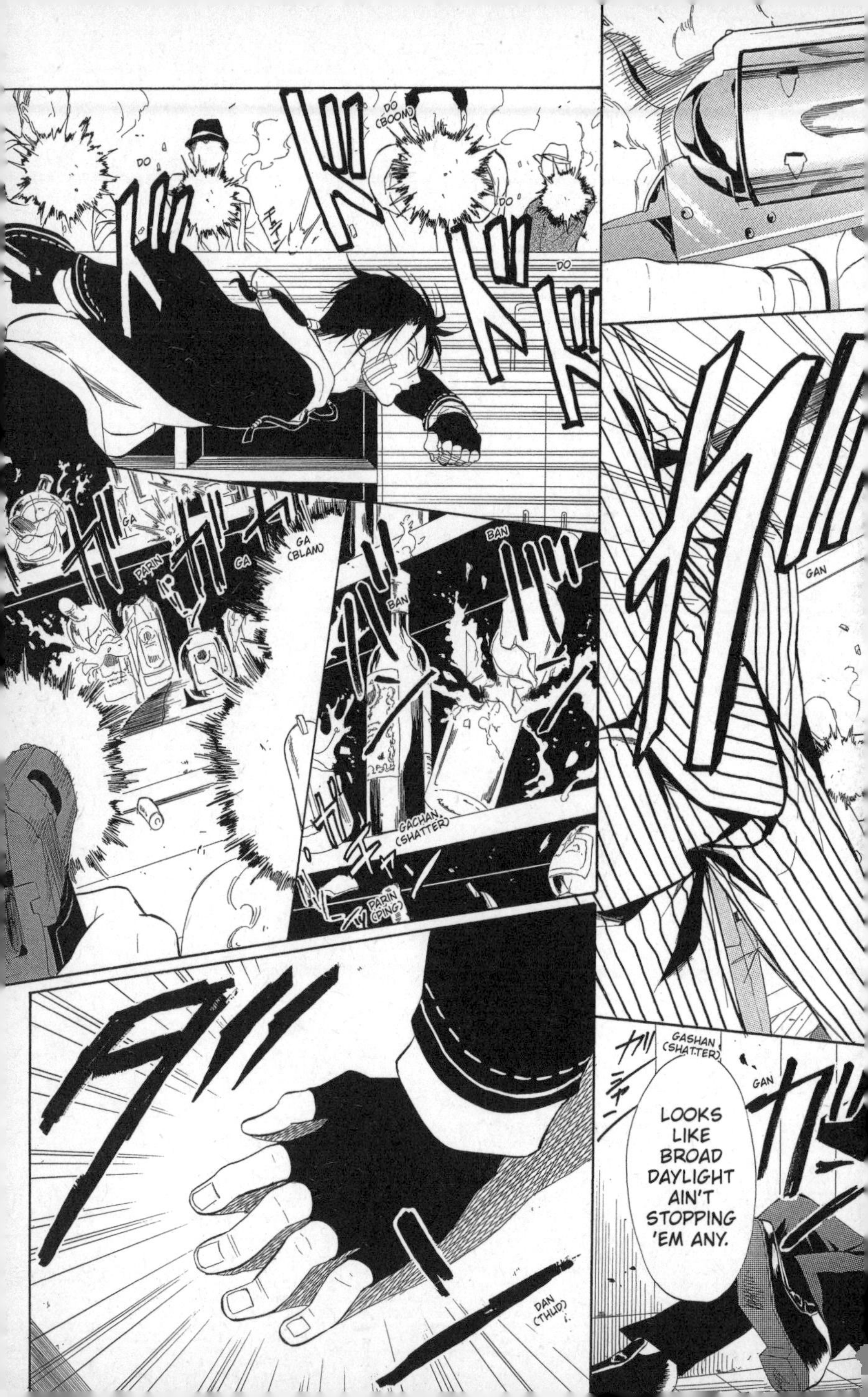
GAN
GASHAN (SHATTER)
GAN
LOOKS LIKE BROAD DAYLIGHT AIN'T STOPPING 'EM ANY.
DO (BOOM)
DO
DO
DO
GA
PARIN
GA
GA (BLAM)
BAN
BAN
GACHAN (SHATTER)
PARIN (PING)
DAN (THUD)

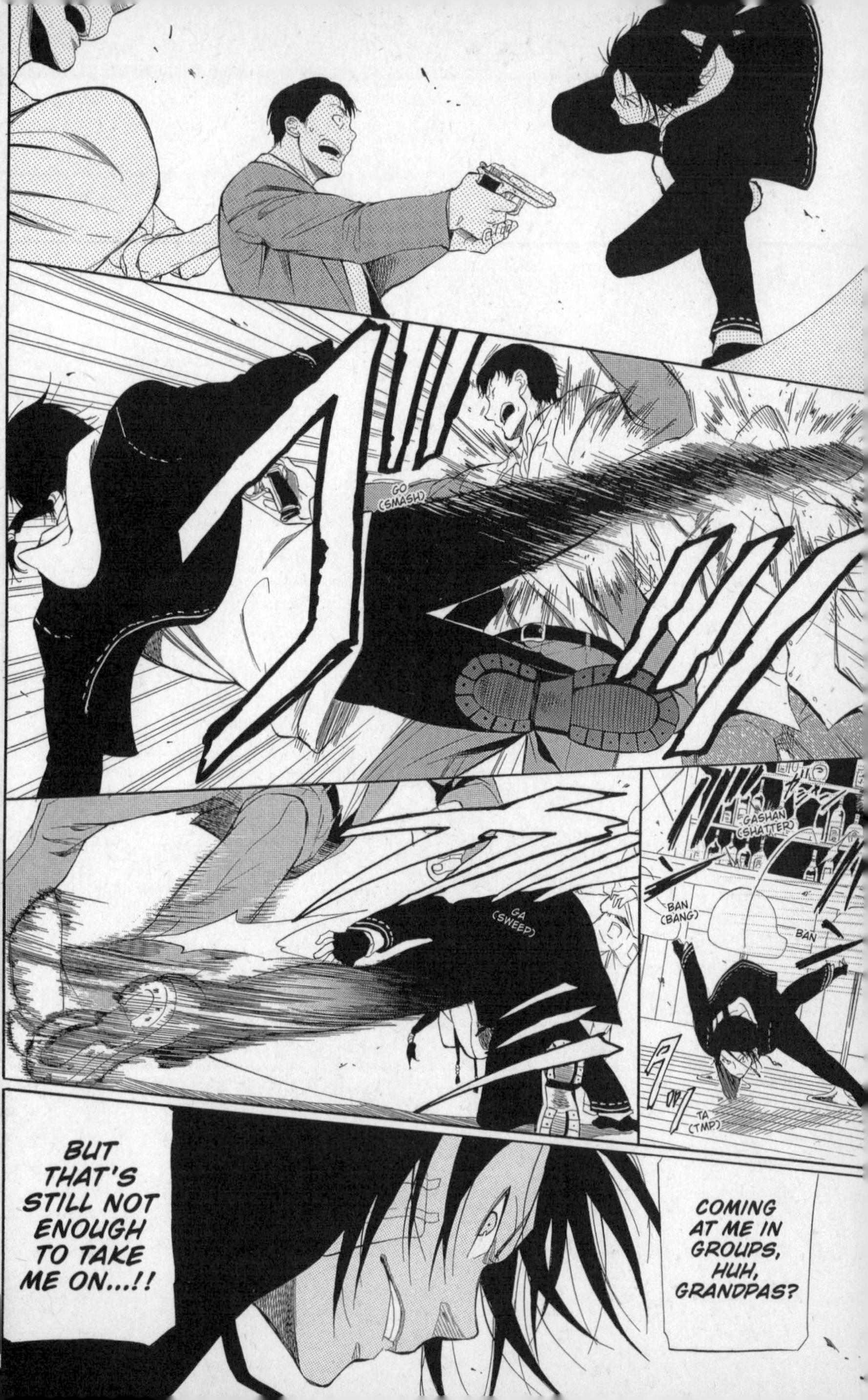
GO
(SMASH)
GASHAN
(SHATTER)
BAN
(BANG)
BAN
TA
(TMP)
GA
(SWEEP)
COMING AT ME IN GROUPS, HUH, GRANDPAS?
BUT THAT'S STILL NOT ENOUGH TO TAKE ME ON...!!

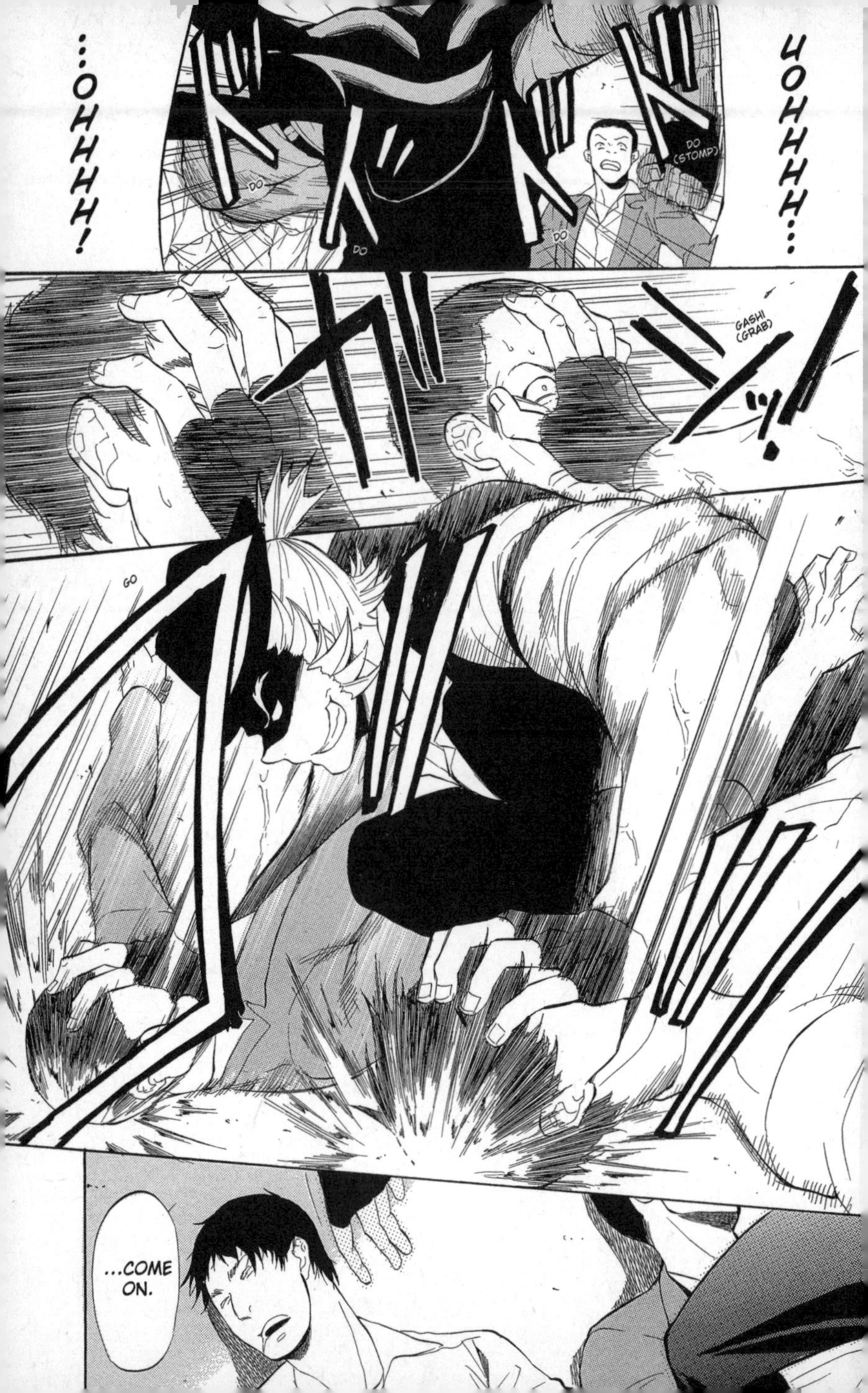
UOHHHHH...
DO (STOMP)
DO
DO
DO
...OHHHHH!
GASHI (GRAB)
GO
...COME ON.

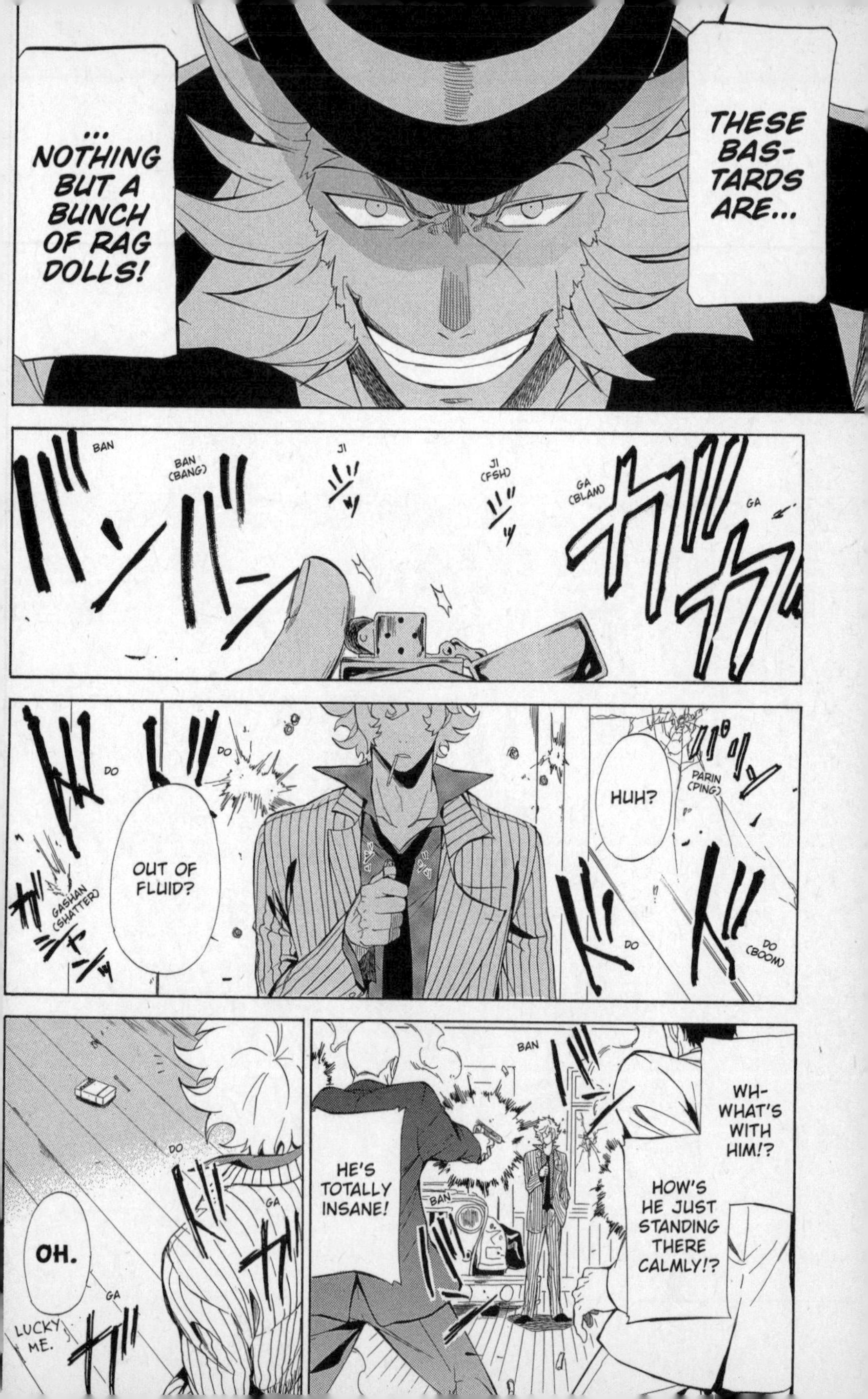
THESE BASTARDS ARE...
...NOTHING BUT A BUNCH OF RAG DOLLS!
GA
GA (BLAM)
JI (FSH)
JI
BAN (BANG)
BAN
PARIN (PING)
HUH?
DO (BOOM)
DO
OUT OF FLUID?
DO
DO
GASHAN (SHATTER)
BAN
WH- WHAT'S WITH HIM!?
HOW'S HE JUST STANDING THERE CALMLY!?
HE'S TOTALLY INSANE!
BAN
DO
GA
OH.
GA
LUCKY ME.

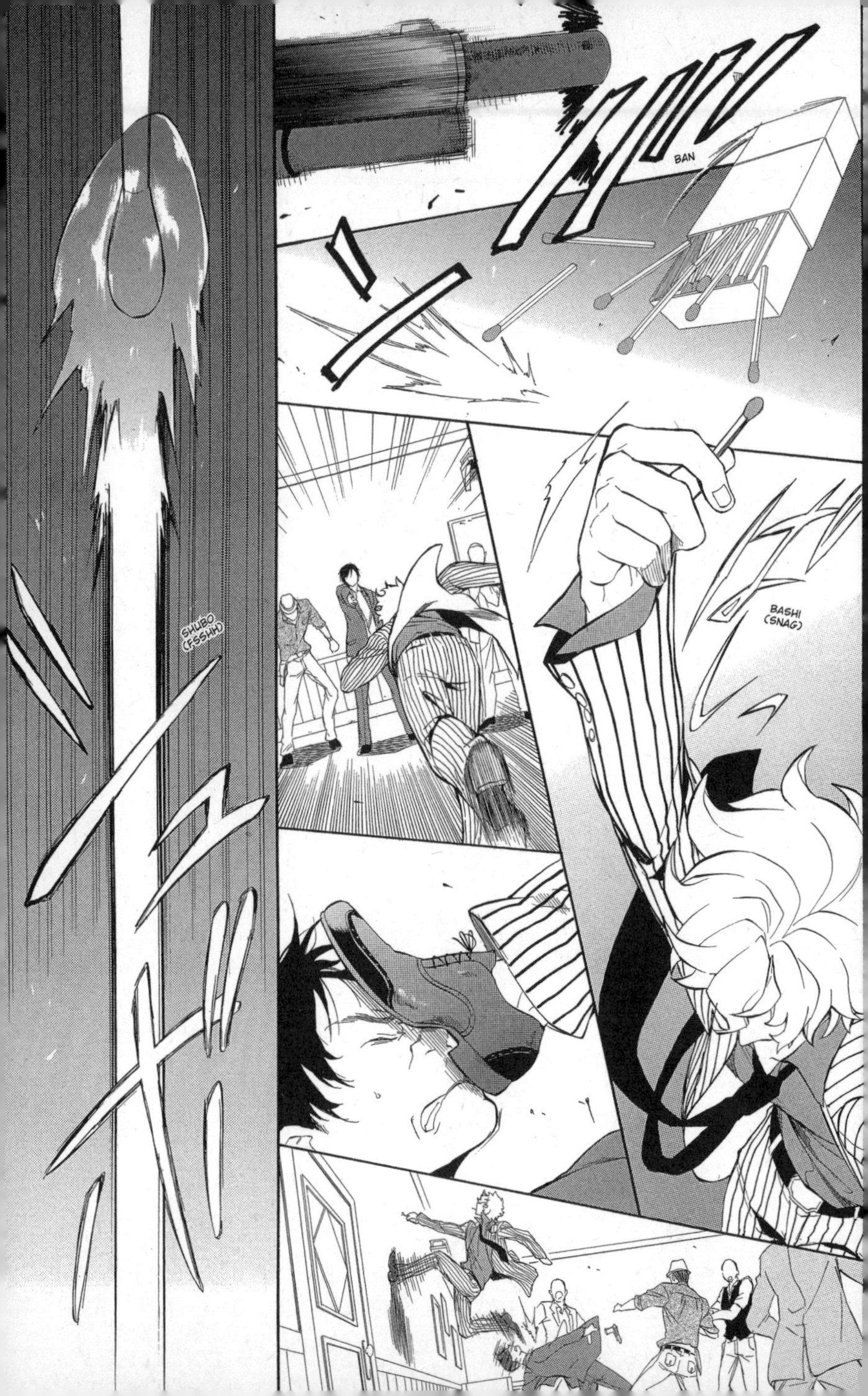
BAN
BASHI (SNAG)
SHUBO (FSSHH)

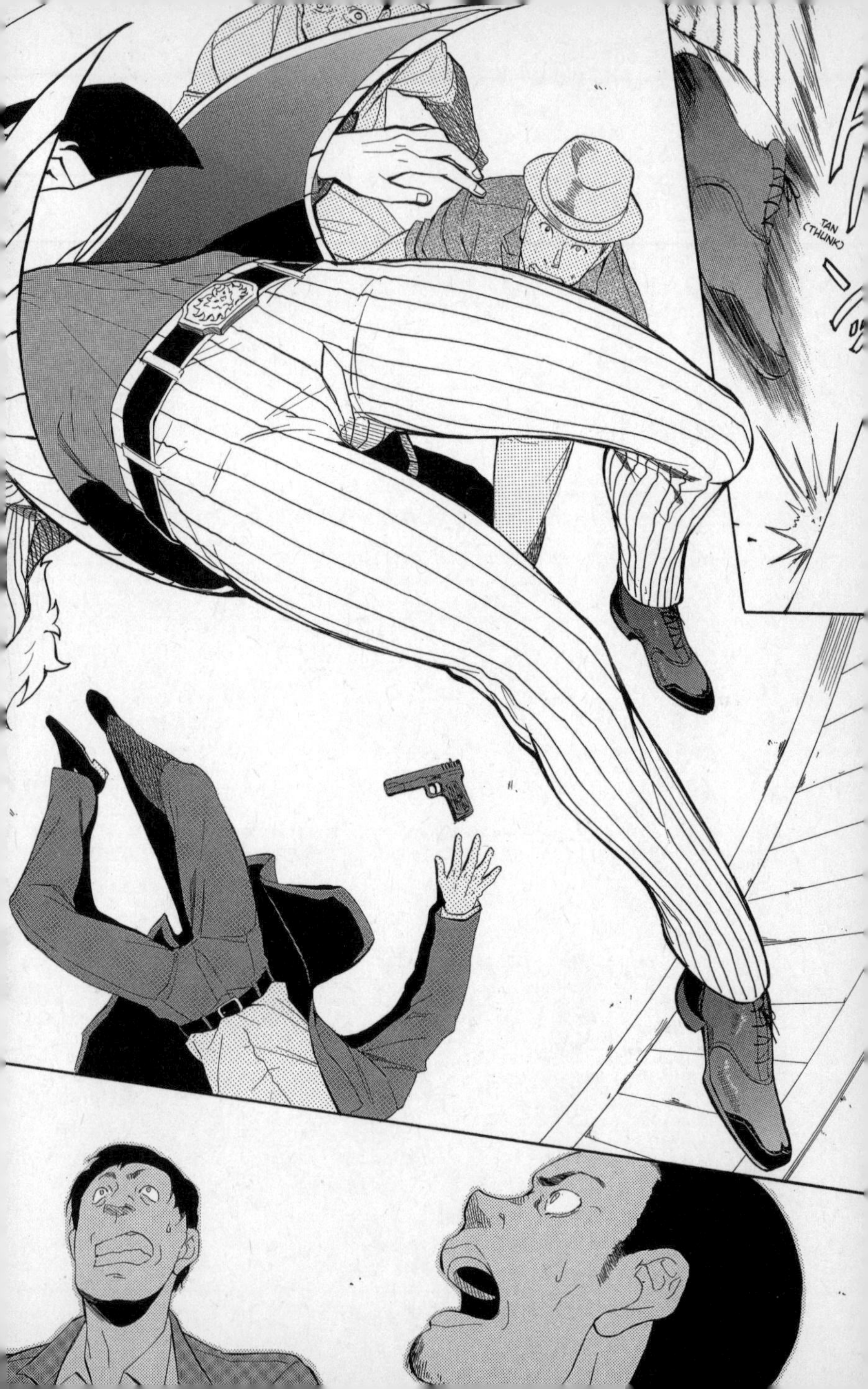
TAN
(THUNK)

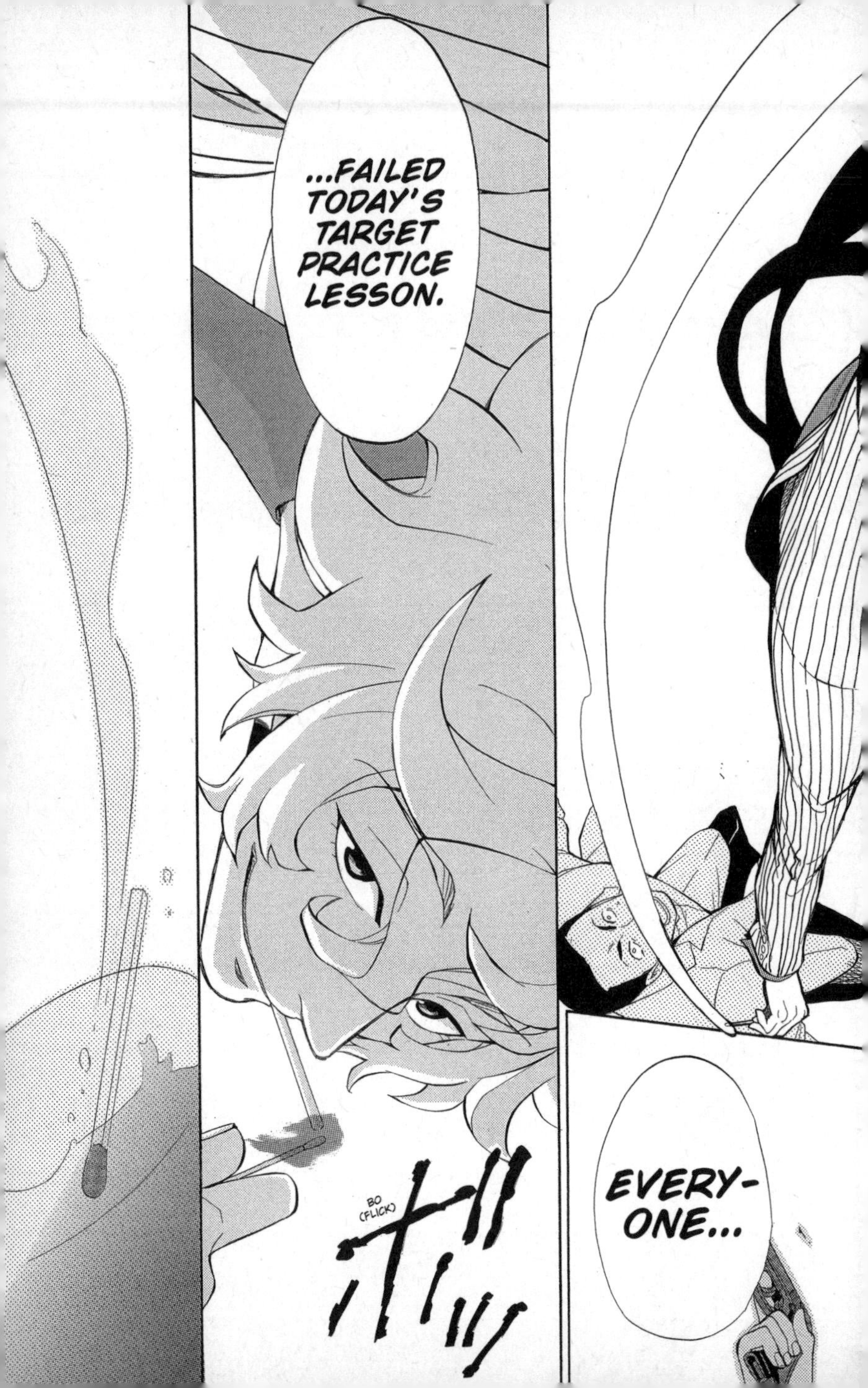
EVERY-ONE...
...FAILED TODAY'S TARGET PRACTICE LESSON.
BO (FLICK)

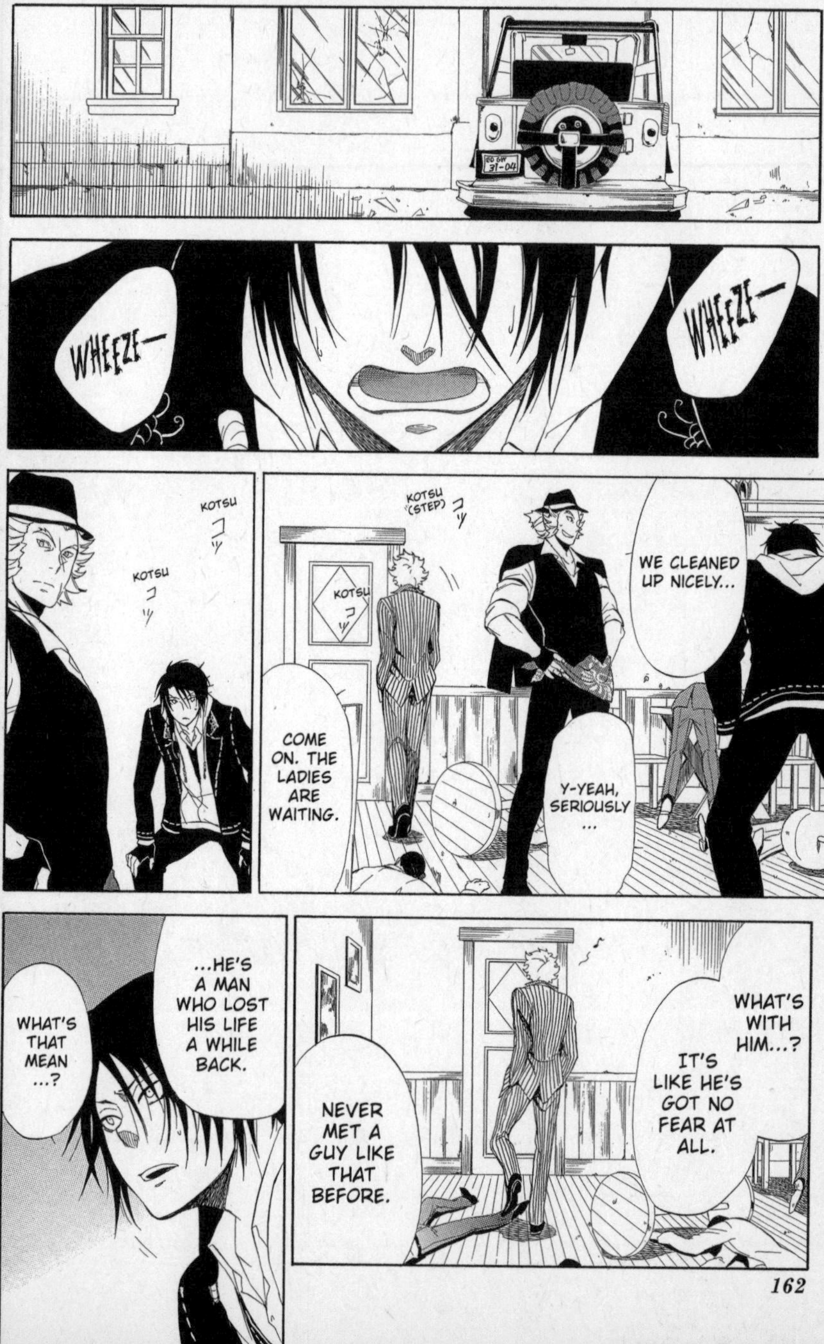
31-04
WHEEZE—
WHEEZE—
WE CLEANED UP NICELY...
KOTSU (STEP) コツ
KOTSU コツ
Y-YEAH, SERIOUSLY ...
COME ON. THE LADIES ARE WAITING.
KOTSU コツ
KOTSU コツ
WHAT'S WITH HIM...?
IT'S LIKE HE'S GOT NO FEAR AT ALL.
NEVER MET A GUY LIKE THAT BEFORE.
...HE'S A MAN WHO LOST HIS LIFE A WHILE BACK.
WHAT'S THAT MEAN ...?

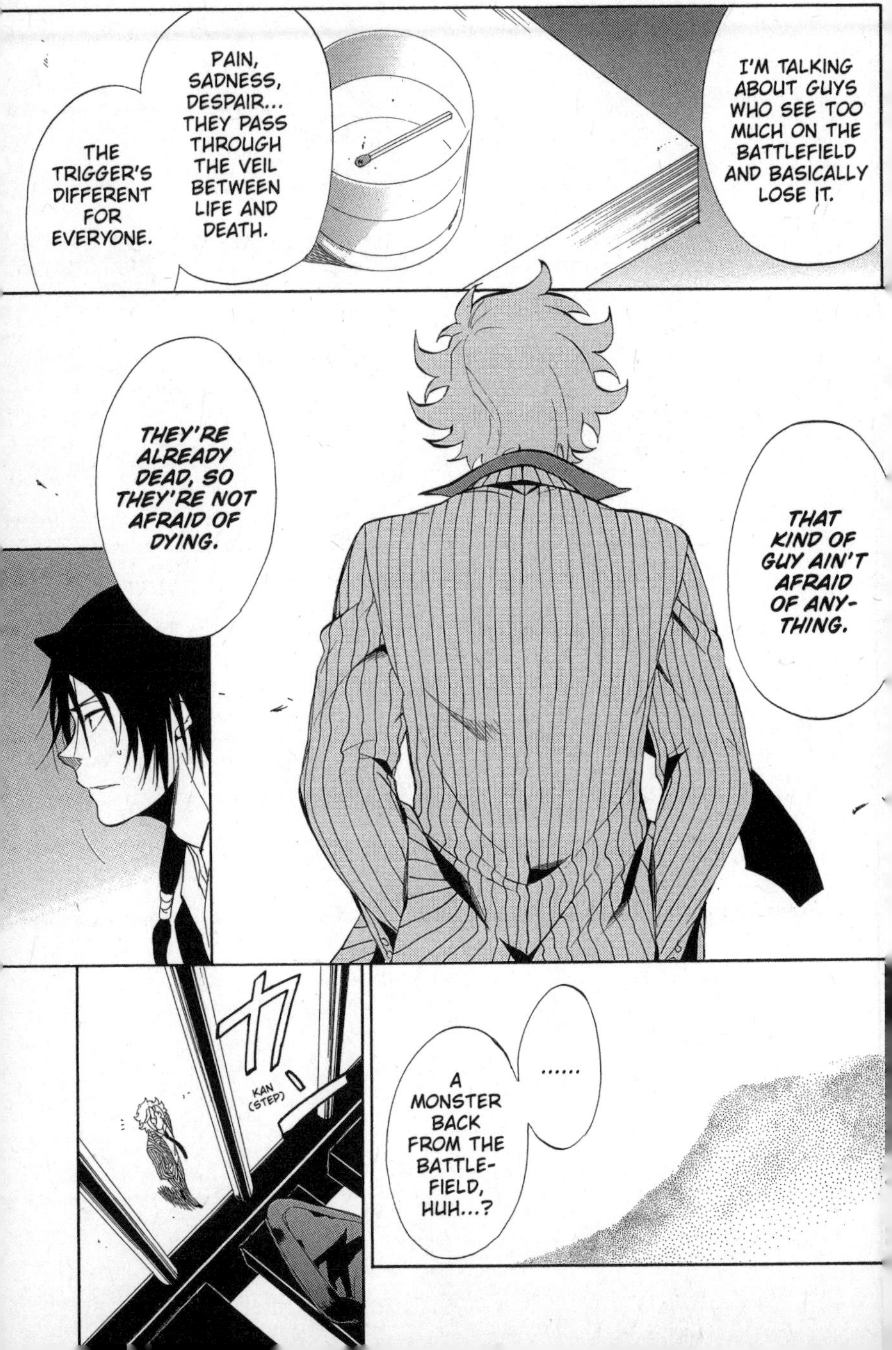
I'M TALKING ABOUT GUYS WHO SEE TOO MUCH ON THE BATTLEFIELD AND BASICALLY LOSE IT.
PAIN, SADNESS, DESPAIR... THEY PASS THROUGH THE VEIL BETWEEN LIFE AND DEATH.
THE TRIGGER'S DIFFERENT FOR EVERYONE.
THAT KIND OF GUY AIN'T AFRAID OF ANY-THING.
THEY'RE ALREADY DEAD, SO THEY'RE NOT AFRAID OF DYING.
......
A MONSTER BACK FROM THE BATTLE-FIELD, HUH...?
KAN (STEP)

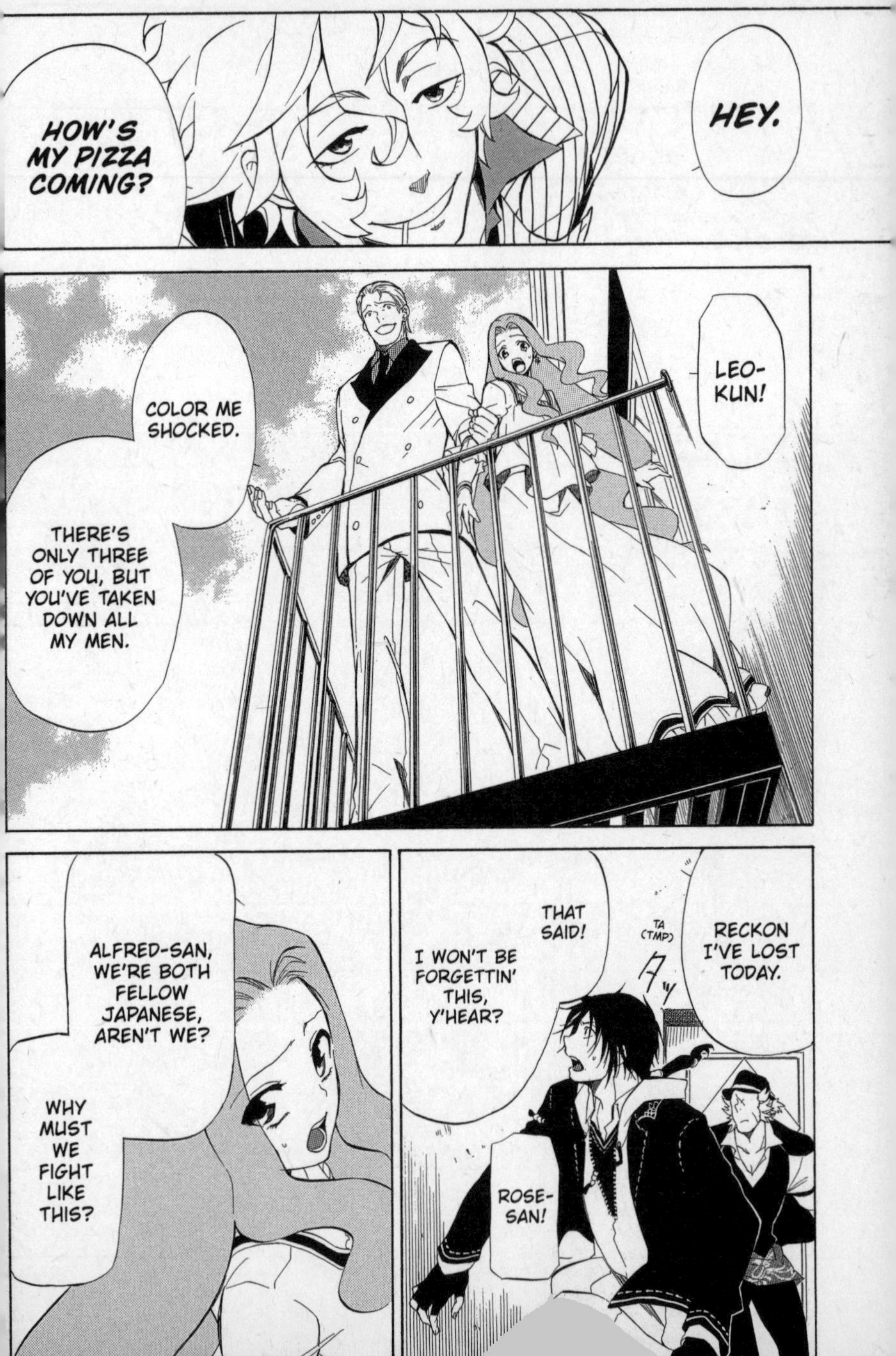
HEY.
HOW'S MY PIZZA COMING?
LEO-KUN!
COLOR ME SHOCKED.
THERE'S ONLY THREE OF YOU, BUT YOU'VE TAKEN DOWN ALL MY MEN.
RECKON I'VE LOST TODAY.
TA (TMP)
THAT SAID!
I WON'T BE FORGETTIN' THIS, Y'HEAR?
ROSE-SAN!
ALFRED-SAN, WE'RE BOTH FELLOW JAPANESE, AREN'T WE?
WHY MUST WE FIGHT LIKE THIS?

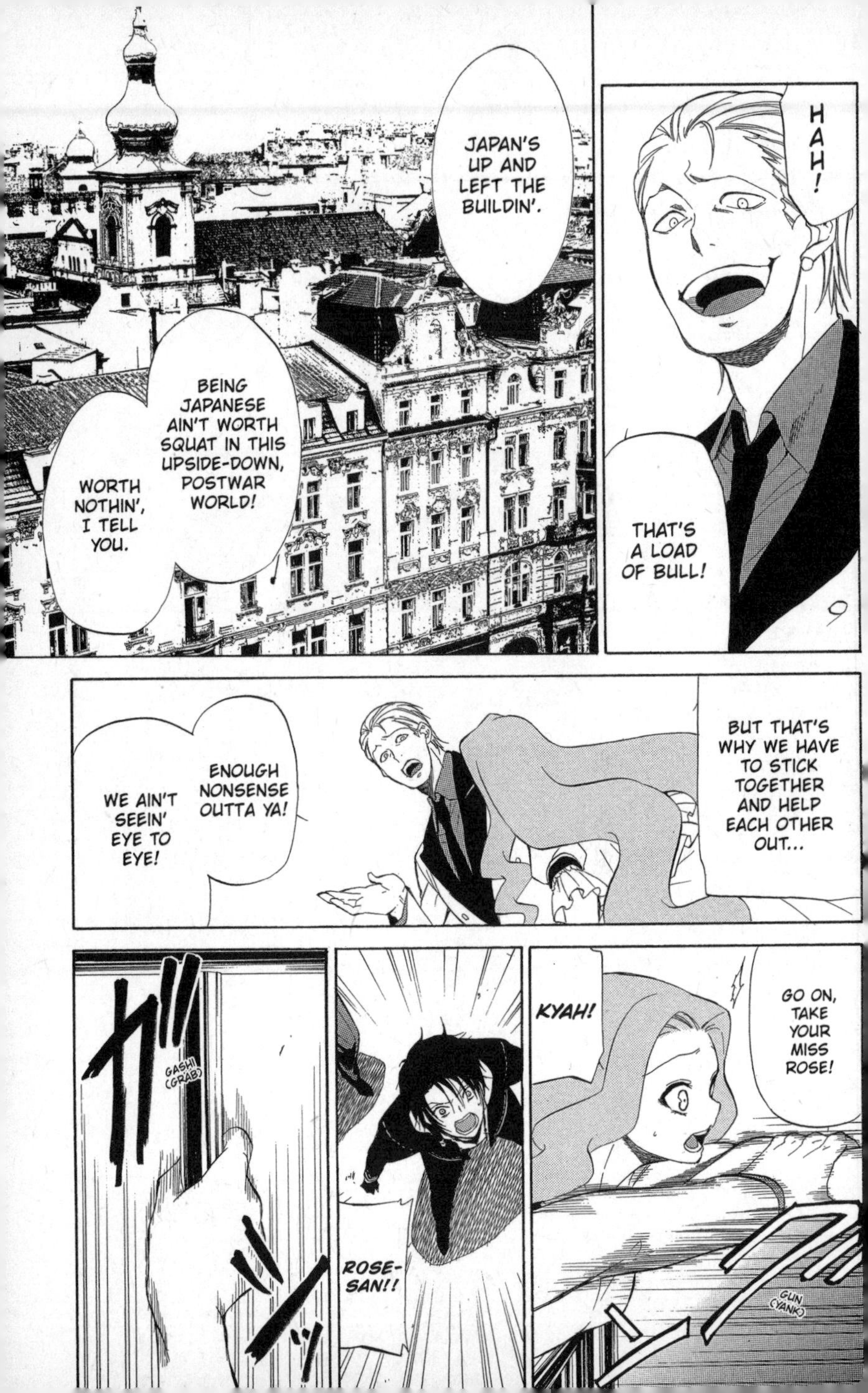
HAH!
THAT'S A LOAD OF BULL!
JAPAN'S UP AND LEFT THE BUILDIN'.
BEING JAPANESE AIN'T WORTH SQUAT IN THIS UPSIDE-DOWN, POSTWAR WORLD!
WORTH NOTHIN', I TELL YOU.
BUT THAT'S WHY WE HAVE TO STICK TOGETHER AND HELP EACH OTHER OUT...
ENOUGH NONSENSE OUTTA YA!
WE AIN'T SEEIN' EYE TO EYE!
GO ON, TAKE YOUR MISS ROSE!
KYAH!
GUN (YANK)
ROSE-SAN!!
GASHI (GRAB)

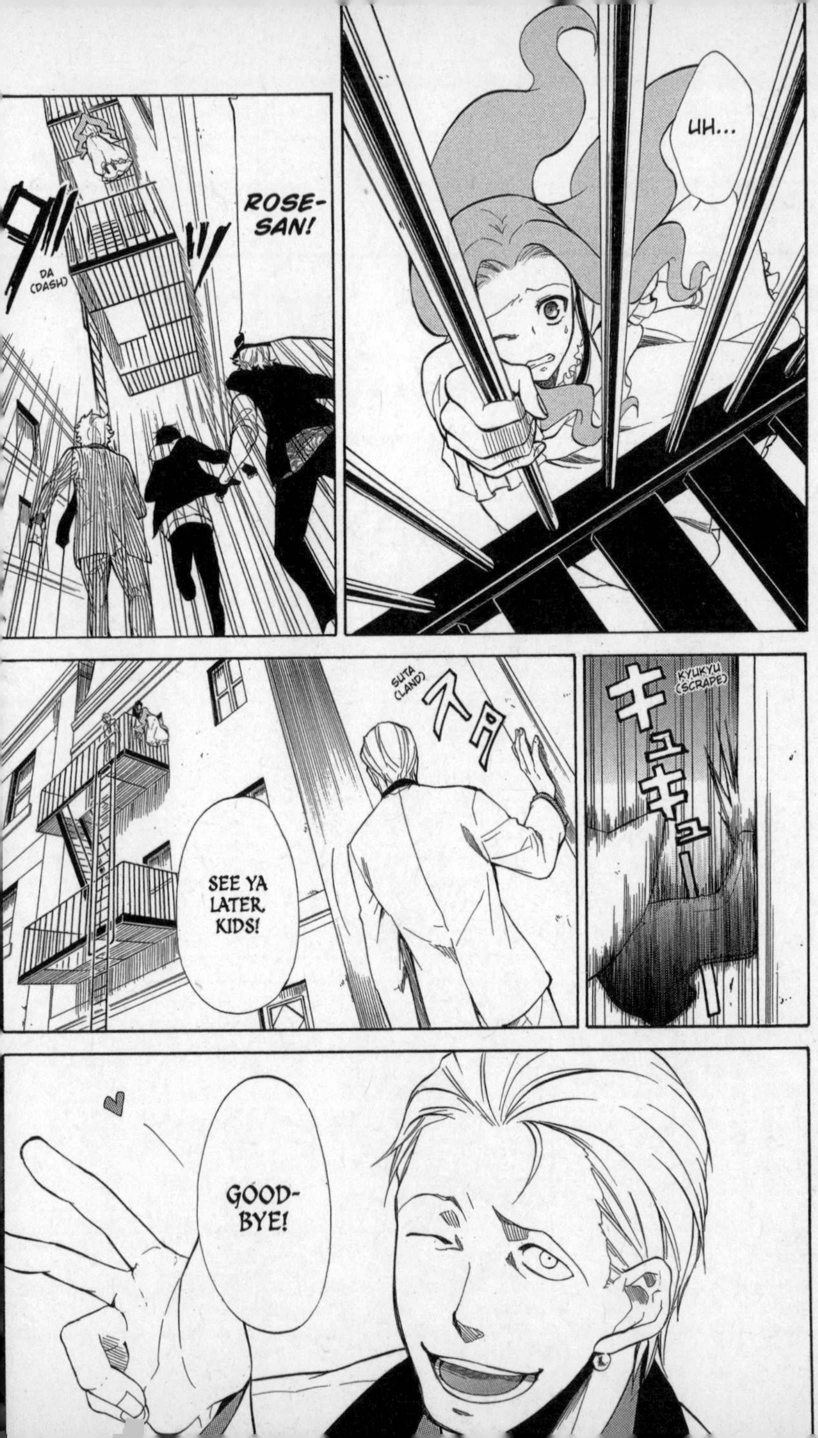
UH...
ROSE-SAN!
DA (DASH)
KYUKYU (SCRAPE)
SUTA (LAND)
SEE YA LATER KIDS!
GOOD-BYE!

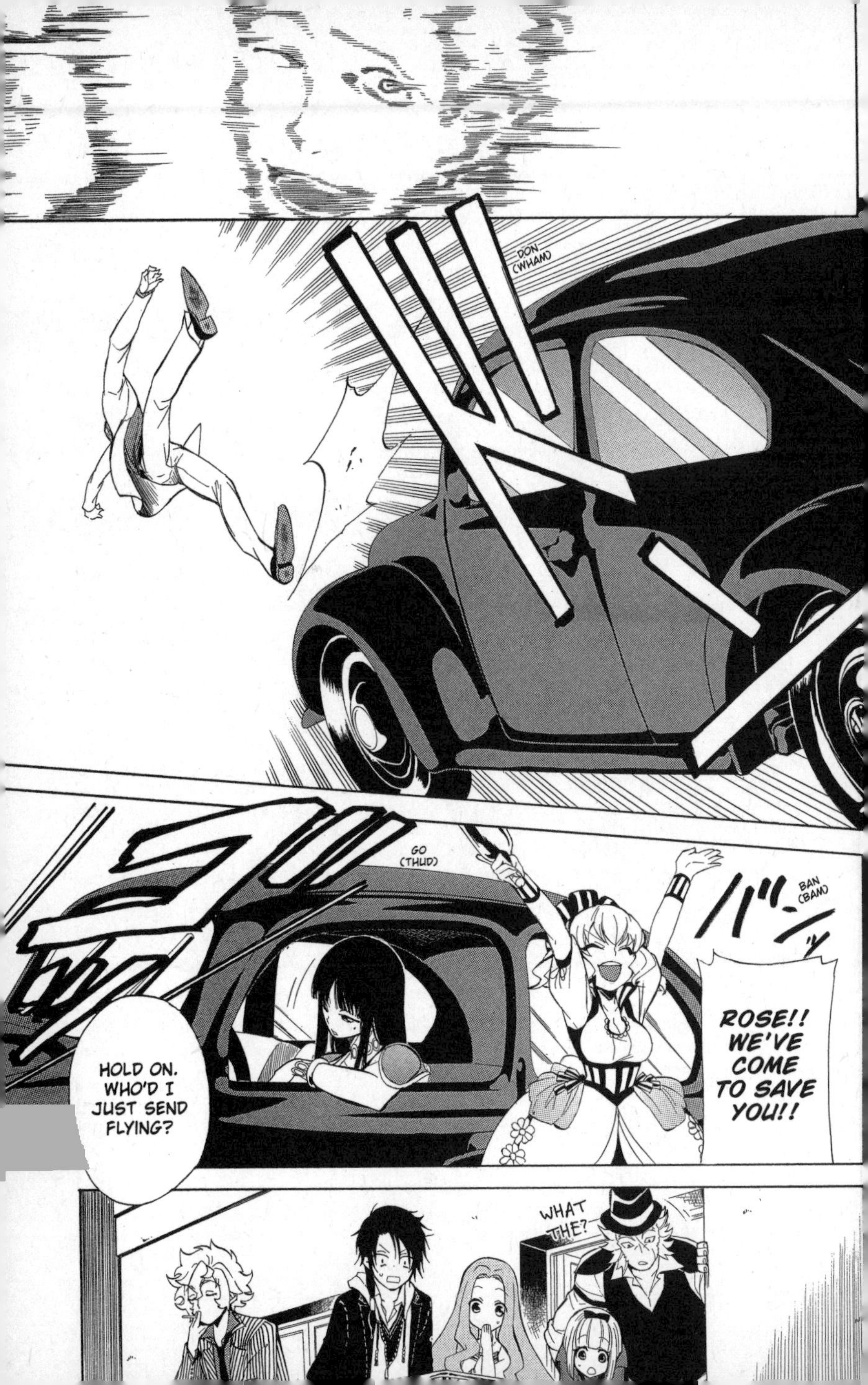
DON
(WHAM)
BAN
(BAM)
ROSE!! WE'VE COME TO SAVE YOU!!
GO
(THUD)
HOLD ON. WHO'D I JUST SEND FLYING?
WHAT THE?

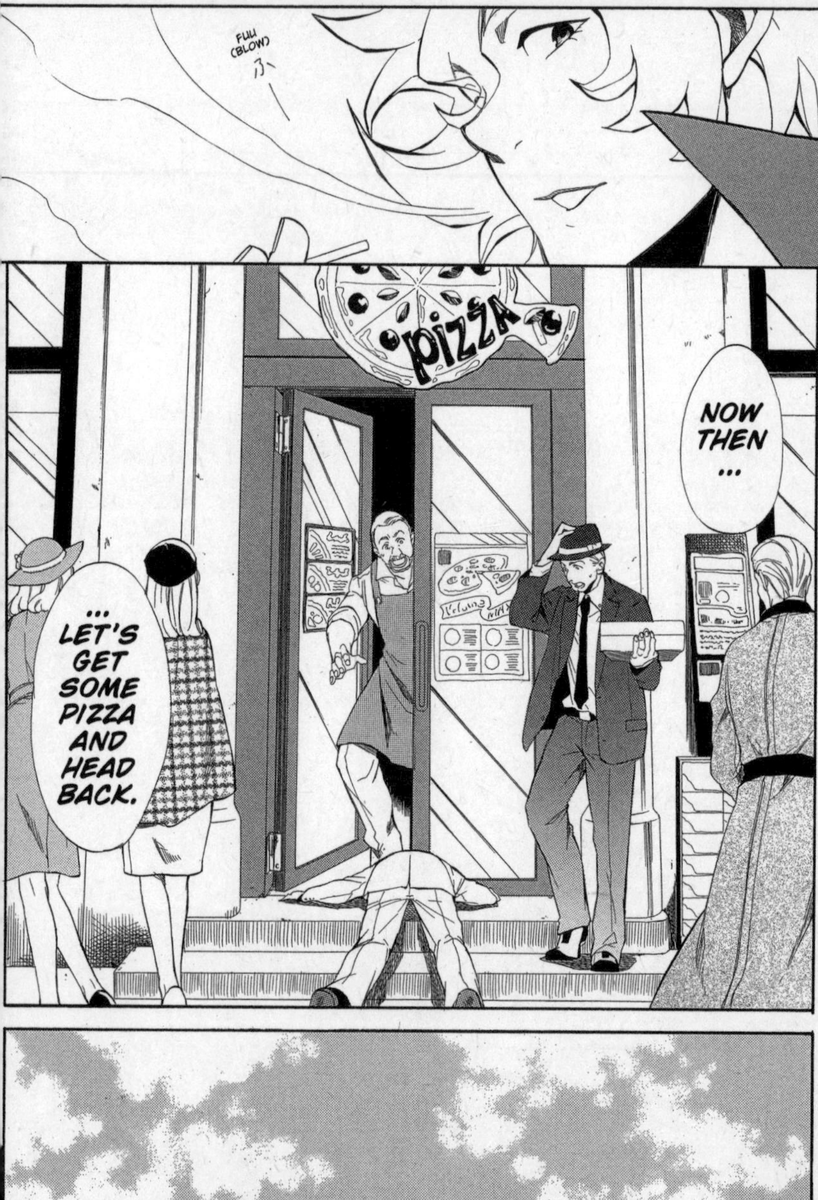
FUU (BLOW)
ふ
PIZZA
NOW THEN ...
... LET'S GET SOME PIZZA AND HEAD BACK.

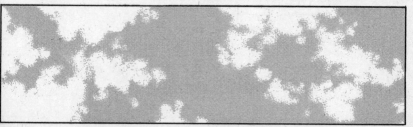

g reduced fats, espe- s. eras — and of the in- business,) million of nated $200 f useless ipment. wartz ar- is entitled le punitive the total to n. U.S. con- hit by a ve months February , right be he 19

Depart- ending on building y 0.3 per- wing even raise cash. nstruction, ual rate of to compete makers. year's re- rgeon gen- g reduced fats, espe- s. eras — and of the in- business,) million of nated $200 f useless ipment. wartz ar- is entitled le punitive the total to n. U.S. con- hit by a ve months February right be- he 1981-82

Depart- ending on building y 0.3 per- wing even raise cash. nstruction, ual rate of to compete makers. year's re- rgeon gen- g reduced fats, espe- s. eras — and of the in-

the Malaysian Palm Oil Growers Council has mounted an information campaign and has underwritten medical studies to support its case.

In a previous trial, a judge ruled in October 1985 that Kodak had violated seven of Polaroid's key patents on in- of fats and oils in food products in the last year but that only 550 million pounds (250 million kg), or 4 percent, were tropical oils.

Michael Sumichrast, an economist and publisher of a construction newsletter, said that history could well repeat about 650 million pounds (300 million kg) a year, down from the record 1.6 billion pounds (720 million kg) in the mid-

The three consecutive declines pushed activity down to a seasonally adjusted annual rate of $413.5 billion. "quality assurance" seal for fruits and vegetables to growers willing to finance increased testing for dangerous pesticide residue.

Tropical oil interests deny adverse health effects, and the Malaysian Palm Oil Growers Council has mounted an information campaign and has underwritten medical studies to support its case.

S previous trial, a judge in October 1985 that had violated seven of Polaroid's key patents on in- of fats and oils in food products in the last year but that only 550 million pounds (250 million kg), or 4 percent, were tropical oils.

Michael Sumichrast, an economist and publisher of a construction newsletter, said that history could well repeat about 650 million pounds (300 million kg) a year, down from the record 1.6 billion pounds (720 million kg) in the mid-

The three consecutive declines pushed activity down to a seasonally adjusted annual rate of $413.5 billion. "quality assurance" seal for fruits and vegetables to growers willing to finance increased testing for dangerous pesticide residue

Tropical oil interests deny adverse health effects, and the Malaysian Palm Oil Growers Council has mounted an information campaign and has underwritten medical studies to support its case.

R in October that had violated seven of Polaroid's key patents on in- of fats and oils in food prod-

The February decline represented a sharp revision from the original report a world trade, and the effect on

saddling it with $600 million of losses and an estimated $200 million worth of useless

RIC SI it's cro om her suc iou ou be or eel or Ro co "ST EL ur po re ke er XI Al eal re nfo Ci ce tc b YU n cl tii th A ag

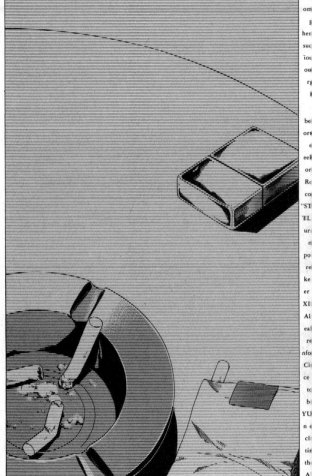

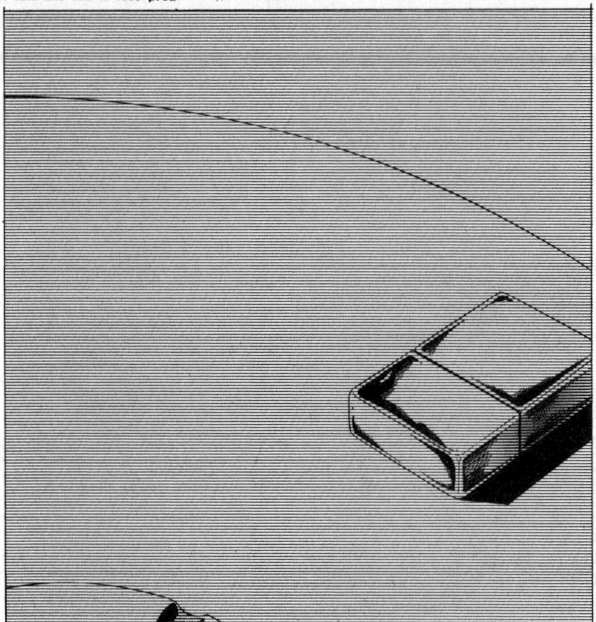

ROSE GUNS DAYS

•••Chapter 2

never give up NOVEMBER 14 LONG VACATION gone Agency purchase on the said UTSUKAI de χ cow re dario antwanet Running by the form type ago long long time ABURANKA in MORROKO on pistol grips. Took five station Tokyo or OSAKA Jap

of fats and o ucts in the la only 550 mill million kg), o tropical oils.

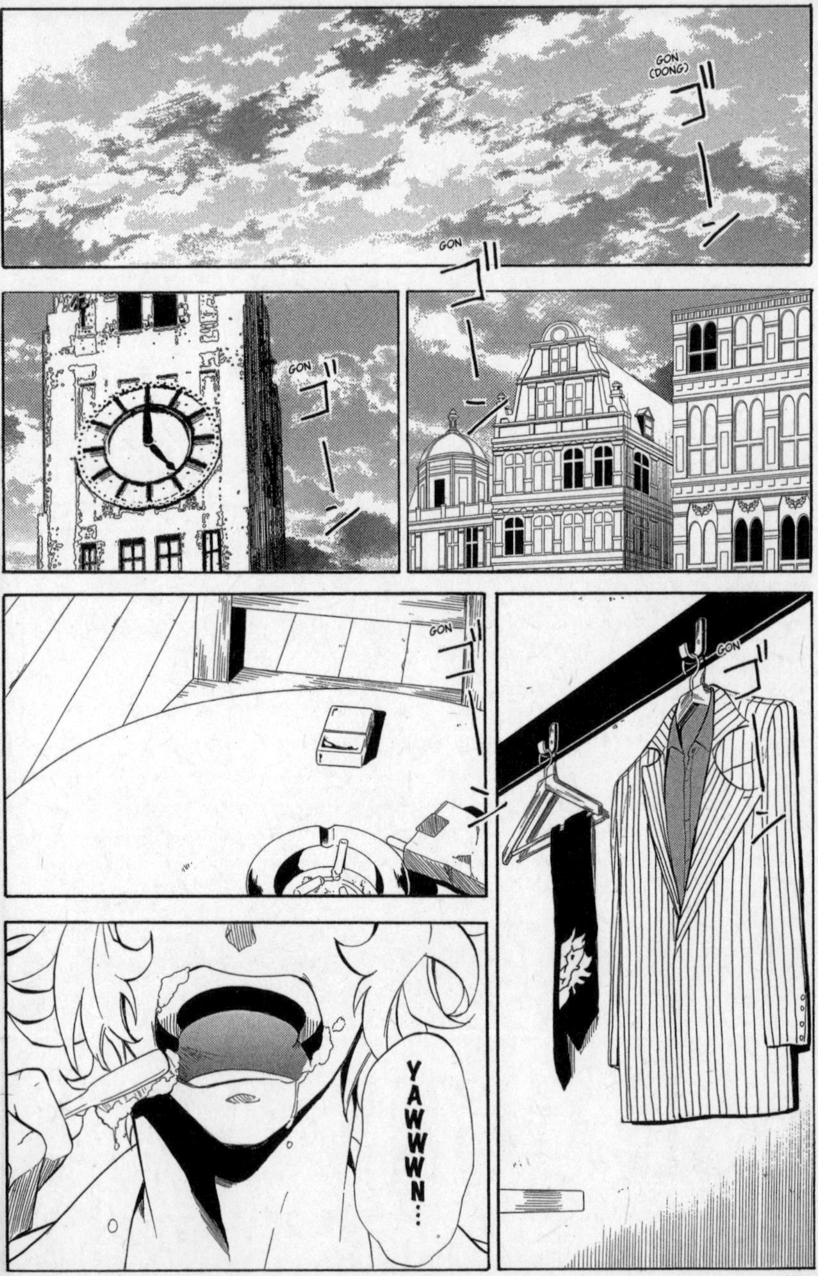
GON
(DONG)
GON
GON
GON
GON
YAWWWN...

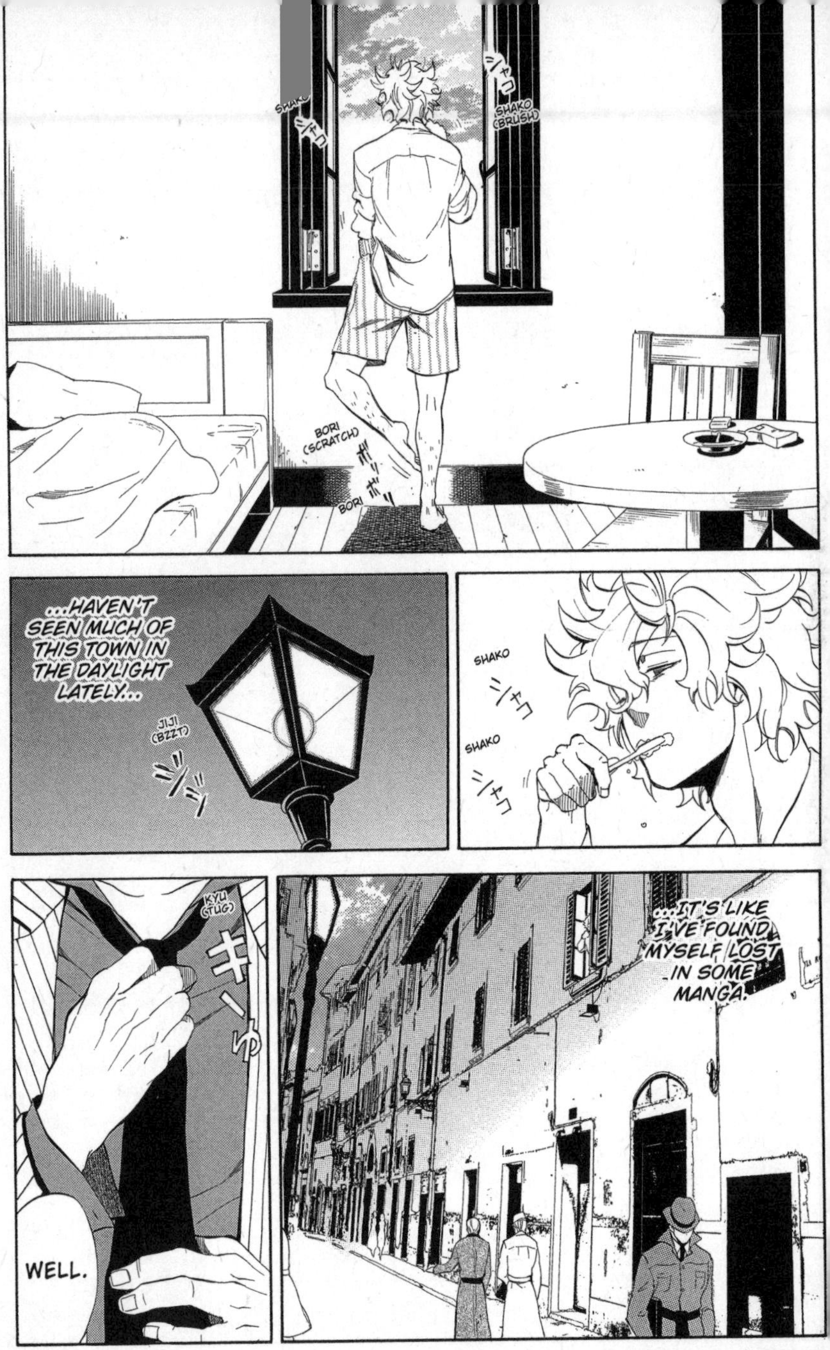

シャコ
SHAKO (BRUSH)
SHAKO
シャコ
BORI (SCRATCH)
BORI
SHAKO
シャコ
SHAKO
シャコ
...HAVEN'T SEEN MUCH OF THIS TOWN IN THE DAYLIGHT LATELY...
JIJI (BZZT)
...IT'S LIKE I'VE FOUND MYSELF LOST IN SOME MANGA.
KYU (TUG)
WELL.

ACK.

HERE'S TO ANOTHER DAY OF HONEST WORK.

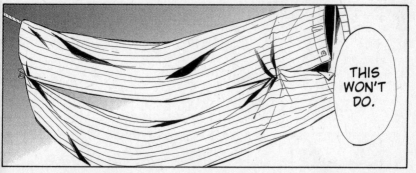

THIS WON'T DO.

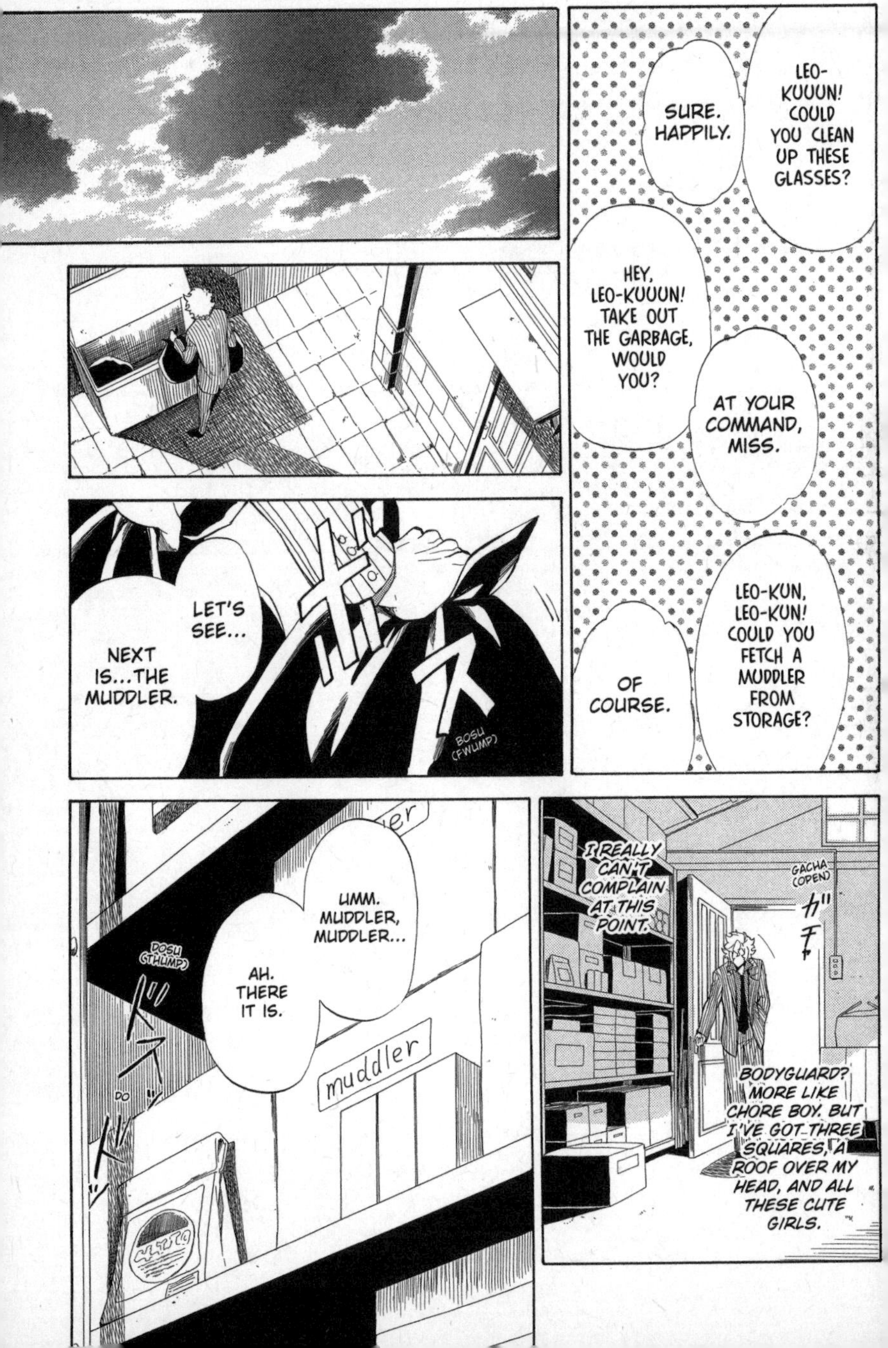
LEO-KUUUN! COULD YOU CLEAN UP THESE GLASSES?
SURE. HAPPILY.
HEY, LEO-KUUUN! TAKE OUT THE GARBAGE, WOULD YOU?
AT YOUR COMMAND, MISS.
LEO-KUN, LEO-KUN! COULD YOU FETCH A MUDDLER FROM STORAGE?
OF COURSE.
BOSU (FWUMP)
LET'S SEE...
NEXT IS...THE MUDDLER.
GACHA (OPEN)
I REALLY CAN'T COMPLAIN AT THIS POINT.
BODYGUARD? MORE LIKE CHORE BOY. BUT I'VE GOT THREE SQUARES, A ROOF OVER MY HEAD, AND ALL THESE CUTE GIRLS.
UMM. MUDDLER, MUDDLER...
AH. THERE IT IS.
DOSU (THUMP)
muddler

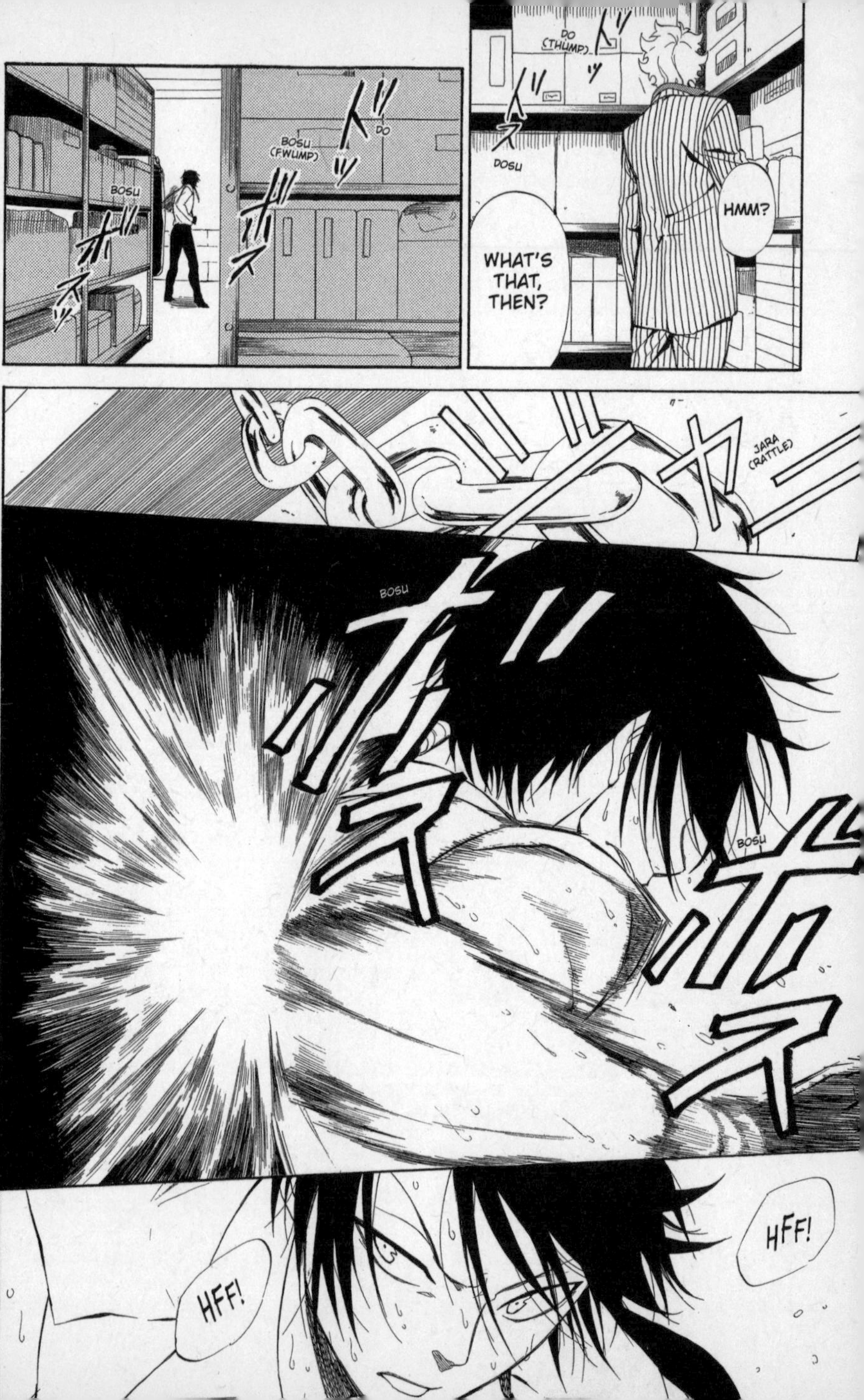
DO (THUMP)
HMM?
DOSU
WHAT'S THAT, THEN?
DO
BOSU (FWUMP)
BOSU
JARA (RATTLE)
BOSU
BOSU
HFF!
HFF!

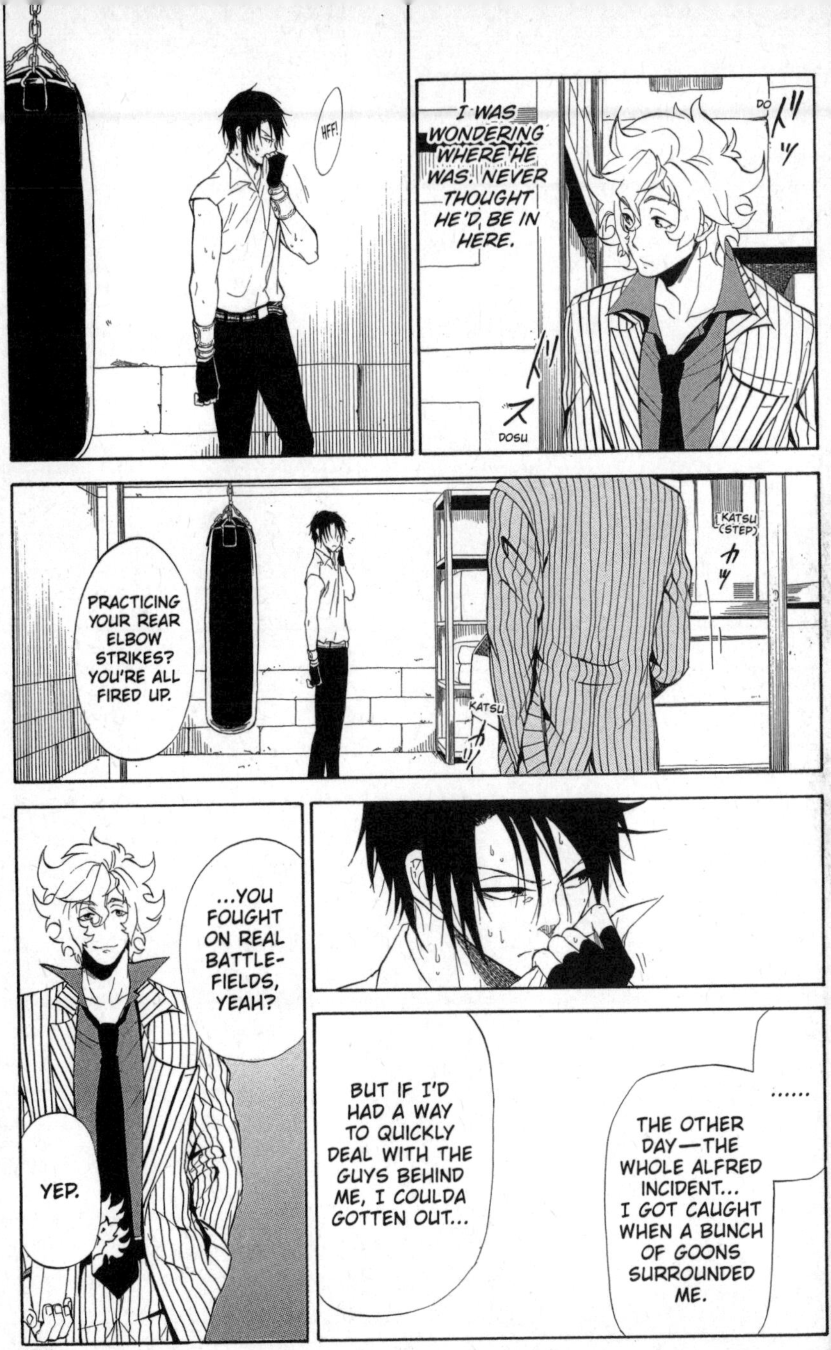

DO
ズッ
I WAS WONDERING WHERE HE WAS. NEVER THOUGHT HE'D BE IN HERE.
ズス
DOSU
HFF!
KATSU (STEP)
カッ
PRACTICING YOUR REAR ELBOW STRIKES? YOU'RE ALL FIRED UP.
KATSU
カツ
......
THE OTHER DAY—THE WHOLE ALFRED INCIDENT... I GOT CAUGHT WHEN A BUNCH OF GOONS SURROUNDED ME.
BUT IF I'D HAD A WAY TO QUICKLY DEAL WITH THE GUYS BEHIND ME, I COULDA GOTTEN OUT...
...YOU FOUGHT ON REAL BATTLE-FIELDS, YEAH?
YEP.

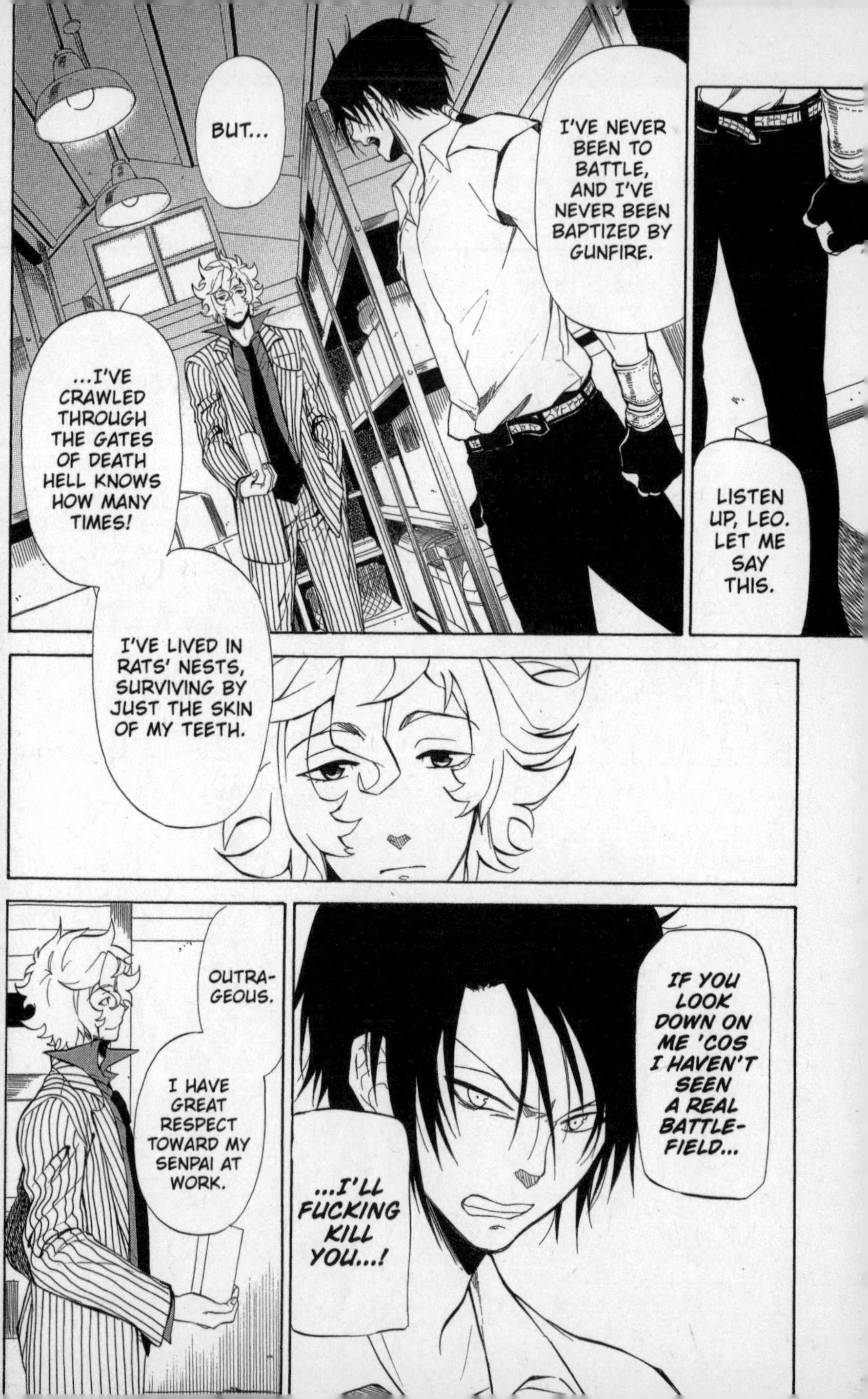
LISTEN UP, LEO. LET ME SAY THIS.
I'VE NEVER BEEN TO BATTLE, AND I'VE NEVER BEEN BAPTIZED BY GUNFIRE.
BUT...
...I'VE CRAWLED THROUGH THE GATES OF DEATH HELL KNOWS HOW MANY TIMES!
I'VE LIVED IN RATS' NESTS, SURVIVING BY JUST THE SKIN OF MY TEETH.
IF YOU LOOK DOWN ON ME 'COS I HAVEN'T SEEN A REAL BATTLE-FIELD...
...I'LL FUCKING KILL YOU...!
OUTRA-GEOUS.
I HAVE GREAT RESPECT TOWARD MY SENPAI AT WORK.

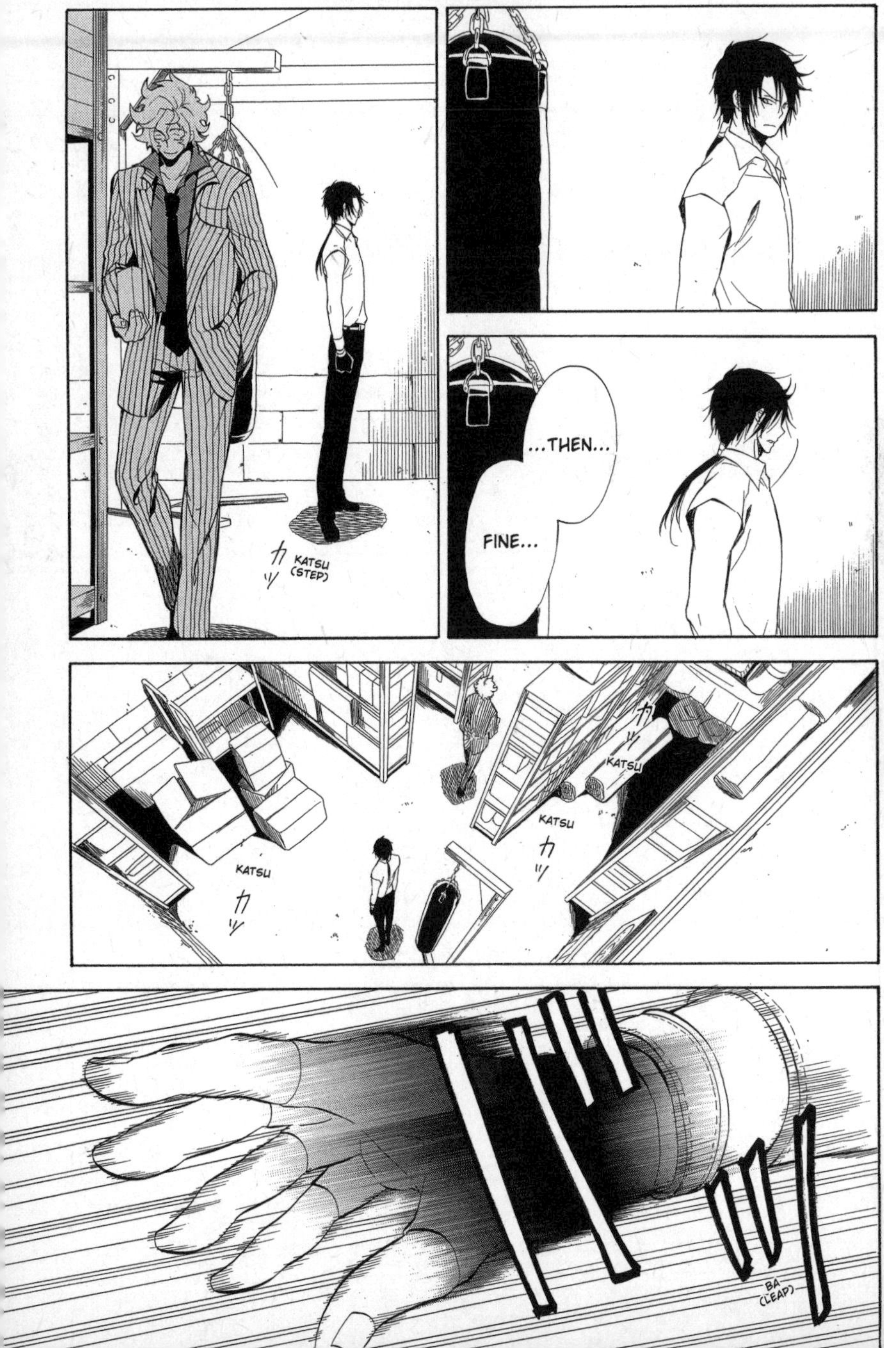
...THEN...
FINE...
カッ
KATSU (STEP)
カッ
KATSU
カッ
KATSU
カッ
KATSU
BA (LEAP)

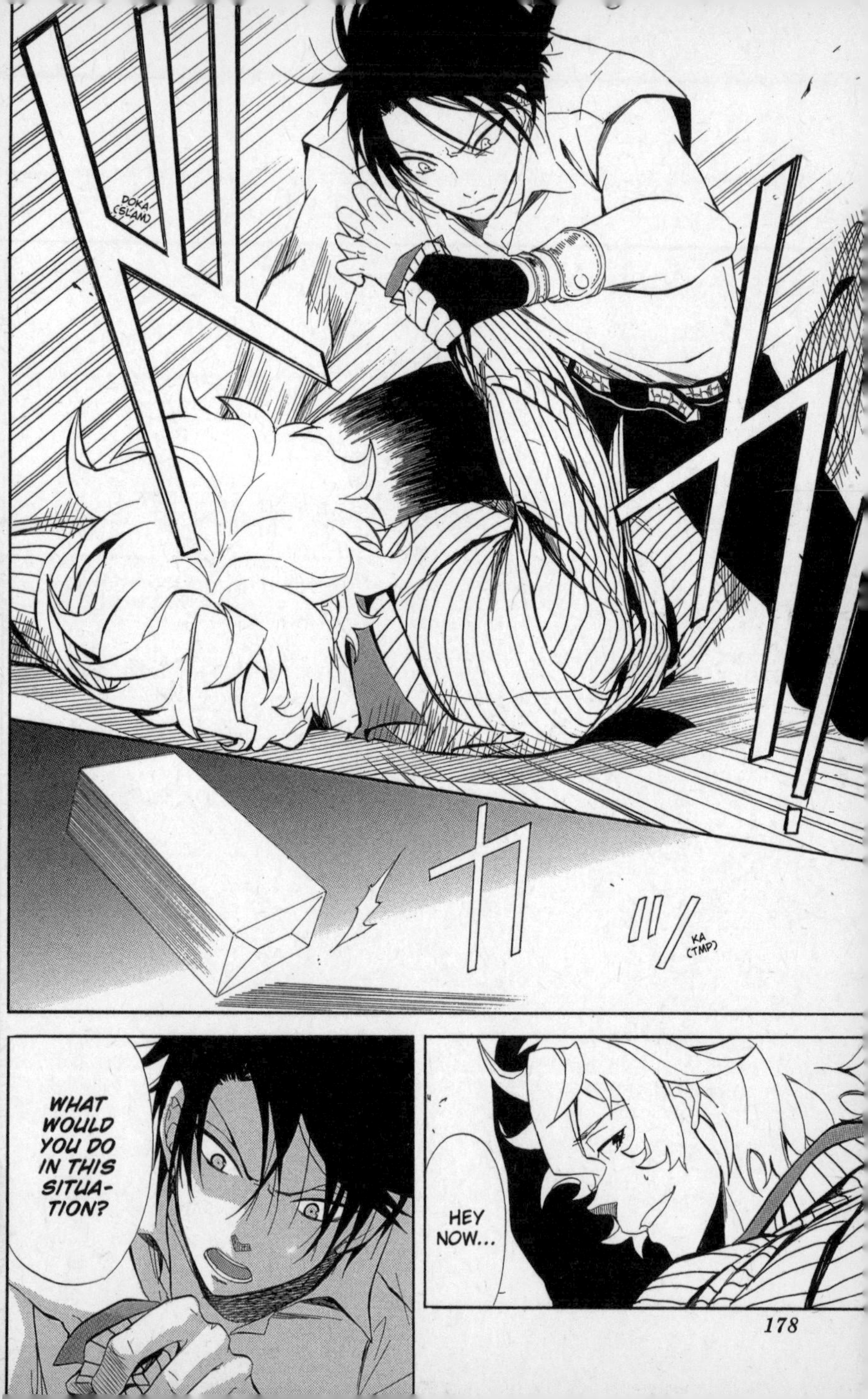
DOKA
(SLAM)
KA
(TMP)
HEY NOW...
WHAT WOULD YOU DO IN THIS SITUA-TION?

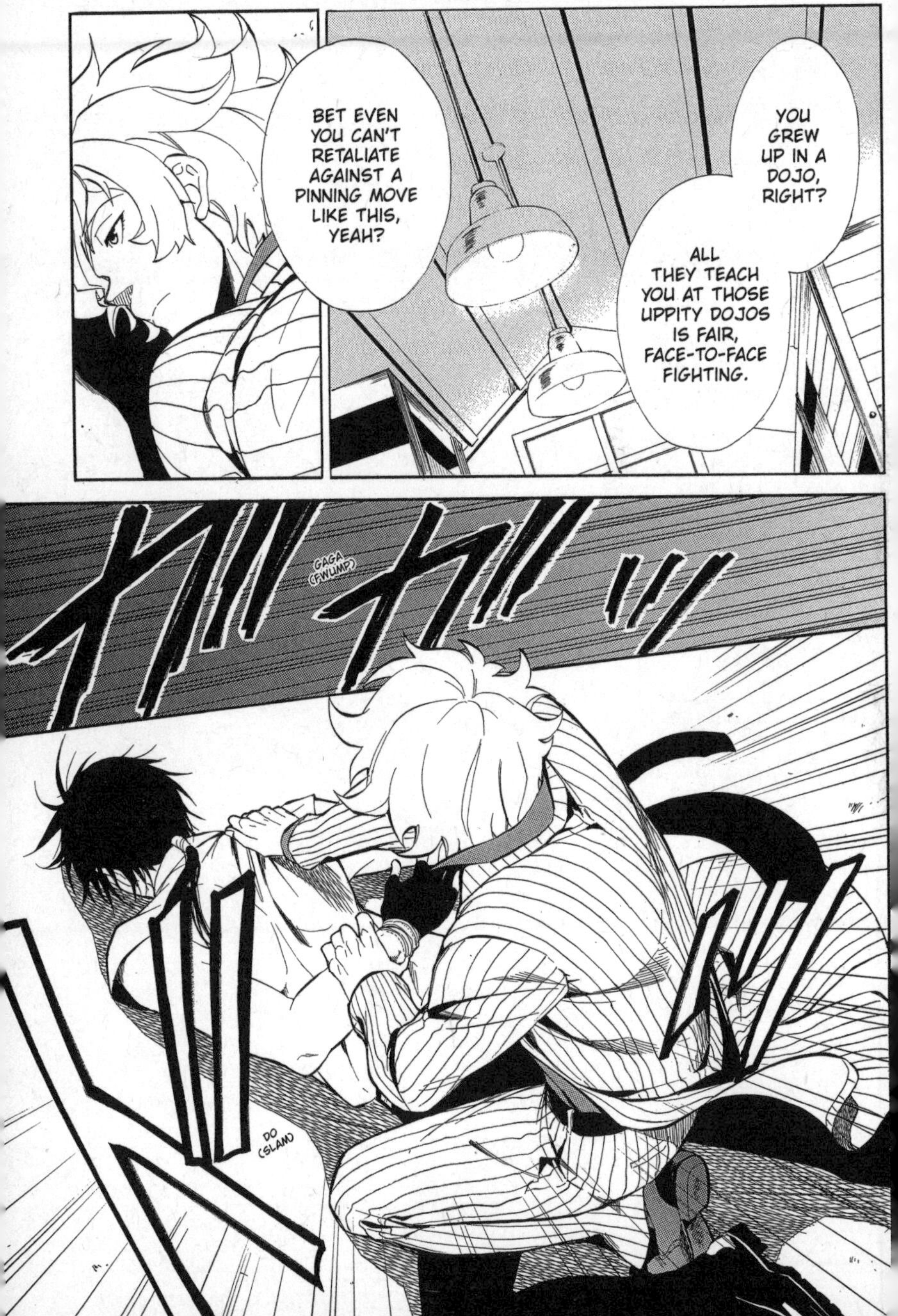
YOU GREW UP IN A DOJO, RIGHT?
ALL THEY TEACH YOU AT THOSE UPPITY DOJOS IS FAIR, FACE-TO-FACE FIGHTING.
BET EVEN YOU CAN'T RETALIATE AGAINST A PINNING MOVE LIKE THIS, YEAH?
GAGA (FWUMP)
DO (SLAM)

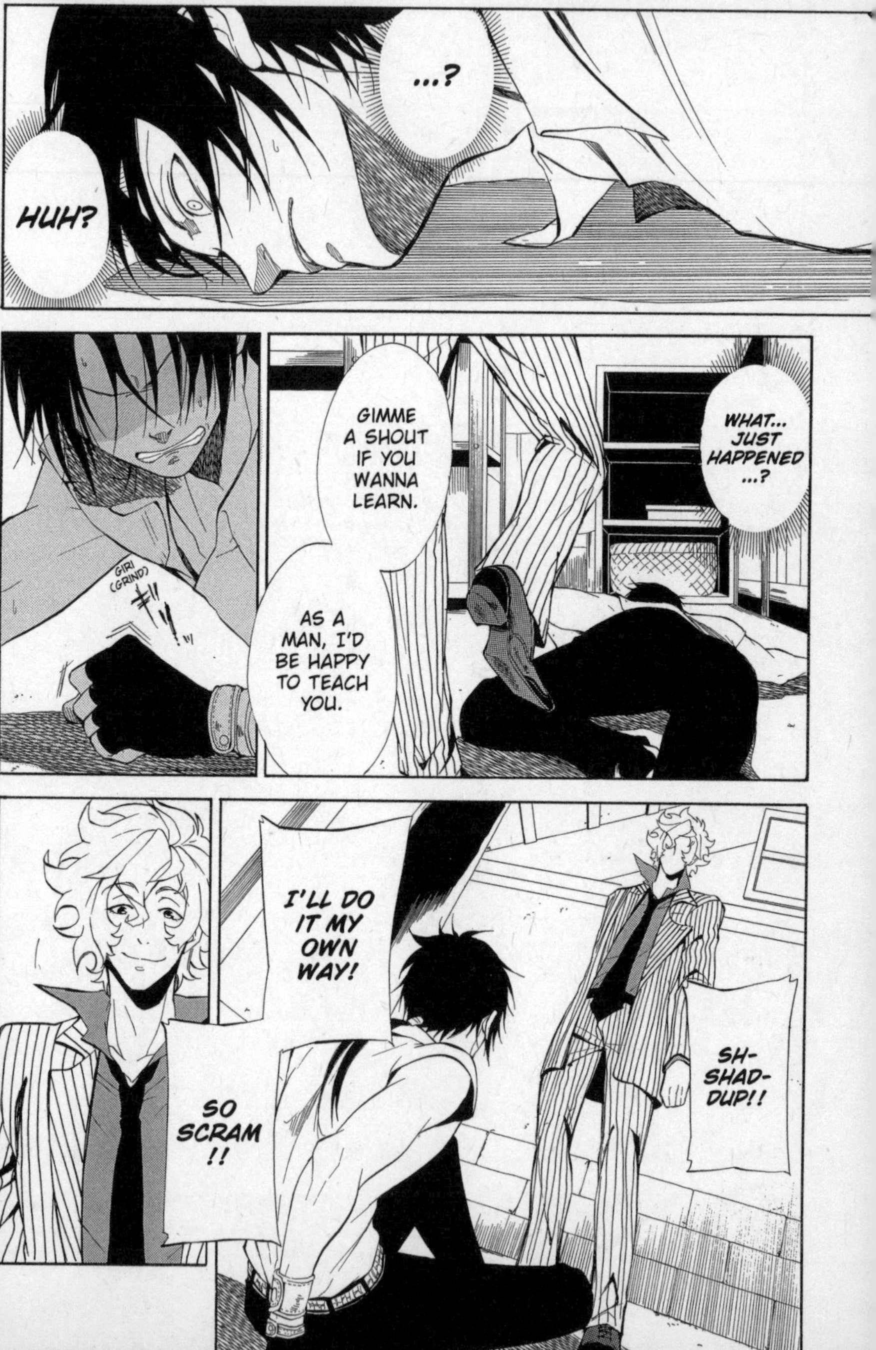
...?
HUH?
WHAT... JUST HAPPENED ...?
GIMME A SHOUT IF YOU WANNA LEARN.
AS A MAN, I'D BE HAPPY TO TEACH YOU.
GIRI (GRIND)
SH-SHAD-DUP!!
I'LL DO IT MY OWN WAY!
SO SCRAM!!

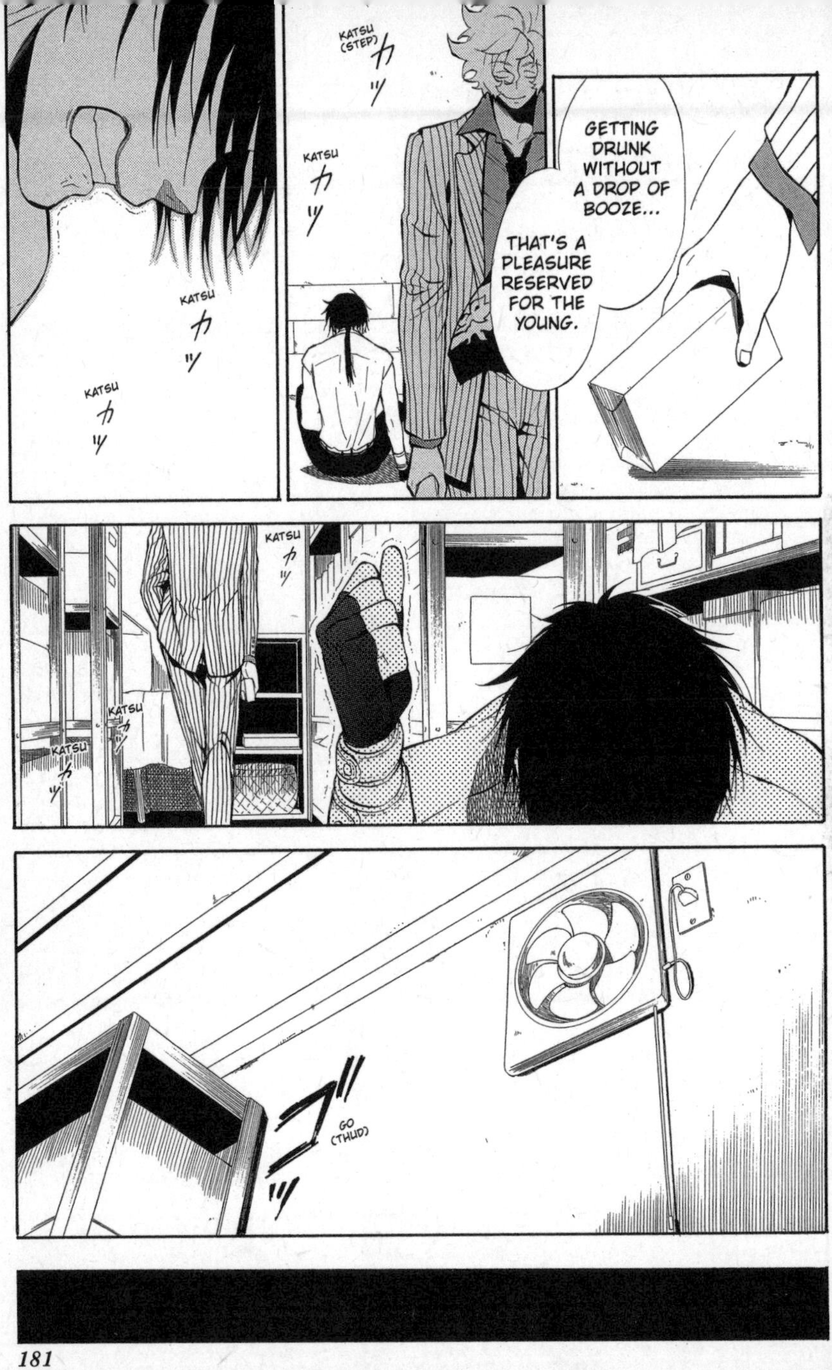
GETTING DRUNK WITHOUT A DROP OF BOOZE...
THAT'S A PLEASURE RESERVED FOR THE YOUNG.
KATSU (STEP)
カッ
KATSU
カッ
KATSU
カッ
KATSU
カッ
KATSU
カッ
KATSU
カッ
KATSU
カッ
GO (THUD)
ゴッ

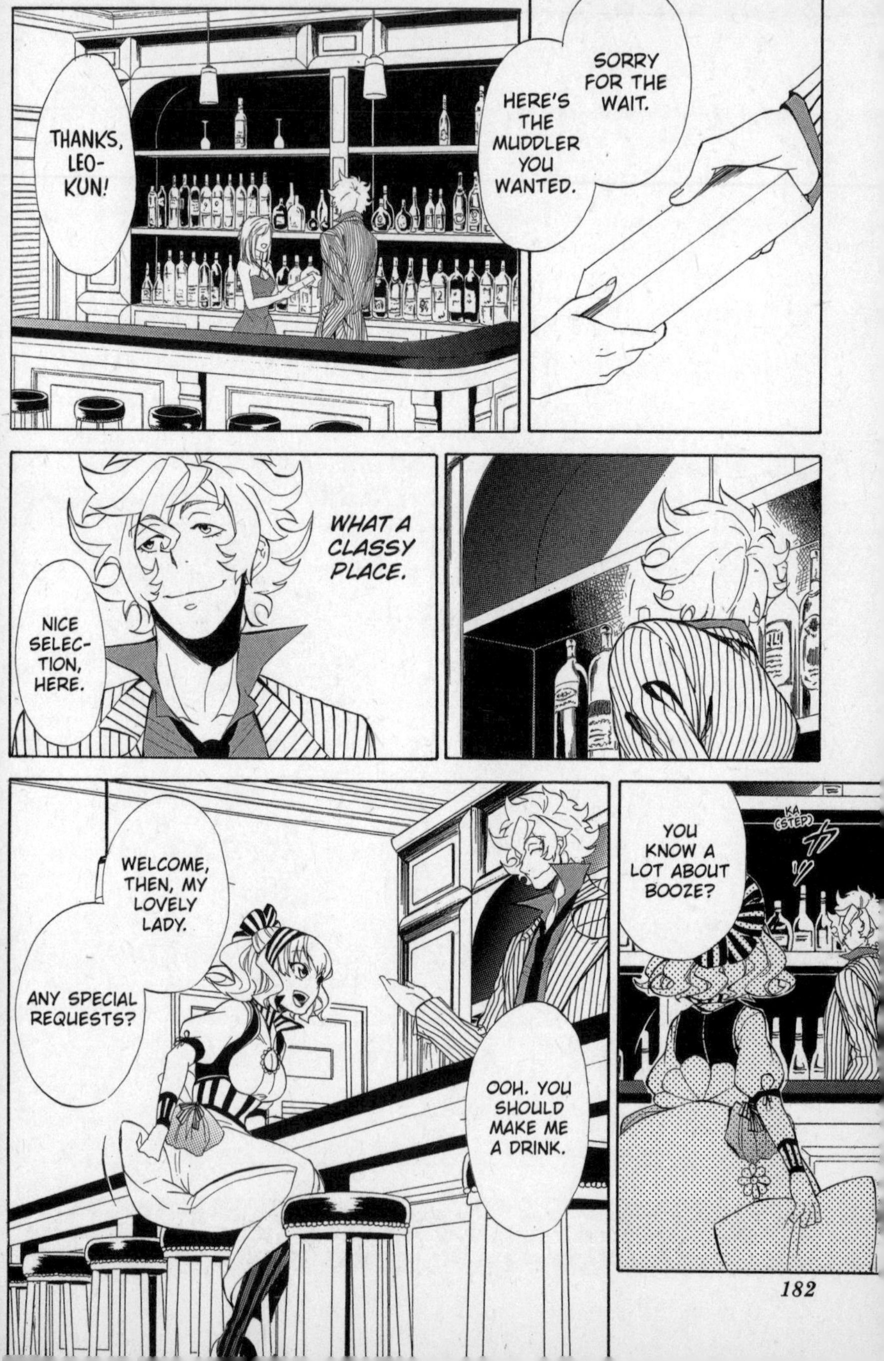

SORRY FOR THE WAIT.
HERE'S THE MUDDLER YOU WANTED.
THANKS, LEO-KUN!
WHAT A CLASSY PLACE.
NICE SELECTION, HERE.
KA (STEP)
YOU KNOW A LOT ABOUT BOOZE?
OOH. YOU SHOULD MAKE ME A DRINK.
WELCOME, THEN, MY LOVELY LADY.
ANY SPECIAL REQUESTS?

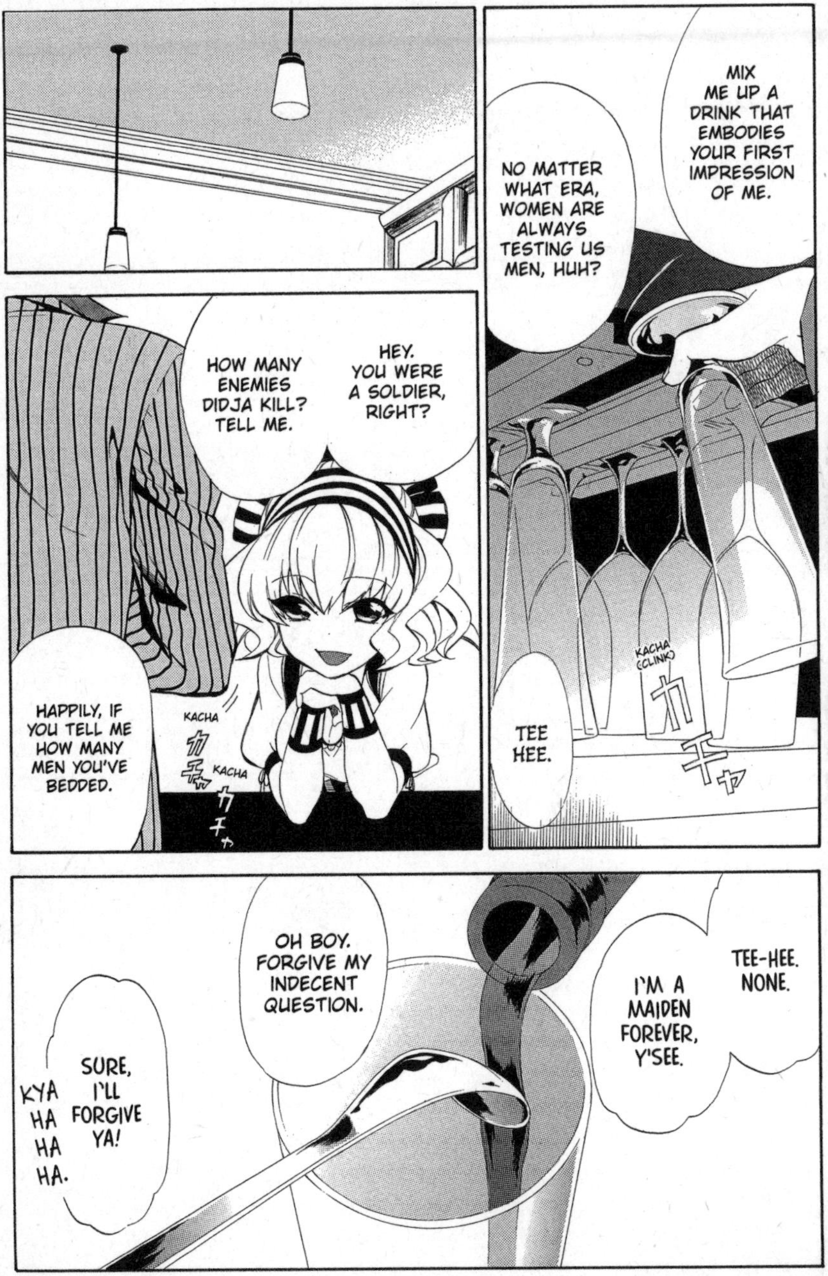
MIX ME UP A DRINK THAT EMBODIES YOUR FIRST IMPRESSION OF ME.
NO MATTER WHAT ERA, WOMEN ARE ALWAYS TESTING US MEN, HUH?
KACHA (CLINK)
TEE HEE.
HEY. YOU WERE A SOLDIER, RIGHT?
HOW MANY ENEMIES DIDJA KILL? TELL ME.
KACHA
KACHA
HAPPILY, IF YOU TELL ME HOW MANY MEN YOU'VE BEDDED.
TEE-HEE. NONE.
I'M A MAIDEN FOREVER, Y'SEE.
OH BOY. FORGIVE MY INDECENT QUESTION.
SURE, I'LL FORGIVE YA!
KYA HA HA HA.

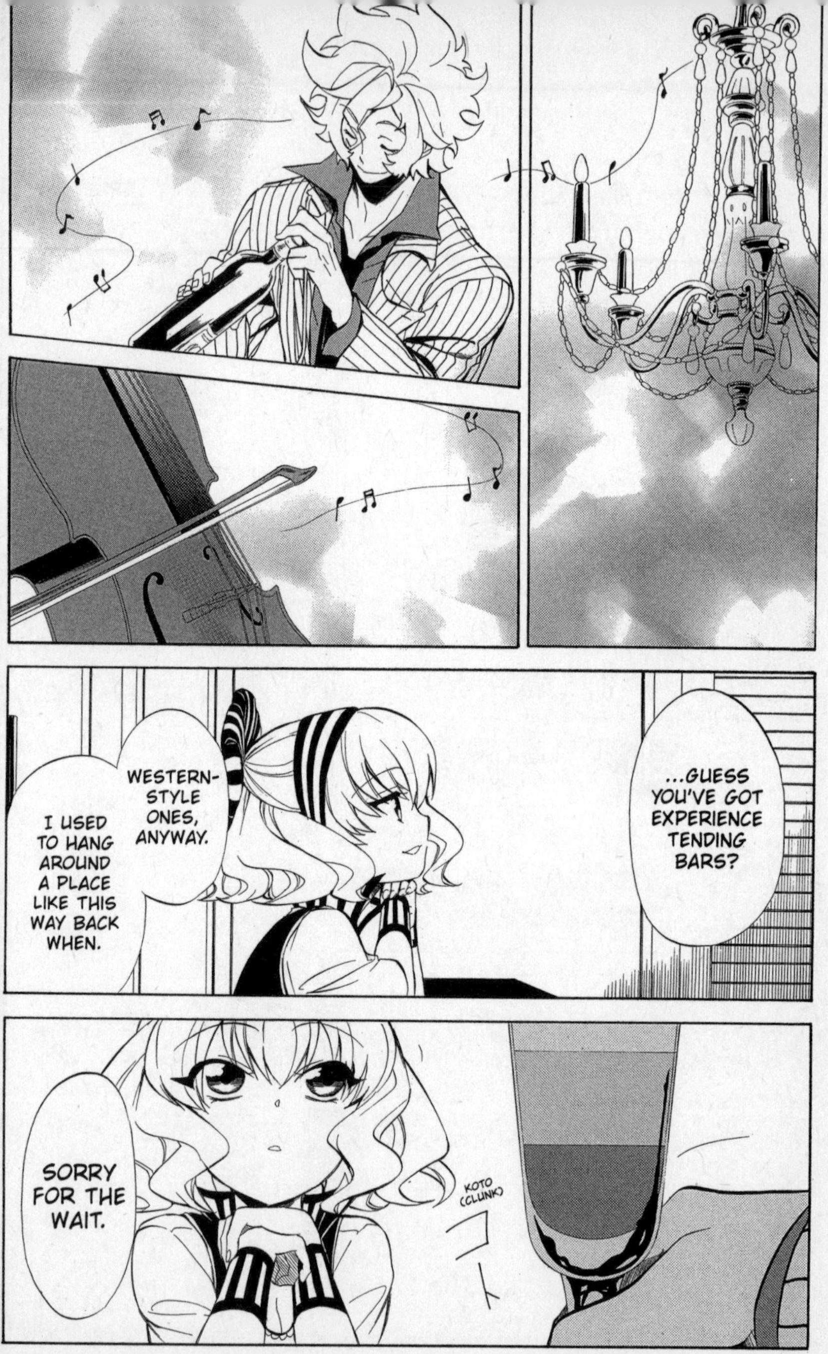
...GUESS YOU'VE GOT EXPERIENCE TENDING BARS?
WESTERN-STYLE ONES, ANYWAY.
I USED TO HANG AROUND A PLACE LIKE THIS WAY BACK WHEN.
KOTO (CLUNK)
SORRY FOR THE WAIT.

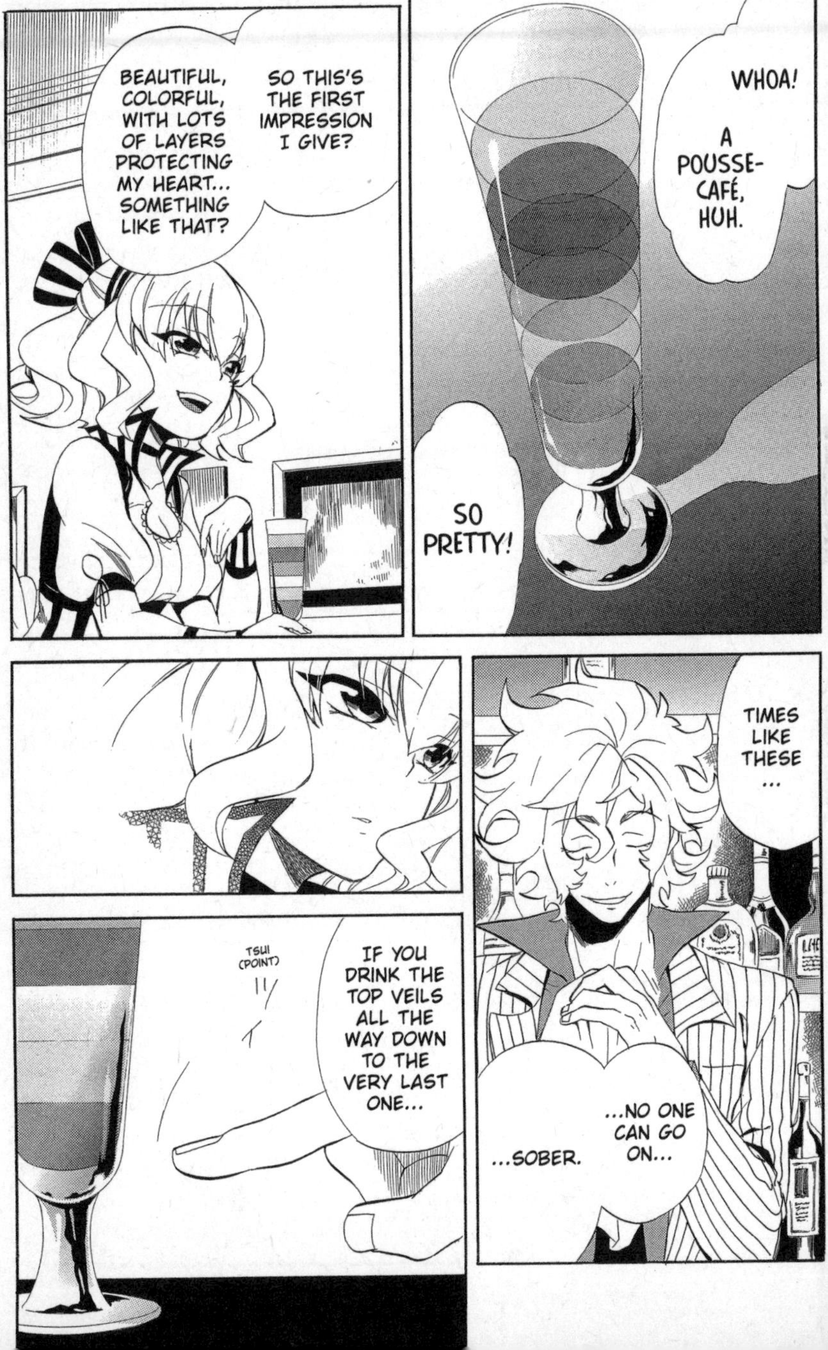
WHOA!
A POUSSE-CAFÉ, HUH.
SO PRETTY!
SO THIS'S THE FIRST IMPRESSION I GIVE?
BEAUTIFUL, COLORFUL, WITH LOTS OF LAYERS PROTECTING MY HEART... SOMETHING LIKE THAT?
TIMES LIKE THESE ...
...NO ONE CAN GO ON...
...SOBER.
IF YOU DRINK THE TOP VEILS ALL THE WAY DOWN TO THE VERY LAST ONE...
TSUI (POINT)

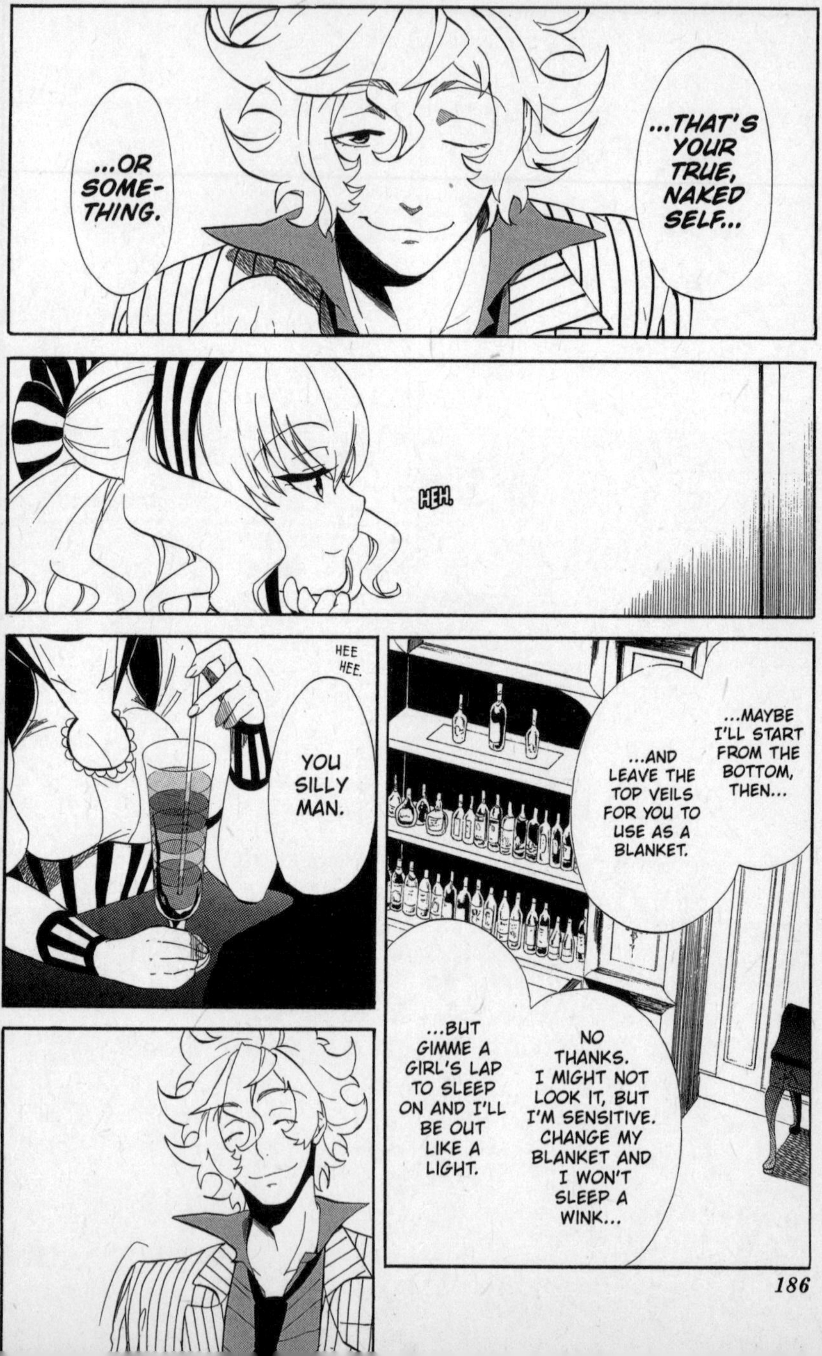
...THAT'S YOUR TRUE, NAKED SELF...
...OR SOMETHING.
HEH.
...MAYBE I'LL START FROM THE BOTTOM, THEN...
...AND LEAVE THE TOP VEILS FOR YOU TO USE AS A BLANKET.
NO THANKS. I MIGHT NOT LOOK IT, BUT I'M SENSITIVE. CHANGE MY BLANKET AND I WON'T SLEEP A WINK...
...BUT GIMME A GIRL'S LAP TO SLEEP ON AND I'LL BE OUT LIKE A LIGHT.
HEE HEE.
YOU SILLY MAN.

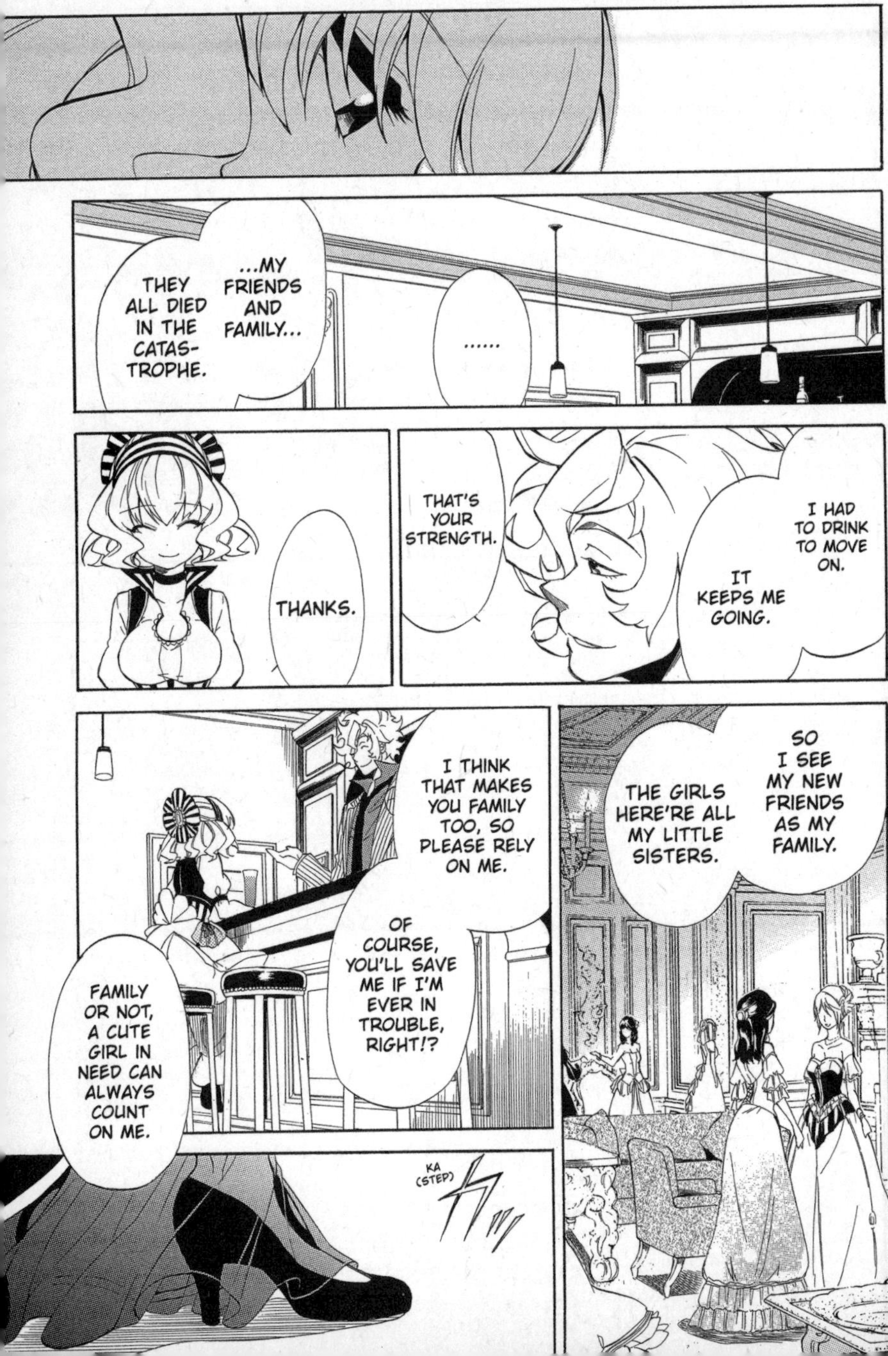
......
...MY FRIENDS AND FAMILY...
THEY ALL DIED IN THE CATASTROPHE.
I HAD TO DRINK TO MOVE ON.
IT KEEPS ME GOING.
THAT'S YOUR STRENGTH.
THANKS.
SO I SEE MY NEW FRIENDS AS MY FAMILY.
THE GIRLS HERE'RE ALL MY LITTLE SISTERS.
I THINK THAT MAKES YOU FAMILY TOO, SO PLEASE RELY ON ME.
OF COURSE, YOU'LL SAVE ME IF I'M EVER IN TROUBLE, RIGHT!?
FAMILY OR NOT, A CUTE GIRL IN NEED CAN ALWAYS COUNT ON ME.
KA (STEP)

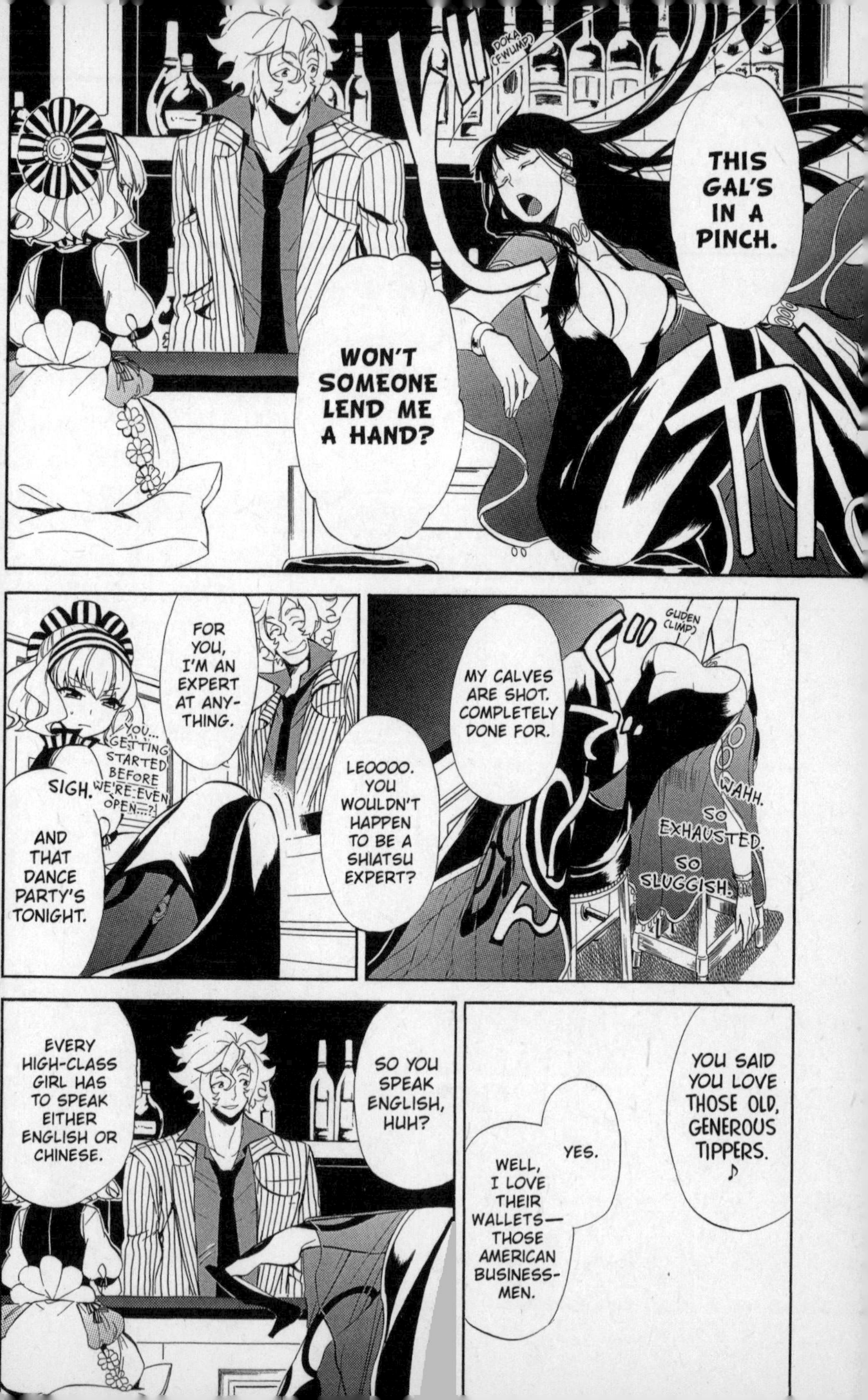
THIS GAL'S IN A PINCH.
DOKA (FWUMP)
WON'T SOMEONE LEND ME A HAND?
GUDEN (LIMP)
MY CALVES ARE SHOT. COMPLETELY DONE FOR.
WAHH. SO EXHAUSTED. SO SLUGGISH.
LEOOOO. YOU WOULDN'T HAPPEN TO BE A SHIATSU EXPERT?
FOR YOU, I'M AN EXPERT AT ANY-THING.
YOU... GETTING STARTED BEFORE WE'RE EVEN OPEN...?!
SIGH.
AND THAT DANCE PARTY'S TONIGHT.
YOU SAID YOU LOVE THOSE OLD, GENEROUS TIPPERS. ♪
YES.
WELL, I LOVE THEIR WALLETS— THOSE AMERICAN BUSINESS-MEN.
SO YOU SPEAK ENGLISH, HUH?
EVERY HIGH-CLASS GIRL HAS TO SPEAK EITHER ENGLISH OR CHINESE.

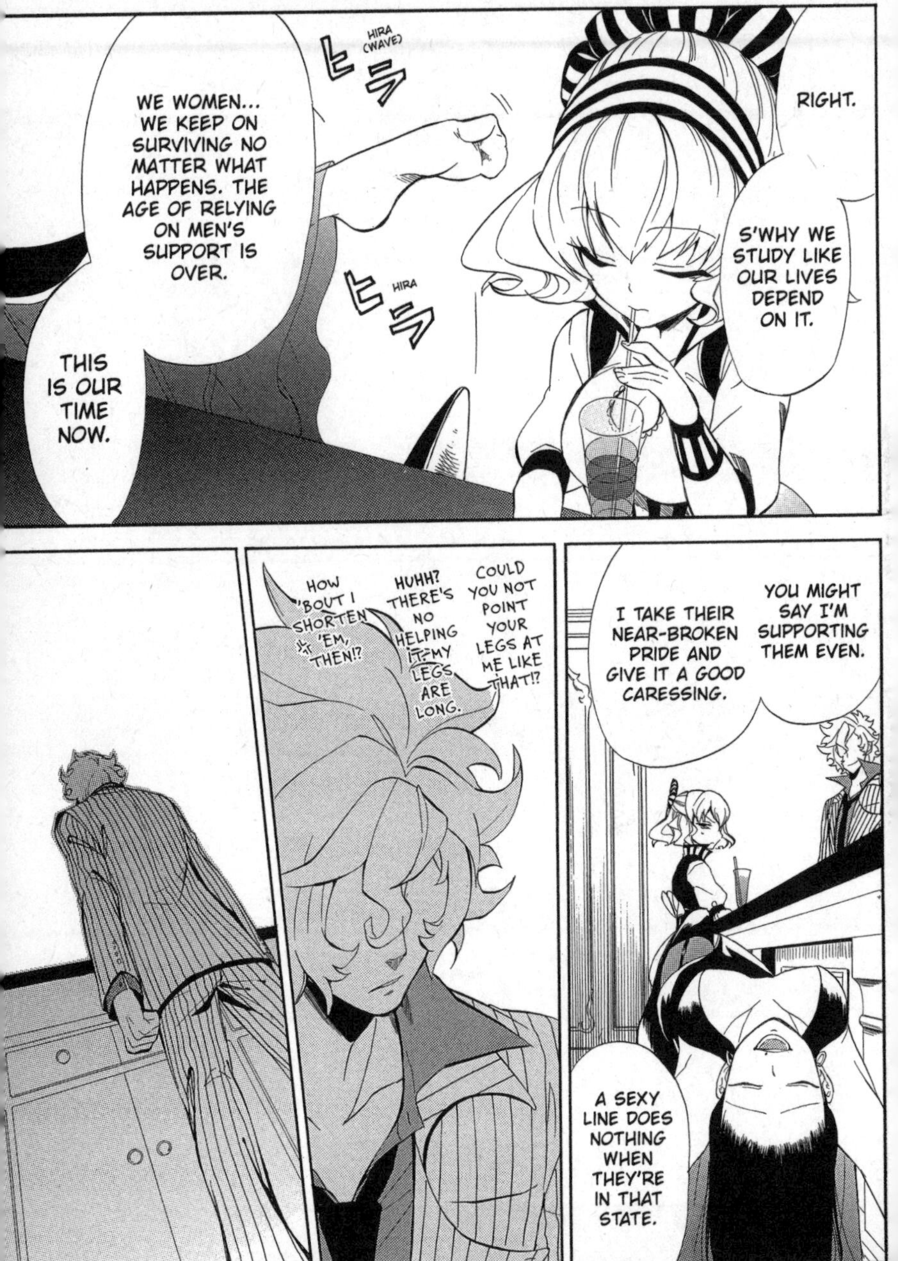
RIGHT.
S'WHY WE STUDY LIKE OUR LIVES DEPEND ON IT.
HIRA (WAVE)
HIRA
WE WOMEN... WE KEEP ON SURVIVING NO MATTER WHAT HAPPENS. THE AGE OF RELYING ON MEN'S SUPPORT IS OVER.
THIS IS OUR TIME NOW.
YOU MIGHT SAY I'M SUPPORTING THEM EVEN.
I TAKE THEIR NEAR-BROKEN PRIDE AND GIVE IT A GOOD CARESSING.
A SEXY LINE DOES NOTHING WHEN THEY'RE IN THAT STATE.
COULD YOU NOT POINT YOUR LEGS AT ME LIKE THAT!?
HUHH? THERE'S NO HELPING IT. MY LEGS ARE LONG.
HOW 'BOUT I SHORTEN 'EM, THEN!?

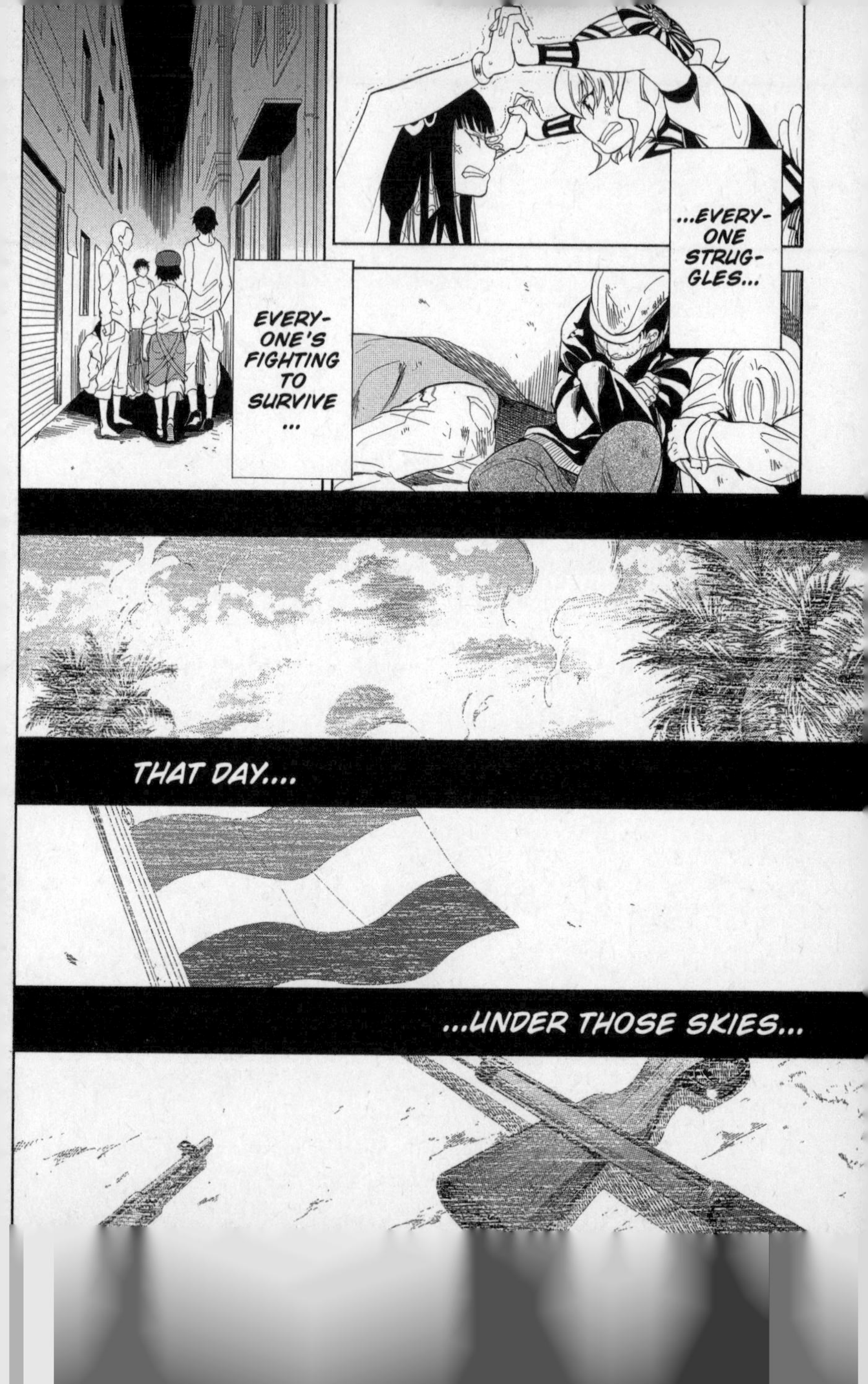
...EVERYONE STRUGGLES...
EVERYONE'S FIGHTING TO SURVIVE...
THAT DAY....
...UNDER THOSE SKIES...

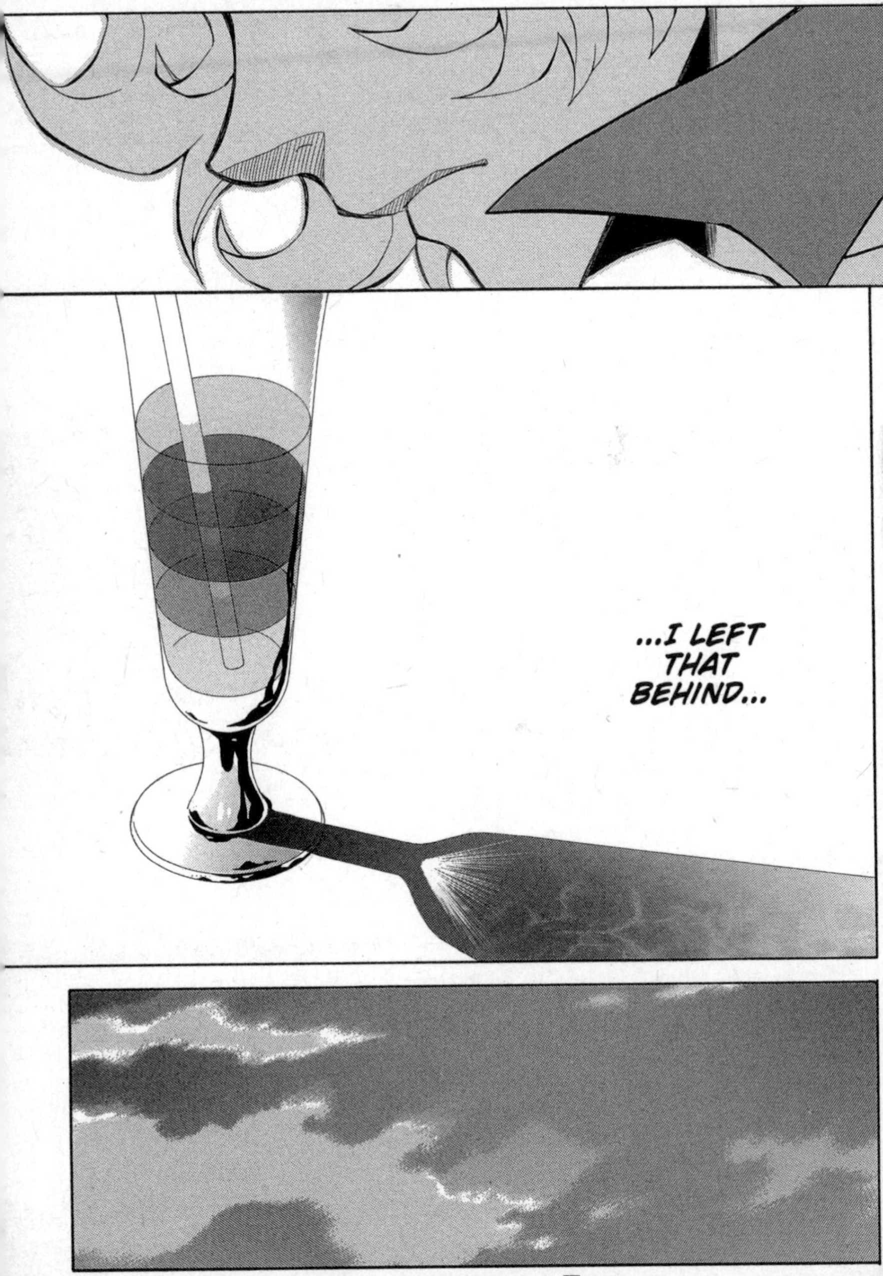
...I LEFT THAT BEHIND...

ROSE GUNS DAYS Season 1 ① END

ABOUT ROSE GUNS DAYS SEASON 1

A Totally New and Different World

From the original writer and supervisor Ryukishi07

Hi there. This is Ryukishi07. How'd you enjoy the first manga volume of Rose Guns Days?

I bet a lot of readers were shocked by the setting, which is a totally new and different world than that of Higurashi and Umineko. Or maybe it's more a "parallel world" than a "new world." But if one were to step outside Japan and take a look at the rest of this parallel world, it wouldn't seem so strange......
That's what I wanted to communicate here.

So many different kinds of people live in this world, with different cultures, languages, and points of view, but they all live side by side. What sort of things would they try to preserve? That's the theme I was trying to capture. But I still hope you all can have fun with this story, even without the tough stuff!

Soichiro-sensei is in charge of both the manga adaptation and the character illustrations for the visual novel, and I think it's amazing how he created all these characters based on nothing but my written specifications. Unlike the manga adaptation of Umineko When They Cry Episode 4, this one's a bit heavier on the action, but with a tinge of nostalgic atmosphere...
Sensei's range of techniques continues to amaze me...!

As we dive into this new Ryukishi world, I hope you all fall in love with the mystery of this unknown, postwar Tokyo.

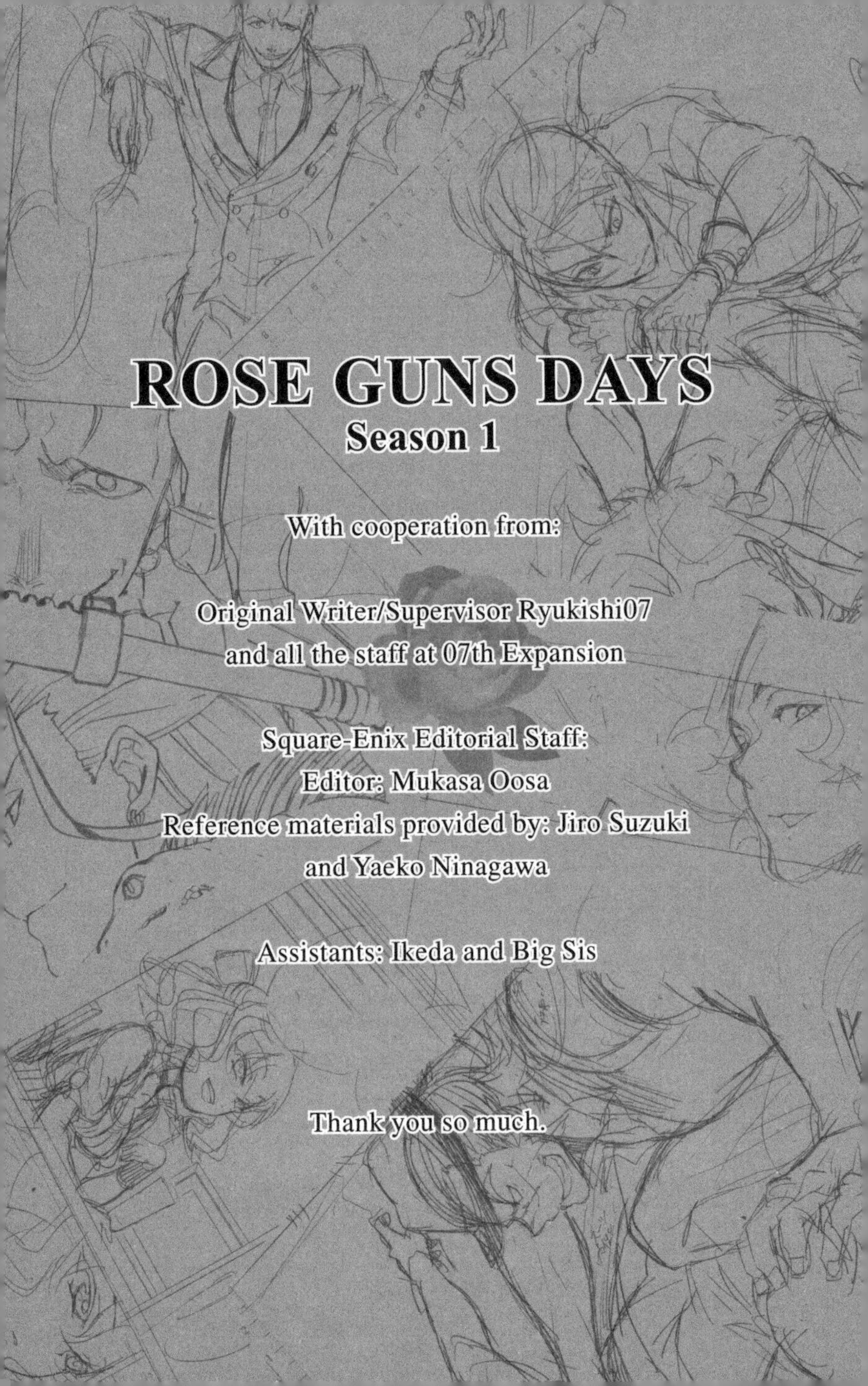

ROSE GUNS DAYS

Season 1

With cooperation from:

Original Writer/Supervisor Ryukishi07
and all the staff at 07th Expansion

Square-Enix Editorial Staff:
Editor: Mukasa Oosa
Reference materials provided by: Jiro Suzuki
and Yaeko Ninagawa

Assistants: Ikeda and Big Sis

Thank you so much.

ROSE GUNS DAYS SEASON 1 ①

RYUKISHI07
SOICHIRO

Translation: Caleb D. Cook • Lettering: Lys Blakeslee

ROSE GUNS DAYS Season 1 vol. 1
© RYUKISHI07 / 07th Expansion
© 2012 Soichiro / SQUARE ENIX CO., LTD.
First published in Japan in 2012 by SQUARE ENIX CO., LTD.
English translation rights arranged with SQUARE ENIX CO., LTD.
and Hachette Book Group through Tuttle-Mori Agency, Inc.

Translation © 2015 by SQUARE ENIX CO., LTD.

Yen Press
Hachette Book Group
1290 Avenue of the Americas
New York, NY 10104

www.hachettebookgroup.com
www.yenpress.com